"A timely and much needed overview of the state of the cultural and creative industries across Europe in the time of pandemic. The three foci of responses: at the local, labour market and national and institutional levels, provide lucid and detailed new evidence that culture matters more than ever; but sadly, that our information sources are deficient, and policy responses are insufficient. Read it and weep: we must do better!"

Andy C Pratt,
Professor of Cultural Economy and Director of
Centre for Culture and the Creative Industries, City,
University of London, UK

"We all missed going to the theatre, a cinema or entering an art gallery, but few outside the industry really understand the depth and breadth of the impact that the Covid pandemic has had on the creative and cultural industries. This volume fills that important void. It presents an insightful, rigorous and heartfelt investigation of the short and longer-term bearing of the pandemic on creative and cultural industries, as well as its people, with a selection of international case studies that provides close up analyses of national responses and policy initiatives, whilst bringing to life a global canvas of adaptation and resilience."

Lisa De Propris,
Professor of Regional Economic Development and Head of the
Business and Labour Economics Group,
University of Birmingham, UK

T0328369

Cultural Industries and the COVID-19 Pandemic

Already dealing with disruptive market forces, the Cultural and Creative Industries (CCIs) faced fundamental challenges resulting from the global health crisis, wrought by the COVID-19 pandemic. With catastrophic changes to cultural consumption, cultural organizations are dealing with short-, medium-, and long-term threats to livelihoods under lockdown.

This book aims at filling the literature gap about the consequences of one of the hardest crises – COVID-19 – severely impacting all the fields of the CCIs. With a focus on European countries and taking into account the evolving and unstable context caused by the pandemic still in progress, this book investigates the first reactions and actual strategies of CCIs' actors, government bodies, and cultural institutions facing the COVID-19 crisis and the potential consequences of these emergency strategies for the future of the CCIs. Solutions adopted during the repeated lockdowns by CCIs' actors could originate new forms of cultural consumption and/or new innovative market strategies. This book brings together a constellation of contributors to analyze the cultural sector as it seeks to emerge from this existential challenge.

The global perspectives presented in this book provide research-based evidence to understand and reflect on an unprecedented period, allowing reflective practitioners to learn and develop from a range of real-world cases. The book will also be of interest to researchers, academics, and students with a particular interest in the management of cultural and creative organizations and crisis management.

Elisa Salvador is Professor (PhD, HDR) of Innovation and Creativity at ESSCA School of Management, France.

Trilce Navarrete is Lecturer in Cultural Economics at the Erasmus University, Netherlands.

Andrej Srakar is Scientific Associate at the Institute for Economic Research (IER) and Assistant Professor of Economics and Business at the University of Ljubljana, Slovenia.

Routledge Research in the Creative and Cultural Industries
Series Editor: Ruth Rentschler

This series brings together book-length original research in cultural and creative industries from a range of perspectives. Charting developments in contemporary cultural and creative industries thinking around the world, the series aims to shape the research agenda to reflect the expanding significance of the creative sector in a globalised world.

Strategic Cultural Centre Management
Tomas Järvinen

The Music Export Business
Born Global
Stephen Chen, Shane Homan and Tracy Redhead

Cultural Management and Policy in Latin America
Edited by Raphaela Henze and Federico Escribal

Transforming Museum Management
Evidence-Based Change through Open Systems Theory
Yuha Jung

The Metamorphosis of Cultural and Creative Organizations
Exploring Change from a Spatial Perspective
Edited by Federica De Molli and Marilena Vecco

Cultural Industries and the COVID-19 Pandemic
A European Focus
Edited by Elisa Salvador, Trilce Navarrete and Andrej Srakar

For more information about this series, please visit: www.routledge.com/ Routledge-Research-in-the-Creative-and-Cultural-Industries/book-series/ RRCCI

Cultural Industries and the COVID-19 Pandemic

A European Focus

Edited by
Elisa Salvador, Trilce Navarrete and
Andrej Srakar

LONDON AND NEW YORK

First published 2022
by Routledge
2 Park Square, Milton Park, Abingdon, Oxon OX14 4RN

and by Routledge
605 Third Avenue, New York, NY 10158

Routledge is an imprint of the Taylor & Francis Group, an informa business

British Library Cataloguing-in-Publication Data
A catalogue record for this book is available from the British Library

Library of Congress Cataloging-in-Publication Data
A catalog record has been requested for this book

ISBN: 978-0-367-65191-6 (hbk)
ISBN: 978-0-367-65190-9 (pbk)
ISBN: 978-1-003-12827-4 (ebk)

DOI: 10.4324/9781003128274

Typeset in Sabon
by KnowledgeWorks Global Ltd.

Contents

List of figures   x
List of tables   xi
List of boxes   xiii
List of contributors   xiv
Preface and acknowledgements   xxi
Foreword   xxii

Introduction: The COVID-19 pandemic and the cultural industries: Emergency strategies and a renewed interest for building a better future?   1
ELISA SALVADOR

SECTION 1
Regional and national policies: The impact of the COVID-19 crisis on the cultural industries   9

1 **The COVID-19 pandemic and cultural industries in the EU and in the United Kingdom: A perfect storm**   11
   ALESSANDRO GIOVANNI LAMONICA AND PIERANGELO ISERNIA

2 **The COVID-19 pandemic and cultural industries in France: Cultural policy challenged**   27
   JEAN PAUL SIMON

3 **The effects of the COVID-19 pandemic on the field of Finnish cultural industries: Revealing and challenging policy structures**   46
   MERVI LUONILA, VAPPU RENKO, OLLI JAKONEN, SARI KARTTUNEN, AND ANNA KANERVA

4   The COVID-19 pandemic and the cultural policy
     response in Slovakia   65
     ZUZANA DOŠEKOVÁ AND ANDREJ SVORENČÍK

SECTION 2
Cultural workers: Resilience and organization during
the COVID-19 pandemic   81

5   The COVID-19 pandemic and cultural workers: Fight,
     flight or freeze in lockdown?   83
     BEATE ELSTAD, DAG JANSSON AND ERIK DØVING

6   The COVID-19 pandemic, cultural work, and resilience   98
     VIKTORIYA PISOTSKA AND LUCA GIUSTINIANO

7   The COVID-19 pandemic, coworking spaces, and cultural
     events: The case of Italy   114
     FEDERICA ROSSI AND ILARIA MARIOTTI

8   Freelance classical musicians in Austria and the
     COVID-19 pandemic   128
     DAGMAR ABFALTER AND SANDRA STINI

9   Artists in the COVID-19 pandemic: Use of lockdown
     time, skill development, and audience perceptions in
     Colombia and Spain   141
     JAVIER A. RODRÍGUEZ-CAMACHO, PEDRO REY-BIEL, JEREMY C. YOUNG
     AND MÓNICA MARCELL ROMERO SÁNCHEZ

SECTION 3
Institutional strategies: First responses in the arts and
culture sectors to the strict lockdown of March 2020   175

10 The COVID-19 pandemic and structural change in
     the museum sector: Insights from Italy   177
     ENRICO BERTACCHINI, ANDREA MORELLI AND GIOVANNA SEGRE

11 The COVID-19 pandemic and cultural industries in Spain:
     Early impacts of lockdown   194
     RAÚL ABELEDO-SANCHIS AND GUILLEM BACETE ARMENGOT

12 The COVID-19 pandemic and cultural industries in
the Nordic region: Emerging strategies in film and
drama productions   208
TERJE GAUSTAD AND PETER BOOTH

13 The COVID-19 pandemic and cultural industries in the
Czech Republic   226
MAREK PROKŮPEK AND JAKUB GROSMAN

14 The COVID-19 pandemic and the European screen industry:
The role of national screen agencies   239
CAITRIONA NOONAN

15 Orchestrating change: The future of orchestras post COVID-19   254
JOHN O'HAGAN AND KAROL J. BOROWIECKI

Conclusions: The legacy of COVID-19 for the cultural industries   268
TRILCE NAVARRETE

Index   271

List of figures

3.1 A concise description of the Finnish cultural policy structure
in relation to the analyzed anti-COVID measures.   48

4.1 Daily new confirmed COVID-19 deaths per mil. people (7-day
moving median) in Slovakia.   71

7.1 The geographical distribution of CSs in Italy.   119

7.2 The agglomerations of CSs in Milan in 2014 (a) and 2021 (b).   122

9.1 Representative screenshot of the experimental setting
presented to each participant when asked to rate a work
(in Spanish). Gabriel Angel with permission for its anonymous
use in the experiment and its inclusion in this chapter.   152

9.2 The two works provided by one artist for our experiment:
pre-pandemic (top), post-pandemic (bottom). Andrés Kal with
permission for its anonymous use in the experiment and its
inclusion in this chapter.   159

10.1 Distribution of visitors aged 18 and over and paid admissions
to Italian State museums, per frequency of visit, year 2018.   188

11.1 Expected revenue losses in the first half of 2020.   198

11.2 Actions deployed in response to lockdown.   199

11.3 Access to COVID-19 subsidies.   202

12.1 Variation in the stringency index across the Nordic countries,
12 March 2020–20 November 2020.   214

13.1 Missing income in March and April 2020.   232

13.2 Lost audience in March and April 2020.   233

13.3 Cancelled performances in March and April 2020.   234

15.1 Trends in attendance at the live orchestra in Germany,
the United States, Finland, and Sweden (normalized scale).   262

15.2 Events organized by publicly funded orchestras and radio
ensembles in Germany, 2003–2004 and 2017–2018.   263

15.3 Income from orchestra activities, New York Philharmonics,
1990–2000 to 2017–2018.   264

15.4 Global classical recorded music revenues 2016–2018 (millions $).   264

15.5 Global classical recorded music revenues by region
2018 (millions $).   265

List of tables

1.1 Typology of public policy responses announced, adopted, or implemented between February and July 2020 in Europe. Distribution by country.   14

2.1 The direct economic weight of culture in 2019.   28

2.2 Budget of the main cultural entities funding the various segments (2018).   30

2.3 Sectoral measures across cultural entities.   33

2.4 Sectorial support for cultural venues.   34

3.1 Examples of the COVID-19 related surveys.   53

3.2 Examples of emergency funding for CCIs from the Finnish government 2020–2021.   56

4.1 Estimated lost revenue in creative sectors, as reported by sector representatives in May 2020.   69

5.1 Coping instances by professional categories, means (1 = does not at all agree to 5 = fully agree), ranked by total mean.   87

5.2 Pearson correlations and descriptives for coping modes, employment status and job satisfaction.   91

5.3 Regression analyses with regard to coping modes and job satisfaction.   93

6.1 Data.   102

8.1 Sample description.   133

9.1 Distribution of fields of artistic specialization in the sample.   153

9.2 Artists' self-reported perception of the time allocated to different activities connected to their creative practice during the lockdown.   155

9.3 Use of time by Colombian and Spanish artists before the pandemic and during the lockdown.   157

9.4 Demographic characteristics of the experiment participants.   161

9.5 Artist-level differences in the pre- and post-pandemic ratings of their work and time invested in developing their skills.   163

9.6 Effect of skill levels and lockdown time allocations: regression results for the post-pandemic audience ratings.   166

10.1 Characteristics and economic facts of Italian state-owned
     museums and heritage institutions – 2018.   187
11.1 Distribution of the survey sample according to sectors.   196
11.2 Lockdown impact assessment.   197
11.3 Assessment of priority needs.   198
11.4 Activities/actions carried out during lockdown (time
     allocation).   200
11.5 Expected long-term changes in the cultural ecosystem.   203
11.6 Preferred measures to counter the effects of COVID-19 on
     cultural ecosystems.   204
12.1 Comparison of national containment and closure policies,
     12 March 2020 to 20 November 20.   214
12.2 Clustering variables by clusters 1 to 4 ($N = 115$).   217
12.3 Project strategy clusters by production phase as of
     12 March 2020 ($N = 115$).   219
12.4 Project strategy clusters 1 to 4 by country ($N = 115$).   221
13.1 Size of the ACS in the Czech Republic vs. sample of
     the survey.   230
14.1 Overview of screen agencies in the project's research
     sample.   241
14.2 Trends in the interventions from screen agencies to
     the pandemic.   244

List of boxes

2.1 Cancelled festivals, an assessment of the losses   32
2.2 Trade associations and professional unions   35
2.3 The main authors' rights management societies   36
2.4 Unions   37

Contributors

Abeledo-Sanchis Raúl is an Associate Professor in the Department of Applied Economics at the Universitat de València (UVEG) and a member of the Research Unit in Economics of Culture and Tourism (Econcult). Since 2008, he has participated and directed different Interreg and Horizon2020 EU projects focused on the development impacts of cultural organizations through creativity and economic and social innovation. He is currently the Academic Director of the Cultural Observatory of UVEG.

Abfalter Dagmar is an Associate Professor at the Department of Cultural Management and Gender Studies at MDW – University of Music and Performing Arts Vienna, Austria. She holds an accreditation to supervise research (habilitation) in Cultural Institutions Studies from MDW (2018) and a PhD in International Economic Sciences from the University of Innsbruck (2008). Her research interests focus on strategizing, management and leadership as well as exclusion practices in arts and cultural organizations.

Bacete Armengot Guillem is a Predoctoral Researcher at the Universitat de València – Social Sciences PhD program. His research is oriented towards cultural and tourism phenomena. He has participated in InterregMed Creativewear and Chebec projects.

Benghozi Pierre-Jean is a Research Director at the National Centre for Scientific Research (CNRS) and is a Professor at the École Polytechnique (Paris) and GSEM (Geneva University). Since the early 1980s, Professor Benghozi has been developing pioneering research on information technology, telecommunications, media, and culture. His latest book deals with videogames as a cultural industry. He is the Co-chair of AIMAC and is on the board of several international editorial and scientific committees.

Bertacchini Enrico is an Associate Professor in Public Economics at the Department of Economics and Statistics at the University of Torino,

Italy. His research interests focus on public and political economic issues related to the arts and heritage sector. His work has addressed the provision of museum services, the determinants of UNESCO World Heritage listing, and the economic and spatial organization of cultural and creative industries.

Booth Peter is an Associate Professor at BI Norwegian Business School connected to the Nordic Centre for Internet and Society and BI's Centre for Creative Industries. He is trained as an economist at The London School of Economics, in visual arts at the Oslo National Academy of the Arts, and completed his doctorate in Cultural Economics at Erasmus University Rotterdam. His research broadly covers sociology of art and finance, creative labour, and the impact of technologies on the Cultural and Creative Sectors.

Borowiecki Karol is a Professor of Economics at the University of Southern Denmark. His pioneering and highly original research in the economic history of the arts regularly makes a societal impact. He is Executive Board Members of the Association of Cultural Economics International, founder and co-editor of EconomistsTalkArt.org, and guest editor at the *Journal of Cultural Economics*.

Došeková Zuzana is a Data Analyst at the Institute for Cultural Policy, the analytical unit of the Ministry of Culture of the Slovak Republic. She has a background in mathematics and musicology, with academic publications in the fields of music cognition and music data analysis.

Døving Erik, Dr.oecon., is an Associate Professor in management at Oslo Business School at Oslo Metropolitan University Oslo. His research and teaching focuses on human resource management in strategic and professional contexts, workplace learning and skills, and working conditions. Døving's research has appeared in books and journals such as *Strategic Management Journal and Leadership*.

Elstad Beate Dr.oecon., is an Associate Professor in management at Oslo Business School at Oslo Metropolitan University. She is a lecturer at the Arts Management and Master of Business Administration Programmes. Her research interests are arts management, freelancers' working conditions and careers, and volunteer management. She is also a freelance big band conductor.

Gaustad Terje is an Assistant Professor in Communication and Culture and Associate Dean for Creative Industries Management at BI Norwegian Business School. He holds a PhD in Strategic Management from BI Norwegian Business School and an M.A. in Communication Management from the University of Southern California. His main research interests are in institutional and organizational economics applied to the entertainment industries.

Giustiniano Luca (PhD) is a Professor of Organization Studies at the Luiss University (Rome, Italy) and is the Director of the Centre for Research in Leadership, Innovation, and Organisation (CLIO). His research interests are focused on organization design. His papers have appeared in top journals such as the *Journal of Management, Management and Organization Review, British Journal of Management*, and *European Management Review.*

Grosman Jakub is a doctoral candidate in Arts Management at the Prague University of Economics and Business. His main research interests are primarily the music industry and performing arts funding. Beyond his academic work, Jakub is a founder and organizer of music festivals and several cultural projects.

Isernia Pierangelo is a Professor of Political Science and Jean Monnet Chair of Culture in International Relations at the University of Siena, Italy. His main research interests are in the field of public opinion, foreign policy, international cultural relations, European integration, transatlantic relations, and anti-Americanism.

Jakonen, Olli is a Researcher at the Center for Cultural Policy Research Cupore and a doctoral student at the Department of Social Sciences and Philosophy, University of Jyväskylä, Finland. He is specialized in funding and steering systems of the Finnish cultural policy.

Jansson Dag PhD, is an Associate Professor of arts management at Oslo Business School at Oslo Metropolitan University. He runs the Arts Management Programme, where he also teaches leadership and organization. His research focus is aesthetic leadership and artistic practices and education. He is also a choral conductor and teaches at music academies in Oslo and Gothenburg.

Kanerva Anna is a Senior Researcher at the Center for Cultural Policy Research Cupore. Her research interests include international comparative cultural policies, cultural and creative industries, and cultural heritage policies. She is the Finnish expert in the Compendium of Cultural Policies and Trends – network.

Karttunen Sari is a Senior Researcher at the Center for Cultural Policy Research Cupore and University Researcher at the University of the Arts Helsinki. She specializes in artistic occupations and cultural policy instrument analysis. Her current interests include equality in art and community art practice.

Lamonica Alessandro Giovanni is a post-doctoral research fellow at the Centre for the Study of Political Change of the University of Siena, where he teaches Cultural Diplomacy. He has been part of various EU-funded research projects on the role of culture in international relations.

Luonila, Mervi is a Senior Researcher in the Center for Cultural Policy Research, Cupore, and at the University of Jyväskylä and also Research Fellow (visiting) in the UNIARTS Helsinki. Her recent research concerning arts and festival management and cultural policy is published f.ex. in the *International Journal of Arts Management, Journal of Policy Research in Tourism, Leisure and Events, Event Management,* and *Journal of Business Research.*

Marcell Romero Sánchez Mónica is an Assistant Professor in the Department of Visual Arts at Pontificia Universidad Javeriana (Bogotá, Colombia). As a researcher she works on social and pedagogical processes involving diverse communities in the arts. Her creative practice is fundamentally collaborative and interdisciplinary, critically exploring the relationship between the arts, affect, entrepreneurship, education, social innovation, and communities. She has worked in the design and implementation of cultural policy programs in Colombia, with an emphasis on arts training and education.

Mariotti Ilaria is an Associate Professor of Urban and Regional Economics at the Department of Architecture and Urban Studies, Politecnico di Milano (IT). She is the Chair of the Cost Action 18214 (2019–2023) and Project Coordinator for the Politecnico di Milano team of the CORAL Project – ITN-2020 (2021–2024).

Morelli Andrea is a Researcher in cultural economics at Santagata Foundation and Symbola Foundation. Consultant at Foundation for Culture Torino and researcher affiliate at OMERO Interdepartmental Research Centre on Urban and Event Studies at the University of Turin. He holds a master's degree in Economics of Culture at the University of Turin.

Navarrete Trilce is a specialist in the economic and historical aspects of digital heritage. She is currently Lecturer in Cultural Economics at the Erasmus University Rotterdam. Navarrete is adviser of the European Group of Museum Statistics (EGMUS) and a board member of the International Committee of Documentation of the International Council of Museums (CIDOC).

Noonan Caitriona is a Senior Lecturer in Media and Communication, Cardiff University. Her expertise is in cultural production, policy, and labour. She is co-author of the book *Producing British Television Drama: Local Production in a Global Era* (Palgrave, 2019). More information about her research is available at www.smallnationsscreen.org

O'Hagan John is a Professor of Economics and Senior Fellow, Emeritus, Trinity College, University of Dublin. He is a leading authority on the political economy of Ireland and is a distinguished expert in cultural economics, a field which he helped to develop.

Pisotska Viktoriya is a PhD Candidate in Management at the Luiss University (Rome, Italy) and a visiting PhD fellow at the Copenhagen Business School, Department of Organization. Her research areas are creative industries, organization theory, and project organizing. Her research focuses on how different competing demands can be managed in the context of Cultural and Creative Industries.

Prokůpek Marek is an Assistant Professor in Arts Management at the Prague University of Economics and Business. Previously, Marek was a Postdoctoral Fellow at the LabEx ICCA (*Industries culturelles et création artistique*) in Paris. His research interests lie primarily in the areas of museum fundraising and philanthropy and its ethical dilemmas and innovative business models of arts and cultural organizations.

Renko, Vappu is a Researcher at the Center for Cultural Policy Research Cupore and a doctoral student at the Department of Social Sciences and Philosophy, University of Jyväskylä, Finland. Her research interests include local and regional cultural policies in Finland and other Nordic countries.

Rey-Biel Pedro is an Associate Professor of Behavioral Economics at ESADE, Ramon Llull University (Barcelona, Spain), where his research combines theoretical and empirical methodologies, as well as laboratory and field experiments to understand economic decision making and how it is affected by the design of proper incentive schemes which take into account the complex array of behavioural traits behind human motivation. He has published articles in leading academic journals in economics such as *The Journal of European Economic Association, The Journal of Economic Perspectives, The Economic Journal*, and *The Journal of Public Economics*. Pedro also collaborates with public and private institutions in the applications of behavioural economics to optimal organizational design and has conducted large RCTs for several leading companies.

Rodríguez-Camacho Javier A. is an Assistant Professor in the Department of Business Administration at Pontificia Universidad Javeriana (Bogotá, Colombia). He works at the intersection of economics of information, entrepreneurship, and the creative industries. His research has explored the role of expert and user reviews, symbolic capitals, and technological change in the production and consumption dynamics of the film and music industries. He has worked as a film and music critic for several media outlets in Bolivia, Spain, Colombia, and the United States. He is the academic organizer of Cultmarts, an International Conference on the Creative and Cultural Industries held in Bogotá every year since 2019.

Rossi Federica is a Postdoctoral Research Fellow in Economics at the Department of Architecture and Urban Studies, Politecnico di Milano (IT).

In 2018, she received a PhD in Economics from Università della Svizzera italiana (Lugano, CH). Her research interests include topics in regional economics, such as firms' location choices and agglomeration economies.

Salvador Elisa (HDR, University of Paris 13; PhD, University of Turin) has worked on innovation policy for the Italian National Research Council (CNR) and was awarded CNR's Promotion of Research 2005 prize. She has collaborated with the Polytechnic of Turin and with the ESCP-Europe Business School; she taught at Iéseg School of Management; she worked as a researcher at Ecole Polytechnique, Paris, investigating R&D and innovation in the cultural and creative industries. Currently she is a Professor at ESSCA School of Management, where she coordinates the master's course in Managing Creativity and Innovation.

Segre Giovanna is an Associate professor in Economic Policy at the University of Turin, where she currently serves as Deputy Director of the Biennial Master in Economics of Environment, Culture and Territory, Deputy Director of the Master in Cultural Property Protection in Crisis Response, Vice-president of the Interdepartmental Research Center for Urban Studies, and member of the Academic Board of the PhD in Technologies for Cultural Heritage. She is also a Research Associate of IRCrES-CNR, and a member of the Scientific Committee of the Santagata Foundation for the Economics of Culture. Her research interests and publications focus on economics of culture, cultural heritage, creative industries, and welfare economics.

Simon Jean-Paul is an independant researcher and consultant specialized in media/telecom law regulation and strategy. He is a frequent speaker on telecommunications and media in Asia, Europe, and the United States. He holds a PhD in Philosophy (1975) and is a graduate (MBA) from the Ecole des Hautes Etudes Commerciales (HEC) (MBA, econometrics, 1971). He has written several books and articles on communications and public policy.

Srakar Andrej is a Scientific Associate at the Institute for Economic Research and an Assistant Professor at the School of Economics and Business, University of Ljubljana. He researches probability and mathematics, mathematical statistics, econometrics, and cultural economics, where he published in most leading international publications and is involved in organizational work in leading international associations.

Stini Sandra is a trained flutist and Cultural Manager. She is currently working at the Department of Cultural Management and Gender Studies at the MDW – University of Music and Performing Arts Vienna as a university assistant for cultural institutions studies. Her doctoral research focuses on the orchestra labour market in Austria.

Svorenčík Andrej is a post-doctoral fellow at the Economics Department of the University of Mannheim in Germany. Since 2017 he has been an advisor to Slovak ministers of culture and has been responsible for the establishment of the Institute for Cultural Policy, the analytical unit of the Ministry of Culture of the Slovak Republic.

Young Jeremy C. is an Assistant Professor in the Department of Business Administration at Pontificia Universidad Javeriana (Bogotá, Colombia). He was a Visiting Researcher at the Department of Social and Behavioral Sciences, Harvard T.H. Chan School of Public Health. His research centres on public health and the behavioural response of citizens to public policies, using experimental and behavioural methods. He hopes to collaborate more with public institutions to apply behavioural science to optimize public policies.

Preface and acknowledgements

The inspiration for this book originated during the first strict lockdown (March 2020) due to the COVID-19 pandemic that profoundly impacted the overall world.

The three co-editors of this edited volume have been confronted with distant working and digital communication. They have had to deal with all the matters related to the construction of the book without having the possibility to discuss face to face along the just over one-year-journey from the starting idea till the manuscript submission. They did their best for assuring the completion of the book in the shortest possible time so to assure current news to readers.

To this respect, the editors thank all the contributors of the book for their reactivity and respect of strict deadlines, but most of all for their effort to contribute original and dedicated work for this book.

The editors are also grateful to two anonymous reviewers as well as to Routledge for enabling this volume. A special thanks to Terry Clague, senior publisher Routledge books, and Professor Ruth Rentschler (University of South Australia) for their enthusiasm shown since the beginning about the idea of this edited volume and for their constant encouragement.

Foreword

Much has been said about the shock and dramatic effects of the pandemic on economic and social life. The cultural sector has naturally not escaped the trauma of the virtual shutdown of society for many months. Moreover, it was undoubtedly one of the areas most affected because of its economic characteristics and its importance for the culture and collective life of everyone, in the anthropological sense of the term. The pandemic has in fact, better than any other events, contributed to underline the importance, for individuals, of cultural and artistic activities in their personal balance, as a factor of integration, and inclusion in communities of experience and tastes: in a word, a dimension that goes far beyond the mere consumption of cultural content.

The editors of this book are to be congratulated for having coordinated the following important work. It provides the basis for an initial assessment, based on research conducted throughout Europe. This picture is backed up, in my opinion, by several important observations.

Firstly, the pandemic has provided the opportunity for a unique public debate on the role of culture in society and therefore on how to conceive or rethink the cultural policies to be implemented. The debate was opened by asking about possible derogations for this sector from a health and economic point of view (opening of theatres or cultural outlets), and defining the collective efforts to be made to support artistic venues, businesses and personnel. The discussion quickly opened up on the basis of the existing gap between the perception of the efforts made by the community and that of the cultural professionals in the face of issues that are not simply economic but also affect their essential relationship with the public, the recognition of the work done, and the opportunity for visibility. Whether it be books, music, shows, museums, online services, etc., the COVID-19 has made it possible to open the debate in society on the place – more or less essential – that cultural activities occupy in it: from an economic, social and psychological point of view, for the actors of culture as well as for its consumers.

What economic and social models for the performing arts and cultural industries' sectors? How can we deal with all kinds of risks, when projects follow one another, when intermittence is omnipresent, in multi-employer activities with different statutes, and an economy of nobody knows? The present crisis has called into question routines, "ways of doing things", "managing emotions", the ability to project oneself into the future, calling into question professional commitment and sometimes vocations. How, then, can we articulate the commitment of artists and technicians to their work, with the meaning given to their creative contribution, and the various forms of recognition (peers, hierarchy, public)?

In this respect, the pandemic has acted as a revelation of the structural tensions that were already running through the world of culture, but it has also acted as a catalyst for transformations that were already in the making in terms of relations with spectators as well as in terms of the animation of artistic collectives, productions and the management of venues: think in particular at the appropriation of digital technology!

Sectors variously affected

Speaking of the opportunities and new roads opened to culture by the pandemic situation, it has to be underlined that the field should not be considered globally and as a whole since the COVID-19 contributed to accentuate the gaps and divides between the different sectors: some benefited highly from the situation (cf. video games, SVOD), others are facing greater difficulties (live events, festivals, museums ...).

The effects of the pandemic thus differed greatly depending on the sector. In some cases, once economic support was assured, the lockdown allowed creators to have time available to write and develop works (cinema, plastic arts), while in other cases (performing arts, heritage), it could only lead to the closure of all activities.

In this respect, the differences created by the crisis are not limited to the consequences on supply. They have also resulted in strong disparities in demand in terms of both volume and consumption structure. Some content (TV, AV streaming, books, recorded music, video games) has been over-consumed due to the availability of consumers who have been locked out of their homes. But other practices, on the other hand, have had to be completely suspended (live shows, heritage, museums, etc.).

The COVID-19: Threat and opportunity

Beyond the differences between sectors, the pandemic has thus constituted, more broadly speaking, as much a crisis and an economic and artistic emergency as well as an opportunity for a number of projects and professionals. If the suspension of usual activities and the successive postponements of projects in development (writing, rehearsals, performances, etc.) were a real psychological suffering for the individuals involved, fortunately it also resulted in strong resilience. For many, the unchosen time off was an opportunity to take a step back and reflect on their own careers.

As recently noted by P. Rondin, the director of the Festival d'Avignon (France), after a one-year break, one is no longer the same: loss of routine, physical fitness, skills, self-confidence ...: a small impairment of which one is not always aware. He cited the case of stagehands who are afraid of vertigo when hanging scenery and lighting at heights, while they never suffered this problem before. Similarly, many dancers were injured during the reprise due to a lack of continuity in their work.

In the face of difficulties and depending on the effectiveness of cultural policy, the reactions of the cultural actors were thus very wide-ranging. Thanks to public support, some were able to continue to live but withdrew completely into themselves, suffering real isolation: if the artists received financing, this did not always compensate for the absence of an artistic challenge, the possibility of performing, the absence of a direct relationship with the public or recognition by audiences. Other professionals also saw their income painfully affected and were forced to cobble together a living from odd jobs or may have chosen to leave a profession that required a particularly strong commitment. But others were also able to take advantage of these periods to boost their creativity and develop their skills (practising their instrument, for example). Reactions have been just as varied, at the collective level, in the capacity of certain organizations to reinvent themselves: in their economic model, their way of working, of animating their collectives, in the artistic formats and in the new relationships created with consumers to renew the spectator's experience in distanced conditions.

The effect of the crisis has also had a differentiated mechanical effect on the cultural supply chain: increased production costs, maintenance of fixed costs (theatres and staff), but also distribution bottlenecks at the end of the lockdown (less visibility of works, on a volume of audience that is itself restricted).

Of course, what was bad before did not get better during the crisis. The world remains the same, but it appears much more labile, giving the opportunity to define new ways of creating and working, building on new skills and ways of doing things, renewing and rethinking new solidarities: "during the crisis, we had to stick together".

What about policies?

If differences exist among the various sectors of the cultural field, a similar diversity takes place among countries in terms of public policy choices as well as financial resources dedicated to support the ecosystem.

The following book reveals the great disparity of the measures taken in the different countries. As a matter of fact, they must address several categories of actors with very different issues and types of problems to be dealt with depending on the country: producers, cultural venues (heritage museums or theatres), artists and technicians leading to difficulties. These issues could sometimes appear contradictory, since it was necessary to reassure cultural professionals about economic and employment support (income, partial activity) and to enable them to maintain artistic collectives, by announcing clear rules to prevent skills from leaving for other sectors. The challenge was to maintain adapted forms of activity (teleworking), and degraded artistic formats (concerts, festivals or online exhibitions) in order to keep the teams committed and prepare for the post-crisis period.

The variety of situations can therefore only raise questions about the effectiveness and calibration of the public support measures implemented, as well as those to be devised in a European framework. Faced with an unexpected crisis, which affected all societies, we could not help but notice the difficulty of public authorities in managing both the continuation of traditional forms of culture and the emergence and support of new formats and new activities driven by digital technology and consumed by users.

It therefore seemed particularly important to rely on contributors from several European countries to feed a systematic work of international comparison based on the experience of many of the countries mentioned in this book. It is even an incentive to go further, particularly regarding the harmonization and collation of data.

Pierre-Jean Benghozi

Introduction

The COVID-19 pandemic and the cultural industries
Emergency strategies and a renewed interest for building a better future?

Elisa Salvador

June 2021

The idea for this book was born during the first strict lockdown of March 2020 for containing the COVID-19 pandemic worldwide.

Since the very beginning of such an exceptional and unexpected situation, the pivotal role played by culture and cultural and creative activities at home was evident. People obliged to stay at home by the repeated lockdowns and, distressed by the brutal effects of the virus, started to consume more cultural products. Reading a book, watching a film, listening to music, visiting virtually a museum, etc. became habits useful not only for spending time but also and most of all for relaxing the mind. It is undeniable that the culture and arts sectors were revealed to be strong resources during the pandemic.

This unusual and unexpected situation brought awareness about the positive contribution that culture and the cultural and creative industries (CCIs) bring to everyday life. A public debate emerged soon about the essential character or not of cultural activities (books, music, concerts, museums), and therefore discussions started about the possible exceptions (to the strict lockdown rules) to be provided for the CCIs, and the collective efforts to be made to support them as well as the artistic personnel.

Thus, a renewed attention toward the importance of culture and the CCIs aroused. Historically, culture has played a pivotal role at the European Union level, and it is part of a central pillar of its actions, not only for fostering cooperation among member states but also for valorizing cultural heritage, national identities, and traditions (Littoz-Monnet, 2007; Benghozi, Salvador, 2019). Notwithstanding, CCIs are hardly considered to live up to other well-established industries in the manufacturing or service sectors. Univocal classifications as well as definitions of what are the CCIs at national and international level do not exist, and, consequently, this complexity is usually reflected in different policy measures at the country level. Nonetheless, the capacity to survive and adapt to a sprouting environment

DOI: 10.4324/9781003128274-1

is at the heart of the challenges of creativity. Consequently, the innate characteristics of the CCIs should place them among the best provided to deal with an exceptional situation like the COVID-19 pandemic, showing creative capacities, original and adaptive solutions. The CCIs had yet recently to address the disruptive changes brought by the Internet and Information and Communication Technologies (Salvador et al., 2019): a reversal model (Benghozi, Salvador, 2015) associated with new strategies appeared. According to Benghozi et al. (2021), nowadays CCIs' companies are facing the alternative between two main specific strategies, not forcedly classifiable according to theories and perspectives existing in the academic literature: a static but flexible strategy *vs* a dynamic and liquid one (Bauman, 2000). This last strategy consists of a proactive and more than agile strategy characterized by quick movements, rapid adaptations, and constant changes for being in tune with the evolutions of the external environment. This strategy seems particularly suitable to the present context.

In other words, if it is true that the COVID-19 pandemic found everyone unprepared from several points of view, it is also true that, among others, it displayed the fundamental contribution of the CCIs for society.

Nonetheless, this situation was also dramatic for the CCIs: since the beginning of March 2020 we assisted in the closure of heritage sites, museums, theatres, cinemas, and several other cultural institutions across the world as well as to the cancellation of events like concerts and festivals. In line with the "dynamic and liquid" strategy, several cultural institutions reacted quickly by providing smart online solutions to the unexpected situation and sudden disconnection from consumers. Virtual tours and online exhibitions flourished, and on social networks hashtags like #museumsfromhome were created, opera houses proposed online programming of their events, and cinemas turned to streaming solutions or rediscovered old formats like the drive-in. But the CCIs and artists started also to experience severe funding difficulties and drastic loss of income for an uncertain period.

Such a situation, never seen before, pushed the Editors of this Book to launch a call for chapters about this edited volume. The call for chapters aroused a lot of interest and the selection of 15 accepted chapters is presented in this volume under three main Sections (cf. *infra*).

Of course, it is far too early to estimate the full effects of the pandemic on the CCIs and the various national cultural systems. Nonetheless, the COVID-19 crisis has certainly obliged to realize some structural problems and needs of the CCIs at the country level, and it could and should be a good opportunity for revising cultural policy priorities and strategies as well as solving undealt issues. When the pandemic is over, also the CCIs will have to adapt to "the new normal" in their activities: actually, we cannot know what and how it will be, but it is to be hoped that the reading of this book would help to reflect on the next future.

The time has come to pay attention and to care about the CCIs on a regular basis and not only in times of critical contexts, like the pandemic that is impacting the lives of people worldwide. The main goal of this book is thus to alert to the need not to turn off the attention on the CCIs *after* the COVID-19 emergency. The lessons learned from this sad experience should lead to a better valorization of the contribution of the CCIs to the heritage of humanity.

Considering the importance and necessity of updated EU policy strategy for the CCIs, given the evolving context influenced by the pandemic, rethinking what the future of these industries would look like has become non-postponable. To this aim, a European action for a dedicated *White Paper* about CCIs policy actions in the next future would be advisable. A team of experts could provide useful suggestions for a revised policy strategy orientation and priorities setting at the EU level about the CCIs.

Culture, like science, can be considered a public good with intrinsic characteristics making its complete transformation into a commodity impossible (Callon, Bowker, 1994; Dasgupta, David, 1994). This reasoning can be someway extended to the overall world of the CCIs. The recent massive digital consumption of cultural products questions a possible rising process of "commodification or commoditization of culture": like in the e-book readers' comparison (Benghozi, Salvador, 2015), recent habits due to the consequences of the pandemic could, among others, originate a shift toward commoditization. In other words, a process could be activated so that a cultural product loses its specific attributes, and it becomes no longer truly distinguishable by customers, that are thus pushed to make consumption decisions mainly because of "price". Following the effects of the pandemic, a reflection on the future orientation of the EU policy about the CCIs should take into account also this aspect: reconciling the market needs of profits with the CCIs mission of producing cultural products seen also as public goods.

Given this framework and taking into account the evolving and unstable context due to the pandemic still in progress, this Book investigates first reactions and actual strategies of CCIs' actors, government bodies, and cultural institutions facing the COVID-19 crisis and the potential consequences of these emergency strategies for the future of the CCIs. Creative solutions adopted during the repeated lockdowns by CCIs' actors could originate new forms of cultural consumption and/or new innovative market strategies when the pandemic is over. This book is thus a collection of original contributions focused on European countries.

More specifically, the book is organized into three main sections.

Section 1 explores "Regional and national policies: the impact of the COVID-19 crisis on the cultural industries", including four chapters focused in general on member states of the European Union and the United Kingdom, and in particular on France, Finland, and Slovakia.

Section 2 deals with "Cultural workers: resilience and organization during the COVID-19 pandemic", including five chapters focused on Norwegian, Italian, Austrian, and Spanish (compared to Colombian) actors.

Finally, Section 3 is focused on "Institutional strategies: first responses in the arts and culture sectors to the strict lockdown of March 2020", including six chapters mainly focused on Italy, Spain, Nordic countries, and the Czech Republic. The great uncertainty that shrouds the present context of the COVID-19 pandemic still in progress as well as the post-pandemic era that is expected to come in the next future makes it difficult to discuss emergency strategies and to envisage future policy responses. Nonetheless, this section provides an interesting collection of first responses.

The book ends with a short concluding chapter written by Trilce Navarrete, co-editor of the Book.

A short summary of individual chapters included in each section is provided here below.

Section 1: "Regional and national policies: The impact of the COVID-19 crisis on the cultural industries"

The book begins with the chapter written by **Alessandro Giovanni Lamonica and Pierangelo Isernia (Chapter 1)**, which looks at the main policy responses put in place by public authorities to support the initial relief of the CCIs during the pandemic in Europe. To this aim, they review and discuss the short-term, first wave reaction policy responses put in place by national governments of the member states of the European Union and the United Kingdom from the beginning of the COVID-19 crisis to the late summer of 2020. Their analysis is focused on a database of 484 policy responses to the COVID-19 crisis (early February–late July 2020) created in the framework of a study commissioned by the Cultural Relations Platform of the European Commission. They show that all EU governments have activated public support for the CCIs relatively quickly and in an articulated fashion, with of course specificities in national approaches.

Chapter 2 is about the case of France, known for the specificities of the role played in general by culture – the so-called "exception culturelle" (Lescure, 2013). **Jean-Paul Simon** thus focuses on the policies and reactions of the main stakeholders in France facing the COVID-19 pandemic: his chapter investigates the resilience of the French cultural bodies through analyzing a wide collection of official documents and reports. He provides a review of the main supporting measures adopted by the French government since the spread of the COVID-19 pandemic for the CCIs. He highlights the difficulty of obtaining comprehensive and reliable data as well as disentangling the real amounts of measures and forecasts. This brings confusion and adds further difficulties to assess the impact of the pandemic on the CCIs. Nonetheless, the French government has not neglected the CCIs: specific financial support to the CCIs' sectors has been implemented.

The case of Finland is then explored in **Chapter 3. Mervi Luonila, Vappu Renko, Olli Jakonen, Sari Karttunen, and Anna Kanerva** explore the various measures that have been designed for and targeted to the CCIs in

Finland facing the pandemic since March 2020. Their analysis is enriched by a survey they carried out among public cultural policy officers in early 2021. They describe the complex combination of different funding instruments, policy programs, and government institutions and organizations that characterize the management and implementation of policies related to the CCIs in Finland. Then, they highlight how Finland launched multiple support initiatives to keep CCIs afloat and compensate at least some of the losses caused by the pandemic. They argue that the crisis seems to have given new impetus to the corporatist tendencies in Finnish cultural policies. Facing the pandemic, multiple stakeholders have been involved in the policy planning and decision making, and the emergency support instruments have been designed and implemented in collaboration with CCIs' actors.

Finally, **Zuzana Došeková and Andrej Svorenčík** analyze the impact of the COVID-19 pandemic on CCIs in Slovakia and the government's policy response (**Chapter 4**). To this aim, they use data from official statistics as well as self-reports collected in surveys. They conclude their chapter with a summary of recommendations for policymakers.

Section 2 "Cultural workers: Resilience and organization during the COVID-19 pandemic"

After the overview on policies at the regional and national levels in some European countries, Section 2 looks at the situation of cultural workers. To this aim, in **Chapter 5 Beate Elstad, Dag Jansson, and Erik Døving** focus on the immediate coping modes among cultural workers in the Norwegian performing arts sector in the spring of 2020: through an original methodology, they explore how different categories of cultural workers in Norway coped with their work situation one month after the full lockdown caused by the COVID-19 pandemic. Their analysis was focused on 1,337 responses coming from an online questionnaire distributed by email to members of Creo – Norway's largest trade union for performing artists. They found that cultural workers predominantly entered "fight" modes, and to a lesser extent "flight" or "freeze" modes in the initial phase of the pandemic.

Then, in **Chapter 6 Viktoriya Pisotska and Luca Giustiniano** explore Italian cultural workers' psychological resilience and adaptation during and immediately after the first COVID-19 lockdown as well as reorganization of their professional lives: 26 semi-structured interviews and several informal conversations with cultural workers and experts in the CCIs, undertaken between March and July 2020, feed their analysis. Their findings revealed how cultural workers hold several resource endowments that helped them facing better the critical situation: besides their personality traits and creative attitude, their flexibility and adaptation capacity fostered improvisation engagement through using available (even if not always optimal) resources.

And **Chapter 7** is about the coworking spaces context. **Federica Rossi and Ilaria Mariotti** explore the consequences of the COVID-19 pandemic on the cultural events' organization, management, and communication strategies by coworking spaces in Italy: the users of these spaces are mostly professionals belonging to the CCIs. These authors analyze data from the national survey by the Italian coworking online platform in 2018 (before COVID-19) and 2020 (during COVID-19), and present the case study of Milan, based on the local survey in 2020 of the project Milano Collabora. As expected, the COVID-19 pandemic has had a strong negative impact on events and training courses: coworking spaces have reacted through massively using social media and messaging channels to keep their community alive and organizing online training courses and webinars as well as virtual events. Tailored policy tools are advocated by the authors that advance interesting suggestions.

Dagmar Abfalter and Sandra Stini in Chapter 8 investigate the situation of freelance classical musicians during the COVID-19 pandemic in Austria. They developed an early explorative online survey among freelance musicians in Austria about the expected loss of earnings for the first pandemic month from 13 March to 13 April 2020. The sample consists of 200 freelance musicians of all genres in Austria. In this chapter they present perceptions of the impact of the COVID-19 on job portfolios and income.

This section ends with the contribution by **Javier A. Rodríguez-Camacho, Pedro Rey-Biel, Jeremy C. Young, and Mónica Marcell Romero Sánchez (Chapter 9)**. These authors focus on the life of artists during the COVID-19 lockdown. They investigate how artists dealt with the effects of the pandemic, notably the availability of more time and the absence of audience in presence. To this aim, 345 artists from different disciplines from Colombia and Spain participated in their survey in 2020–2021. This survey was followed by an experimental design between April and May 2021 to evaluate experts and audience reactions to the works (pre- and post-pandemic) of 18 Colombian visual artists who participated in the survey. This experimental stage aimed at linking the ways artists used their time during the lockdown with potential market results. This original experiment is presented in the chapter as well as the econometric model they estimated.

Section 3 "Institutional strategies: First responses in the arts and culture sectors to the strict lockdown of March 2020"

This section is finally focused on first responses and strategies at the institutional level, with a focus on some EU countries.

In **Chapter 10, Enrico Bertacchini, Andrea Morelli, and Giovanna Segre** focus on cultural heritage and museums, one of the most hit CCIs' sectors: they use the Italian context as a seminal case study for addressing how the impact of the COVID-19 crisis has highlighted the need to find new solutions and is obliging museums to rethink their strategies toward new models of audience involvement and economic sustainability. With a cultural heritage often considered one of the largest and most diversified globally, Italy is one of the best case studies for such an analysis. The authors argue about the need to shift from a transactional to a relationship orientation as well as to explore new network governance models. They advance very interesting and original policy proposals, like the design of a universal membership scheme.

After the focus on Italy, in **Chapter 11 Raúl Abeledo Sanchis and Guillem Bacete Armengot** focus on the Spanish context: they analyze the first reaction of the CCIs in Spain following the lockdown measures implemented in March 2020 by providing descriptive data coming from 784 respondents to a survey undertaken one month after the beginning of the strict lockdown. Overall, respondents showed some mistrust in policymakers' support in the short and long term: a support scheme specific to the CCIs was absent and a strategic recovery plan dedicated to the CCIs was desirable.

The pandemic also severely affected film and drama series projects. Thanks to a survey of theatrical film and documentary as well as TV-drama producers across the Nordic countries (Denmark, Iceland, Finland, Norway, and Sweden), supplemented by in-depth interviews, **Terje Gaustad and Peter Booth (Chapter 12)** identify the emergency project strategies developed by film and drama producers for reacting to the unexpected COVID-19 crisis coming from outside the production. These authors argue that producers have responded to the initial disruption brought by the COVID-19 with emergency strategies that are gradually turning into new emergent strategies alongside new patterns of work. A two-step cluster analysis completes their study: they identify four strategic clusters representing different types of strategic responses to the pandemic.

Then, **Marek Prokůpek and Jakub Grosman in Chapter 13** explore the impact of the COVID-19 pandemic on the arts and cultural sector in the Czech Republic. They analyze data coming from a survey undertaken between March and June 2020. During this period, the authors collected responses from 317 arts and cultural organizations and 860 individual cultural workers.

Finally, **Caitriona Noonan (Chapter 14)** examines national screen agencies as key public bodies mediating the impact of the pandemic, and she provides some reflections on the challenges and threats screen agencies will have to face in the next future because of the consequences of the pandemic. And **John O'Hagan and Karol J. Borowiecki (Chapter 15)** thoroughly discusses the likely implications for the production and consumption of live orchestral music during the COVID-19 crisis and the long-term changes, with a focus on symphony orchestras.

To conclude, **Trilce Navarrete** highlights some common messages coming from the various chapters: the role of culture in our society, the difficulty of obtaining data about the CCIs, and the insights to deepen investigations about the CCIs coming from the pandemic. She concludes with some considerations about the possible implications of the pandemic on the CCIs.

References

Bauman Z. (2000), Liquid Modernity, Cambridge, Cambridge University Press.

Benghozi P.-J., Salvador E. (2015), Technological Competition: a Path Towards Commoditization or Differentiation? Some Evidence from a Comparison of e-book Readers, Systèmes d'Information et Management (SIM), vol. 20, n. 3, pp. 97–135.

Benghozi P.-J., Salvador E. (2019) "The place of the Cultural and Creative industries in the EU policy orientation: the point of view of Communications from the European Commission", 15th International Conference on Arts and Cultural Management, AIMAC 2019, Ca' Foscari University of Venice, Italy, June 23–26.

Benghozi P.-J., Salvador E., Simon J.-P. (2021), "Strategies in the cultural and creative industries: static but flexible vs dynamic and liquid. The emergence of a new model in the digital age", Revue d'Economie Industrielle, vol. 174, n. 2, pp. 117–157.

Callon M., Bowker G. (1994), "Is Science a Public Good?", Fifth Mullins Lecture, Virginia Polytechnic Institute, 23 March 1993, Science, Technology & Human Values, vol. 19, n. 4, pp. 395–424.

Dasgupta P., David P. A. (1994), "Toward a New Economics of Science", Research Policy, vol. 23, pp. 487–521.

Lescure P. (2013), "Mission Acte II de l'exception culturelle. Contribution aux politiques culturelles à l'ère numérique", Culture-Acte 2, Ministère de la culture et de la communication, Paris, Mai, p. 719.

Littoz-Monnet A. (2007), The European Union and Culture: Between Economic Regulation and European Cultural Policy, Manchester, Manchester University Press.

Salvador E., Simon J.-P, Benghozi P.-J. (2019), "Facing Disruption: The Cinema Value Chain in the Digital Age", International Journal of Arts Management, vol. 22, n. 1, pp. 25–40.

Section 1

Regional and national policies

The impact of the COVID-19 crisis on the cultural industries

1 The COVID-19 pandemic and cultural industries in the EU and in the United Kingdom

A perfect storm[1]

Alessandro Giovanni Lamonica and Pierangelo Isernia

Introduction

The COVID-19 pandemic has deeply impacted economies, societies, and political systems worldwide. Culture, as an economic sector and a social phenomenon, has not been spared either. To face this emergency, public authorities have announced, adopted, and sometimes implemented measures to mitigate the impact of the pandemic on the Cultural and Creative Sectors (CCSs) and to support and revitalize the economic and social fabric. This chapter is intended to contribute to an understanding of the contribution of public authorities to the immediate relief of the cultural ecosystem in Europe in the face of the pandemic. To do so, it reviews and discusses the key policy responses put in place by the member states of the European Union (EU) and the United Kingdom from the beginning of the COVID-19 health crisis to the late summer of 2020.

An analysis of the policy responses aimed at addressing the effects of the pandemic on the CCSs implies an understanding of the impact of the pandemic on the CCSs in Europe. This impact largely depends on the peculiar nature of the cultural and creative "ecosystem". Accordingly, in this chapter, we first analyze the economic characteristics of the CCSs in Europe before COVID-19 and the main effects of COVID-19 on the CCSs. After setting out this context, we then discuss the main policy responses put in place by public authorities to support the initial relief of the CCSs during the pandemic in Europe, looking at their content, variety, and cross-national applications.

Background: The economic and socio-cultural characteristics of a fragile ecosystem

In discussing the economic characteristics of culture in Europe, we focus on three dimensions: government spending, the nature and size of sectoral employment, and the characteristics of the business actors involved. If government expenditures are a reliable indicator of policy relevance, culture

DOI: 10.4324/9781003128274-3

occupies only a marginal role among governments' activities in Europe. In 2019, social protection and health accounted for 19.3% and 7.0% of gross domestic product (GDP), respectively. Conversely, culture[3] accounted for only 0.7% of GDP (and approximately 1.4% of general government expenditure, as compared to 41.4% for social protection and 15.1% for health). In gross figures, these percentages hover around Eur 90 billion, a rather modest figure that has not changed significantly from 2013 to date (Eurostat 2020a).

The low priority of culture in government spending in Europe is in contrast with the significance of the cultural sector in terms of employment[4] and revenues. In 2019, 7.4 million individuals were employed in the cultural sector in Europe, amounting to 3.7% of the total number of people employed in the European economy. Prior to the pandemic, cultural employment was steadily growing, with an increase of 8% (or half a million more workers) between 2014 and 2019 in most European countries (Eurostat 2020b). The vitality of the CCSs before the pandemic is also confirmed by the fact that more than 1.1 million cultural enterprises[5] were operating in Europe in 2017, amounting to 5% of all enterprises (excluding those in the financial sector). The sector's value added (€145 billion or 2.3% of the total) was higher than that of motor trades or chemical products manufacturing. And between 2012 and 2017, European cultural enterprises have been growing at an average rate of 1.5% per year, higher than the continent's total of the non-financial business economy.

Despite these positive economic fundamentals, even before the pandemic, the CCSs in Europe were characterized by an inherent and structural fragility (OECD 2020:9–11; IDEA Consult et al. 2021:15). The creative and cultural sectors are characterized by discontinuity, poor social protection, and fragmented nature of the economic infrastructure. On the one hand, many cultural workers have either precarious or part-time jobs with peculiar contractual forms that regulate the sector. On the other hand, the small (10–49 employees) and even micro (fewer than 10 employees) size of most cultural business activities in Europe (that account for more than half of the workforce in the sector, Eurostat 2020c) add a further layer of complexity. Finally, the overly specific, fragmented, and diversified business models of the CCSs make government struggle to recognize and protect them and it makes access to private finance difficult (UNESCO 2020; IDEA Consult et al. 2021:18).

Impact: The economic effects of COVID-19 on the CCSs in Europe

Qualitative and quantitative estimates clearly indicate that COVID-19 has been deeply and vastly disruptive to the world of culture (see, e.g. OECD 2020; IDEA Consult et al. 2020; KEA 2020). Looking at percentage changes over the same quarter of 2019 for employment and gross value added (GVA) at the EU level, the "arts and entertainment" sector experienced one of the sharpest contractions, with a 5.6% decrease in employment in the second quarter of 2020 (–3% in the third quarter, and –3.2% in the fourth quarter), and a loss of GVA of 29.2% in the second quarter (–13.6% in the third quarter, and –23.7% in the fourth quarter) (Eurostat 2020d). This drop is the direct effect of the anti-COVID-19 containment measures put in place by the various European countries as of March 2020 (see Politico 2020). Recent survey data (see, for example, Live DMA 2020; NEMO 2020; CCV 2021) shows how the halting of non-essential activities and mobility has affected the entire chain of creative value – creation, production, distribution, and access, including ancillary services and the hospitality sector – and it is significantly weakening the professional, social, and economic standing of artists and cultural professionals across the EU.

This impact is asymmetric in nature, varying with the cultural sub-sector involved. The loss of income involved all cultural sectors, with differences arising from the position in the value chain and status of the worker. The most affected were performing arts, due to their visitor and venue-based nature (CINARS 2020; IDEA Consult et al. 2021:19). Along with the performing arts, the film industry has been hit hard (Isernia and Lamonica 2021:19). According to the OECD (2020:21), the book publishing sector at the global level lost up to 7 billion dollars in 2020, or 7.6% of revenues achieved in 2019, with repercussions in the activities of publishers, writers, and bookshops. Containment measures have nearly wiped-out live music industry revenues due to the cancellation of music events and festivals (see, for example, EFA 2020), resulting in shrinking ticket and merchandise revenues and a collapse in sponsorship (OECD 2020:15).

Responses: Public policy measures in EU member states and in the United Kingdom

As the pandemic started to spread from February 2020 on, all European countries announced, adopted, and implemented measures aimed at containing the negative effects of the crisis on their economic and social fabric. In this section, we discuss the public policy responses put in place by national governments to support the CCSs during the pandemic in the EU and the United Kingdom.[6]

Our analysis, which is intended as a first descriptive exercise and not a systematic policy assessment, relies upon a standardized database of 484 policy responses to the COVID-19 crisis[7] created in the framework of a study commissioned by the Cultural Relations Platform of the European Commission. The period covered goes from early February to late July 2020, and therefore it examines the short-term, first-wave reaction policy responses adopted by the EU governments and the United Kingdom.

The policy measures were classified into different categories (see Table 1.1), based on a distinction between economic and non-economic

Table 1.1 Typology of public policy responses announced, adopted, or implemented between February and July 2020 in Europe. Distribution by country.

Country	Structural fund/grant	Loans	Fiscal measures	Economic policy Extension/ referral of pre-existing support measures	Unemployment schemes	Income support/ cash transfers	Exemption/ postponement/ referral of obligations	Debt/ contract relief	Closure and reopening	Health	International support	Digital infrastructure	Access to culture
Austria	✓	✓								✓			
Belgium	✓	✓		✓	✓	✓	✓		✓				
Bulgaria	✓	✓	✓	✓	✓		✓						✓
Croatia	✓		✓	✓	✓	✓	✓		✓				
Czech Republic						✓			✓			✓	
Denmark	✓		✓	✓									
Estonia	✓		✓	✓		✓			✓	✓			
Finland	✓	✓	✓	✓	✓	✓	✓		✓			✓	✓
France	✓	✓	✓	✓	✓	✓	✓	✓	✓				✓
Germany	✓	✓	✓	✓		✓	✓		✓			✓	✓
Greece	✓	✓	✓										
Hungary													

(Continued)

Table 1.1 Typology of public policy responses announced, adopted, or implemented between February and July 2020 in Europe. Distribution by country. (Continued)

Country	Structural fund/grant	Loans	Fiscal measures	Extension/referral of pre-existing support measures	Unemployment schemes	Income support/cash transfers	Exemption/postponement/referral of obligations	Debt/contract relief	Closure and reopening	Health	International support	Digital infrastructure	Access to culture
					Economic policy								
Ireland	✓	✓	✓	✓									
Italy	✓	✓	✓			✓	✓		✓				✓
Latvia	✓	✓	✓	✓		✓	✓		✓				✓
Lithuania	✓	✓	✓	✓	✓	✓	✓		✓				
Luxembourg	✓		✓	✓	✓							✓	
Malta	✓		✓		✓	✓	✓		✓				
Netherlands	✓	✓	✓	✓	✓	✓	✓		✓				
Poland	✓		✓	✓	✓	✓	✓		✓				
Portugal	✓			✓	✓		✓		✓			✓	
Republic of Cyprus	✓		✓		✓			✓					✓
Romania	✓		✓	✓	✓	✓	✓		✓				
Slovakia	✓	✓	✓	✓	✓	✓	✓						
Slovenia	✓		✓	✓	✓		✓		✓				
Spain	✓	✓		✓			✓						
Sweden	✓	✓				✓			✓	✓			
United Kingdom													

measures. One-third of the measures we report are horizontal and designed to protect many economic and productive sectors also including the CCS. A vast majority (71%), however, are more selective and cover only one, a few, or the whole range of cultural sectors in different combinations. Finally, while only three out of ten measures also[8] act at the individual level – e.g. in favour of self-employed people – 80% of measures include provisions benefitting organizations (e.g. micro, small, and medium-sized enterprises, non-governmental organizations).

Economic measures

Measures of an economic nature represent the overwhelming majority (82%) of the public measures put in place in response to the pandemic and reported over the period covered by this analysis. These measures can be broken down into income support, structural funds/grants, loans/loan guarantees, unemployment schemes, exemption/postponement/referral of obligations, extension/referral of pre-existing measures, fiscal measures, and debt contract/relief. Most of these measures are direct in nature (85%). Out of the total of economic measures, the most frequent one is the structural funds/grants (44%), while debt contract/relief (0.5%) is the least common.

Income support/cash transfer

European countries have put in place income support measures for both individuals and organizations. The latter mainly concern compensation for losses during periods of virus containment, in the form of reimbursement schemes or maintenance of funds already allocated for events that were later cancelled. Some countries (e.g. Italy, United Kingdom) have supplemented these measures with initiatives specifically aimed at supporting individual workers to guarantee the continuity of cultural production during periods of social distancing and interruption of venue-based activities. Measures of this type have been constructed having self-employed professionals and micro-enterprises in mind, and they take the form of a monthly or one-off income supplement. Income support measures, which make up a modest portion of the total collected (6%), were planned by more than half of the European countries (18). As of July 2020, Belgium, Latvia, and Slovenia were those countries in which income support measures reached the highest percentage (both over 15%).

Structural funds/grants

Public support has also taken the form of direct funding to cultural organizations, either as part of broader measures in favour of small and medium-sized businesses or as distinctly reserved for the CCSs alone.

Grants are usually provided on a one-off basis and allow organizations to continue operating and ensure the employment of staff by covering fixed costs or any emergency expenses. In some cases, the provision of support is linked to investments in upgrading digital infrastructure and digital production or securing premises. In smaller numbers, there are also grants directed not to organizations but to individuals to support cultural production. Structural funds account for four out of six of all economic measures implemented between February and July 2020, and they are the most frequent type of intervention overall. Over the period considered here, virtually all EU countries had introduced measures to introduce direct forms of financing. The share of these measures out of the total number of initiatives undertaken by each country varies widely, from approximately 15% in Latvia to 59% and 61%, respectively, for Ireland and Finland.

Loans/loan guarantees

Several countries have also made use of low-interest loans to guarantee liquidity to cultural activities and thus the continuity of their production, betting on the ability of cultural organizations and businesses to pay off debt in the long term. In other cases, loan guarantees have been introduced or simplified and extended; more rarely, debt payments have been suspended. Many of these measures are cross-sectoral and not limited to the creative and cultural sectors. At the end of the summer of 2020, loans, especially those devoted to culture, were not widespread among European countries (constituting only 6% of all economic initiatives). In fact, less than half of the countries had made provisions for them. Among the countries that have activated them, the United Kingdom stands out with 20% of the total of measures introduced.

Unemployment schemes

By July 2020, most countries had put in place unemployment schemes for workers who have lost their jobs due to the virus. In some cases, these measures also extended to those occupational categories in the CCS that are recognized by the social security system. However, despite their importance, they represent a tiny portion of the economic measures surveyed (4%). In the period discussed here, only 12 countries – Austria, Belgium, Bulgaria, France, Germany, Lithuania, Luxembourg, Poland, Cyprus, Romania, Slovenia, and Spain – had planned them. Among the countries mentioned, Slovenia stands out for having dedicated 17% of all its measures to unemployment support schemes. More recently, countries such as Germany and the Netherlands have been able to extend social safety nets to previously excluded cultural workers (as confirmed by CCV 2021). This is an important step, considering the non-standard nature of many cultural occupations.

Fiscal measures, exemption/postponement/referral of obligations

The creative and cultural sectors have also been fuelled to maintain the liquidity they need to operate by exempting and delaying tax obligations for both individuals and cultural and creative businesses. In some cases, countries have delayed the expiration dates of taxes such as corporate and income tax payments, social security payments, pension contributions, and value-added tax. In other cases, the same taxes have been reduced or waived. Finally, efforts have been made to simplify access to public administrations and make administrative procedures more flexible. Virtually all European countries have planned measures of this type, making up 21% of the total measures collected. Also, in this case, the frequency of measures of a fiscal nature varies greatly depending on the country under consideration. Ireland (4.5%) and the United Kingdom (5%) have given thought to fiscal aspects, but without these being preponderant, while countries such as Slovenia (50%) and Italy (37%) have used this in a great proportion.

Non-economic measures

If economic measures have played a key role in the first phase of the crisis response, and non-economic measures constitute a smaller proportion (around 18%) of those recorded, still their role is not insignificant, and it could be argued that, over time, these measures will become more and more important to redress the difficult situation of the CCSs.

Closure and reopening

All European countries have put in place containment measures, many of them specifically tailored for CCS activities (100% of those discussed here). This has led, at different times and in different ways, to the closure of cinemas, theatres, concert halls, and other venues dedicated to cultural events. Beginning in March 2020 and continuing today, these measures alternate depending on each state's approach to containment and on the pace of the epidemic (UNIC 2020). These measures are by far the most frequent non-economic measures undertaken (14%). Out of 28 countries mapped, 21 have adopted containment measures aimed specifically at the CCS.

Health

All national authorities have implemented health-related measures to contain the spread of the virus. As of July 2020, only Austria (3.7% of national measures), Estonia (10%), and the United Kingdom (5%) had issued health and safety guidelines directed exclusively at the CCSs. These measures represent a very modest portion of the total (1%). The reason is probably to be found in the fact that they can be considered recovery measures rather than relief measures, and therefore were not particularly widespread in the first phase of the emergency. In many cases, professional associations have independently produced safety protocols to be used in coordination with public authorities. This is the case, for example, with many associations in the film industry (UNIC 2020:14).

Digital infrastructure

Measures to support the digitization of the production and enjoyment of culture were not widespread as of July 2020. However, some countries have linked *ad hoc* initiatives aimed at fostering innovation and structural change in the CCSs to digitization processes. Some of these initiatives are connected to the digital production of culture; others make available incentives, tools, or capacity building to foster the creation or the strengthening of digital infrastructure. The goal is to strengthen the resilience and the innovation capacity of the world of culture and its sustainability, but also to make culture accessible in times of distancing and in a digital divide. In absolute terms, measures related to digitization represent only 1.5% of those collected and have been deployed by five countries only and in modest proportions when compared to other national measures: Czech Republic (5%), France (3%), Hungary (7%), Lithuania (7%), and Portugal (10%).

Access to culture

Finally, several states in Europe have introduced measures to support social cohesion. These include access to culture as a vehicle for greater psycho-physical well-being and social integration. In practice, these initiatives mainly concern the creation of digital platforms capable of aggregating and disseminating cultural content and encouraging dialogue between producers and users of culture. These measures represent only 2% of the total. Compared to purely digital measures, social cohesion initiatives were fielded by a greater number of countries (7): Croatia (7% of total national measures), France (3%), Greece (8%), Hungary (7%), Ireland (4%), Italy (4%), and Cyprus (9%). Like the health security measures, it is possible that the lack of attention given to social cohesion in the first stage of the health crisis is due to the urgent need to address the negative economic consequences of the containment measures. Addressing the social consequences of the pandemic for the CCSs, the importance of which has already been recognized and made explicit in various studies (IDEA Consult et al. 2021; OECD 2020; CCV 2021; Radermecker 2021), could possibly become the focus for the recovery phase, in which specific measures could be designed and implemented to limit the social and psychological repercussions of the crisis and to re-establish the enjoyment of culture and cultural products.

General considerations

To summarize this rich and variegated set of policy responses, we stress four major points. *First*, the public sector in Europe seems to have focused on the adoption of economic measures aimed at strengthening income and reducing costs. Some of these measures were aimed at supporting the economy by targeting enterprises and workers on a cross-sectoral basis that included also the CCSs. Conversely, many of the initiatives we collected specifically aim to offer relief to cultural organizations and workers. Direct disbursements of resources, via grants, loans, and cash transfers, have represented the main avenue along which these economic measures have been channelled. Only a minority of these measures were forms of indirect support, such as exemptions, referrals of obligations, and fiscal measures.

Second, the measures surveyed show substantial variability, due above all to differences in approach by individual countries. Some of these differences are merely quantitative: some countries have implemented more measures than others – e.g. France with 8% of all measures, or Germany, Italy, and Austria (with 6%) – while Eastern European countries have been less prolific (18%) than Western European countries (32% of total measures). Other differences are instead qualitative, depending on the nature of the chosen measures. In countries, such as Bulgaria, Denmark, Slovakia, Slovenia, and Sweden, virtually all measures are of an economic nature. In others, such as Croatia, Czech Republic, Estonia, Hungary, and Portugal, non-economic measures exceed 30% of the total.

Third, there is considerable variation in the priority given to different CCSs. The cultural sector in which most measures were adopted is the audio-visual sector and film distribution and production (72% of cases), and the one in which less measures were adopted is the visual arts sector (44% of cases)[9] with wide differences across countries. The gap between the most and least assisted sectors is wide in Latvia (69% film, 8% visual arts) or Sweden (83% film, 17% visual arts), whereas other countries have a more balanced distribution of measures, as it is the case with the United Kingdom or Malta (with 15% points difference between the most and least supported sector).

Fourth, the COVID-19 pandemic also spurred a supranational response. A certain number of measures have been put in place by European institutions in favour of Member States (2% of the total). These initiatives are substantially different from those of individual countries. First, almost all EU measures are economic in nature (92%), while the rest is in support of the digital infrastructure. Second, the EU has relied more heavily on structural funds and grants (50% of total EU measures) than member countries (average 35%). Third, the European institutions show a more balanced distribution of initiatives across the various CCSs, ranging from 75% of measures targeting museums and historical sites to 100% of those addressing the music sector. At the same time, a large part of these measures

(58%) is not limited to the CCSs but includes them within broader initiatives affecting all productive and commercial sectors of the EU. These include the temporary employment support measures in the SURE scheme, which allows member countries to open credit lines on easy terms that can provide up to Eur 100 billion in public spending to fight unemployment. Two other instruments put in place during the pandemic are the pan-European guarantee fund of the European Investment Bank (EIB), which offers low-interest loans of up to Eur 200 billion for European small and medium-sized companies, and the credit line for public spending on healthcare provided by the European Stability Mechanism (with loans for eurozone countries of up to 2% of GDP). Last, the EU has also implemented support measures devoted to the CCSs, albeit infinitesimally smaller than the general ones just mentioned (see, for example, EPRS 2020; Montalto et al. 2020). Apart from a few million euros in funding redirected towards the performing arts sector and the creation of an emergency fund for the film sector, the targeted measures mainly concern the postponement of administrative deadlines for Creative Europe projects and the strengthening of digital infrastructures to facilitate access to culture (e.g. the creation of the Creatives Unite platform).

Conclusion

The crisis due to COVID-19 had a devastating impact on CCSs, which proved to be one of the hardest hit sectors in the European economy. With due differences between countries and between sub-sectors, the data show that CCSs have experienced an overall freeze in activity since the beginning of the pandemic, with a consequent collapse in revenues and an important drop in jobs (see, for example, OECD 2020; IDEA Consult et al. 2021; CCV 2021).

In response to this perfect storm, our analysis shows that all EU governments have activated public support for the sector relatively quickly and in an articulated fashion. The specificities of national approaches notwithstanding, the measures put in place range from direct and indirect economic measures aimed at supplementing the income and revenues of cultural operators and reducing costs up to measures concerning public health, social cohesion, and digitalization. The role of public actors in mitigating the risks and alleviating the negative economic and social effects of COVID-19 varies from country to country, and it depends on the structural relationship between non-governmental actors and public authorities in the cultural sector.

It can be said that as compared to other economic sectors, the authorities have had more difficulty in identifying the cultural categories most in need and implementing *ad hoc* measures for them. The cause of this partial inefficiency and ineffectiveness is to be found in the specific characteristics of the cultural ecosystem and the inadequacy of public support schemes to face them. It is possible to surmise that cross-sectoral measures, insensitive to the peculiarities of the cultural sectors, might have only partially fulfilled the needs of the CCS. On top of that, social security schemes have proved unable to protect the weakest categories of the CCSs – non-standard workers – who frequently cannot even access the support measures put in place due to their status (see Johnson 2020; IDEA Consult et al. 2021:35).

Our contribution, we should also stress, has its own limits as well. In this chapter, we have focused on public actions. However, it is undeniable that non-governmental actors, and society at large, have also played a key role in complementing national initiatives. On the one hand, in many countries collective management organizations, CCS firms, and non-profit and philanthropic bodies have carried out effective advocacy that has prompted several governments and EU institutions to intervene in support of the cultural sector (see, for example, Isernia and Lamonica 2021; Comunian and England 2020). On the other hand, these same actors have quickly acted to provide economic relief to the cultural sectors most in need. This has been done by supplying alternative funding and support programmes or by working in tandem with public authorities at different levels to prepare emergency measures.

The second limit of our analysis is that it focused on the short-term responses to COVID-19 for the CCSs. Extending our gaze beyond the short-term horizon to assess the viability of the European CCSs over the long term and to predict how and when they will recover from the impact of the health emergency is, however, more difficult. The COVID-19 pandemic is likely to have profound and lasting effects on how culture is produced and enjoyed. The recovery and eventual transformation of the sector will depend on several factors.

The major known unknown is how the pandemic will evolve, how effective the health response of individual countries and of EU coordination will be, and what consequences all this will have on social distancing and containment measures. COVID-19 is still spreading in Europe, and governments are reluctant to allow their citizens back to normal life. This has implications for the ability of many CCSs, especially venue-based ones, to move from an emergency phase to a recovery and innovation one and for the possibility of members of the public to resume in-person cultural consumption. The sustainability of public expenditure and private funding is also at stake. Despite commitments, both government and non-government actors are unlikely to be able to rescue the CCSs as much as they need. It is very possible that the cultural sectors still have to pass their harder resilience test.

Notes

1. This chapter benefits from and partially relies on the primary and secondary data collected by the authors during the national lockdown periods as part of a research commissioned by the European Commission from the

Consortium responsible for the execution of the Cultural Relations Platform (EUROPAID/140334/DH/SER/MULTI). The research was conducted between June and October 2020. The full report is here: https://www.cultureinexternalrelations.eu/2021/02/10/study-is-out-impact-of-covid-19-on-ccs-in-partners-countries/. Its content is the sole responsibility of the authors and does not reflect the views of the European Union. We thank Sana Ouchtati and Jermina Stanojev, the consortium partners (Goethe-Institut, IETM [International network for contemporary performing arts], the ECF [European Cultural Foundation]), and Prof. Richard Higgott for their input during the different stages of preparation of the original report. The dataset on which this chapter is based is available from the authors upon request.

2. In line with the Regulation 1295/2013 of the European Parliament and the Council of the European Union establishing the Creative Europe Programme (2014–2020), article 2 (1), we define the cultural and creative sectors (CCSs) as "all sectors whose activities are based on cultural values and/or artistic and other creative expressions, whether those activities are market- or non-market-oriented, whatever the type of structure that carries them out, and irrespective of how that structure is financed ..."

3. The notion of culture we use includes two economic functions: "cultural services" and "broadcasting and publishing services", in line with the classification of government functions offered by Eurostat (COFOG). See: https://ec.europa.eu/eurostat/statistics-explained/index.php?title=Glossary: Classification_of_the_functions_of_government_(COFOG).

4. We adopt the definition of "cultural employment" suggested by Eurostat, and that includes those who are employed in the cultural sector, those who perform a cultural function in a non-cultural sector, and those who perform a non-cultural function in a cultural sector.

5. For a detailed discussion of the notion of "cultural enterprises" and what it includes, see https://ec.europa.eu/eurostat/statistics-explained/index.php/ Culture_statistics_-_cultural_enterprises#Business_demography.

6. For a more detailed analysis of the effects of COVID-19 on CCSs in the United Kingdom and the policy responses of the English government and non-governmental actors, see Banks M., O'Connor J. (2021); Macfarland C., Agace M., Hayes C. (2020).

7. For the mapping of the relief measures that have been taken to support the CCSs during the COVID-19 pandemic, the following sources were used and standardized for analysis: Compendium of Cultural Policies & Trends, KEA, and European Audiovisual Observatory (EAO). These sources were complemented by further online mapping and a series of interviews with area experts. A total of 749 datasets have been generated to analyze major trends. For the scope of this chapter, the data analysis is limited to all public policy responses put in place by the 27 EU member states plus the United Kingdom and the EU institutions ($N = 484$). The dataset refers to a percentage count of measures that were reported by a given country, and it does not refer to the allocation of economic resources. Our collection is not intended as an exhaustive compilation of all measures taken in all the states under scrutiny, but rather a sample of major types of relief measures that may reflect a certain institutional responsiveness and adaptability. It is not possible to hypothesize a positive correlation between the number of policy responses and their effectiveness in combating the emergency.

8. In some cases, measures include actions at both individual and organizational levels; in other cases, initiatives are targeted at only one of the two groups of potential recipients.

9. This holds true among traditional cultural sectors. Related and contiguous sectors such as Cultural and Creative Industries and the world of fashion and design score even less in terms of cases, 35% and 38%, respectively.

References

Banks, M. and O'Connor, J. (2021) "A plague upon your howling": art and culture in the viral emergency, *Cultural Trends*, 30:1, 3–18, DOI: 10.1080/09548963.2020.1827931

CCV, Center for Cultural Value (2021) *Impacts of Covid-19 on the cultural sector*. Available at: https://www.culturalvalue.org.uk/the-team/covid-19-research-project/ (last accessed: April 12, 2021).

CINARS (2020) *International survey on the Impacts of COVID-19 on performing arts international mobility*. Available at: https://www.cjoint.com/doc/20_05/JElvjeeTDaK_ReportSurvey-CINARS.pdf?fbclid=IwAR19iwZA9yAd3vmdj_7sEUtS2yoD1juAhlEYfd02qGM5I6TsIv3D0xR1wQY (last accessed: November 3, 2021).

Compendium of Cultural Policies & Trends (2020) *Financial measures*. Available at: https://www.culturalpolicies.net/covid-19/comparative-overview-financial/ (last accessed: April 20, 2021).

Comunian, R. and England, L. (2020) Creative and cultural work without filters: Covid-19 and exposed precarity in the creative economy, *Cultural Trends*, 29:2, 112–128, DOI: 10.1080/09548963.2020.1770577

EAO, European Audiovisual Observatory (2020) *COVID-19 audiovisual sector measures*. Available at: https://www.obs.coe.int/en/web/observatoire/COVID-19-audiovisual-sector-measures (last accessed: December 20, 2021).

EFA, European Festivals Association (2020) *Report on the occasion of the COVID-19 survey*. Available at: https://www.efa-aef.eu/en/news/1978-report-covid-19-survey-festivals-needs-and-commitments/ (last accessed: November 16, 2021).

EPRS, European Parliamentary Research Service (2020) *EU support for artists and the cultural and creative sector during the coronavirus crisis*. Available at: https://www.europarl.europa.eu/thinktank/en/document.html?reference=EPRS_BRI(2020)649414 (last accessed: February 2, 2021).

European Parliament and Council of the European Union (2013) *Regulation (EU) No 1295/2013 of the European Parliament and of the Council of 11 December 2013 establishing the Creative Europe Programme (2014 to 2020) and repealing Decisions No 1718/2006/EC, No 1855/2006/EC and No 1041/2009/EC*. Available at: https://eur-lex.europa.eu/legal-content/EN/TXT/?uri=CELEX%3A32013R1295 (last accessed: February 15, 2021).

Eurostat (2020a) *Cultural statistics – government expenditure on cultural, broadcasting and publishing services*. Available at: https://ec.europa.eu/eurostat/statistics-explained/index.php?title=Culture_statistics_-_government_expenditure_on_cultural,_broadcasting_and_publishing_services&oldid=524139 (last accessed: March 10, 2021).

Eurostat (2020b) *Cultural statistics – cultural employment*. Available at: https://ec.europa.eu/eurostat/statistics-explained/index.php?title=Culture_statistics_-_cultural_employment (last accessed: March 10, 2021).

Eurostat (2020c) *Cultural statistics – cultural enterprises.* Available at: https:// ec.europa.eu/eurostat/statistics-explained/index.php?title=Culture_statistics_-_ cultural_enterprises (last accessed: March 12, 2021).

Eurostat (2020d) *Quarterly national accounts – GDP and employment.* Available at: https://ec.europa.eu/eurostat/statistics-explained/index.php?title=Quarterly_ national_accounts_-_GDP_and_employment&oldid=491753 (last accessed: March 2, 2021).

IDEA Consult, Goethe-Institut, Amann S. and Heinsius J. (2021), *Research for CULT Committee – cultural and creative sectors in post-Covid-19 Europe: crisis effects and policy recommendations.* European Parliament, Policy Department for Structural and Cohesion Policies, Brussels.

Isernia, P. and Lamonica, A. G. (2021) *The assessment of the impact of COVID-19 on the cultural and creative sectors in EU's partner countries: policy responses, and their implications for international cultural relations,* Report, Cultural Relations Platform. Available at: https://www.cultureinexternalrelations.eu/cier-data/uploads/2021/02/CRP_COVID_ICR_Study-final-Public.pdf (last accessed: March 20, 2021).

Johnson, R. (2020) *Policy review: social security and the status of the artist.* Centre for Cultural Value, Leeds.

KEA (2020) *COVID-19 national measures for CCS across the EU.* Available at: https://keanet.eu/research-apps/c19m/ (last accessed: December 15, 2020).

Live DMA (2020) *Key numbers – impact of the Covid-19 pandemic on 2600 live music venues and clubs in 2020.* Available at: https://vi.be/files/artikels/ attachments/key-numbers-impact-of-the-covid-19-pandemic-on-2600-live-dma-european-music-venues-and-clubs-in-2020-september-2020.pdf (last accessed: February 9, 2021).

Macfarland C., Agace M. and Hayes C. (2020) *Creativity, culture and connection. Responses from arts and culture organisations in the COVID-19 crisis.* COVI Common Vision. Available at: http://covi.org.uk/dev4/wp-content/ uploads/2020/09/Creativity-Culture-and-Connection_Common-Vision-report_ September-2020.pdf (last accessed: January 9, 2021).

Montalto V., Sacco P. L., Alberti V., Panella F. and Saisana M. (2020) *European cultural and creative cities in COVID-19 times: jobs at risk and the policy response,* EUR 30249 EN, Publications Office of the European Union, Luxembourg. ISBN 978-92-76-19433-0, doi:10.2760/624051, JRC120876. Available at: https://pub-lications.jrc.ec.europa.eu/repository/handle/JRC120876 (last accessed: February 20, 2021).

NEMO, Network of European Museums Organisations (2020) *Survey on the impact of the COVID-19 situation on museums in Europe.* Report. Available at: https://www.ne-mo.org/fileadmin/Dateien/public/NEMO_documents/NEMO_ COVID19_Report_12.05.2020.pdf (last accessed: February 15, 2021).

OECD, Organization for Economic Cooperation and Development (2020) *Culture shock: COVID-19 and the cultural and creative sectors.* OECD Policy Responses to Coronavirus (COVID-19), OECD Publishing, Paris, https://doi. org/10.1787/08da9e0e-en.

Politico (2020) "Europe's coronavirus lockdown measures compared". *Politico.* Available at: https://www.politico.eu/article/europes-coronavirus-lockdown-measures-compared/ (last accessed: March 1, 2021).

Radermecker, A-S. V. (2021) Art and culture in the COVID-19 era: for a consumer-oriented approach, *SN Bus Econ* 1, 4. https://doi.org/10.1007/s43546-020-00003-y

UNESCO (2020). *Museums around the world in the face of COVID-19.* UNESCO. Available at: https://unesdoc.UNESCO.org/ark:/48223/pf0000373530 (last accessed: February 12, 2021).

UNIC, Union Internationale des cinémas (2020) *The impact of the Coronavirus outbreak on the European cinema industry.* Report, UNIC. Available at: https://www.unic-cinemas.org/fileadmin/user_upload/Publications/Public_-_UNIC_research_-_Coronavirus_impact_on_the_cinema_industry_v96.pdf (last accessed: January 5, 2021).

2 The COVID-19 pandemic and cultural industries in France

Cultural policy challenged[1]

Jean Paul Simon

Introduction

It is almost a *cliché* to highlight the substantial action of French public authorities in the field of culture. As stressed by Ahearne (2002, p. 1): "Indeed, France and the USA are commonly taken to indicate opposite ends, as it were, of the spectrum of cultural policy framework instituted by modern democratic liberal states ...". These cultural policies are all-encompassing: national, regional and local governments allocate meaningful funds to various segments of the Cultural and Creative Industries (CCIs), besides administrating legal and regulatory aspects. An impressive array of public entities (cf. Section 2 is in charge of managing these various fields and of liaising with the main stakeholders. France is known as a strong promoter of the so-called "cultural exception" (Lescure, 2013).

Therefore, one may expect some strong reactions from the authorities to deal with the impact of the COVID-19 pandemic. Some of these actions may be easy to track (for example, to maintain employment or support cultural venues, etc.). However, the real issues stem from various factors. First, it looks difficult to perform any early assessment of the impact of the pandemic still in progress on the CCIs, and the extent of persistent damage (scarring) as it combines "the effects of shocks in the same sector (own effect) and from other sectors (spill over effects) on the cumulative change in real gross value added" (IMF, 2021, p. 51). Because of lingering and dynamic effects as well as delayed impacts, the precise dimensions are far from being clear. As stressed by a recent report for the European Parliament (de Vet et al., 2021, p. 29): "No comprehensive data is currently available on the estimate job losses in European CCI since the outbreak of COVID-19 ..." Furthermore, the lack of reliable data is linked to "the often informal and unstable nature of 'cultural' work in virtually all Member States ..." (European Euro FIA/EFJ/FIM/UNI Europa, 2016). In France "one third of cultural sector workers are self-employed, compared to only 12% of the total labour force in all sectors" (Turner, 2021).

On top of this structural aspect, the very notion of CCIs still remains vague (Benghozi et al., 2015, 2021). The definitions of the sectors and data

DOI: 10.4324/9781003128274-4

availability vary.[2] The 2019 report for the European Parliament (2019) noted: "the difficulty in clearly delimitating cultural domains of activity, for instance, performing arts do not include live musical performances, which are included under the cultural industry 'music' sector".

Against this backdrop, the goal of the chapter is to marshal data and to document the policies and reactions of the main stakeholders in France facing the COVID-19 pandemic. The chapter aims at investigating the resilience of the French cultural bodies confronted with the pandemic. The research is based on desk research and an analysis of the available official documents and reports from or commissioned by trade associations will be undertaken.

The chapter opens with a brief presentation of the weight of culture in France, followed by a presentation of the main bodies involved in the implementation and funding of the cultural policies. The third section reviews the initiatives adopted to support the industries during the pandemic. The last section gives the viewpoint of some leading stakeholders. It introduces some elements about the demand side.

The economic weight of culture: A quick overview[3]

According to the Ministry of Culture (see Table 2.1): "in 2019, the direct economic weight of culture, that is to say the added value of all cultural branches, is 49.2 billion euros" (Turner, 2021, press release). "In 2018, 692,900 people worked in the cultural sectors (2.6% of the labour force), mainly in books and the press (19%), visual arts (15%) and audiovisual (15%)" (Turner, 2021, press release).

Table 2.1 The direct economic weight of culture in 2019.[4]

Distribution across cultural domains	Production (commercial and non-commercial) Value (billion euros)	Production (commercial and non-commercial) Weight (%)	Added value Value (billion euros)	Added value Weight (%)
Audiovisual[a]	31.8	33.3	13.7	27.8
Performing arts	12.3	12.9	7.6	15.4
Book industry and newspaper	14.8	15.6	7.1	14.4
Advertising	11.5	12.0	5.5	11.2
Heritage	7.7	8.1	4.8	9.7
Visual arts	8.4	8.9	4.3	8.7
Architecture	6.1	6.4	4.1	8.3
Education	2.7	2.8	2.2	4.5
Total	95.3	100.00	49.3	100.0

Source: Compiled by the author from Turner (2021, p. 4), Ministry of Culture (2020a,b,c,d).
[a] Includes recorded music and video games.

By contrast with these figures, the recent EY study for the GESAC[5] (EY/GESAC 2021)[6] claims that in France 1.3 million jobs are directly threatened by the pandemic, a number of jobs that is almost double the official data. The study forecasts a decrease of 32% of the turnover. However, these dire figures may not be ground_d in robust evic_nce, as illus__ated by the discrepancy with the official data: "For the year 2020, revenues from the market cultural sectors fell by 11 billion euros compared to 2019, a decrease of 12%. Film projection (–65%) and live entertainment (–43%) are the two sectors most affected, while video games show an annual growth of 21% in sales" (Bourlès & Nicolas, 2021). The European Parliament report notes, for instance, that: "Television, streaming, music and radio services endured a solid uptake" (de Vet et al., 2021, p. 30).

Indeed, in the case of music in Europe, EY predicts a decrease of 76%. This figure may hold for the live events segments. However, IFPI (2021) reported that the global recorded music market grew by 7.4% in 2020. No wonder that Le Diberder (2021) can describe their forecasts, in the case of France, as "alarmist and fanciful", adding that the gloomy picture is just a tool to get some funds at the national or EU level. By the same token, he also deems that all these forecasts are grossly exaggerated, including the level of the exceptional measures adopted by the French authorities. Their real amount appears rather difficult to disentangle. Such confusions add further difficulties so as to assess the impact of the pandemic.

Cultural bodies in France: A "cornucopia"[7]

Without going into any details, one can stress that the French cultural policies went through a progressive institutionalization (Perrin et al., 2016, Poirrier, 2000, Négrier, 2017). The organization and scope of the dedicated ministry has been evolving over the last sixty years, since its creation in 1959. According to Fondu and Vermerie (2015), this evolution has been characterized by two major moves: first, its very creation, then a major broadening of its remit after 1981. Since that date, the national policies have been weakening,[8] to some extent, as cultural policies were decentralized on the one hand, or left to the market forces and/or hit by "austerity" measures, on the other hand. As of 2019, local authorities (cities, counties ("départements"), and regions) account for 55%[9] of the public support for culture (leaving aside the case of Paris) (Observatoire des politiques culturelles (OPC), 2021, p. 4).

André Malraux, French minister of culture in the 60s, received for missions "to make the capital works of humanity, and first of all France, accessible to as many French as possible; to ensure the widest possible audience for our cultural heritage, and to encourage the creation of works of art and the spirit that enrich it" (conference 60th anniversary of the Ministry of Culture, 2019, press release). The cultural policies, although they did evolve, are still structured around three main lines: "heritage, creation, knowledge transmission and cultural democratization, in particular via cultural and artistic education" (Perrin et al., 2016, p. 7).

Table 2.2 sums up some of the amount available for the cultural agencies to allocate funds to a range of cultural fields, directly or indirectly, supported by various sources (ministries, specific taxes and fees). There are other means to support these industries. For example, taking into account the highly prevalent status of self-employment and/or freelance; artists and technicians commonly called "intermittents du spectacle"[10] when employed on short-term contracts benefit from a special status derogatory to the national unemployment provision convention to receive a specific social security coverage. The preservation of this exceptional status created a lot of tensions over the last decade. A specific social insurance regime applies to authors and to "artists-authors" (writers, music composers, film and television authors, software authors, choreographers, photographers, visual artists, graphic artists, etc.).

The sub-sectors were granted reduced VAT rates: 7% instead of 19.6% for cinemas, festivals, and the entrances to zoos, museums, monuments, exhibitions and cultural sites; 5.5% for books (paper and digital) and book rental activities, ticket-selling for the performing arts (Perrin et al. 2016, p. 36).

These institutionalized bodies of cultural agencies appear rather comprehensive and all encompassing. The very existence of these cultural bodies, the working relationships with the various segments involved, with the

Table 2.2 Budget of the main cultural entities funding the various segments (2018).

Entity	Budget[a] (million euros)
Centre national du cinéma et de l'image animée (CNC)	675.3
Centre national du livre (CNL)	34.7
Centre national de la chanson, des variétés et du jazz Centre national de la musique (CNM) since 2020	32.4
Centre national de la danse (CND) There are 19 National Choreographic Centres	10.8
Centre national des arts plastiques (CNAP): manages the contemporary works bought by the Fonds national d'art contemporain (FNAC)	1
Association pour le soutien au théâtre privé (ASTP): funds private theaters	6.6
Fund for newspapers, direct support for newspapers (aides directes à la presse)	93.9

Source: Compiled by author from "Morphologie et économie du champ culturel" (Ministry of Culture, 2020d, p. 17), ministère de la culture, CNAP (https://www.cnap.fr/rapport-dactivite-2018), CND (https://www.cnd.fr/fr/page/2-rapport-d-activite).

[a] Based on the amount of specific taxes collected and allocated by the law of finance, with the exception of CNAP and CND. Taxes and fees are specific to certain cultural sectors, e.g. tax on cinema tickets (TSA).

trade associations and unions may have helped to tailor the aids quickly and finely.

A review of the main supporting measures adopted by the French government since the spread of the COVID-19 pandemic

By and large, the impact of the pandemic on the various segments and sub-segments of the CCIs varies. Some segments are worse off than others, typically live events/performing arts. As stressed in the European Parliament report (de Vet et al., 2021, p. 30), because of the fragmentation of the CCIs, "cultural industries were generally more affected than creative ones". As noted earlier, there is actually a paucity of robust data.

As of July 2020, the research department of the Ministry of Culture released a first study[11] on the economic impact of the pandemic, highlighting a decrease of 25% of the total turnover between 2019 and 2018. It confirmed that the performing arts and heritage sectors were severely hit: a decrease of 74% for music,[12] 69% for theatres, 68% for dance/circus/street arts, 65% for heritage, and 64% for museums. The study highlights variations among sub-segments within each segment (Ministry of Culture, 2020, p. 18)

The National Centre of Music (CNM) estimates the losses generated by COVID-19 on live performances to be between 1.7 and 2 billion euros (KEA, 2020, p. 3). In a study commissioned by France Festival (see Box 2.1), Négrier and Djakouane (2020, p.12) provide a tentative assessment of the economic losses due to the cancellation of music festivals: 1, 5 billion euros (lower range), up to 1, 8 million (higher range). Le Diberder (2021) states that the resources for the audiovisual sector[13] decreased by nearly 19% in 2020, but stresses that decreases are uneven: a loss of 70% of the turnover for movie theatres, contrasting with an increase of nearly 40% for online video (VOD and SVOD). On the book market sales were down 20% in France (SNE, 2021).

This situation called for ad hoc forms of support (see Table 2.3). The "intermittents du spectacle" were granted what was described as "a white year" ("année blanche"): a maintained protection for 2020. The measure has been extended to 2021. Mostly targeted to the people working in performing arts: 949 million euros in total (half in 2020, half in 2021) (Le Diberder, 2021).

To compensate for the sharp decline of the revenues in cultural venues (such as movie theatres and live entertainment) some sectorial support schemes have been introduced (Table 2.4).

At the same time, beyond the national general measures adopted by the French government,[14] a 2 billion euros national recovery plan for CCIs was set up in September 2020.[15] The plan blends support for the renovation of the model of creation (426 million), for the modernization of cultural

Box 2.1
___

Cancelled festivals, an assessment of the losses

The analysis of the costs of the cancellation during 2020 (April–August) is based on a sample of 129 festivals (mostly music festivals), part of a panel of 184 festivals followed by the authors for their seminal work on music festivals.

The authors produce three kinds of indicators for their assessment:

- Direct negative economic impact (retombées économiques négatives directes: REND).
- Indirect negative economic impact (retombées économiques négatives indirectes: RENI).
- Total economic losses (pertes économiques totales: PET).

They add REND to RENI and then multiply by a factor of 1.5 to take into account the induced losses. The results are the following:

- For music festivals: lower range 1.53 euros, higher range 1.8 billion.
- Extrapolation to the 4,000 cultural festivals: lower range 2.3 billion euros, higher range 2.6.

The second part of the study provides indicators about the social impact:

- Social impact on jobs: number of jobs at risk, between 34,640 and 72,974.
- Social impact on activity: reduction of the activity of the persons involved (paid or voluntary).
- Social impact on artistic work: number of hiring cancelled.

Source: Compiled by author from Négrier and Djakouane (2020),
https://www.francefestivals.com/media/francefestival/189240-sofest_
festivals_annules_estimer_la_perte_economique_et_sociale-2.pdf

industries (428 million), measures to improve employment and employability (including through an improvement of education, 113 million), funding of heritage (614 million) to promote both activities and attractiveness of the territory, and the definition of a strategy for the future (19 million and an additional 400 million over the next five years). As of April 2021, about a third of the budget has already been allocated to the territories.[16]

Early 2021, another set of measures was announced[17] meant to support employment, protect the cultural scene all throughout France, and facilitate the future restart of cultural activities. A first scheme of 45 million euros (as of February): a 30 million euros fund for cultural festivals to

Table 2.3 Sectoral measures across cultural entities.

Sector	Budget (million euros)	Nature
Centre national du cinéma et de l'image animée (CNC)	165	Ad hoc fund to compensate for the costs generated by the interruption of the shootings.
Centre national du livre (CNL)	5	Emergency plan set up by the CNL. Subsidies received for cancelled book festivals can be kept.
Centre national de la musique (CNM)	11.5	Relief fund set up by the CNM for the most vulnerable professionals. The collection of ticketing taxes for the month of March 2020 was suspended.
Centre national des arts plastiques (CNAP)	2	Emergency plan for the most vulnerable professionals. Two additional schemes:
	+1.2	• an exceptional session of the Acquisition and Commissioning Committee for galleries and an emergency fund for artist authors in addition to government support.
	+0.800	• an exceptional aid may be awarded by the Ministry to places of creation and dissemination which encounter difficulties that call into question the continuity of their activity.
Association pour le soutien au théatre privé (ASTP)	5	"Fonds d'urgence pour le spectacle vivant privé (FUSV)": emergency fund for the live musical entertainment sector, in particular the private theatre sector, in order to meet the difficulties encountered, in conjunction with professional organizations, and with particular attention to maintaining employment. The FUSV is also available for street art and puppets shows. "Fonds de compensation du spectacle vivant (FCSVP)": Box Office compensation fund. Also available for circuses.
"White year" conditions	10	Artists and technicians.

Source: Compiled by author from Ministry of Culture, http://traduction.culture.gouv.fr/url/Result.aspx?to=en&url=https://www.culture.gouv.fr/Divers/Crise-sanitaire-informations-et-recommandations-aux-structures-soutenues-par-le-ministere-de-la-Culture-au-titre-de-la-creation-et-de-la-diffusion, Le Diberder (2021) for the CNC.

Table 2.4 Sectorial support for cultural venues.

Sector	2020 (million euros)	2021 (million euros)
Movie theatres (managed by CNC)	75	
Performing arts (managed by CNM)		
• emergency fund,	52	
• compensation fund,	50	
• "captation" (shooting),		10
• festivals.		20
Performing arts (outside music)		
• emergency fund for live events (managed by ASTP),	30	
• subsidized theatres,	11	
• support for labels and networks,	16	20
• "captation" (shooting),		5
• festivals.	10	10

Source: Compiled by author from Senate report (Sénat, 2021).

enable them to modify their standards format so as to adapt to the new sanitary conditions, and another 15 million funds to record all categories of live shows as long as the locations remain closed. A second scheme of 52 million euros (as of March): 22 million for artists-authors whose status did not allow them to have access to the general support mechanisms (10 million for the music sector, 5 for theatres, 5 for the visual arts, 1 for cinema and 1 for book publishing), 20 million euros to support local artistic teams within the region, an emergency fund of 17 million euros (Fonds d'urgence spécifique de solidarité pour les artistes et les techniciens du spectacle: Fussat) to deal with the case of artists and technicians that do not meet the conditions to benefit from the "année blanche" fund.

Territories and local authorities[18] intervened to complement the national initiatives setting up various schemes. For instance, the French Region Grand Est[19] introduced a specific support scheme[2] for independent bookshops (subsidies of 1,000 euros for investing in safety equipment, between 1,000 and 3,000 euros to purchase books), in addition to other specific support measures for local CCIs (KEA, 2020, p.18). The Hauts-de-France Region[20] set up a support fund of EUR 3 million for the year 2020 dedicated to cultural actors impacted by the COVID-19 crisis. Most regions[21] introduced an emergency fund (8 out 10 regions), as well as "counties" (24 out of 41 counties) (Observatoire des politiques culturelles (OPC), 2021, p.8).

The views of stakeholders: Half-full or half-empty glass?

The sectorial organization of the management of culture gave birth, as noted, to a wealth of entities. They are usually matched by parallel trade associations (see Box 2.2) and unions (Boxes 2.3 and 2.4). These entities

---

Box 2.2

Trade associations and professional unions

- Fédération des Entreprises du Spectacle Vivant, de la Musique, de l'Audiovisuel et du Cinéma (Fesac) regroups the unions of employers in live events, music, audiovisual and cinema.
- Forces Musicales: operas houses and orchestras.[a]
- Syndicat Professionnel des Producteurs, Festivals, Ensembles, Diffuseurs Indépendants de Musique (PROFEDIM): union of producers, festivals, ensembles, independent distributors of music.[a]
- Fédération des structures indépendantes de création et de production artistiques (FSICPA), includes the Syndicat des Cirques et Compagnies de Création (SCC): federation of independent entities of artistic creation and production (includes circuses).[a]
- Syndicat National des Arts Vivants (SYNAVI): national union of living arts.[a]
- Syndicat National de l'édition (SNE): national union of book publishing.
- Syndicat national de l'édition phonographique (SNEP): national union of recorded music.
- Syndicat National du Jeu Vidéo (SNJV): national union of video games.
- Syndicat des Musiques Actuelles (SMA): union of contemporary music.[a]
- Syndicat National des Scènes Publiques (SNSP): national union of public theatres.[a]
- Syndicat National des Entreprises Artistiques et Culturelles (SYNDEAC): national union of artistic and cultural enterprises.

[a] Members of CCNEAC.

Source: Compiled by author from Audiens/AFDAS (2019), rapport de branche de la Convention collective nationale des entreprises artistiques et culturelles (CCNEAC)

---

liaise with the Ministry of Culture, participate in the negotiations of the contractual working agreements and status, organize public relations and lobbying campaigns. They deliver all kinds of services to their constituents. For instance, France Créative,[22] an entity that brings together stakeholders from all the segments of CCIs, publishes economic documents and reports so as to emphasize the weight of the economics of culture. France Festivals[23] commissions research to document the evolution of the field. SGDL or SNAC provides legal, social, and fiscal advice. Trade associations can also intervene to provide help and assistance, in particular the bodies that collect and redistribute copyright income (Box 2.3). Authors' rights management societies supply funds to support creativity, diffusion of live performances, and artists' training schemes.

Box 2.3

The main authors' rights management societies

- Société des auteurs et compositeurs dramatiques (SACD): union of authors and playwrights.
- Société des auteurs, compositeurs et éditeurs de musique (SACEM): union of authors, composers and publishers of music.
- Société des auteurs dans les arts graphiques et plastiques (ADAGP): union of authors in graphic and plastic arts.
- Société des arts visuels et de l'image fixe (SAIF): union of authors of visual arts and fixed image.
- Société civile des auteurs multimédia, (SCAM): union of multimedia authors.
- Société civile pour l'administration des droits des artistes et musiciens interprètes (ADAMI): administration of rights for artists and musicians.
- Société des gens de lettre (SGDL): union of writers.
- Société des producteurs de phonogrammes en France (SPPF): union of producers of sound recordings in France.
- Société des droits de reproduction mécanique (SDPM): union of mechanical reproduction rights.

Source: Compiled by author from Internet searches

Some of them devised their own initiatives to cope with the pandemic, as illustrated by the case of SACEM[24] adopting an emergency response plan that consists of a rescue fund, exceptional royalty advances, and increased support for the programme to assist publishers. It introduced a system for exceptional remuneration more suited to the live streams played during the pandemic period, designing a new method to remunerate those live sessions, and inking contracts with YouTube, Facebook/Instagram, and other platforms (KEA, 2020, pp. 19–20). Jointly with the CNC, an emergency fund was set up for composers who have contributed to the music of film, documentary, or TV series: an allowance up to 1,500 euros per month, depending on each composer's income. Most of these bodies have been providing advices during the pandemic,[25] serving as a platform for the sharing of various questionnaires aiming at impact assessment and other researches.

Like any industry, the CCIs also tried to become a top priority of the government. Taking into account the very scope and number of the economic measures adopted to address the fragility of the value chain and to prop up the sector's resilience, it would be difficult to argue that the French government has neglected the CCIs by failing to extend specific financial support to these vital industries in their moment of need. International comparisons show that France has implemented a full range of stimulus plans

Box 2.4

Unions[a]

Employees' unions	Employers' unions
Syndicat national des journalistes (SNJ): journalists.	Association des Producteurs de Cinéma (APC): film producers.
Syndicat National des Techniciens et Travailleurs de la Production Cinématographique et de Télévision (SNTPCT): technicians and workers.	Syndicat des producteurs de films d'animation (SPFA): animation film producers.
Syndicat national des auteurs et des compositeurs (SNAC): authors and composers.	Union de Producteurs de Films (UPF): film producers.
Syndicat des Professionnels des Industries de l'Audiovisuel et du Cinéma (SPIAC-CGT): audiovisual and cinema profesionals.	Syndicat de producteurs indépendants (SPI): independent film producers.
Fédération nationale des syndicats du spectacle, de l'audiovisuel et de l'action culturelle (FNSAC): national federation of the unions of audiovisual, performing arts, and cultural activities.	Union Syndicale de la Production Audiovisuelle (USPA): audiovisual production. Association Française des Producteurs de Films et de programmes audiovisuels (AFPF): film and audiovisual production.
Société des réalisateurs de films (SRF) : film directors.	
Union Nationale des Syndicats d'Artistes Musiciens de France CGT (SNAM-CGT: unions of musicians.	

[a] Sample not exhaustive, meant to give an overview.

Source: Compiled by the author.

(economy-wise, and targeted) (SNE, 2021, p. 17). Nevertheless, Bourlès and Nicolas (2021) remain cautious about the outcome: "State and local and regional government support for cultural sectors may have helped to limit the extent of the decline in activity".

There is some consensus about the relevancies of the economic measures, about the principles adopted (Wahl, 2020), but at the same time there are some questions and criticisms about their implementation,[26] for instance, about a specific contractual commitment with the entire industry ("Contrat de Filière entre les ICC") announced in 2019 but not fully deployed.[27] Stakeholders are asking for more cooperation with the state agencies,[28] with their proposals often echoing the national recovery plan for the role of the CCIs in the economy.

Not surprisingly, the main criticism is about the agenda for re-opening. Stakeholders, mostly from the performing arts segment, claim that "culture has been sacrificed" and that this agenda has been rather erratic: an unpredictable and iterative "stop & go" (SYNDEAC, 2021).[29] The cultural bodies resent being classified as "non-essential" while supermarkets were not. They claim the distinction was neither fair considering the new conditions to welcome the audience, nor grounded as they consider their activity essential ("supplément d'âme"[30]), especially during troubled times. They lobby for using culture as a major pillar for economic recovery (da Empoli, 2020, EY/GESAC, 2021).

As of 2021, the government announced a progressive re-opening of cultural activities, setting up an agenda: museums and monuments first, cinema second, and lastly theatres. However, due to strong lobbying from the performing arts sector, the latter will not be delayed and will follow the same deadline (mid-May as of April) (Guerrin, 2021). This is, first and foremost, a public health issue, of course with strong economic consequences, especially with uncertainty about the duration of the pandemic. Similar fluctuations are observable in other EU countries about the timing, duration of the lockdown, and agenda for re-opening. While criticizing the "stop& go", the April 2021 report from the French senate stresses that re-opening should not lead to an increase in contamination and that this agenda should accompany the evolution of the sanitary situation.

On the demand side, Jonchery and Lombardo (2020) reveal that the "economic situation which led to widening the gap between social groups in terms of social inequalities, the outcome is slightly different when it comes to cultural participation". This may not be a paradox as research on cultural participation by educational attainment and income[31] shows that attendance to performing arts (theatres, concerts, operas, etc.) is correlated to privileged social positions; therefore closing down these facilities has a low impact on unequal access to culture.[32] Besides, during lockdown, people staying at home seized the opportunity "to develop their own creativity and self-expression playing music, drawing, painting, writing a diary or a novel for instance and those who did were younger and from less privileged social backgrounds than usual".

Governmental agencies have been providing data to assess the impact, allocating new ad hoc funds to the various segments; however, the issue of the agenda of opening/re-opening remained pending, perceived rightly or wrongly as some kind of failure or lack of interest. Managing funds, building on working relationships is one thing, aligning the agenda on a fast-changing sanitary evolution is another thing: half-full or half-empty glass? Typically, the "année blanche" was designed with a double goal: to guarantee the continuity of social rights and to accompany the progressive re-opening. The first one was achieved, according to the Gauron report (2021, p. 43), but not the second one. Per se, these measures cannot anticipate the scope of recoveries amid high uncertainty. The Senate report states that support have been available but remained inferior to the needs, which is hardly a surprise.

Discussion and conclusion

We noted that some sectors are faring better than others; besides the industry is not unified, there are major differences, for instance, in terms of the status of the employees. There is an unbalance between upstream players (artists/technicians) and downstream players (publishers, distributors, producers, etc.), generating some tensions (Racine, 2020 p. 3).[33] Therefore, no wonder that Banks (2020) could sound less optimistic about the consequences of the pandemic in progress on the CCIs, stating that: "We can be more certain, however, that one immediate effect of C-19 is likely to be the exacerbation of some familiar inequalities in cultural work". A view shared by de Vet et al. (2021, p. 32): "The pandemic exposed "the existing fragility of our cultural or 'creative' economy" (Banks, 2020). However, these fragilities are not new; they are structurally linked to the fragmentation of the CCIs' sectors, to the fact already noted that "Cultural workers are more often self-employed, work part-time, combine two or more jobs, and do not have a permanent job" (EP, 2019, p. 8), with performing arts being the most labour intensive sector. Racine (2020, p. 21), in a report commissioned by the Ministry of Culture, highlighted that the situation of "artist-authors"[34] has been deteriorating for some time.

In the case of France, the derogatory status and the extended protection deployed during the pandemic may have mitigated the issue. However, it remains to be seen if, under higher economic pressure, such extensive protective schemes can be maintained as the continuing conflicts about "intermittents du spectacle" has shown. As noted and illustrated by Table 2.1, the funding of the agencies is grounded in specific tax and fees (movie theatres, theatres, etc.), the drastic fall of the box office may jeopardize the subsidy scheme, an issue that may be worsen on the demand side if the patterns of leisure have been negatively altered after the pandemic.

On the positive side, shifting online several cultural activities opened opportunities for further democratization that may signal a deeper modification of the access to culture. Montalto et al. (2020, p. 27) argued that "the pandemic provides a unique opportunity to upscale innovation and the use of online/digital tools to further democratise cultural participation". On the supply side, leaving aside the sectors that maintain a steady growth (online video, videogames), in some other segments the consequences may be mixed. In the case of music, the live events have been devastated, but the recorded segment has been growing. The analysis of the distribution of the turnover for 2019 and 2020 reveals even a continued rise of independent artists, ushering in "a new breed of record label". (Mulligan 2021). In the case of France, innovative new companies like "Believe" played a pioneering role in the digital distribution of independent artists and companies

(Benghozi et al., 2021). It may be too early to predict how these evolutions will play out; however, not only in the music sectors[35] but also in the other CCIs' sectors, the pandemic acted as a catalyst of changes, speeding up the digitization. Sectors like the performing arts (live streaming) or museums have been innovative.

Answering the question "to what extent government support for cultural sectors may have reduced the decline in activity?" is indeed difficult, as stressed by Bourlès and Nicolas (2021). However, the institutional system appeared to have been resilient enough to provide some needed measures. It is nevertheless possible to argue that the system was not proactive enough, but mostly due to public health issues and choices under uncertainty. The fragilities exposed by the pandemic need to be dealt with. The strategy for the future part of the recovery plan for culture could focus on pending issues that have to be addressed. For instance, measures are being taken to facilitate the digitization of the CCIs (such as support for shooting of events). At the same time, digitization is ushering in a new distribution of value. The ministry and the public bodies have a role to play to build up a consensus on fair forms of sharing, updating the existing contractual arrangements.[36]

Notes

1. The author would like to thank Elisa Salvador and Alain Busson for their fruitful comments.
2. See, for a discussion and presentation, Box 0.1 in De Prato et. al (2014, pp. 8–12), see also the methodological discussion in ESSnet-CULTURE (2012) and the data from Eurostat (2020).
3. For a more comprehensive overview, see Busson and Evrard (2013, pp. 3–7).
4. For the methodology to measure culture, see Appendix, pp. 12–19. One should stress that the department of research (DEPS) of the Ministry of Culture provides a wealth of robust data.
5. GESAC: European Grouping of Societies of Authors and Composers.
6. The study covers: Advertising, Architecture, Audiovisual, Books, Music, Newspapers and magazines, Performing arts, Radio, Video games, Visual arts. See also ECBN (2020).
7. For a detailed list of Cultural institutions financed by public authorities, by domain, see Perrin et al. (2016, p. 52). See also Ministry of Culture (Ministère de la Culture), (2021a).
8. They came under various criticisms, the most well-known being Fumaroli (1991) and Schneider (1993).
9. Totally, 9.830 million euros, and 7.989 million euros for the state (Ministry of Culture: 3.690, other ministries: 4.299).
10. A population of 276,000 as of 2019 (Rapport Gauron, 2021, p. 32).
11. "L'impact de la crise du COVID-19 sur les secteurs culturels", based on a survey of 7,829 stakeholders, but as spotted by Le Diberder the study disappeared from the website of the ministry, one can only find a press release under the link: https://www.culture.gouv.fr/Regions/Dac-de-La-Reunion/A-la-une/Les-resultats-importants-de-l-etude-du-DEPS-sur-L-impact-de-la-crise-du-Covid-19-sur-les-secteurs-culturels-presentee-par-le-ministere-de-la-Cu
12. Only the segment of live music, recorded music, went down by 11% only (p. 11).

13. Unlike the data from the ministry in Table 2.1, it does not include recorded music and video games.
14. https://www.economie.gouv.fr/coronavirus-soutien-entreprises
15. https://www.culture.gouv.fr/Presse/Communiquesde-presse/Plan-de-relance-un-effort-de-2-milliards-d-euros-pour-la-Culture (2021b)
16. https://www.culture.gouv.fr/Presse/Communiques-de-presse/Crise-sanitaire-premieres-mesures-du-ministere-de-la-Culture-en-soutien-au-secteur-culturel
17. https://www.culture.gouv.fr/Presse/Communiques-de-presse/ Pres-de-100-M-d-aides-d-urgence-supplementaires-en-faveur-de-la-culture (2021c)
18. The "Fédération nationale des collectivités territoriales pour la culture" (national federation of local authorities for culture: FNCC) has over 450 constituents, all categories of local authorities: municipalities, cities, metropolis, départements (counties) and regions.
19. https://www.grandest.fr/covid19-culture/
20. https://www.aides-entreprises.fr/actualites/6964
21. Regional councils have budgets running to billions of euros and are responsible for schools, transport, and economic development.
22. https://www.france-creative.org/
23. https://www.francefestivals.com/
24. Rescue fund (non-recoupable financial reliefs of €300, €600, €900, €1,500, €3,000, or €5,000): https://createurs-editeurs.sacem.fr/en/news/our-society/covid-19-sacem-launching-plan-emergency-measures-its-members
25. See, for instance, the guidelines released by SYNDEAC: https://www.syndeac.org/covid-19-guide-pour-nos-adherents-10552/
26. See for instance https://www.lemonde.fr/culture/article/2020/05/07/culture-des-aides-sous-conditions_6038960_3246.html
27. https://www.entreprises.gouv.fr/fr/numerique/enjeux/industries-culturelles-et-creatives-icc, https://www.entreprises.gouv.fr/files/files/industrie/ICC/egicc-fiche-explicative.pdf
28. https://www.france-creative.org/rapport-ey-gesac-france-creative-appelle-a-sauver-la-culture-et-a-en-faire-le-1er-partenaire-de-la-relance-europeenne-et-francaise/
29. https://www.syndeac.org/un-an-sans-public-la-culture-sacrifiee-11447/
https://www.france-creative.org/rapport-ey-gesac-france-creative-appelle-a-sauver-la-culture-et-a-en-faire-le-1er-partenaire-de-la-relance-europeenne-et-francaise/
30. In English: "spiritual supplement", Cf. F. Mayor, DG UNESCO (1993, p. 6): https://unesdoc.unesco.org/ark:/48223/pf0000095877_fre
31. See for instance the EU Eurostat, *Culture statistics 2019* pp. 134–139.
32. The author would like to thank A. Busson for this remark.
33. For the case of music see Simon (2019a).
34. "artistes-auteurs": writers, authors of books of comic strips, illustrators, graphic designers, photographs, designers, screenwriters, visual artists. A population of around 270,000.
35. Racine (2020, p. 51) considers that self-production may increase the vulnerability of the weakest segments. On self-production and UGC see Simon (2019b).
36. For instance, the French streaming company Deezer has been testing fan-licensing as a way to rebalance the royalty equation. The CNM (2021) released a study on the impact of adopting User Centric Payment System (UCPS).

References

Ahearne, J., (2002), *French cultural policy debates: A reader* (texts selected, edited, translated and introduced), London, Routledge.

Audiens/AFDAS, (2019) *Rapport de branche. Entreprises artistiques et culturelles. Exercice 2018.* http://revuedepresse.syndeac.org/rapports-de-branche/rdb-ccne-ac-2019-exercice2018.pdf

Banks, M., (2020), "The work of culture and C-19", *European Journal of Cultural Studies.* https://journals.sagepub.com/doi/full/10.1177/1367549420924687.

Benghozi P.-J., Salvador E., Simon J.-P., (2015) *Models of ICT innovation. A focus on the cinema sector,* edited by Bogdanowicz M., European Commission, JRC Science and Policy Report, JRC95536, EUR 27234 EN, ISBN 978-92-79-48170-3 (PDF), ISSN 1831-9424 (online), doi:10.2791/041301, pp. 1–144. http://is.jrc.ec.europa.eu/pages/ISG/EURIPIDIS/documents/JRC95536.pdf

Benghozi P.-J., Salvador E., Simon J.-P., (2021), "Strategies in the cultural and creative industries: Static but flexible *vs* dynamic and liquid. The emergence of a new model in the digital age", *"Créativité", Revue d'Economie Industrielle* 2021(n. 174), pp. 109–149.

Bourlès, L., Nicolas, Y., (2021), Short-term analysis of culture turnover in the 4th quarter 2020. http://traduction.culture.gouv.fr/url/Result.aspx?to=en&url=https://www.culture.gouv.fr/Sites-thematiques/Etudes-et-statistiques/Publications/Collections-de-synthese/Note-de-conjoncture/Analyse-conjoncturelle-du-chiffre-d-affaires-de-la-culture-au-4e-trimestre-2020?filter%5Btype_tag_ids_mi%5D%5B0%5D=70

Busson, A., Evrard, Y., (2013), *Les industries culturelles et créatives – économie et stratégies,* Paris, Vuibert.

Centre National de la Musique (CNM), (2021), Impact of adopting User Centric Payment System (UCPS). https://cnm.fr/en/studies/impact-of-online-music-streaming-services-adopting-the-ucps/

da Empoli, G., (2020), "Seven ideas for a European Cultural Recovery Plan", *Le Grand Continent.* https://legrandcontinent.eu/fr/wp-content/uploads/sites/2/2020/07/GEG_culture_recovery_plan-2.pdf

De Prato, G., Sanz, E., Simon, J. P., (2014), *Digital media worlds. The new media economy,* Houndmills Basingstoke, Palgrave McMillan.

de Vet, J. M, et al., (2021), *Impacts of the COVID19 pandemic on EU industries,* Luxembourg, Publication for the committee on Industry, Research and Energy, Policy Department for Economic, Scientific and Quality of Life Policies, European Parliament. https://www.europarl.europa.eu/RegData/etudes/STUD/2021/662903/IPOL_STU(2021)662903_EN.pdf

ECBN, (2020), White paper: Breaking out of the COVID-19 crisis: Restarting the Cultural Creative Industries is at the centre of an open, sustainable and democratic Europe. https://www.ecbnetwork.eu/ccis-coronacrisis-update-15-white-paper-restarting-the-cultu ra lcreative-industries-in-europe/

ESSnet-CULTURE, (2012), *European Statistical System Network on Culture. Final Report.* https://ec.europa.eu/eurostat/cros/system/files/ESSnet%20Culture%20Final%20report.pdf

European Group of the International Federation of Actors (Euro FIA), European Federation of Journalists (EFJ), International Federation of Musicians (FIM), UNI Europa – Uni Global Union (Media, Entertainment & Arts), (2016),

The Future of Work in the Media, Arts & Entertainment Sector. Meeting the Challenge of Atypical Working. https://www.fim-musicians.org/wp-content/uploads/atypical-work-handbook-en.pdf#page=10

European Parliament, (2019), *Employment in the cultural and creative sectors, Employment in the cultural and creative sectors.* https://www.europarl.europa.eu/RegData/etudes/BRIE/2019/642264/EPRS_BRI(2019)642264_EN.pdf

Eurostat, (2020), Culture statistics – cultural employment. https://ec.europa.eu/eurostat/statisticsexplained/index.php/Culture_statistics_-_cultural_employment

EY/GESAC, (2021), *Rebuilding Europe. The cultural and creative economy before and after the COVID-19 crisis,* January 2021. https://1761b814-bfb6-43fc-9f9a-775d1abca7ab.filesusr.com/ugd/4b2ba2_1ca8a0803d8b-4ced9d2b683db60c18ae.pdf

Fondu, Q. Vermerie, M., (2015), "Les politiques culturelles: évolution et enjeux actuels", *Informations sociales* 2015/4 (n 190), pp. 57–63. https://www.cairn.info/revue-informations-sociales-2015-4-page-57.htm

Fumaroli, M., (1991), *L'État culturel. Essai sur une religion moderne*, Paris, Fallois.

Gauron, A., (2021), *Situation des intermittents du spectacle à l'issue de l'année blanche. Diagnostics et propositions.* https://www.culture.gouv.fr/content/download/288172/3306419?version=11

Guerrin, M., (2021), Le monde du spectacle, bien plus puissant que celui de l'art, a promis le feu s'il rouvrait après les musées: il a gagné. https://www.lemonde.fr/idees/article/2021/04/09/le-monde-du-spectacle-bien-plus-puissant-que-celui-de-l-art-a-promis-le-feu-s-il-rouvrait-apres-les-musees-il-a-gagne_6076089_3232.html

IFPI, (2021), *Annual Global Music Report, 2021.* https://www.ifpi.org/ifpi-issues-annual-global-music-report-2021/

IMF, (2021), *Managing Divergent Recoveries.* https://www.imf.org/en/Publications/WEO/Issues/2021/03/23/world-economic-outlook-april-2021

Jonchery, A., Lombardo, P., (2020), Pratiques culturelles en temps de confinement. https://www.culture.gouv.fr/content/download/280448/3240401?version=30

KEA, (2020), *The impact of the COVID-19 pandemic on the Cultural and Creative Sector.* Report for the Council of Europe. https://keanet.eu/wp-content/uploads/Impact-of-COVID-19-pandemic-on-CCS_COE-KEA_26062020.pdf.pdf?fbclid=IwAR2nGtKVc1vqz2bcgMhfYQjJJZy9v6dfkeQF7FlrSwhu3yDVeusjf8qaFNY

Le Diberder, A., (2021), L'économie du système audiovisuel français en 2020 et 2021. https://alain.le-diberder.com/leconomie-du-systeme-audiovisuel-francais-en-2020-et-2021/

Lescure P., (2013), Mission Acte II de l'exception culturelle. Contribution aux politiques culturelles à l'ère numérique, Culture-Acte 2, Ministère de la culture et de la communication, Paris, Mai, p. 719

Ministry of Culture (Ministère de la Culture), (2019), 60th anniversary of the Ministry of Culture, press release. http://traduction.culture.gouv.fr/url/Result.aspx?to=en&url=https://www.culture.gouv.fr/Nous-connaitre/Decouvrir-le-ministere/Histoire-du-ministere/Evenements/Journees-d-etudes/

Du-partage-des-chefs-d-aeuvre-a-la-garantie-des-droits-culturels-Ruptures-et-continuite-dans-la-politique-culturelle-francaise?filter%5Bcontent_type_id_id%5D%5B0%5D=117

Ministry of Culture (Ministère de la Culture), (2020a), Key figures on culture and communication.   https://www.culture.gouv.fr/Media/Medias-creation-rapide/01-Morphologie-et-economie-du-champ-culturel.pdf

Ministry of Culture (Ministère de la Culture), (2020b), Médias et industries culturelles: cinéma, musique enregistrée, presse écrite, radio, télévision. https://www.culture.gouv.fr/Media/Medias-creation-rapide/07-Medias-et-industries-culturelles.pdf

Ministry of Culture (Ministère de la Culture), (2020c), Création artistique et diffusion: arts visuels, danse, spectacles musicaux. https://www.culture.gouv.fr/Media/Medias-creation-rapide/06-Creation-artistique-et-diffusion.pdf

Ministry of Culture (Ministère de la Culture), (2020e), Morphologie et économie du champ culturel. https://www.culture.gouv.fr/Media/Medias-creationrapide/01-Morphologie-et-economie-du-champ-culturel.pdf

Ministry of Culture (Ministère de la Culture), (2020d), The direct economic weight of culture in 2019.

Ministry of Culture (Ministère de la Culture), (2021a), Plan de relance: 460 millions d'euros d'opérations d'ores et déjà territorialisées. https://www.culture.gouv.fr/France-Relance/Plan-de-relance-460-millions-d-euros-d-operations-d-ores-et-deja-territorialisees

Ministry of Culture (Ministère de la Culture), (2021b), Plan de relance: un effort de 2 milliards d'euros pour la Culture (2020). https://www.culture.gouv.fr/Presse/Communiquesde-presse/Plan-de-relance-un-effort-de-2-milliards-d-euros-pour-la-Culture

Ministry of Culture (Ministère de la Culture), (2021c), Cultural institutions. http://traduction.culture.gouv.fr/url/Result.aspx?to=en&url=https://www.culture.gouv.fr/Sites-thematiques/Developpement-culturel/Le-developpement-culturel-en-France/Culture-et-Monde-rural/Les-acteurs-et-les-outils-au-service-du-maillage-culturel-du-territoire/Les-partenaires/Les-institutions-culturelles

Montalto, V., et al., (2020), *European Cultural and Creative Cities in COVID-19 times: Jobs at risk and the policy response.* https://publications.jrc.ec.europa.eu/repository/bitstream/J RC120876/kjna30249enn_1.pdf

Mulligan, M., (2021), Smaller independents and artists direct grew fastest in 2020.   https://www.midiaresearch.com/blog/smaller-independents-and-artists-direct-grew-fastest-in-2020

Négrier, E., (2017), Le ministère de la Culture et la Politique culturelle en France: Exception culturelle ou exception institutionnelle?. https://hal.archives-ouvertes.fr/hal-01442310/document

Négrier, E., Djakouane, A., (2020), *Festivals annulés, L'empreinte sociale et territoriale des festivals.* https://www.francefestivals.com/media/francefestival/189240-sofest_festivals_annules_estimer_la_perte_economique_et_sociale-2.pdf

Observatoire des politiques culturelles (OPC), (2021), Note de conjoncture sur les dépenses culturelles des collectivités territoriales et leurs groupements (2019–2021). http://www.observatoire-culture.net/fichiers/files/note_de_conjoncture_sur_les_depenses_culturelles_des_collectivites_2019_2021.pdf

Perrin, T., Delvainquière, J. C., Guy, J. M., (2016), "Country Profile: France". *Compendium. Cultural Policies and Trends in Europe.* https://www.culturalpo-licies.net/wp-content/uploads/pdf_full/france/france_112016.pdf

Poirrier, P., (2000), *L'État et la Culture en France au XXe siècle*, Paris, Le Livre de Poche, collection Références.

Racine, B., (2020), *L'auteur et l'acte de création.* https://www.culture.gouv.fr/content/download/261853/2984031?version=2

Schneider, M., (1993), *La comédie de la culture*, Paris, Seuil.

Sénat, (2021), *La réouverture des lieux culturels*, Report n°528. http://www.senat.fr/rap/r20-528/r20-528_mono.html

Simon, J. P., (2019a), "New players in the music industry: Lifeboats or killer whales? The role of streaming platforms", *Digital Policy, Regulation and Governance Journal* 21 (n. 6), pp. 525–549. https://doi.org/10.1108/DPRG-06-2019-0041.

Simon, J. P., (2019b), "Media: Innovation, Self-production, Creativity", in Chamoux, J.P. (Ed), *The digital era 2. Political economy revisited*, London, ISTE Editions, pp. 23–54. DOI: 10.1002/9781119468967.ch2

Syndicat National de l'Edition (SNE), (2021), *Consequences of the covid-19 crisis on the book market.* https://www.sne.fr/app/uploads/2020/12/FEE-20190707_covid_european-book-market.pdf

Turner, L., (2021), The direct economic weight of culture in 2019. http://traduc-tion.culture.gouv.fr/url/Result.aspx?to=en&url=https://www.culture.gouv.fr/Sites-thematiques/Etudes-et-statistiques/Publications/Collections-de-synthese/Culture-chiffres-2007-2021/Le-poids-economique-direct-de-la-culture-en-2019-CC-2021-1?filter%5Btype_tag_ids_mi%5D%5B0%5D=70

Wahl, J., (2020), Françoise Benhamou, économiste, sur le plan de relance de la culture: "Il faut que le plan soit affiché, et affiché dans la durée", *Toute la culture.* https://toutelaculture.com/actu/politique-culturelle/francoise-benhamou-economiste-sur-le-plan-de-relance-de-la-culture-il-faut-que-le-plan-soit-affiche-et-affiche-dans-la-duree/

3 The effects of the COVID-19 pandemic on the field of Finnish cultural industries

Revealing and challenging policy structures

Mervi Luonila, Vappu Renko, Olli Jakonen, Sari Karttunen, and Anna Kanerva

Introduction

Worldwide, the fields of arts, culture, and creative economy have been widely affected by the outbreak of the COVID-19 pandemic in early 2020 (e.g. Florida and Seman, 2020; OECD, 2020; UNESCO, 2020). The first effects of the pandemic in these fields (Cultural and Creative Industries, henceforth CCIs[1]) have been mapped out in several countries and economic areas. Researchers as well as organizations and government agencies have conducted surveys for both individuals and institutions, which indicate major losses in opportunities and income in the CCIs. It has also been suggested that cultural workers in the most vulnerable positions may have had to seek other employment. (See e.g. Banks, 2020; Betzler et al., 2020; Comunian and England, 2020; Eikhof, 2020; Serafini and Novosel, 2020; GESAC, 2021) Writing this chapter in May 2021, the pandemic's long-term effects on the CCIs cannot yet be seen. The effects also vary depending on industry, actor, or country.

In Finland, the short-term impacts related to the CCIs have included income loss (e.g. Mankkinen and Mattila, 2021) and rising unemployment (Statistics Finland, 2020; see also Center for the Cultural Policy Research Cupore, 2021). The pandemic and resultant government restrictions have hindered cultural production, consumption, and participation (e.g. The Compendium of Cultural Policies and Trends, 2020). In judicial terms, people's right to participate in culture and artists' right to make art have been violated (e.g. Mattila, 2021). In economic terms, a decrease in sales, salaries, and employment is clearly visible (e.g. GESAC, 2021; Weckström, 2020). These indicate significant impacts in a field with nearly 120,000 employees and approximately 18,000 businesses with a combined turnover of 13.4 billion euros in Finland in 2019 (Saari, 2021).[2]

In the following, we will explore the various COVID measures that have been designed for and targeted to the CCIs in Finland. As Betzler

DOI: 10.4324/9781003128274-5

and others (2020, p. 2) point out, the different measures need to be scrutinized "against the background of their specific national character-istics and selected social and economic contextual factors" to present a framework for crisis management. The Finnish cultural policy context is characterized by an established role of the public sector and a multi-tude of third sector organizations. CCI policy responsibilities are divided into several ministries within the state administration. Hence, at the out-break of the pandemic, not only nominal cultural policy agencies but also many other government actors conducted policy measures in relation to the CCIs.

Currently, the pandemic constitutes one external factor that affects the prevailing Finnish system and challenges it. It may also open up possibilities for new ways of thinking, modes of action, and structural changes (see e.g. Committee on the Future, 2020). We agree with Betzler et al. (2020) that the COVID crisis presents a possibility to critically examine the current cultural policy structures and priorities and may also give opportunities to rectify the exposed gaps and vulnerabilities.

In this chapter, our purpose is to examine crisis management in Finnish cultural policy. We focus on two interlinked key measures targeted at the CCIs in Finland during the pandemic in 2020: data collection and emer-gency funding. First, we explore how and for whom these measures were conducted. Second, drawing on the conducted measures, we discuss if there are any features in the Finnish cultural policy structure that the pan-demic and following crisis management have revealed and challenged in the context of the CCIs. Our interest is on the policy change that usu-ally results from changes in "political or economic environments, such as budget crises and international talks" (Kangas and Vestheim, 2010, p. 282). In the development of cultural policies, an important role has been played by 'policy transfer', the adoption of ideas and models from other jurisdictions (Paquette and Redaelli, 2015). The COVID pandemic represents a sudden, external factor that shakes established structures and ways of doing, while crisis management may adopt models from other countries. Our examination draws on data gathered in relation to the recognized key measures: funding calls and decisions, surveys conducted in the CCIs, and media monitoring since March 2020, as well as a sur-vey carried out by the authors among public cultural policy officers in early 2021.

The chapter is organized as follows. First, we briefly describe the Finnish cultural policy structure and aims as a context for the examination. Second, we present an overview of the evolvement of the pandemic and the CCIs in Finland in 2020. Third, we analyze the policy measures for collecting information and supporting the CCIs during the pandemic. We conclude by presenting the key findings and discussing the policy effects and further research needs.

The established cultural policy structure as a framework for crisis management

The structure of Finnish cultural policy on a national level consists of multiple government institutions, quasi-autonomous non-governmental organizations, and interest organizations (Figure 3.1), with the Ministry of Education and Culture (MEC) responsible for the statutory art and cultural policy. In a country of 5.5 million citizens, Finland's cultural policy structure constitutes a relatively stable, organized, and institutionalized system for the implementation of public policy.

Following the Nordic welfare state model, Finland's cultural policy system was built from the 1960s onwards. To this day, its key characteristics include a strong role of the state and municipalities, a multi-dimensional financial system, the arms-length principle (including peer review bodies), the use of gambling revenues as a part of state cultural funding, a state subsidy system for museums, theatres, and orchestras, as well as an important role of the independent actors outside the state-subsidized organizations (so-called "free field") (e.g., Häyrynen, 2015; see also Oinaala and Ruokolainen, 2017). The public funding system for arts and culture has been created over time in close collaboration among the state and arts and the culture institutions and organizations, representing a corporatist tradition (e.g. Heiskanen et al., 2005). In 2019, the state funding for

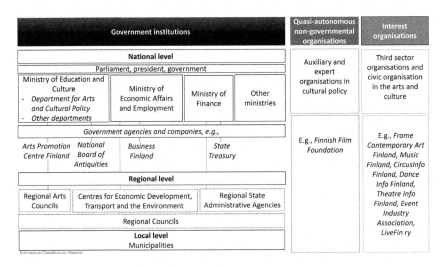

Figure 3.1 A concise description of the Finnish cultural policy structure in relation to the analyzed anti-COVID measures.

Source: Figure by authors; The Compendium of Cultural Policies and Trends (2020); Kangas and Pirnes (2015).

culture from all government sectors was 1 328 million euros,[3] of which the MEC's earmarked cultural budget was 452 million euros, representing around 0.8% of the total state expenditure. (Jakonen et al., 2020, pp. 34, 65.)

Since the economic recession in the 1990s, neoliberal tendencies have been identified that challenge the traditional welfare state model in Finnish cultural policies (e.g. Häyrynen, 2018). These have included increasing efficiency expectations, results-based steering, knowledge-based management, and auditing arrangements (e.g. Karttunen, 2012). The state has also promoted new forms of partnerships in cultural policy implementation, including outsourcing. Since the 2000s, the role of the expert agencies has been increasingly strengthened as the MEC has delegated more responsibilities to agencies such as Arts Promotion Centre Finland (henceforth Taike), established in 2013 based on the former arts council system. Other expert bodies include the Finnish Heritage Agency placed under the MEC, Business Finland promoting innovation funding and trade, travel, and investment promotion under the Ministry of Economic Affairs and Employment (henceforth MEAE), and the State Treasury under the Ministry of Finance.

Policies related to the CCIs in Finland are implemented through a complex combination of different funding instruments, policy programmes, and government institutions and organizations (cf. also Wyatt and Trevena, 2020). In the early 2000s, in line with the international discussion, the concepts 'creative industries' and 'creative economy' were adopted in Finnish policy making (Heiskanen, 2015; see also Pratt, 2009). During the past 20 years, cultural activities have been regarded more and more intensively from the point of view of employment and business policy in national strategies (see Jakonen 2017). The current government programme's goals written just under a year before the outbreak recognize the CCIs in the context of providing more jobs, growing ratio in the GDP, and improving the employment conditions (VN, 2019). It has not, however, been easy for the different government sectors to locate common visions for mapping and developing the creative economy. Up to this date, there is no agreed standard definition of the creative sectors or industries in Finland (Kangas, 2001; Heiskanen, 2015; Oksanen et al., 2018). Many dichotomies also persist, for instance, the notion of keeping cultural entrepreneurship separate from the artistic core activities (cf. Heiskanen, 2015).

Evolvement of the pandemic and the CCIs in Finland in 2020

On 16 March 2020, a national state of emergency was announced by the Finnish government, with the aim of protecting the population and safeguarding the functioning of society in the face of the COVID-19 pandemic.

The CCIs were affected in many ways. The public indoor premises, including many cultural premises such as public libraries, museums, cultural houses, and hobby spaces, were immediately closed. As a result, many performances, exhibitions, and productions were cancelled or indefinitely postponed. The measures were to be in force until 13 April but were later extended until 13 May. As of 1 June, only public events with a maximum attendance of 50 persons were allowed, forcing many festivals and other large-scale events to cancel their activities.[4]

During summer 2020, as the COVID situation in Finland improved and the incidence rate decreased, large-scale restrictive measures were replaced by more targeted ones. The restrictions were gradually loosened, including the opening of cultural premises for limited audience numbers. However, large-scale public events with more than 500 attendees were prohibited until 31 July. In practice, the pandemic led to the cancellation of the whole festival summer (cf. Davies, 2020) and significantly hampered the event industry in general (Wirén et al., 2020).

In Autumn 2020, the restrictive measures focused on the regional and in many cases local level as the pandemic spread unevenly across the country. Instead of large-scale restrictive measures, the Finnish government formulated regional recommendations divided into three categories based on the phase of the pandemic. The Ministry of Social Affairs and Health issued official healthcare and social welfare instructions to the municipalities, hospital districts, Regional State Administrative Agencies, and other relevant parties. The Regional State Administrative Agencies then made the decisions on the restriction of performances, concerts, shows, and other public events under the Communicable Diseases Act.

At the end of 2020, the pandemic accelerated again and public gatherings and the number of visitors in public spaces were restricted. All publicly run organizations such as cultural centres and museums were forced to close in many regions, the capital city of Helsinki included.[5]

In a country with a low population density and only a few large cities, the regional recommendations and restrictions have been effective, and the need for hospital care has remained relatively stable throughout 2020 and at the beginning of 2021 (Finnish Institute for Health and Welfare, THL, 2021). As the situation has not radically worsened, the justifications for the COVID restrictions have been increasingly challenged by the CCI actors. For example, at the beginning of 2021, a number of well-known artists along with established representative bodies, businesses, and experts presented sharp criticism towards the suppression of cultural activities (e.g. Kajander, 2021; Vedenpää, 2021; see also e.g. Näyttelijäliitto, 2021; Taike, 2021). It was proposed that cultural venues such as museums, libraries, theatres, and concert halls have been closed to create an impression of efficiency in tackling the pandemic while at the same time restaurants and shopping centres have remained open (see Mattila, 2021).

Anti-COVID measures and the CCIs

The data collection efforts

The immediate first step in crisis management in the context of Finnish cultural policy was to start the collection of data on the effects of the pandemic. In line with the Finnish cultural policy framework characterized by close collaboration between the state and the arts and culture institutions and organizations, data collection as an emergency measure has also included close collaboration between multiple government institutions, quasi-autonomous non-governmental organizations, and interest organizations.

According to the cultural policy officers survey, the MEC first called actors from the field to a meeting on 17 March 2020 to get an overview of the ongoing situation. A summary of the COVID actions in other Nordic countries was prepared for internal use. Since March 2020, the MEC has conducted multiple surveys on the impacts of the pandemic in the CCIs in Finland.

The first main survey regarding the wider sectors of arts, culture, and creative industries was sent out in April 2020 to gather information on the effects of the pandemic "both to support the formulation of rapid conclusions and policy responses and to plan longer-term policies and actions" (VNK, 2020a, p. 8). Around 1,600 actors responded to the survey. In disseminating the survey and, more importantly, in analyzing the results, the MEC collaborated with various third sector expert bodies and interest organizations. Different arts information centres analyzed the results related to their respective field of operations (such as music, visual arts, theatre, dance, and circus). The MEC then summarized the key findings.

Half of the survey respondents felt that their activities had been essentially compromised by the pandemic. One-quarter of the respondents stated that the pandemic had caused significant changes in their activities, while another quarter reported only minor changes. The respondents estimated that the situation would deteriorate over the next three months but improve in the latter part of the year. (VNK, 2020a.) According to the survey, the net income losses caused by the pandemic were estimated to be approximately 130 million euros. The amount is most likely much higher, as the respondents represented only a part of the field. The results are at best indicative as the representativeness of the responses varied significantly by field, which also makes comparisons between the fields difficult.

At the beginning of May 2020, the MEC sent out a survey to Finnish municipalities regarding the local effects of the pandemic on cultural activities (VNK, 2020c). According to the results, the pandemic affected the municipal cultural activities largely by suspending them. However, new forms of activity and innovations such as digital cultural services and distance learning had also been developed or improved. The data collection has continued along with the pandemic. In January 2021, the MEC launched a third COVID survey on the impacts of the pandemic on the activities and economy of the creative industry actors during 2020, as well as on their assumptions concerning the first half of 2021. According to the MEC, the information will be used in creating situation awareness and designing longer-term policy interventions (cf. also Creative FLIP, 2021).

The MEC was the main initiator of the data collection efforts conducted by the state in the CCIs. The surveys were made by the Department for Art and Cultural Policy and the Finnish Heritage Agency (in collaboration with the Finnish Museums Association and the MEC). According to the interviews of public officers, also the MEAE and Centres for the Economic Development, Transport, and the Environment conducted targeted inquiries among interest groups involved with the CCIs.

In addition to the state, many interest organizations, universities, and research institutes developed methods to monitor and evaluate the impacts of COVID-19. Statistics Finland, the national statistical agency, took the initiative to curate statistical information on the COVID situation, including a subsection for "Culture and Leisure" and drawing upon official statistical sources as well as industry statistics and surveys (see Weckström, 2020). Data collection was also one of the first steps taken by Finland's Event Industry Association, a new central organization established to support the enterprises in the event industry. Live music clubs and venues were also scrutinized by the association LiveFIN, also quite recently established, with the aim of following up on the COVID impacts in the Finnish music industry.

Despite the extensive data collection, it seems that the various surveys and analyses were not systematically used for example by the government when deciding about the restrictions and creating support measures in the CCIs. According to the ministry officers, the survey findings were mostly utilized in the funding decision stage rather than in the design of the first measures. The first surveys coincided with the implementation of the first financial measures, facing the pace pressures of COVID crisis management (Table 3.1).

Emergency funding and other supporting measures for CCIs

During 2020, the Finnish state launched multiple support initiatives to keep CCIs afloat and compensate at least some of the losses caused by the pandemic (see also Banks and O'Connor 2021). In comparison to the general arts and culture funding, the amounts channelled through various emergency funding instruments were significant. The state co-operated with private foundations in some funding initiatives, but mostly the emergency funding was channelled through various government institutions. In addition to the state, several third-sector organizations in the CCIs have launched their own crisis support mechanisms and initiatives.

Table 3.1 Examples of the COVID-19 related surveys.

Examples of COVID-19 related surveys for CCIs by the government institutions in Finland during 2020

Executor	Purpose	Target group
Ministry of Education and Culture (MEC), Finnish Heritage Agency, in collaboration with Finnish Museums Association and the Ministry	To gather information on the effects of the pandemic on museums	Professional museums
Department for Art and Cultural Policy	To map the effects of the pandemic on the fields of art and culture in Finland. Two-part questionnaire. In the first part respondents were asked to assess the effects from 15 March to 31 May 2020, and in the second part from 1 June to 31 August 2020	Actors in the arts, culture and CCI. The questionnaire was distributed mainly through national arts organizations
	To map the effects of the pandemic on municipal cultural activities, including basic arts education. The questionnaire did not cover libraries	Municipalities

Examples of COVID-19 related surveys for CCI interest organizations in Finland during 2020

Frame Contemporary Art Finland	To gather information on the effects of the pandemic in visual arts.	Visual arts organizations and visual artists.
Music Finland	To gather information on the effects of the pandemic on the incomes of Finnish music professionals	Professionals in the field of music
CircusInfo Finland	To gather information on the effects of the pandemic in the field of circus	All actors in the field of circus with loss of income due to the pandemic were eligible, including circus groups and producers, freelance artists, circus teachers, actors in applied circus activities (social circus, circus in social welfare and health sector, etc.), festivals, and event organizers
Dance Info Finland	To gather information on the effects of the pandemic in the field of dance	All actors in the field of dance with loss of income due to the pandemic were eligible, including dance groups and producers, freelance dance artists and producers, actors in applied dance activities (community dance, dance in social welfare and health sector, etc.), festivals, and event organizers
Event Industry Association	Surveys for actors in the field	Enterprises in the event industry
LiveFin ry	To gather information on the effects of the pandemic in the field of live music	Live music clubs and venues

The COVID-19 emergency funding targeted at various sections of the CCIs was channelled through different government institutions. In addition to the MEC, the MEAE supported creative industries through several government agencies and companies. Business Finland gave emergency funding to CCI businesses. Similar measures were implemented by the Centres for Economic Development, Transport, and the Environment. In addition, the State Treasury steered by the Ministry of Finance has also channelled support for CCIs. The CCI domains funded especially by the MEAE include such areas as creative, arts and entertainment activities, audio-visual production, mass communications, and advertising and marketing activities. Also, the State Treasury has channelled funding to a diverse group of companies representing almost 40 subcategories of CCI businesses, from book publishing to advertising and graphic design. The MEAE and the State Treasury have funded also "core creative arts" such as visual and performing arts.[6]

The emergency funding and other supporting measures in the CCIs have included emergency aid and discretionary crisis grants, special working grants, provision of work opportunities, diverse aid for artists and freelancers, and lists of good practices (European Parliament, 2020). In addition, but less frequently, funding has been provided for artistic proposals or projects and documentation of the COVID-19 crisis. Apart from the financial aid, the MEC has also stated that the closing of cultural institutions and the resulting cutbacks in activities or personnel do not affect the amount of state subsidies to cultural institutions in 2020 and that the MEC will not impose recoveries of payments. The government and the private foundations have also allowed extensions to grant periods. Rather soon after the outbreak of the pandemic, the MEC, Taike, and major Finnish foundations together provided emergency aid to assist arts and culture professionals affected by the pandemic. The first emergency funding was channelled through Taike as short-term grants for artists and freelancers in April 2020. A new application round was opened at the beginning of May. Followingly, according to a public officer, Taike also received applications from various CCI professionals outside its usual "artistic" remit, such as producers, sound technicians, sound and lighting engineers, stand-up comedians, magicians, and gallerists. The multiplicity of CCIs in the funding recipients (Taike, 2020) would require, according to the officer, more knowledge concerning the operation logic and production structures of the CCIs from the decision makers and public officers. As the Taike officer stated, creative industries are an undefined, vague concept.

During 2020 and 2021 the Finnish government reached an agreement on various supplementary budget proposals, which also included emergency support for art, culture, and CCI actors. The altogether seven budget proposals during 2020 included approximately 110 million euros of crisis support for culture through the MEC. This represents nearly 25% of the regular cultural budget of the MEC. The ministry has granted funding to the established sectors of Finnish cultural policy: organizers of cultural festivals and other cultural organizations, and to theatres, orchestras and museums receiving state subsidies, national art and heritage institutions, and the providers of basic art education and liberal adult education. However, some of the funding forms received applications from a wider and more diverse group than usual (interview with public officer). In addition, Taike allocated aid to individual artists and freelancers in artistic fields but also in CCIs more broadly. Among the applicants there were also supporting personnel from the CCIs. Organizations from other administrative sectors have also been allocated "non-earmarked" funding for CCIs since 2020 (see Table 3.2).

At the beginning of 2021 two supplementary budget proposals included over 140 million euros to be allocated for art and culture through the MEC. This funding includes nearly 80 million to be allocated from Taike within two application periods to individuals and groups within the CCIs. Furthermore, the second supplementary proposal allocates 80 million euros to the event industry from the MEAE as a part of business cost support. According to a public officer, creative work related to events has risen more strongly than planned on the MEAE agenda. These crisis funding decisions were preceded by intense pressure from the artistic fields and interest organizations (see Figure 3.1) and continuous, heated media debate concerning inadequate crisis support, particularly for events and freelancers within the wider CCIs. For example, Taike is expected to widen the scope of its corona grants even further within the CCIs during autumn 2021.

Discussion and conclusions: Towards a wider recognition of creative sectors?

The key anti-COVID measures adopted in Finnish cultural policies have included information gathering efforts and emergency funding tools, in line with the approaches taken in the other Nordic countries (e.g. Kulturanalys Norden 2021). The crisis management has highlighted many structural features in Finnish cultural policies. Close collaboration between the government institutions and the CCI actors has been characteristic in Finland, and the emergency measures have in many cases been implemented in a similar manner. Contacts have been created and strengthened between various actors and sectors of society, reflecting the traditionally close relationship between the public sector and the civil society. Surveys conducted by the MEC seem to manifest the government's recently adopted and increasingly demanded aim of evidence-based policy making (see also Häyrynen, 2018).

The crisis seems to have given new impetus to the corporatist arrangements in Finnish cultural policies that have appeared to be dissolving in the recent decades (see e.g. Mangset, 2009). Facing the pandemic, the government's aim has been to take note of multiple stakeholders in the policy planning and decision making and the emergency support instruments

Table 3.2 Examples of emergency funding for CCIs from the Finnish government 2020–2021.

Organization	Funding scheme(s) implemented due to COVID-19 pandemic[a]	Target institutions and group(s)	Earmarked funding scheme for art and culture	Notions from the viewpoint of CCIs/creative sectors
MEC/Department for Art and Cultural Policy	Subsidies for national art organizations	The National Gallery, the National Theatre, the National Opera	Yes	No funding especially for CCIs. Targeted to established national art institutions
	Subsidies for museums, theatres, and orchestras	Theatres, orchestras, and museums within the network of state-subsidized cultural organizations	Yes	No funding especially for CCIs. Targeted to established network of art institutions
	Subsidies for community/club houses	Communities maintaining community/club houses	Yes	No funding especially for CCIs. Targeted to small civil society organizations
	Subsidies for basic art education	Maintainers of basic art education institutions	Yes	No funding especially for CCIs. Targeted to educational organizations
	Subsidies for art, Cultural and Creative Sector organizations	Associations, cooperatives, foundations, companies in cultural sector	Yes	Targeted also to creative sectors and companies within the CCIs. New applicants and more companies as applicants compared to previous years
	Subsidies for cultural events and festivals	Communities and companies organizing art and cultural festivals and events	Yes	No funding especially for CCIs. Intended for communities that organize cultural events regularly
The Finnish Film Foundation[b]	Subsidies for regional cinemas and movie productions	Movie festivals, productions, and regional cinemas	Yes	No funding especially for CCIs but audio-visual culture has been generally regarded as a part of the CCIs

(*Continued*)

Table 3.2 Examples of emergency funding for CCIs from the Finnish government 2020–2021. (Continued)

Organization	Funding scheme(s) implemented due to COVID-19 pandemic[a]	Target institutions and group(s)	Earmarked funding scheme for art and culture	Notions from the viewpoint of CCIs/creative sectors
MEC/Arts Promotion Centre Finland (Taike)	Corona grants[c]	For individual professionals and private traders within the art, Cultural and Creative Sectors	Yes	Targeted also to professionals and private traders within the CCIs. New applicants from CCIs compared to regular artistic grants
MEAE/Business Finland	Funding for business development in disruptive circumstances	Businesses with more than five employees	No	Businesses within the CCIs could apply[d]
MEAE/Centres for Economic Development, Transport and the Environment	Funding for companies in the exceptional circumstances caused by the coronavirus	Businesses employing a maximum of five people at the time of application	No	Businesses within the CCIs could apply[d]
The Ministry of Finance/State Treasury	Business cost support	Businesses whose turnover has fallen due to the coronavirus pandemic	No	Businesses within the CCIs could apply[d]
Finnish Municipalities	Corona aid for sole entrepreneurs	Maximum of 2,000 euros to cover costs incurred in carrying out the activities of a sole entrepreneur	No	Sole entrepreneurs within the CCIs could apply[d]

[a] This table includes only emergency funding that could be applied for through specific application periods. Crisis funding allocated directly for the operating costs of cultural policy agencies etc. through the state budget is not listed.
[b] Independent foundation operating under the supervision of the MEC, which receives its funding through the MEC to implement film industry policies.
[c] Altogether five different application periods during 2020–2021. The fourth and fifth application periods of TAIKE are to be implemented during the spring and autumn of 2021.
[d] Based on a national "Standard Industrial Classification TOL 2008", comprising such industry categories as "Arts, entertainment and recreation" or "Information and Communication" with multiple subcategories. Statistics Finland's Classification Services maintain and publish national classification recommendations.

have been designed and implemented in collaboration with CCI actors. For example, a new representative organization, Finland's Event Industry Association (*Tapahtumateollisuus ry*), was established in 2020. Moreover, in October 2020, the MEC established an "event rescue team" in which, for example, the music industry is represented (Nevalainen, 2020). The state and the private grant-awarding foundations gathered joint crisis funding to support artists. (Cf. Banks 2020, 653.) Additionally, it seems that surveys have emerged not only as a method of data collection but also as a medium of interaction between the government and the CCI representatives, reflecting their traditionally close relationship as well as the government's aims of evidence-based decision making. The Parliamentary Committee on the Future hopes that the co-operation will continue in the future: "A critical examination of the traditional division of roles will be important in the future from the perspective of the development of the field" (Committee on the Future, 2020, p. 164).

The crisis has hit small creative enterprises and freelancers hard. Crisis management efforts have brought up the lack of a comprehensive CCIs policy framework and an unequivocal operational definition of the CCIs that fall under the remit of several ministries. The general concept was transferred from other environments to Finland and has not been thoroughly domesticated in Finland (cf. Alasuutari 2013). For example, channelling emergency funding for CCIs from different ministries (MEC, MEAE) reflects the complexity as well as different understandings of the CCIs as a policy field (see also Wyatt and Trevena, 2020). The division of labour between different government sectors in supporting the CCIs seems ambiguous and in need of coordination and conceptual clarification (see also Tarjanne, 2021).

At the same time, key measures targeted the CCIs in Finland during the pandemic point to certain policy shifts. The MEC has channelled funding for CCI enterprises that it has hardly ever supported before. Admittedly, the amounts granted to freelancers and small enterprises during 2020 have been marginal compared to the amounts granted to the established recipients such as the national cultural institutions. In Nordic countries and internationally, the COVID measures have been poorly adapted to the conditions in which the cultural sector operates, especially in the case of self-employed and small-scale actors (see Kulturanalys Norden, 2021). In Finland freelance actors and the "free field" art organizations operating outside the established cultural institutions systems have felt left out of the pandemic support (Saari, 2021).

Our analysis nevertheless shows that the emergency funding measures have opened opportunities for new types of applicants to enter the cultural policy support system. The scope of funding has been increasingly extended from the traditional core artistic areas to creative industries. Moreover, the artist as an entrepreneur functioning as a part of the CCIs has risen on the cultural policy agenda. Our presumption is that the pandemic situation has been especially hard on those actors who normally operate on the market and in CCI value networks without direct state subsidies. The emergency seems to have put pressures to broaden and diversify the group of recipients and hence the scope of cultural policy within different administrative sectors. Thus, the anti-COVID measures might work as an incentive to improve coordination and reform the governmental CCI activities in the future (cf. e.g. Peters, 2018, p. 318). The Finance Committee of the Parliament recently stated (April 2021) that joint coordination is needed to support the Cultural and Creative Sectors.

The state has undeniably put notable efforts into aiding the CCIs in the crisis in Finland. However, it is exactly the state restrictions that have severely complicated the actors' operating possibilities. The state has been able to terminate the operations of public actors, especially. Reflecting the CCIs' entwined chains and networks of production in the field of arts and culture, the containment measures have widely affected not only the arts but the whole creative economy as well as the related sectors, e.g. the hospitality industry. As the information gathering efforts and close contacts with the CCIs during the crisis have increased the government's awareness of the varied operating structures of the CCIs and the interdependencies in the CCI ecologies, some of the policy shifts may last beyond the emergency situation.

While there is abundant information available on the short-term impacts of the pandemic on the CCIs in Finland, no comprehensive overview has been produced yet. In any case, the economic, social, and cultural difficulties are expected to recur and continue well into the future (see also VNK, 2020a, 2020b). The Finnish state has declared that after the pandemic, the arts and culture actors will have to adapt to "the new normal" in their activities (see e.g. VNK, 2020a, 2020b; VM, 2020). It is far too early to estimate the full effects of the pandemic in the Finnish cultural system, which has traditionally been rigid and slow to respond to new cultural developments and needs. The pandemic has in many ways revealed the structural problems in the CCIs and the vulnerability of the cultural economy and its relation to the state. In this way, the pandemic not only represents a temporary crisis after which things will go back to "normal", but it may also have more profound effects on the CCIs and the related cultural policy priorities (cf. Haugsevje et al., 2021).

The responses to the pandemic have brought forth some new operating models that have shaken the rigidity of the cultural policy system in Finland, and this may also mean a spark for institutional change. It is evident, though, that the problems faced by the Finnish cultural policy system even before the pandemic, such as diminishing public resources, remain and may endanger the opportunities to implement the cultural policy objectives outlined in for example the current government programme (VN, 2019) and the administrative cultural policy strategy (Opetus – ja kulttuuriministeriö, 2017) in the future. Indeed, further research on the effects of the pandemic in the CCIs is needed to understand and develop flexible and sustainable policy measures that could also be applied upon the arrival of the black swans of the future. There are signs that due to COVID-19 awareness of the nature and importance of the CCIs has increased in public debate and among administrators and politicians.

Notes

1. Totally aware of the wide discourse regarding the definition of CCIs (e.g. Flew, 2012; Hesmondhalgh, 2013; UNESCO, 2009) and recent discussion on the Cultural and Creative Sector (CCS; see e.g. European Commission, 2021), we lean in this chapter on the ESS-net definition of CCIs (2012) and recognize the set of cultural domains as presented in that conceptualization. Furthermore, CCIs can be also defined empirically by the data from the crisis funding instruments and other sources. These investigations are still ongoing at the time of writing this chapter.
2. These statistics define CCIs more widely than the ESS-net definition.
3. Direct funding allocated through the state budget. Note that some cultural funding streams were impossible to separate from the state budget within the limits of the research. For example, the sum does not include the costs of professional training in the arts on different educational levels.
4. https://valtioneuvosto.fi/en/-/10616/muutoksia-koronavirusepidemian-vuoksi-asetettuihin-rajoituksiin-1-kesakuuta [retrieved 25 Jan. 2021]
5. https://yle.fi/uutiset/osasto/news/new_coronavirus_restrictions_and_recommendations_in_force_in_december/11673834 [retrieved 25 Jan. 2021]
6. These industry classifications are based on national classification recommendations maintained and published by Statistics Finland's Classification Services. Several of them are based on international standards confirmed by EU directives.

References

Alasuutari, P. (2013) 'Spreading global models and enhancing banal localism: the case of local government cultural policy development', *International Journal of Cultural Policy* 19 (1), pp. 103–119.

Banks, M. (2020) 'The work of culture and C-19', *European Journal of Cultural Studies* 23 (4), pp. 648–654. https://journals.sagepub.com/doi/full/10.1177/1367549420924687 (Accessed: 8 May 2020).

Banks, M. and O'Connor, J. (2021) '"A plague upon your howling": art and culture in the viral emergency', *Cultural Trends*, 30 (1), pp. 3–18, DOI: 10.1080/09548963.2020.1827931 (Accessed: 10 December 2020).

Betzler D., Loots, E., Prokůpek, M. Marques, L. and Grafenauer, P. (2020) 'COVID-19 and the arts and cultural sectors: investigating countries' contextual factors and early policy measures', *International Journal of Cultural Policy*. DOI: 10.1080/10286632.2020.1842383 (Accessed: 23 Sep 2020).

Center for the Cultural Policy Research Cupore. (2021) *Impacts of the corona pandemic on artistic work have been significant or even devastating.* Available at: https://www.cupore.fi/en/information/news/-110911-01022021 (Accessed: 2 February 2021).

Comunian, R. and England, L. (2020) 'Creative and cultural work without filters: Covid-19 and exposed precarity in the creative economy', *Cultural Trends*, 29 (2), pp. 112–128, DOI: 10.1080/09548963.2020.1770577 (Accessed: 23 September 2020).

Creative FLIP. (2021) *Creatives Unite*. Available at: https://creativesunite.eu/one-place/ (Accessed: 16 June 2021).

Davies, K. (2020) 'Festivals Post Covid-19', *Leisure Sciences*, DOI:10.1080/01490 400.2020.1774000 (Accessed: 23 September 2020).

Eikhof, D.R. (2020) 'COVID-19, inclusion and workforce diversity in the cultural economy: what now, what next?', *Cultural Trends*, 29 (3), pp. 234–250, DOI: 10.1080/09548963.2020.1802202 (Accessed: 23 September 2020).

ESSnet-CULTURE European Statistical System Network on Culture. (2012) *Final Report*. Eurostat. Available at https://ec.europa.eu/assets/eac/culture/library/reports/ess-net-report_en.pdf (Accessed: 27 September 2021).

European Commission. (2021) *Cultural and creative sectors*. Available at: https://ec.europa.eu/culture/sectors/cultural-and-creative-sectors (Accessed: 5 March 2021).

European Parliament. (2020) *Euroopan parlamentin päätöslauselma Euroopan kulttuurisesta elpymisestä*. Available at: https://www.europarl.europa.eu/doceo/document/B-9-2020-0249_FI.html (Accessed: 16 June 2021).

Flew, T. (2012) *Creative Industries: Culture and Policy*. London: SAGE Publications.

Florida, R. and Seman, M. (2020) *Lost Art: Measuring COVID-19's Devastating Impact on America's Creative Economy*. Washington, DC: The Metropolitan Policy Program at Brookings. Available at: https://www.brookings.edu/wp-content/uploads/2020/08/20200810_Brookingsmetro_Covid19-and-creative-economy_Final.pdf (Accessed: 16 June 2021).

GESAC – The European Grouping of Societies of Authors and Composers. (2021) *Rebuilding Europe. The cultural and creative economy before and after the COVID-19 crisis*. Available at: https://www.rebuilding-europe.eu/ (Accessed: 16 June 2021).

Haugsevje, Å.D., Stavrum, H., Heian, M.T. and Gunn, K.A.L. (2021) 'Bridging, nudging and translating: facilitators of local creative industries in Norway', *International Journal of Cultural Policy*, DOI: 10.1080/10286632.2021.1895131 (Accessed: 16 June 2021).

Häyrynen, S. (2015) *Kulttuuripolitiikan liikkuvat rajat. Kulttuuri suomalaisessa yhteiskuntapolitiikassa*. Tietolipas 248. Suomalaisen Kirjallisuuden Seura.

Häyrynen, S. (2018) 'Renegotiating Cultural Welfare: The Adoption of Neoliberal Trends in Finnish Cultural Policy and How It Fits the Nordic Model of a Welfare State', in Alexander, V., Hägg, S., Häyrynen, S. and Sevänen, E. (eds.), *Art and the Challenge of Markets Volume 1. National Cultural Politics and the Challenges of Marketization and Globalization*. London: Palgrave MacMillan.

Heiskanen, I. (2015) 'Taiteen ja kulttuurin uusi asemointi talouteen: kulttuuriteollisuus, luovat alat ja luova talous', in Heiskanen, I., Kangas, A. and Mitchell, R. (eds.), *Taiteen ja kulttuurin kentät. Perusrakenteet, hallinta, lainsäädäntö ja uudet haasteet*, pp. 109–190. Helsinki: Tietosanoma.

Heiskanen, I., Ahonen, P. and Oulasvirta, L. (2005) *Taiteen ja kulttuurin rahoitus ja ohjaus: kipupisteet ja kehitysvaihtoehdot*. Cuporen julkaisuja 6. Kulttuuripolitiikan tutkimuksen edistämissäätiö.

Hesmondhalgh, D. (2013) *The Cultural Industries* (3rd Ed.). London: SAGE Publications.

Jakonen, O. (2017) 'Cultural policy and nationalism in a Finnish competition state: Innovative creative economy', *Kulttuuripolitiikan Tutkimuksen Vuosikirja*, pp. 20–37, DOI: 10.17409/kpt.60100 (Accessed: 16 June 2021).

Jakonen, O., Luonila, M., Renko, V. and Kanerva, A. (2020) 'Katsaus koronan vaikutuksista taiteen ja kulttuurin alojen toimintaedellytyksiin ja kulttuuripolitiikkaan Suomessa', *Kulttuuripolitiikan tutkimuksen vuosikirja*, 5 (1), pp. 50–59.

Kajander, R. (2021) *Suomen elokuva-ala pitää koronarajoituksia lainvastaisina ja vaatii niiden muuttamista.* Available at: https://yle.fi/uutiset/3-11787098 (Accessed: 12 Dec 2021).

Kangas, A. (2001) 'Cultural Policy in Finland', *The Journal of Arts Management Law, and Society*, 31 (1), pp. 57–78.

Kangas, A. and Vestheim, G. (2010) 'Institutionalism, cultural institutions and cultural policy in the Nordic countries', *Nordisk Kulturpolitisk Tidskrift*, 13 (2), pp. 267–286. Available at: https://www.idunn.no/file/pdf/47501136/art03.pdf (Accessed: 16 June 2021).

Kangas, A. & Pirnes, E. (2015). 'Kulttuuripoliittinen päätöksenteko, lainsäädäntö, hallinto ja rahoitus', in Heiskanen, I., Kangas, A. and Mitchell, R. (eds.), *Taiteen ja kulttuurin kentät. Perusrakenteet, hallinta, lainsäädäntö ja uudet haasteet*, pp. 23–108. Helsinki: Tietosanoma.

Karttunen, S. (2012) 'Cultural policy indicators: Reflections on the role of official statisticians in the politics of data collection', *Cultural Trends*, 2012 (1), pp. 1–15.

Kulturanalys Norden. (2021) *Covid-19-pandemiens effekter på kultur-sektoren i de nordiske landene.* A report prepared by Kulturanalys Norden on behalf of the Nordic Council of Ministers. Available at: https://kulturanalys.se/publikation/covid-19-pandemiens-effekter-pa-kultursektoren-i-de-nordiske-landene/ (Accessed: 16 June 2021).

Mangset, P. (2009) 'The Arm's Length Principle and the Art Funding System: A Comparative Approach', in Pyykkönen, M., Simanainen, N. and Sokka, S. (eds.), *What about Cultural Policy? Interdisciplinary Perspectives on Culture and Politics* (2nd Ed.), pp. 273–297. SoPhi 114. Helsinki: Minerva Kustannus Oy. Available at: https://jyx.jyu.fi/bitstream/handle/123456789/41953/978-952-492-320-0.pdf (Accessed: 16 June 2021).

Mankkinen, J. and Mattila, M. (2021) *Kulttuurialoilta katosi satojamiljoonia euroja ja töitä tuhansilta, ilmenee Ylen selvityksestä – musiikin sekatyöläinen Paavo Malmberg sinnittelee.* Available at: https://yle.fi/uutiset/3-11807085 (Accessed: 25 Feb 2021).

Mattila, M. (2021) *Kulttuurialasta tuli korona-ajan hylkiö, eivätkä taiteilijat koettele rajoituksia – asiantuntijan mukaan oikeuksiin kajoaminen on hyväksytty hiljaa.* Available at: https://yle.fi/uutiset/3-11755060 (Accessed: 27 Jan 2021).

National Institute for Health and Welfare [THL]. (2021) *Situation update on coronavirus.* Available at: https://thl.fi/en/web/infectious-diseases-and-vaccinations/what-s-new/coronavirus-covid-19-latest-updates/situation-update-on-coronavirus#Coronavirus_situation (Accessed: 24 February 2021).

Näyttelijäliitto. (2021) *Näyttelijäliitto vaatii freelancereiden tulonmenetysten korvaamista.* Available at: https://www.nayttelijaliitto.fi/?x18074=3224114 (Accessed: 7 Feb 2021).

Nevalainen, A. (2020) *Musiikkialaa uhkaa musertava lasku – Ministeri Saarikko kutsuu Paula Vesalan ja muut alan toimijat tapahtuma-alan pelastusryhmään.* Available at: www.yle.fi/uutiset/3-11606991 (Accessed: 22 Oct. 2020).

OECD. (2020) *OECD Policy Responses to Coronavirus (COVID-19).* Culture shock: COVID-19 and the cultural and creative sectors. Available at: http://www.oecd.org/coronavirus/policy-responses/culture-shock-covid-19-and-the-cultural-and-creative-sectors-08da9e0e/ (Accessed: 16 June 2021).

Oinaala, A. and Ruokolainen, V. (2017) 'Esittävän taiteen vapaa kenttä osana muuttuvaa kolmatta sektoria', *Kulttuuripolitiikan tutkimuksen vuosikirja,* pp. 124–139. DOI: 10.17409/kpt.60106 (Accessed: 16 June 2021).

Oksanen, J., Kuusisto, O., Lima-Toivanen, M., Mäntylä, M., Naumanen, M., Rilla, N., Sachinopoulou, A. and Valkokari, K. (2018) *In Search of Finnish Creative Economy Ecosystems and Their Development Needs – Study Based on International Benchmarking.* Publications of the Government's analysis, assessment and research activities 50/2018. Prime Minister's Office.

Opetus – ja kulttuuriministeriö (2017) *Strategy for Cultural Policy 2025.* Opetus – ja kulttuuriministeriön julkaisuja 2017:20. Available at https://julkaisut.valtioneuvosto.fi/bitstream/handle/10024/80577/okm22.pdf?sequence=1&isAllowed=y (Accessed: 25 Octobre 2021).

Paquette, J. and Redaelli, E. (2015) *Arts Management and Cultural Policy Research.* Palgrave Macmillan.

Peters, B.G. (2018) *The Politics of Bureaucracy. An Introduction to Comparative Public Administration.* Routledge.

Pratt, A.C. (2009) 'Policy Transfer and the Field of the Cultural and Creative Industries: What Can Be Learned from Europe?', in Kong, L. and O'Connor J. (eds.), *Creative Economies, Creative Cities,* pp. 9–23. Springer.

Saari, L. (2021) *Kulttuurin puolesta. 24 keinoa kulttuuri- ja taidealan tukemiseksi COVID-19 pandemian jälkeen.* [For Culture. 24 Ways to Support the Cultural and Artistic Sector in the Aftermath of the COVID-19 Pandemic]. KULTA ry.

Serafini. P. and Novosel, N. (2020) 'Culture as care: Argentina's cultural policy response to Covid-19', *Cultural Trends,* DOI: 10.1080/09548963.2020.1823821 (Accessed: 16 June 2021).

Statistics Finland. (2020) Koronakriisi iski voimakkaasti esittäviin taiteisiin. Available at: https://www.stat.fi/uutinen/koronakriisi-iski-voimakkaasti-esitta viin-taiteisiin (Accessed: 27 September 2021).

Taike. (2020) *Taike jakoi luoville aloille korona-apurahoja 8,7 miljoonaa.* Available at: https://www.taike.fi/fi/uutinen/-/news/1316227 (Accessed: 17 June 2020).

Taike. (2021) *Taideneuvosto vaatii tulevaisuudennäkymää ulos kulttuurialan kriisistä – vaarana peruuttamattomat vauriot työllistävälle, kasvavalle ja hyvinvointia luovalle alalle.* Available at: https://www.taike.fi/fi/uutinen/-/news/1346874 (Accessed: 16 February 2021).

Tarjanne, P. (2020) *Roadmap to the creative economy.* Publications of the Ministry of Economic Affairs and Employment 2020:48. Available at: https://julkaisut.valtioneuvosto.fi/bitstream/handle/10024/162474/TEM_2020_48.pdf?sequence=1&isAllowed=y (Accessed: 25 Octobre 2021).

The Compendium of Cultural Policies and Trends. (2020) Available at: https://www.culturalpolicies.net/ (Accessed: 26 October 2020).

Tulevaisuusvaliokunta [Committee on the Future]. (2020) *Koronapandemian hyvät ja huonot seuraukset lyhyellä ja pitkällä aikavälillä.* Eduskunnan tulevaisuusvaliokunnan julkaisu 1/2020. Available at: https://www.eduskunta.fi/FI/naineduskuntatoimii/julkaisut/Documents/tuvj_1+2020.pdf (Accessed: 27 September 2021).

UNESCO. (2009) *The 2009 UNESCO Framework for Cultural Statistics* (FCS). Available at: http://uis.unesco.org/sites/default/files/documents/unesco-framework-for-cultural-statistics-2009-en_0.pdf (Accessed 27 September 2021).

UNESCO. (2020) *Culture in Crisis. Policy Guide for a Resilient Creative Sector.* UNESCO.

Vedenpää, V. (2021) *Kulttuurialalla meni hermo koronarajoituksiin – Paula Vesala vaatii hallitukselta tekoja: "Olisi aika tehdä päätöksiä ja estää itsemurhat".* Available at: https://yle.fi/uutiset/3-11788872 (Accessed: 13 February 2021).

VM. (2020) *"Uusi normaali" puhutti 12.5. järjestetyissä poikkeusajan dialogeissa.* Available at: https://vm.fi/-/uusi-normaali-puhutti-12-5-jarjestetyissa-poikkeusajan-dialogeissa (Accessed: 20 May 2020).

VN. (2019) *Osaamisen, sivistyksen ja innovaatioiden Suomi.* Marinin hallitus. Hallitusohjelma.

VNK. (2020a) *Koronapandemian vaikutukset kulttuurialalla. Raportti kyselyn vastauksista.* [Effects of the COVID-19 pandemic on the cultural sector. Report on the responses to the survey]. Publications of the Finnish Government 2020:14. Available at https://julkaisut.valtioneuvosto.fi/bitstream/handle/10024/162255/VN_2020_14.pdf?sequence=1&isAllowed=y (Accessed: 26 October 2020).

VNK. (2020b) *Government decides on plan for hybrid strategy to manage coronavirus crisis and for gradual lifting of restrictions. Bulletin 4.5.2020 Government Communications Department.* Available at: https://valtioneuvosto.fi/-/10616/hallitus-linjasi-suunnitelmasta-koronakriisin-hallinnan-hybridistrategiaksi-ja-rajoitusten-vaiheittaisesta-purkamisesta?languageId=en_US (Accessed: 26 October 2020).

VNK. (2020c) *Koronapandemian vaikutukset kuntien kulttuuritoimintaan.* [Effects of the COVID-19 Pandemic on the Cultural Activities of Municipalities]. Publications of the Finnish Government 2020:23. Available at: https://julkaisut.valtioneuvosto.fi/bitstream/handle/10024/162352/VN_2020_23.pdf?sequence=1&isAllowed=y (Accessed: 26 October 2020).

Weckström, K. (2020) *Korona pisti kulttuuri- ja viihdetoiminnan polvilleen.* Available at: http://www.stat.fi/tietotrendit/artikkelit/2020/korona-pisti-kulttuuri-ja-viihdetoiminnan-polvilleen/ (Accessed: 13 February 2021).

Wirén, M., Westerholm, T. and Liikamaa, A. (2020) *Tapahtumateollisuuden toimialatutkimus 2020 osa 2.* Available at: https://www.tapahtumateollisuus.fi/wp-content/uploads/2020/09/Tapahtumateollisuuden-toimialaraportti-2020_osa-2_high.pdf (Accessed: 13 February 2021).

Wyatt, D. and Trevena, B. (2020) 'Governing creative industries in the post-normative cultural condition', *International Journal of Cultural Policy*, DOI: 10.1080/10286632.2020.1849167 (Accessed: 16 June 2021).

4 The COVID-19 pandemic and the cultural policy response in Slovakia[1]

Zuzana Došeková and Andrej Svorenčík

Introduction

The COVID-19 pandemic deeply affected individuals, societies, and economies worldwide. In order to slow down the spread of the virus, prevent loss of lives, and manage the burden on health care systems, many countries adopted policies of social isolation. As a result, business activities in many sectors, including the Cultural and Creative Sectors (CCS), were interrupted for months. Countries took different approaches to the trade-off between health and economic impacts. This chapter zooms on one of the affected countries – Slovakia.

In particular, we describe the impact of COVID-19 on the CCS in Slovakia and the subsequent central government policy responses over a one-year period. Using data from official statistics and tax records, as well as self-reports collected in surveys, we analyze the situation in the CCS and its development throughout the pandemic. A step-by-step account of the financial and non-financial relief policies undertaken by the state highlights the challenges of tailoring help to the specifics of this sector. To provide context and allow comparison with other countries, we also furnish background information about the spread of COVID-19, attitudes of the public to the epidemic prevention measures, and some qualitative insights. The chapter concludes with a summary of recommendations for policymakers to tackle similar situations in the future.

Background: CCS in Slovakia

Estimated size of the CCS varies from one source to another. Based on the 2018 data from the Satellite Account on Culture and Creative Industry of the Slovak Republic, the CCS in Slovakia accounted in 2018 for 1.69% GDP with EUR 1.52 bil. and had a 1.83% share on total value added of the economy with EUR 1.47 bil. There were 66,000 overall job positions in the CCS domains but only 40,000 jobs in creative professions[2] (Horecká and Némethová, 2020[3]). According to tax records, there were about 56,000 workers in the CCS in 2018 (30,000 employees and 26,000 self-employed).

DOI: 10.4324/9781003128274-6

Eurostat estimates cultural employment in Slovakia at 72,000 in 2018 and 74,000 in 2019. That makes it 2.9% of the total labour force, lower than the European Union (EU) average of 3.7% (Eurostat, 2019). It needs to be emphasized that quantifying the real contribution of CCS on a national economy is generally challenging because of the non-standard nature of contracts, difficulty to distinguish cultural from non-cultural activities in some sectors, and the fact that part of it falls into informal economy (Isernia and Lamonica, 2021). As a result, the official numbers are likely to be underestimated (OECD, 2020).

Public expenditure on culture corresponds to the EU average. In 2018, Slovakia allocated 0.87% of GDP on culture,[4] the same percentage as the EU 28 average (0.87% of GDP) but less than in Visegrad Group countries[5] (1.24% of GDP, due to high cultural spending in Hungary). In terms of spending, the central government plays a larger role than the local governments, contributing 64% of the total public expenditure on culture. Central government funds the largest and best-known cultural institutions, public broadcasting, churches, and three cultural public grant funds: Slovak Arts Council, Audiovisual Fund, and Fund for the Support of Minorities' Culture. An important part of independent cultural infrastructure is run by non-profit and civil society organizations (CSO). These are often subsidized from public sources, such as state or municipal grant schemes, and can receive tax assignment. The share of private resources in culture is lower than in other countries.[6] Around 80% of products and services of the CCS in Slovakia are bought by the private sector; in other countries,[7] the share of the private sector accounts for more than 85%. Investments in the form of donations and sponsorship are especially low by comparison (Institute for Cultural Policy, 2020).

First wave: March to May 2020

General situation

The government's response to the first wave of COVID-19 in March 2020 was quick and radical. A week after the first identified case on March 6, the Slovak government proclaimed an emergency situation and imposed a ban on public gatherings including cultural events on March 10, followed by a nationwide lockdown on March 12. Schools, shops, offices, cultural venues, and all public institutions were closed, with the exception of food stores, pharmacies, and gas stations. Face masks became mandatory and citizens were encouraged to stay at home unless absolutely necessary. The strict measures were broadly endorsed (although not unanimously) by medical experts, the media, and political leaders. As a result, the general public largely accepted the measures and complied with them.

At first, the unprecedented situation raised a wave of solidarity. Musicians performed free gigs online or played outdoor shows under the windows of hospitals and nursing homes, as well as in their neighbourhoods, to cheer up the residents. Actors took turns in reading children's books online, in an effort to support both children and their parents staying at home. Visual artists' community started social media groups to share their art created in self-isolation.

A number of individual artists took their performances online. As for cultural institutions, not all were prepared for a quick shift into online space. While all Slovak public institutions have at least a website and a Facebook page, not all were able to attract audiences with online content. Those who did were generally those who had actively worked with online content before the pandemic, such as the National Philharmonic Orchestra that had a pre-existing streaming service it could readily use. The cinema run by the Slovak Film Institute introduced "cinema at home" screenings, and Slovak audiovisual production also profited from a video-on-demand service, dafilms.sk, that had started in February 2020. Public theatres made individual efforts offering pre-recorded performances, with little new online content; a shared platform for watching theatre shows online was launched only in November. As for museums and libraries, the pandemic showed the unsatisfactory results of the heritage digitization project running since 2012 and costing over EUR 300 mil. For instance, on Europeana, the European portal for digitized cultural heritage, Slovakia is one of the countries with the fewest digital objects on display. Slovakia has presented 2,072 objects per 100,000 population, far below the EU average of 13,337 objects. That puts it near the bottom of the list, before Portugal, Bulgaria, and Romania (Institute for Cultural Policy, 2020).

On the positive side, the wide net of public cultural institutions[8] provided at least some protection for its employees: even if staying at home, they received most of their wages. As bonuses are usually paid for performances, and actors or musicians often top up their budgets with private projects in their free time, their income sank to the comparatively low base pay.

The first lockdown did successfully flatten the curve. By the end of May, Slovakia had a total of only 280 confirmed cases per mil. population, and only 28 deaths (5 per mil. people): one of the best results in the EU. By the end of May, most restrictions were lifted. Museums re-opened on May 6, cinemas and theatres on May 20 (with restrictions on visitor numbers). The phases of gradual re-opening of the economy progressed faster than originally planned, and state borders re-opened as well. This resulted in a wave of relief and even optimism. Several restrictions stayed in place, most notably, limits on the number of visitors at public events. Therefore, during the summer, some event organizers decided to run their events on a smaller scale. Others re-scheduled events to later dates (typically in autumn) or cancelled them, hoping to come back in 2021. Museums, on the other hand, were able to make up for some of their losses, as many Slovaks opted for a domestic summer holiday.[9] Still, revenues in tourism went down nearly 50% (Statistical Office of the Slovak Republic, 2021).

Financial losses

Using data from online cash registers, the National Bank of Slovakia estimated that revenues in the arts, entertainment, and recreation sector dropped during the lockdown in March and April 2020 by 73%–88% in comparison to the previous year – more than in any other sector, including accommodation and food services (National Bank of Slovakia, 2020).

In May, when some of the restrictions were lifted, the Institute of Cultural Policy, the analytical unit of the Ministry of Culture of the Slovak Republic, modelled two scenarios for the economic impact of the pandemic on the CCS using tax records from 2018. In the best-case scenario, for every month of the pandemic it was assumed that the CCS suffer a 20% decrease in revenue compared to the previous year, and 50% in the worst-case scenario. The pandemic-induced revenue loss in the CCS would then be EUR 57 mil. per month in the best-case scenario and EUR 140 mil. per month in the worst-case scenario.

These scenarios were complemented by data reported by representatives of various cultural sectors in May 2020. The highest revenue loss in total numbers was experienced by the audiovisual sector, followed by media publishing (Table 4.1). The sector of architecture, not included in the table, reported no substantial changes in income. Designers did not provide an estimate but hazarded that 10% of individual designers and 50% of product design manufacturers were having serious financial difficulties. Note that each sector used a different source of data, methodology, and time frame. Some sectors, such as visual arts, are not represented at all, due to a data gap. This is symptomatic of the difficulties in gathering reliable data about the CCS; a recurring issue throughout the pandemic.

Relief measures

Financial

Like most countries, Slovakia launched a set of financial and non-financial relief measures (for an overview of measures taken by other states, see e.g. European Commission, 2021; UNESCO, 2020). The main financial instrument chosen was a horizontal program called "First Aid" that offered wage compensations to all sectors of the economy. It was designed and administered by the Ministry of Labour, Social Affairs and Family (for details, see Social Policy Institute, 2020a, 2020b). The first round of the scheme received criticism for being insufficient, over-bureaucratic, and restrictive in its eligibility conditions. With its one-size-fits-all approach it was not well suited to CCS for several reasons.

Maximum compensations were available only to employers whose establishment was closed by decree. This was not applicable to employers without fixed establishments, such as event organizers who normally rent venues.

Table 4.1 Estimated lost revenue in creative sectors, as reported by sector representatives in May 2020.

Sector	Estimated Lost Revenue (EUR)	Time period
Audiovisual		March–December[c]
TV + audiovisual production	43.0 mil.	
Cinemas + distribution	15.8 mil.	
Radio	5.0–6.0 mil.	
Booksellers + publishers	4.0 mil.	Monthly
Print and digital media		March–June
Newspapers, journals	20.0–25.0 mil. advertising income 30–95% sales, depending on title (down to 15% by the end of May)	March–June
Distribution	4.3 mil.	
Music		March–December[c]
Event organizers[a]	2.5 mil.	March–December[c]
Royalties[b]	5.1 mil.	March–December[c]
Musicians	2.3 mil.	Monthly
Theatres	1.4–1.6 mil.	Monthly
Independent cultural centres	0.5 mil.	March–June
Game development	10.0 mil.	March–December[c]

Source: Online consultations of the Ministry of Culture of the Slovak Republic with various stakeholders in the CCS.

[a] Excluding festivals

[b] Due to no live events, closed venues and businesses paying for music licenses (bars, hotels, etc.)

[c] Estimates spanning the period March to December were based on the assumption of a 3-month lockdown period

The former were reimbursed 80% of each employee's monthly wages up to EUR 1,100[10] (corresponding to the national average wage), but the latter could only be compensated up to EUR 880 per employee. Self-employed workers' wage compensations depended on the degree of income loss. Even those who lost 100% of revenues could receive EUR 540 at most and were still required to pay health and social insurance contributions (with a possibility to postpone them). The most restrictive eligibility condition was that freelancers who had any income, albeit minimal, from contracts with an employer, were ineligible for the self-employed workers' aid. That proved a serious barrier for creative workers with hybrid contracts: according to the 2018 tax records, half of the 26,000 self-employed creative workers had had concurrent income from employee contracts in addition to their income from freelance work. Another group excluded from full aid were so-called single-person limited companies, a micro-business form used by some freelancers to optimize social insurance and liability. Freelancers operating as single-person Ltds. were only eligible for a so-called "S.O.S" compensation of EUR 210. The cultural community and the Ministry of

Culture representatives had been communicating the shortcomings of the scheme from early on, but it was altered only in October (non-retroactively), bringing up the support for freelancers to EUR 880, incorporating workers with hybrid contracts, and raising the "S.O.S" payments to EUR 315. Businesses residing in rented spaces could also take advantage of a rent support scheme administered by the Ministry of Economy.

In the first wave, there was no sector-specific financial package for the CCS. Devising targeted help for creative workers proved difficult for two reasons. First, there was a lack of reliable data. Slovakia, unlike some other European countries (e.g. Germany, Slovenia, Estonia; see Krausová, 2021), does not have an official artists' register that would allow prompt identification of individual creative workers. The Business Register and Tax Office only record entrepreneurs' self-reported NACE code,[11] which is not a reliable enough indicator for identifying all businesses and individuals working in the creative industries.[12] Second, public grant distribution bodies in the cultural sector were not prepared to handle relief programs due to limits in legislation. Disbursement of grants for artists and non-state cultural organizations is normally carried out by three cultural public grant funds operating on arm's length principle: Slovak Arts Council, Audiovisual Fund, and Fund for the Support of Minorities' Culture. Some grant programs are also administered directly by the Ministry of Culture. The three funds proved useful with their resources and know-how of administering grant support. Under existing legislation, however, they could only offer project-based support. They were unable to distribute quick all-purpose compensations, or support non-artistic professionals hit by the pandemic, such as event technicians. Nevertheless, they quickly responded by adapting grant programs and opened special calls to strengthen support for the sectors in most acute need. Slovak Arts Council extended their existing scheme for libraries' acquisitions, encouraging libraries to buy books from local bookstores, and the Audiovisual Fund opened a special call for cinemas, worth EUR 500,000, to encourage them to screen Slovak movies (and partially compensate them for their losses). Amendments to respective laws passed in autumn allowed both Ministry of Culture and the grant funds to pay out social and crisis support, and they made use of it later during the second wave of COVID-19.

Non-Financial

Non-financial measures included pandemic care support that allowed parents to receive sick/nursing pay when staying at home with their children as their schools closed down or when in quarantine. Self-employed workers had the option to postpone health and social insurance contributions until September.

Three public grant funds reviewed criteria for existing projects, allowing postponements or cancellations. Non-refundable costs were reimbursed, but the rest of the funds was to be returned. As a tax relief, the payments of mandatory 2% of authors' earnings to the Arts Funds[13] were made voluntary. A temporary relaxation of mandatory quotas for Slovak music allowed radios to top up their budgets with extra advertising time.

Second wave: September–December 2020

General situation

After the summer holidays, the number of new cases of COVID-19 soared, and mortality rates followed in October (Figure 4.1). The public response to the second wave was in stark contrast to the first wave. The relative mildness of the first wave led many to perceive the dangers of the pandemic as overrated. As a result, they became less willing to accept or observe tightened regulations, and every added restriction raised protesting voices.

The authorities failed in imparting pandemic measures in a clear, consistent, and unambiguous fashion. Rules were introduced (and reversed) often, with little or no prior warning. Performers and event organizers repeatedly found themselves in situations where they cancelled an event due to another lowering of the visitors' quota, only to discover, a few days later, that the quota did not apply to their specific case or that the original quota was not going to change after all.

In October, a massive operation was launched to test the entire adult population with rapid antigen tests within two days (October 31 to

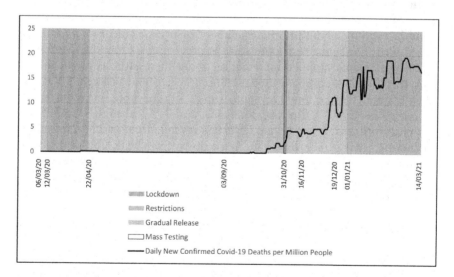

Figure 4.1 Daily new confirmed COVID-19 deaths per mil. people (7-day moving median) in Slovakia.

Source: National Health Information Centre (2021).

November 1). The testing was voluntary and had a relatively high turnout – 3.6 out of 4.4 mil adult population. Although the exponential growth of infection rates slowed down, the effect was only temporary. As it was not followed consistently by complementary measures and as negative tests led some to lose their caution, infection rates started growing again.

With continued restrictions on public gatherings, representatives of the CCS became even more active in the media and public debates, demanding that cultural events resume or that compensations become more adequate. In September, public television screened a documentary in which various professionals from the music industry talked about the uncertainty and difficulties (including financial) they faced since the onset of COVID-19. It is worth noting that the CCS in Slovakia do not have a strong representative body. While unions, professional associations, and interest groups do exist, they tend to be fragmented and rarely represent a critical number of actors in a given sector. During the crisis, CCS workers were motivated to join forces. New informal groups and initiatives emerged on social networks. As a notable example, Slovak Music Union was started by a group of promoters and event organizers in June 2020. It quickly gained ground with people working not only in the music industry but also in other areas of the CCS, attracted more than 9,000 followers, and became a strong negotiator.

Financial losses

In an effort to obtain a better estimate of the financial losses in the CCS, the Ministry of Culture ran an online survey in October, asking actors from the CCS to submit information about their losses incurred as a direct result of the pandemic restrictions in the preceding six months. A total of 7,028 participants supplied information about themselves as physical persons, their business companies, or their non-profit organizations (NPO) and CSO. Estimated interannual revenue drop of 50% or more was reported by 79% legal persons, 71% physical persons, and 74% cultural NPOs/CSOs. A typical business company had 72% less revenue than in 2019; in monetary terms, their 6-month revenue went down from EUR 25,000 to EUR 7,000 (median values). A typical self-employed worker lost 65% revenue, earning EUR 2,545 compared to EUR 7,297 for the respective six months of 2020 and 2019. On the other hand, the downturn in business activities also led to cost-cutting. Business companies lowered their costs by 50%, while self-employed workers were only able to cut off 22%. The main limitation of these results is assumed selection bias. As anyone was free to fill out the online questionnaire, it is likely that those whose income was significantly affected during the pandemic had a stronger motivation to participate than those with little change in the volume of business conducted. Therefore, these findings cannot be applied to all creative sectors in equal measure.

Relief measures

Financial

The "First Aid" income support scheme underwent a revision together with a general policy shift to offer additional sector-specific support schemes. Income support payments to employers and the self-employed were raised by 50%, starting with payouts for October. Also, eligibility conditions were relaxed, making some allowances for workers with parallel incomes, and for those late with their social security payments. However, concerns remained that a number of freelancers with hybrid income left out in the first round of the scheme were at risk, having received no or minimal support in the first six months of restricted work conditions. It was assumed that the principal group at risk were technical and assisting professions, seeing as artists and authors had a parallel grant scheme open at the Slovak Arts Council (see below).

A special one-off scheme was therefore designed to re-compensate non-artistic professionals up to the level of the horizontal income support program: all who fell short of the EUR 880 per month because of a small-scale work contract with an employer, or because of receiving other state support, such as retirement or disability pension, were encouraged to apply. The scheme was administered by the Ministry of Culture. Based on tax records of creative workers, it was estimated that some 1,300 individuals would satisfy the eligibility conditions. However, only 270 applied and were granted the compensation. There are several factors that may have contributed to low interest in the compensation program. First, creative professionals with parallel incomes may have dropped their contracts early on in the pandemic in order to benefit from full income support. Second, a combination of income from work contracts and freelancing may be more typical of artists than of technical and assisting professions, a fact not apparent from the available data. Third, these workers might have found another line of work in the meantime. It is also conceivable that the number of technical and assisting professions most affected was lower than expected, for example, if they worked in television productions rather than live events. Still, it is fair to say that the reasons for the low number of applicants are not entirely clear.

In the meantime, the Ministry of Economy opened a dedicated aid scheme for business companies in the CCS. Its aim was to reimburse fixed costs, keeping businesses afloat during the time of limited business opportunities. The design, however, was not well-suited to businesses with high turnovers and low fixed operating costs, such as promoters and event agencies. The call has not been closed as yet (March 2021), so the number of beneficiaries is not known. Another sector-specific scheme, aimed at enterprises in tourism, was administered by the Ministry of Transport and Construction. Eligible entities included museums, historical sites, zoological and botanical gardens, as well as bars and pubs, a category that music clubs might find themselves in. Payouts were based on revenue difference between 2019 and 2020. Public cultural organizations also received partial compensations for income lost in the form of an extra budget transfer of EUR 7 mil. Performing arts institutions in Slovakia typically have permanent ensembles, leading to high fixed costs they are unable to cover without box office earnings.

In support of individual authors, Slovak Arts Council opened a special call at the beginning of September with an allocation of EUR 9.5 mil., granted on top of its typical annual budget of EUR 20 mil. Artists could apply for grants to cover their living expenses for up to 6 months while they worked on their projects. The call attracted a record number of 3,840 applications, out of which 3,026 were successful. Because the number of projects submitted was much higher than the Fund normally processes, the payments were not sent out before December.

Non-financial

To better identify creative workers, a new regulation was passed to start a register of artists and other professional workers in the creative sectors, administered by the Slovak Arts Council. Its aim was to have a list ready for a speedier distribution of funds in the future. Artists such as writers, professional musicians, visual artists, actors, theatre, or film directors were added to the register based on proof of professional training or self-reported results, such as books published, concerts, plays, exhibitions featured, etc. Register of other creative professionals included a wider set of professions: technicians, editors, journalists, translators, researchers, art, music or drama teachers, producers, or organizers. At the moment, registration does not come with social or other benefits; it serves the purpose of speeding up administration of support.

In co-operation with the music sector, Radio and Television Slovakia commissioned 20 music clubs throughout the country to organize gigs with local musicians and record them on-site for screening, with the intention to support local music communities. The program was granted EUR 150,000 from the state budget.

Second wave: January–March 2021

General situation

The pandemic situation worsened in December and was further exacerbated by increased mobility over the Christmas holidays. By February, Slovakia found itself on top of daily per capita COVID-related mortality charts (Figure 4.1), second only to the Czech Republic. At the time of writing this chapter (March 2021) Slovakia was in its second lockdown.

Vaccination started in late December with senior groups and medical staff, but the share of population fully vaccinated was as yet too low to have a substantial impact on the viral spread.

Continued isolation took its toll not only on the economy but also on the general well-being of the population. During the second lockdown, self-reported perception of COVID-19 as a threat to oneself went up, reaching similar levels to those in the first wave in March 2020 (MNFORCE, Slovak Academy of Sciences, Seesame, 2020–2021). Mental health issues have been on the rise, and barriers in treatment provision are likely to further aggravate the problem (Winkler et al., 2020). Children and young adults are especially at risk. Research shows that non-clinical Slovak students reported increased levels of depression, anxiety, perceived stress, and loneliness (Hajdúk et al., 2020).

While it would be difficult to isolate the cultural deprivation factor from other pandemic-induced stressors (such as acute health danger, loss of social interactions, substantial restrictions in daily routines, economic uncertainty, etc.), it can be hypothesized that limited access to culture as a social and self-expressive activity is likely to have an adverse effect on well-being, especially that of habitual consumers of cultural goods. In a 2019 representative survey on cultural consumption (Národné osvetové centrum, 2019), the most popular cultural activity was visiting museums (81% of the respondents had visited one in the last 12 months), followed by cinemas (71%), traditional music/art events (64%),[14] concerts of popular music (55%), and discos/dance events (50%). Slightly less than half of those questioned had seen a theatre play in the last year (46%). In contrast, internet was most often used for music listening and video viewing (82% at least once a year), radio listening (62%), watching TV (60%), and watching films (56%). Changes in cultural consumption over the year require additional research: at the moment, it is not clear if Slovak consumers substituted preferred cultural activities with available ones or if they spent less time on cultural activities as such.

COVID-19 restrictions also changed the education process. Slovak schools were closed for months, and the re-opening strategy prioritized on-site education of younger children, as they were more reliant on parental care when staying at home. As a result, elementary schools were partially open but high schools and universities stayed closed throughout the year. The efficiency of skill transfer through online tuition raises some concerns, especially in arts education, which does not lend itself well to distance learning. On the elementary school level (ages 6–15), music and art education in Slovakia are organized through "elementary art schools" – public or private institutions offering after-school tuition. It is not known how many teachers were able to continue classes online or how many parents decided to discontinue their children's lessons. At universities and arts colleges, students were assigned limited time in workshops and studios due to the need for social distancing, and music students were left without the opportunity to play together in orchestras and ensembles. For college programs such as restoration of cultural objects, it is virtually impossible to get the full value of courses in home settings. Pandemic measures are likely to have caused some degree of skill loss to students as well as adult professionals.

Relief measures disbursed and planned

The horizontal "First Aid" went through a third review in February, non-retroactively extending eligibility to workers who only started their job in 2020, raising wage compensation from 80% to 100% (up to EUR 1,100), compensations to the self-employed up to EUR 870 and the "S.O.S". aid to EUR 360. An aid package with an allocation of EUR 24.6 mil. was introduced on March 1, 2021, to compensate employees of elementary art schools for the time they were closed since the previous year. This pertains to more than 4,000 full-time and almost 3,700 part-time teachers.

After dedicated schemes for business companies and individual creative workers in the CCS followed a grant scheme for non-profit and civil society cultural organizations, such as theatres and theatre ensembles, independent cultural centres, historical sites, orchestras and music ensembles, festivals, etc. Again, there is a lack of reliable data about their numbers. The public register of non-government organizations does not categorize them by sector.[15] In the absence of better data, the best estimate – based on the number of unique NPOs/CSOs that have applied for support from the public grant funds since 2012 – is approximately 2,400. As non-profits typically have limited financial reserves, a support scheme was opened in March with the aim of helping them overcome the difficult period and continue their activities in 2021. Payments of up to 50,000 euros are based on the organizations' revenue loss between 2020 and 2019 (80%) and their operating costs (20%).

As of March 1, 2021, financial measures to support the CCS have amounted to EUR 45 mil. Out of that, EUR 21.5 mil. were granted to 12,000 individuals (employees or self-employed) as income support, and EUR 10.2 mil. as individual grants. Around EUR 3 mil. have so far been disbursed to enterprises in cultural tourism (the scheme is ongoing). Cinemas received EUR 540,000 and audiovisual producers, EUR 610,000. In addition, EUR 7 mil. was allocated to state cultural institutions, and EUR 2.3 mil. to the public broadcasting service. The support package for NPO has been tentatively allocated EUR 10 mil.

As the pandemic goes into its second year, creative sectors (as well as other sectors) depend on continued financial support. Another one-off payment round for individual entrepreneurs in the creative sectors (both artistic and non-artistic) is in preparation, to be launched in May. Its design is being consulted with representatives of the sectors. Even if the scheme is successful, for some, it may come too late. Some freelancers had already given up on their jobs in the CCS and moved into other lines of work.

Businesses have closed with no plans to re-open. As of now, it is too early to count all the losses. They will transpire in the coming years.

Conclusion

The COVID-19 pandemic has plunged countries around the globe into crisis. Public authorities had to make difficult decisions fast and with limited information available, adapt existing policies, design new ones, and fine-tune them on the go. While it remains difficult to make accurate predictions about the future and the "new normal", the information and experience collected in Slovakia present several generalizable lessons for policymakers. The areas that proved most challenging and will need to be addressed in order to provide optimal support for the CCS in the following months and years can be summed up in six points.

1 **Proactivity.** Post-hoc relief measures will continue to be necessary but planning ahead is crucial to recovery. The CCS need a policy strategy, preparing for best- and worst-case scenarios.
2 **Communication.** The CCS need a comprehensive step-by-step plan for re-opening the economy as the pandemic recedes, with specific conditions for cultural activities in every stage (Ireland is an example of good practice, see Government of Ireland, 2021) to help CCS actors prepare for the recovery phase. Also, it must be clearly stated what relief and recovery aid they can expect, and for how long. Preparing policies in a dialogue with the creative community will improve the information base and make decisions more accepted.
3 **Recognizing sectoral specifics.** Culture belongs to the sectors most sensitive to shocks but many of its actors have non-standard work arrangements and fall out of cross-sectoral aid schemes. Specifics of the sector should be reflected in policies and better explained in public discourse. In Slovakia, public reaction to culture support campaigns revealed that an artist is seen by many as a celebrity with high income who does not work especially hard and is paid for what is essentially a hobby. Yet, as noted in the Status of the Artist Report by UNESCO (2019), a typical artist earns less than most other workers and subsidizes the arts with her unpaid or underpaid labour. The issue of public image of creative workers needs to be addressed with education and awareness campaigns coming from public authorities, influencers, and the artists themselves.
4 **Data collection.** If existing statistics do not capture the complex realities of the CCS, their structure, and their actors' work arrangements, alternative methods of data collection such as regular surveys, need to be put in place. Monitoring working conditions of creative workers can help to address their needs with policies and provide evidence of their real situation to both policymakers and the general public.

5 **Upskilling.** The changed circumstances will require that public cultural organizations become more flexible, work with their audiences through multiple channels, and acquire new skills with digital and interactive content. Venues and ensembles should prepare their own strategies of reconnecting with their audiences – both short-term, working with different scenarios, and long-term, envisaging the eventuality of recurring periods of restricted public events. Digital and presentation skills development would also benefit creative workers.

6 **Flexibility.** Rigid regulations and an inability to strengthen administrative capacities at short notice imply that it takes a long time to set up mechanisms to distribute funds and even longer for the funds to reach their recipients.

The good news is that the tools and mechanisms put in place to allow for crisis support to artists will remain available for future needs. Both the Ministry of Culture and the Slovak Arts Council now have the means to administer direct income support, and the official register of creative professionals could become a basis for future Status of the Artist regulations.

Notes

1. The views and opinions expressed in this chapter are those of the authors and do not necessarily reflect the official policy or position of the Ministry of Culture of the Slovak Republic.
2. As classified by the International Standard Classification of Occupations.
3. Due to data availability and methodological complexity, the Satellite account is published with a 2-year lag.
4. Subclasses 08-2 to 08-6 in the classification of government expenditures (SK COFOG), including cultural services, broadcasting and publishing services, religious and other community services, R&D recreation, culture and religion, and recreation, culture and religion not elsewhere classified.
5. Czech Republic, Hungary, Poland, and Slovakia.
6. Private resources include the support and income from gainful activities obtained from individuals, enterprises, and non-profit organizations, whether they invest, sponsor, donate, or consume cultural goods.
7. Tentative estimate based on the satellite accounts of CCS of countries that use similar methodologies (CZ, NL, AT, USA).
8. Slovakia has a large number of publicly funded cultural institutions, including 27 theatres, 3 orchestras, 82 museums, 24 galleries, 1,461 public libraries (excluding academic and school libraries), and hundreds of local cultural centres.
9. Slovak castle museums are especially popular with tourists. In a survey carried out before the pandemic (Národné osvetové centrum, 2019), 81% Slovak respondents claimed to have visited one in the last 12 months.
10. In the first quarter of 2020, the average monthly salary in Slovakia was EUR 1,086.
11. European Industry Standard Classification system for business activities.
12. The codes are not being used consistently, especially by businesses with multiple activities. An event agency, for example, might choose to categorize their

business as "consulting services", and an audio engineer might be classified under "electrical services".

13. Different to the public grant funds, the Literature Fund, the Music Fund, and the Visual Arts Fund are solidarity funds established by law and self-governed by artists. They receive contributions from authors (2% of remuneration paid to authors), copyright users, and TV licence fees and pay out grants and awards. They operate on a much smaller budget than the public grant funds and, accordingly, offer lower payouts. In 2019, authors contributed EUR 1.1 mil, half of the funds' total budget of EUR 2.1 mil. In comparison, the three public grant funds operated with a budget of EUR 41.7 mil.

14. Traditional music and dance are popular activities in Slovakia, with high active and passive participation. A town or village typically has at least one folk ensemble, or a separate one for children and adults. The members have regular training meetings and perform in local or regional festivities. Three professional and semi-professional folk ensembles are funded by the state.

15. There is an opportunity to address this issue in the ongoing review of Statistical classification of economic activities in the European community (NACE) by making distinctions within category 94.9–Activities of other membership organizations and assigning cultural membership organizations a separate sub-code.

References

European Commission (2021). *Policy Measures Taken against the Spread and Impact of the Coronavirus.* [online] Available at: https://ec.europa.eu/info/sites/info/files/coronovirus_policy_measures_12_february_2021.pdf [Accessed on March 30, 2021]

Eurostat (2019). *Cultural Employment by Sex.* [online] Available at: https://appsso.eurostat.ec.europa.eu/nui/show.do?dataset=cult_emp_sex&lang=en [Accessed on March 30, 2021]

Government of Ireland (2021). *Covid-19 Recovery and Resilience 2021: The Path Ahead.* [online] Available at: https://www.gov.ie/en/campaigns/resilience-recovery-2020-2021-plan-for-living-with-covid-19/ [Accessed on March 30, 2021]

Hajdúk, M. et al. (2020). Psychotic experiences in student population during the Covid-19 pandemic. *Schizophr. Res.*, 222, 520–521. doi: 10.1016/j.schres.2020.05.023

Horecká, J. and Némethová, R. (2020). *The Summary Results of the Satellite Account on Culture and Creative Industry of the Slovak Republic (2013–2018).* Bratislava: Infostat. [online] Available at: https://www.culture.gov.sk/wp-content/uploads/2019/12/Summary-results-SA-CCI-SR-2013-2018.pdf [Accessed on May 1, 2021]

Institute for Cultural Policy (2020). *Culture Spending Review.* [online] Available at: https://www.culture.gov.sk/wp-content/uploads/2020/01/Culturalspending review_FINAL_ENG.pdf [Accessed on May 1, 2021]

Isernia, P. and Lamonica, A. G. (2021). *The Assessment of the Impact of Covid-19 on the Cultural and Creative Sectors in the EU's Partner Countries, Policy Responses and their Implications for International Cultural Relations.* [online] Available at: https://www.cultureinexternalrelations.eu/cier-data/uploads/2021/02/CRP_COVID_ICR_Study-final-Public.pdf [Accessed on March 30, 2021]

Krausová, M. (2021). *Právní úprava statusu umělce [Regulation of the Status of the Artist]*, Parliamentary Institute, Chamber of Deputies of the Parliament of the Czech Republic, Study 5.405. [online] Available at: https://www.psp.cz/sqw/ppi.sqw?lp=1

MNFORCE, Slovak Academy of Sciences, Seesame (2020–2021). *Ako sa máte, Slovensko? [How are you, Slovakia?]*. Continuous survey, data available on request: http://sasd.sav.sk/sk/ [Accessed on March 30, 2021]

Národné osvetové centrum (2019). *Spotreba kultúry (reprezentatívny kvantitatívny prieskum)*. [online] Available at: https://www.nocka.sk/vyskum-a-statistika/ [Accessed on March 30, 2021]

National Bank of Slovakia (2020). *Financial Stability Report*. [online] Available at: https://www.nbs.sk/_img/Documents/ZAKLNBS/PUBLIK/SFS/FSR_052020.pdf [Accessed on March 30, 2021]

National Health Information Centre (2021). *Coronavirus (COVID-19) in the Slovak Republic in numbers*. [online] Available at: https://korona.gov.sk/en/coronavirus-covid-19-in-the-slovak-republic-in-numbers/ [Accessed on March 30, 2021]

OECD (2020). *Culture Shock: COVID-19 and the Cultural and Creative Sectors*. [online] Available at: https://read.oecd-ilibrary.org/view/?ref=135_135961-nenh9f2w7a&title=Culture-shock-COVID-19-and-the-creative-sectors [Accessed on March 30, 2021]

Social Policy Institute (2020a, July). *"First Aid" for Slovakia*. [online] Available at: https://www.employment.gov.sk/files/slovensky/ministerstvo/analyticke-centrum/analyticke-komentare/spi_first_aid_sr_aug2020_final.pdf [Accessed on March 30, 2021]

Social Policy Institute (2020b, November). *"First Aid" for Slovakia*. [online] Available at: https://www.employment.gov.sk/files/slovensky/ministerstvo/analyticke-centrum/analyticke-komentare/isp_first_aid_nov2020.pdf [Accessed on March 30, 2021]

Statistical Office of the Slovak Republic (2021). *Vývoj cestovného ruchu v ubytovacích zariadeniach SR v roku 2020*. [online] Available at: https://slovak.statistics.sk/wps/portal/ext/themes/sectoral/tourism [Accessed on March 30, 2021]

UNESCO (2019). *Culture & Working Conditions for Artists: Implementing the 1980 Recommendation Concerning the Status of the Artist*. [online] Available at: https://unesdoc.unesco.org/ark:/48223/pf0000371790 [Accessed on March 30, 2021]

UNESCO (2020). *Culture in Crisis: Policy Guide for a Resilient Creative Sector*. [online] Available at: https://en.unesco.org/creativity/publications/culture-crisis-policy-guide-resilient-creative [Accessed on March 30, 2021]

Winkler, P. et al. (2020). Increase in prevalence of current mental disorders in the context of COVID-19: analysis of repeated nationwide cross-sectional surveys. *Epidemiol Psychiatr Sci*, e173. doi: 10.1017/S2045796020000888

Section 2

Cultural workers

Resilience and organization
during the COVID-19 pandemic

5 The COVID-19 pandemic and cultural workers

Fight, flight or freeze in lockdown?

Beate Elstad, Dag Jansson and Erik Døving

Introduction

The creative industries have been particularly vulnerable to the lockdowns following the outbreak of the COVID-19 pandemic. This sector is in double jeopardy because it depends on open social arenas and many of its actors are in precarious work situations (Elstad, Døving and Jansson, 2020; Kalleberg and Vallas, 2018). The situation is particularly dramatic when audiences are not allowed to attend performances and rehearsal venues cannot comply with social distancing rules. Existing revenue sources easily dry up and the opportunities for alternative income are somewhat limited. At the outbreak of the pandemic, cultural workers therefore faced substantial uncertainty about current and future income as well as their overall career outlook.

At the same time, the crisis called for innovative responses and the development of new products and services, and even for the emergence of novel industries. A society that still needed human interaction, artistic expression, and culture in extraordinary times created new opportunities. Given this ambiguous outlook, cultural workers have chosen different approaches to cope with the pandemic and the ensuing government interventions. In this chapter, we focus on the immediate coping modes among cultural workers in the Norwegian performing arts sector in the spring of 2020. We apply the coping response framework of *fight*, *flight*, and *freeze* (Skinner et al., 2003; Webster, Brough and Daly, 2016) to analyse survey data from 1,337 respondents.

Given the precarious employment relations in the creative industries where a substantial proportion are self-employed, it is of particular interest to compare the coping differences between the self-employed and those with permanent full-time employment. For example, does a precarious situation imply more or less innovative modes of coping? Are the self-employed, to a greater extent, paralyzed by the situation or do they seek a career change? Based on the particular vulnerability of the cultural sector, a pertinent issue is also how different work arrangements and coping are

DOI: 10.4324/9781003128274-8

related to overall satisfaction with the job situation, as suggested by previous research (Welbourne et al., 2007).

To address these issues, we investigate how categories of cultural workers responded to the initial lockdown by posing two closely related research questions:

1 To what extent do cultural workers renew their professional practice, in terms of rearranging their job situation and considering changing jobs, or conversely, become paralysed and remain stuck in their current situation?
2 How is coping related to work arrangements and job satisfaction, and how does coping vary across the occupational sub-groups?

The coronavirus, creative industries, and coping

The labour market in the creative industries is characterized by a large proportion of self-employed. Work situations are commonly described as precarious, where self-employment, freelancing, short-term project work, low artistic income, and excess supply of recruits and portfolio careers prevail (Bennett, 2009; Bennett and Bridgstock, 2015; Bridgstock et al., 2015; Hennekam, 2017; Hennekam and Bennett, 2016; Mangset et al., 2018). Among Norwegian members of artist trade unions, a majority run their own businesses (60%) or are freelancing (10%) (Heian, Løyland and Kleppe, 2015). Only 17% are employed by an organization.

Previous studies of the immediate economic consequences of the lockdown in Norway from 12 March 2020, show that many sectors experienced dramatic income losses and the national unemployment rate jumped from 2.3% to 10.4% from 10 to 24 March 2020 (Alstadsæter et al., 2020; Holden et al., 2020). In the creative industries, including music, performing art, visual art, museums and literature, Grünfeld et al. (2020) estimated an income loss of 32% between 12 March and September 2020. Elstad, Døving and Jansson (2020) found that self-employed cultural workers expected a fourfold income loss compared with full-time employees from 2019 to 2020.

The initial lockdown in the spring of 2020 created a high level of uncertainty in the short and medium-term that entailed a very stressful situation for those who were most impacted by it. A considerable body of literature describes how employees cope with stress, using a variety of approaches to classify, conceptualize and measure coping behaviours (Skinner et al., 2003; Webster et al., 2016). Coping is an adaptive process, at times unconscious and involuntary, that intervenes between a stressor and its psychological, emotional, and physiological outcomes (Skinner et al., 2003). Coping can be classified at different levels, where higher-order categories are subdivided into finer-grained categories (Skinner et al., 2003; Webster et al., 2016). Based on a review of extensive empirical research, Skinner et al.

(2003) established different levels of measurable coping from higher-order families of coping into specific coping instances. Examples of coping families are problem solving and escape. Coping instances are specific behaviour such as "I tried to figure out what to do" (Skinner et al., 2003, p. 220). In our study, we build on a similar hierarchical logic. At the highest level we have fight, flight, and freeze while coping instances are specific behaviour connected to the pandemic situation. The coping instances may reflect different coping modes as an intermediate level between coping families and coping instances. Since an instrument has not been specifically designed for measuring coping among cultural workers during the pandemic, we had to develop our own instrument.

For the quantitative part of the study, we developed a list of coping instances that were applicable for cultural workers in a pandemic situation. The list of coping instances intended to cover a reduced set of coping families, which included fight, flight and freeze. *Fight* is closely related to problem solving and support seeking in the framework developed by Skinner et al. (2003), defined as actively trying to solve the challenges imposed by the lockdown. *Flight* implies an intended or realized escape from the present situation by pursuing job opportunities elsewhere, within or outside the cultural sector. This is closely related to the escape dimension in Skinner et al. (2003) and Webster et al. (2016) frameworks. *Freeze* implies non-action, a paralysis of sorts, lingering confusion, or simply waiting out the situation. It is closely related to a state of helplessness, lack of coping, and inclination to give up (Skinner et al., 2003, p. 224). For the qualitative part of the study, the respondents were at liberty to frame their own notions of coping as short narratives crossing the survey categories. Previous research has indicated that coping by problem solving and cognitive restructuring is linked to general wellbeing and job satisfaction, while avoidance coping is frequently associated with more negative outcomes (Welbourne et al., 2007).

Method and material

We conducted a survey of members of *Creo* – Norway's largest trade union for performing artists. *Creo* members include musicians, singers, conductors, composers, music and drama teachers, organists, cantors, dancers, choreographers, actors, dramaturgs, directors, audio/light/studio engineers, scenographers, costume designers, producers, stage managers and administrative staff. We collected data in the period 17–25 April 2020 to study the initial impact of the full lockdown, which in Norway began on 12 March and was eased slightly from mid-May. An online questionnaire with standardized as well as open-ended questions was distributed by email to 8,742 members of *Creo*. We received 1,337 responses – a response rate of 15.3%.

The two largest occupational sub-groups in the sample are *musicians* (including composers and conductors) and *music teachers*. Distribution by occupational sub-group in our sample closely corresponds to the distribution among all Creo members, indicating little bias. There is an equal number of men and women in the sample. The most common main work arrangement is full-time employment and part-time employment, followed by self-employed. However, 56% of the respondents combine multiple work arrangements, where the most common combination is being a freelancer and having one's own company. Creo has a higher proportion of artists employed by an organization than the Norwegian creative sector as a whole.

We developed a measurement instrument with coping instances adapted to the particular situation at hand. We decided *a priori* that the items should reflect the three higher-order coping families of fight, flight, and freeze. However, we did not a priori assume any stringent structure of the coping hierarchy but left it to emerge from the statistical analysis. The pool of coping instances was generated by reviewing newspapers, the *Kulturplot* newsletter for the cultural sector in Norway, as well as social media. In addition, we reviewed the items with *Creo*, drawing on feedback from their members about how they dealt with the new situation.

The survey respondents were asked the following overall question: "We have listed a number of possible instances of dealing with the coronavirus situation. To what degree have you [...]". Examples of subsequent items are "increased the use of digital media in my job", "considered finding a job outside the cultural sector", and "been at a loss with regard to what to do". The list of 20 coping instances (in abbreviated format) is shown in Table 5.1. The answers were captured on a five-point Likert scale from 1 = does not at all agree to 5 = fully agree. To measure job satisfaction, we used an existing, validated measurement instrument with three items such as: "All in all, I am satisfied with my job" (Cammann et al., 1979). The answers were captured on a five-point Likert scale (1 = does not at all agree to 5 = fully agree). Survey items were presented in arbitrary order, without any numbering or grouping, and where the different coping families were mixed.

Respondents were also invited to describe in their own words how they dealt with the situation. 28% of the respondents in the survey, across all work arrangements, provided written accounts with varying levels of detail, some of them quite elaborate. We used the qualitative data as an interpretive tool to elucidate the statistical results. The approach is therefore a mixed-method design, albeit with emphasis on the quantitative component. In the taxonomy described by (Cresswell and Clark, 2003), our design falls within the category of 'explanatory sequential design'.

Findings: Coping and consequences

Prominent coping instances

Table 5.1 shows the scores for 20 coping instances, for the total sample as well as for each of the five occupational sub-groups. The items are ranked according to total scores. We observe that the top-ranking activities are

Table 5.1 Coping instances by professional categories, means (1 = does not at all agree to 5 = fully agree), ranked by total mean.

	Total		Musicians	Teachers	Church musicians	Backstage workers	Dancers/ actors	p^a
	Mean	St. dev.						
1 Increased use of job-related digital media	3.9	1.4	3.4	4.8	4.3	3.2	3.8	<0.001
2 Rotated work plans	3.8	1.2	3.9	3.5	4.1	3.7	3.8	<0.001
3 Contacted friends through digital media	3.6	1.1	3.6	3.6	3.3	3.9	3.8	0.011
4 Supported people	3.6	1.0	3.6	3.7	3.4	3.7	3.5	0.067
5 Developed new professional skills	3.5	1.2	3.4	3.7	3.8	3.3	2.9	<0.001
6 Contacted colleagues through digital media	3.4	1.2	3.3	3.7	3.1	3.6	3.8	<0.001
7 Spent time maintaining professional skills	3.4	1.2	3.6	3.2	3.8	3.1	3.1	<0.001
8 Learned to use new technologies	3.2	1.3	2.8	4.0	3.4	2.9	2.8	<0.001
9 Been at loss with what to do	2.9	1.3	3.1	2.6	2.3	3.4	3.3	<0.001
10 Sought social support among family and friends	2.8	1.4	2.8	2.9	2.7	2.7	2.9	0.566
11 Developed new products/projects	2.7	1.4	2.5	2.8	3.6	2.5	2.5	<0.001
12 Stayed put and waited	2.6	1.2	2.8	2.4	2.3	2.9	3.0	<0.001
13 Prepping home office	2.6	1.3	2.4	3.0	2.4	2.3	2.7	<0.001
14 Participated in new projects/services	2.6	1.4	2.5	2.3	3.6	2.6	2.6	<0.001
15 Delayed tasks	2.5	1.2	2.6	2.3	2.6	2.6	2.7	0.030
16 Looked for new income opportunities	2.4	1.3	2.7	2.0	1.5	3.2	2.6	<0.001
17 Will look for job openings	2.3	1.3	2.4	2.1	1.6	2.8	3.0	<0.001
18 Considered another job within arts and culture	1.8	1.1	1.8	1.6	1.3	2.0	2.4	<0.001
19 Considered jobs outside arts and culture	1.7	1.2	1.8	1.4	1.3	2.4	2.0	<0.001
20 Will retrain for another job next three years	1.6	1.0	1.7	1.5	1.2	2.0	1.8	<0.001
N^b	1,041		487	325	91	108	30	

[a] p-values for differences across professional groups obtained from analysis of variance and F-test
[b] Excluded all respondents with missing data on one or more variable

of a proactive and constructive nature. The use of digital media and flexible job rotation are the most prevalent approaches, combined with seeking social support from close relations as well as colleagues. Job rotation means that respondents exploited the portfolio nature of their work situation and shifted towards activities such as composing, home-studio recording, and administration. High scores for the development of new professional skills and the maintenance of existing ones can both be seen as coping options in their own right and elements in a flexible task portfolio. We observe that the development of new products and concepts receives medium-level scores among all the coping activities.

Some medium-level coping instance scores are non-action. This includes waiting for the situation to pass, procrastination, or merely bewilderment as to what to do. The least important coping instances in our sample is the inclination to run away. Respondents sought to a limited extent other jobs in their current sector or planned to leave the arts and cultural sector. The overall pattern was that the initial phase of the pandemic did not change cultural workers' commitment to their profession. Instead, they actively exploited assets at hand and nurtured their capabilities.

Coping across occupations

Table 5.1 reveals some notable differences between occupational sub-groups. For example, church musicians appear to be the most innovative and least inclined to leave the sector. Conversely, backstage workers seemed to have less manoeuvrability and considered other job opportunities. In the following, we describe the situation for each sub-group, where the qualitative data allows additional and specific interpretation.

Musicians, which includes singers, conductors, and composers, are the largest group and whose coping most resembles the total sample. The majority of musicians (67%) are self-employed as freelancers and independent businesses. They rotated their work portfolios and prioritized tasks that could be sustained when physical venues were shut down. Examples include moving up recording sessions, composing and producing new music. They have also spent more time practising and enhancing their skills, as exemplified by these three musicians:

> I have started recording an album that was meant to take three to four years to record because it was supposed to happen 'between battles'. The music has quite a large number of parts that were supposed to be recorded one by one – very time-consuming in busy musicians' lives – but now is the perfect time to get it done.
> I practise new and old repertoire.
> I have tried to keep busy by working more on song-writing, composing and music production. In addition, I have spent time learning to use the application *Ableton Live*, that is, the part of my profession that does not provide immediate income.

Teachers are the second largest group in the sample, which comprises educators in schools at all levels, from primary schools through universities as well as the large sector of municipal cultural schools. Practically everyone in this group is employed (93%), full-time or part-time. Schools and nurseries were closed at the time of the survey and teachers were obliged to work from home. This group stands out with regard to embracing digital media, new technology and prepping home offices. The pandemic became a golden opportunity for them to finally start using existing educational tools:

> I learned how to use the digital dance teaching platform so that I can observe my pupils in more peace and with greater attention to detail.
> Net-based teaching works beautifully. I made it possible to invent new things. I have been compelled to adapt my teaching even more to the individual pupil and that has been a good thing.

Church musicians include organists and cantors, predominantly employed by the Norwegian Lutheran Church. The great majority have permanent employment (96%), whose positions often include a range of tasks such as performing music, leading choirs, arranging music, and producing concerts. *Church musicians* score higher than the other groups for job rotation, skill development, and new concepts. They seemed to be able to combine the time to practise and innovate their modes of delivery. This phenomenon was also observed in that a number of churches started to offer digital religious services and funerals as well as various media platforms to convey their teachings and communicate with their members:

> Great fun to make web-based [religious] services.
> We have become rather good at making digital productions. A priest has become indispensable as photographer and producer. We go the extra mile and are positive and flexible.
> We have learned to think differently. We have worked digitally, posted on Facebook and the church website, and see that we reach a lot more people than we do in the church room.

One group that experienced particular hardship was those working in various *backstage* functions – audio/light/studio engineers, scenographers, costume designers, producers, and stage managers. The majority (60%) are self-employed and, alongside actors and dancers, they score higher on both freeze and flight items. They were immediately hit by the shutdown of venues and cancellation of performances and festivals. Many lost their assignments overnight or were furloughed from their employment. Consequently, they searched for new sources of income and considered retraining for a job outside the arts and cultural sector to a greater extent than other groups:

I have lost 100% of my jobs.

I am at a loss as what to do as a sound engineer when there are no technical jobs around.

I actively search for jobs in several sectors. As a technician, my social security is way too poor up against the fee rates my customers are willing to pay.

Dancers and actors, including choreographers and dramaturgs, represent the smallest group in the sample. Although the majority have permanent employment (60%), which is more than for musicians, they express a higher degree of freeze coping. When theatres and opera houses shut down, dancers and actors were either furloughed or lost freelance assignments, or both.

The emerging pattern is that groups with a high degree of permanent employment *and* who were not furloughed (church musicians and teachers) became more active problem-solvers when the initial shutdown kicked in. Conversely, the groups that were self-employed or furloughed (dancers, actors, backstage workers) to a greater extent went into a flight or freeze mode.

Coping modes and work arrangements

For further analyses, we conducted factor analyses of the 20 coping instances, resulting in six coping modes. Factor analysis is a method that clusters empirically the specific instances into higher-order concepts. The modes show satisfactory discriminant validity. Internal consistency indicators for multi-item measures are in the range of 0.66–0.82, except for *freeze*, which is in the lower end of the satisfactory range ($\alpha = 0.53$).

Four of the modes reflect problem solving that we interpret as aspects of *fight*. Innovation is developing and participating in new concepts and delivery formats, whether digital (such as streaming) or physical (such as drive-in). *Skill nurturing* encompasses the maintenance and development of professional proficiency as well as job rotation. Technology adoption involves expanded use of digital media and learning new technologies as a part of prepping a home office. Social support means providing or actively seeking social support from colleagues, friends or family to cope with the situation. While innovation is externally oriented by serving audiences and the public at large, the other factors are oriented towards individual mastery of the work situation. *Flight* implies an intended or realized escape from the present situation by pursuing job opportunities elsewhere, within or outside the cultural sector. *Freeze* implies non-action, a paralysis of sorts, lingering confusion, or simply waiting out the situation.

Table 5.2 shows correlations between coping modes and how they are scored differently by self-employed and employed cultural workers. The most prevalent coping modes are the *fighting* modes, while *flight* scores are lowest. *Flight* and *freeze* are strongly correlated. Unsurprisingly,

Table 5.2 Pearson correlations and descriptives for coping modes, employment status and job satisfaction.

	Total		Employment status (means)[a]		Correlations (Cronbach's internal consistency alpha on diagonal)						
								Fight			
	Mean	St. deviation	Employed	Self-employed	Flight	Freeze	Social support	Skill nurturing	Innovation	Technology adoption	Job satisfaction
Flight	1.9	1.0	1.7	2.3***	0.83						
Freeze	2.7	1.0	2.5	2.9***	0.41***	0.53					
Fight: social support	3.4	0.8	3.4	3.4	0.16***	0.12***	0.70				
Fight: skill nurturing	3.6	0.9	3.5	3.6*	0.06	-0.09**	0.25***	0.68			
Fight: innovation	2.6	1.3	2.8	2.4***	-0.04	-0.11***	0.25***	0.27***	0.81		
Fight: technology adoption	3.2	1.0	3.5	2.8***	-0.10**	-0.16***	0.33***	0.24***	0.40***	0.66	
Job satisfaction	3.7	1.0	3.8	3.6***	-0.45***	-0.25***	0.07*	0.19***	0.11***	0.10*	0.79

[a] Welch's t-test for difference between means.

*$p < 0.05$ **$p < 0.01$ ***$p < 0.001$

N = 982 (excluded all respondents with missing data on one or more variables).

self-employed suffer greater consequences of the shutdown, become less active, and have a stronger tendency to look for other job opportunities. There is a strong and significant correlation between *Technology adoption* and *Innovation* (r = 0.40; *p* < 0.001), which suggests that an adaptive behaviour tends to combine an internal and external orientation.

Employed cultural workers include those who have a permanent job as their main affiliation with the labour market. The self-employed are those who primarily run their own business or earn a living by freelancing. The self-employed experienced a more challenging situation than the employed, indicated by the significantly higher scores for flight and freeze. A more surprising observation is that the self-employed are less innovative in terms of exploring new products and concepts and have adopted new technologies and made use of digital media to a lesser extent.

While Table 5.2 shows correlations between pairs of coping modes and job satisfaction, Table 5.3 displays the results of linear regression analyses with each of them as a dependent variable. Multiple regression allows us to isolate the differences across occupational sub-groups and between employees and the self-employed from a respondent background such as gender, age, income bracket, and educational level. The last column shows results with regard to job satisfaction, where coping modes are included as independent variables.

These multiple regressions confirm the findings in Table 5.2 that the self-employed innovate and adopt new technologies to a lesser extent than the employed and, at the same time, are more inclined to flight and freeze. Church musicians stand out from other musicians in terms of more extensive innovation, technology adoption, and skill nurturing as coping modes. Compared to musicians, teachers adopt new technology and engage in social support activities to a greater extent, and they were less inclined to freeze in response to the lockdown. In contrast, those working backstage were most inclined to flight among the occupational sub-groups.

Most coping modes are related to overall job satisfaction when controlling for work arrangements, occupational sub-group, and demographic variables. Whereas flight and freeze are negatively related to job satisfaction, fight through social support and skill nurturing are significantly and positively related to job satisfaction. Unlike the bivariate analysis, fight in terms of innovation and technology adoption does not appear to be related to overall job satisfaction when controlling for other coping modes. A possible interpretation is that, despite a positive orientation, innovation and technology adoption seems to come with some reservations:

> [I] felt some sort of anxiety or shame as I didn't know ... or didn't have enough knowledge to get good productions online.
>
> In any case, I don't think streaming is the answer to everything. It's live music and concerts that matter – it has surely become clearer to me after this.

Table 5.3 Regression analyses with regard to coping modes and job satisfaction.[a]

	Flight	Freeze	Fight				Job satisfaction
			Social support	Skill nurturing	Innovation	Technology adoption	
Intercept	2.59***	3.32***	3.43***	3.47***	2.96***	3.00***	3.76***
Backstage worker[d],[b]	0.31**	0.02	0.10	-0.14	-0.17	-0.11	0.05
Church musician[d],[b]	-0.28**	-0.21*	-0.07	0.41***	1.00***	0.38***	-0.05
Music teacher[d],[b]	-0.04	-0.25***	0.17*	-0.04	-0.14	0.92***	-0.11
Female[d]	-0.04	0.19***	0.40***	-0.04	0.04	0.13*	0.02
Age (5-year intervals)	-0.11***	-0.10***	-0.09***	-0.01	-0.09***	-0.05***	-0.01
Gross income (100,000 NOK)	-0.02	0.00	0.03*	0.01	0.08***	0.05**	0.07***
Graduate degree[d],[c]	0.04	-0.10	0.14*	0.09	-0.06	0.09	0.00
Non-degree higher education[d],[c]	0.05	-0.03	0.22	-0.06	0.33	0.14	-0.08
Upper secondary education[d],[c]	0.08	0.06	0.20	-0.15	-0.05	-0.25	-0.10
Self employed[d],[e]	0.39***	0.17*	-0.02	0.19*	-0.40***	-0.23**	0.05
Flight							-0.45***
Freeze							-0.09**
Fight: social support							0.14***
Fight: skill nurturing							0.11***
Fight: innovation							0.01
Fight: technology adoption							-0.03
R^2	0.23	0.15	0.14	0.03	0.11	0.27	0.26

[a] Ordinary least squares, unstandardized coefficients
[b] Reference category is musicians
[c] Undergraduate degree is the reference category
[d] Dummy variables
[e] Employed is the reference category

*$p < 0.05$; **$p < 0.01$; ***$p < 0.001$ (two-tailed test); N = 982

Cultural workers seem to be strongly committed to delivering high quality to pupils, audiences, and churchgoers. New concepts and digitization appear to be mixed blessings. Although renewal is an exciting endeavour, it puts increased pressure on the individual in an unchartered encounter with the audience. In another study with the same sample, 22% of the respondents reported to have performance anxiety in connection with digital events (Elstad, Jansson and Døving, 2020).

Discussion and conclusions

This study shows that the broad categories of fight, flight, and freeze are indeed useful in accounting for cultural workers' coping in the first phase of the pandemic. A methodological contribution of the study is the development of a new measurement instrument for cultural workers' coping with a ruinous interruption in their professional practice. As a theoretical contribution, the coping framework of fight, flight, and freeze was successfully subdivided into six dimensions, where fight comprises skill nurturing, giving and seeking social support, technology adoption, and innovation.

Precarity and innovation

The results presented here show that cultural workers predominantly entered fight modes in the initial phase of the pandemic. Those who were coping through social support and skill nurturing were also more satisfied with their situation, while flight responses to the lockdown were particularly negatively related to job satisfaction.

We observed notable differences between occupational groups because the various subgroups have different opportunities for adapting their working situations. For example, church musicians reached their audiences in new channels and music teachers adopted new technologies, while neither of these options was available to backstage workers to the same extent, who simply lost their market. Musicians rotated their work portfolios and prioritized tasks that could be sustained when physical venues were shut down. A striking and rather unexpected finding, on the other hand, is that innovative coping modes were more prevalent among the employed than the self-employed. We expected stronger creativity and flexibility demands to be imposed on the self-employed as their markets were shut down and contracts cancelled, whereas the employed would not depend on innovation to the same extent. Instead, the self-employed went into freeze and flight mode to a greater extent than the employed and also tended to be less happy with their situation. One of the rationales for a free and unbounded cultural sector alongside institutions is the expectation that it provides renewal and stimulus beyond official policies and mainstream tendencies. In this sample, precarity is *not* the mother of invention.

Table 5.3 shows that income level is positively related to innovation and technology adoption. Income levels were at the outset lower for the self-employed, which unleashed immediate financial stress as the pandemic erupted (Elstad, Døving and Jansson, 2020). Developing new concepts, services, and delivery formats requires a space for trial and error, which was less available to the self-employed when in need of quick fixes to make ends meet. According to Borrup (2018), social structures both enable and constrain entrepreneurial capability in the arts. In our study, the balance between enablement and constraint seems most favourable for church musicians and music teachers, where almost all of them are employed.

Observing less creativity and innovation in the self-employed category seems to be consistent with previous research. Generally, poverty has been found to limit entrepreneurs' capacity to exploit their creativity (Doering, 2016). One of the reasons is that the lack of support structures for self-employed cultural workers creates administrative burdens that often crowd out time for making art (Jackson, 2004). It should be noted that poverty among artists is no less common in prosperous countries. In fact, the opposite is the case because precarity in the arts is largely structurally given (Abbing, 2008); a constant influx of new entrants occurs when economic conditions improve. The converse process may be what we observe in our results: when conditions deteriorate, the self-employed have the strongest inclination to exit (flight).

Beyond the pandemic

The study captured coping activity in the early phase of the pandemic. Nonetheless, the qualitative data point at adaptive behaviour with implications beyond the shutdown itself:

> I have started to live-stream funerals and hope to build a market that endures beyond the quarantine. (Church musician)
>
> I have been able to play three streamed concerts in three different arenas, which I believe has contributed to giving me a larger audience than I otherwise would have had. (Musician)
>
> [I have acquired] new knowledge about streaming and made new acquaintances on YouTube. (Backstage worker)

Building the market by expanding reach, accustom audiences to new channels of encounter, and widening the applicability of skills may prove to be lasting effects. Conversely, it is also imaginable that the innovators have enjoyed a certain initial enthusiasm for creative endeavours and that novelty eventually wears off. How the pandemic continues to unfold, not least how economic impacts and policies vary across countries, will determine the long-term picture for our short-term observations. We can, for example, easily foresee a worst-case exodus scenario where the coping mode of flight becomes much more prominent. Backstage professionals are already at risk as they contemplate other types of jobs to a greater extent. Key competencies in the sector may be permanently lost if a greater level of normalcy is far off.

Even moderate scenarios may imply structural changes in the cultural sector. The balance may shift for some of the traditional dichotomies, for example, between large-scale versus intimate events, click-friendly versus niche expressions, conservative versus high-risk artistic endeavours and between government-funded and privately funded cultural workers. The ubiquity of digitization raises specific issues with regard to how artistic and cultural expressions are perceived and consumed. It is clearly too early to tell what the longer-term impact will be. However, we should expect digital delivery formats to shift how the sector operates, for example, from cinemas to home streaming, video-friendly staging/scenography of opera and theatre, and even religious services on demand. At the same time, audiences will probably rediscover the preciousness of scheduled events, physical encounters, and unmediated performing art. In fact, we would expect multiple, competing trends to coexist, leading to a more varied cultural sector, where concepts, services, and expressions will, to a greater extent, exploit their specific and unique characteristics. The obvious limitation of the study is that it offers a snapshot picture of a phenomenon that is still unfolding. Follow-up research is needed to enable analyses of the dynamics of cultural workers' coping as well as to understand the real impact of shutting down cultural arenas.

References

Abbing, H. (2008) *Why Are Artists Poor? – The Exceptional Economy of the Arts*: Amsterdam: Amsterdam University Press.

Alstadsæter, A., Bratsberg, B., Eielsen, G., Kopczuk, W., Markussen, S., Raaum, O. and Røed, K. (2020) The first weeks of the Corona crisis: Who got hit, when and why? Evidence from Norway. *Covid Economics*, 1(15), pp. 63–87. CEPR Press.

Bennett, D. (2009) Academy and the real world: Developing realistic notions of career in the performing arts. *Arts and Humanities in Higher Education*, 8(3), pp. 309–327. doi:10.1177/1474022209339953

Bennett, D. and Bridgstock, R. (2015) The urgent need for career preview: Student expectations and graduate realities in music and dance. *International Journal of Music Education* 33(3), pp. 263–277. doi:10.1177/0255761414558653

Borrup, T. (2018) Creative disruption in the arts – Special issue introduction. *The Journal of Arts Management, Law, and Society*, 48(4), pp. 223–226. https://doi.org/10.1080/10632921.2018.1497392

Bridgstock, R., Goldsmith, B., Rodgers, J. and Hearn, G. (2015) Creative graduate pathways within and beyond the creative industries. *Journal of Education and Work*, 28(4), pp. 333–345. doi:10.1080/13639080.2014.997682

Cammann, C., Fichman, M., Jenkins, D. and Klesh, J. (1979) The Michigan organizational assessment questionnaire. *Unpublished manuscript, University of Michigan, Ann Arbor*, pp. 71–138.

Cresswell, J. and Clark, V. P. (2003) *Designing and Conducting Mixed Method Research*: Thousand Oaks, CA: Sage Publications, Inc.

Doering, L. (2016) Necessity is the mother of isomorphism: Poverty and market creativity in Panama. *Sociology of Development*, 2(3), pp. 235–264.

Elstad, B., Døving, E. and Jansson, D. (2020) Usikkerhet i koronaens tid. En studie av kulturarbeidere med ulike tilknytningsformer til arbeidslivet. [Uncertainty in the time of the corona virus. A study of cultural workers with different work arrangements]. *Søkelys på arbeidslivet*, 37(4), pp. 299–315. doi:10.18261/ issn.1504-7989-2020-04-06

Elstad, B., Jansson, D. and Døving, E. (2020) *Umiddelbare konsekvenser av covid-19-pandemien i Norge. En studie av kulturarbeidere. [Immediate consequences of the COVID-19 pandemic in Norway. A study of cultural workers]*. Research report 2020 nr 8. Oslo: Oslo Metropolitan University.

Grünfeld, L., Gran, A.-B., Westberg, N. B., Stokke, O. M., Guldvik, M. K., Scheffer, M., Gaustad, T. and. Booth, P. (2020) *Koronakrisen og kultursektoren. Endringer i aktivitet fra mars og april 2020. [The Corona Crisis and the Cultural Sector. Activity changes from April to May 2020]*. Menon-rapport 56/2020. Oslo: Menon/BI Centre for Creative Industries.

Heian, M. T., Løyland, K. and Kleppe, B. (2015) *Kunstnerundersøkelsen 2013. Kunstnernes inntekter. [The Artist Survey 2013. The Artists' Income]*. TF-rapport nr.350. Telemark: Telemarksforskning. http://hdl.handle.net/11250/2439569

Hennekam, S. (2017) Dealing with multiple incompatible work-related identities: The case of artists. *Personnel Review*, 46(5), pp. 970–987.

Hennekam, S. and Bennett, D. (2016) Involuntary career transition and identity within the artist population. *Personnel Review*, 45(6), pp. 1114–1131.

Holden, S., von Brasch, T., Torstensen, K. N., Magnussen, J., Sæther, E. M., Evje, T., Hirch, V.H., Hansson, L.F., Sælensminde, K., Aavitsland, P. and Røttingen, J.-A. (2020) *Samfunnsøkonomisk vurdering av smitteverntiltak – covid-19. [Sosio-Economic Assessment of Infection Control Measures – Covid-19]*: Oslo: Helsedirektoratet.

Jackson, M.-R. (2004) Investing in creativity: A study of the support structure for US artists. *The Journal of Arts Management, Law, and Society*, 34(1), pp. 43–58.

Kalleberg, A. L. and Vallas, S. P. (2018) Probing precarious work: Theory, research, and politics. *Research in the Sociology of Work*, 31(1), pp. 1–30.

Mangset, P., Heian, M. T., Kleppe, B. and Løyland, K. (2018) Why are artists getting poorer? About the reproduction of low income among artists. *International Journal of Cultural Policy*, 24(4), pp. 539–558. doi:10.1080/10286632.2016. 1218860

Skinner, E. A., Edge, K., Altman, J. and Sherwood, H. (2003) Searching for the structure of coping: A review and critique of category systems for classifying ways of coping. *Psychological Bulletin*, 129(2), pp. 216–269.

Webster, V., Brough, P. and Daly, K. (2016) Fight, flight or freeze: Common responses for follower coping with toxic leadership. *Stress and Health*, 32(4), pp. 346–354. doi:10.1002/smi.2626

Welbourne, J. L., Eggerth, D., Hartley, T. A., Andrew, M. E. and Sanchez, F. (2007) Coping strategies in the workplace: Relationships with attributional style and job satisfaction. *Journal of Vocational Behavior*, 70(2), pp. 312–325. doi:10.1016/j.jvb.2006.10.006

6 The COVID-19 pandemic, cultural work, and resilience

Viktoriya Pisotska and Luca Giustiniano

Introduction

Cultural and Creative Industries (CCIs) host activities that have their origin in individual creativity, skill, and talent (DCMS, 2001). They have been often viewed as templates for other organizations (Lampel et al., 2000; Eikhof and Haunschild, 2007; Townley et al., 2009; Wu and Wu, 2016). Cultural workers are considered the motor of CCIs. They are characterized by creativity, flexibility, adaptability to constant challenges, improvisation, and bricolage (Duymedjian and Rüling, 2010). Recently, research into the dark side of CCIs stressed the precarious working conditions of cultural workers, working under conditions of stress, anxiety, hardship, and blurred boundaries between work and personal life (Ekman, 2015; Wright, 2018; Cinque et al., 2020). The unexpected COVID-19 outbreak has produced a profound psychological and professional impact on cultural workers, showing the fragility of this sector, which is based on extensive human interaction.

COVID-19 has spread across the globe at an unprecedented pace. Since the COVID-19 outbreak, world, EU, and national governmental bodies have adopted serious measures, such as large-scale quarantines, travel restrictions, and social-distancing measures. In September 2020, the Organisation for Economic Co-operation and Development (OECD, 2020) announced that CCIs were among the most affected by the current crisis, with jobs at risk ranging from 0.8 to 5.5% of employment across OECD regions. The International Labour Organization (ILO, 2020) revealed the contrast between massive job losses in hard-hit sectors, such as arts and culture, and the positive job growth evident in a number of higher-skilled service sectors, such as information and communication, suggesting that this divergence will tend to increase inequality within countries. In December 2020, the United Nations Educational, Scientific and Cultural Organization (UNESCO, 2020) reported some dramatic estimates: ten million lost jobs in the film industry; the reduction of staff by half in one-third of art galleries; more than $10 billion in lost sponsorships in the music industry in six months of lockdown; and the reduction of the

DOI: 10.4324/9781003128274-9

global publishing market by 7.5%, as a consequence of the COVID-19 pandemic.

In the light of the unexpected global emergency, the purpose of this chapter is to explore cultural workers' psychological resilience – a capacity and a process of individuals to bounce back from adversity (Fletcher and Sarkar, 2013) – and reorganization of their professional lives. Drawing on 16 cultural workers interviewed prevalently from Italy, we answer the following research question: *How do cultural workers positively adapt and reorganize their work during and immediately after the first COVID-19 lockdown (Europe, March–May 2020)?*

Theoretical background

Psychological resilience

The concept of resilience has been extensively used in COVID-19 times. It derives from the Latin *resalio/resilire*, which means to jump back.

Existing studies conceptualize psychological resilience either as a personality trait, a process, or an outcome. For instance, Bonanno (2004, pp. 20–21) defines psychological resilience as "the ability of adults in otherwise normal circumstances who are exposed to an isolated and potentially highly disruptive event ... to maintain relatively stable, healthy levels of psychological and physical functioning ... as well as the capacity for generative experiences and positive emotions". The author highlights that resilient individuals are those that report little or no psychological symptoms and evidence the ability to continue fulfilling personal and social responsibilities and to embrace new tasks and experiences.

Many scales to measure individual resilience, intended as a trait, exist. However, in the early 90s, resilience started being conceptualized as a process. For example, Luthar et al. (2000, p. 543) refer to psychological resilience as a "dynamic process encompassing positive adaptation within the context of significant adversity". The processual view implies that resilience can change with changing circumstances and over time. Recent research (e.g. Giustiniano et al., 2018; Lombardi et al., 2021) proposes to consider resilience as composed of two interrelated dimensions: adaptive and reactive resilience. The former requires the capacity to absorb the impact of a negative incident, whereas the second implies the capacity to look at the negative incident as a source of learning.

Despite its numerous definitions in the psychology research literature, resilience is based around two core concepts: adversity and positive adaptation (Fletcher and Sarkar, 2013). Adopting a holistic view, we define resilience as a capacity and a process of bouncing back from adversity.

Previous literature stresses the importance of several resource endowments, such as personality (Dunn et al., 2008), social support (Brennan, 2008), and material and work resources (Bonanno et al., 2007) to face an adversity. With regard to personality, protective factors such as self-esteem (Kidd and Shahar, 2008) and positive emotions (Tugade and Fredrickson, 2004) have been stressed as beneficial for harnessing individual resilience. This book chapter intends to unveil the supporting resources that help cultural workers face the COVID-19 adversity.

Psychological resilience of cultural workers

CCIs account for 5.3% of the European Union's GDP and 7.5% of the EU's employment (European Commission, 2018). Cultural workers constitute its driving force by virtue of their creativity, skills, and talent (DCMS, 2001). According to the DCMS (2001) classification, a creative worker is someone who is either unemployed but creatively occupied (e.g. a scriptwriter without a contract) or employed but not necessarily creatively occupied (e.g. an accountant in any of creative industries).

Although culture is increasingly recognized as a key enabler for sustainable development (UNESCO, 2019), the evidence suggests that cultural workers have to deal with precarious working conditions. They often accept low pay, long hours, insecure employment, material and existential hardships, and blurred boundaries between work and personal life (Gill, 2014; Ekman, 2015; Wright, 2018; Cinque et al., 2020).

Despite precarious and insecure working conditions, extant studies highlight cultural workers' need for artistic freedom and autonomy (Eikhof and Haunschild, 2006), creativity, and passion (Florida, 2002; McRobbie, 2015; Endrissat et al., 2016; Bennett, 2018; Gaim, 2018). Cultural workers have a great capacity to improvise – get involved in a spontaneous process of creation (Vera and Crossan, 2004) – using available rather than optimal resources (Giustiniano et al., 2018). Research suggests that cultural workers continue to persist despite hardship (e.g. Cinque et al., 2020). However, to the extent of our awareness, there is relatively little research that directly explores the resilience of cultural workers. Our intuition is that creative workers might be used to stress and insecure work, experiencing challenges on a constant basis. They tend to focus on solutions rather than problems. Our book chapter aims to investigate the impact of COVID-19 on the psychological and professional lives of creative workers, a subject that is particularly relevant as COVID-19 still appears full of "unknown unknowns" and the post-pandemic era to come is characterized by even higher uncertainty.

Methodology

A qualitative research approach is adopted for the purpose of this book chapter. There are several reasons why we went for a qualitative approach. First, the nature of COVID-19 adversity is not yet fully understood. Second, a holistic approach of resilience, intended as both capacity and process, requires a qualitative approach. Third, the nature of our research question demands a qualitative approach. Qualitative data provide evidence on people's lived experience, going beyond snapshots of what and how many to grasp why and how things happen (Huberman and Miles, 1994).

For the purpose of this book chapter, a convenience sampling was used: cultural workers who were in the personal network of one of the authors of this chapter were contacted. All the informants were Italian, despite their geographical location. Therefore, we kept the insights of two informants located in Spain and Germany as we reputed them similar to the informants located in Italy. In total we conducted 26 semi-structured interviews with 16 cultural workers working in different CCIs, such as film, performing arts, and fashion, 9 of which were follow-up interviews. Although this constitutes a relatively small sample, we judged that the necessary theoretical saturation was reached (with the involvement of the 15th informant) as all the relevant categories were identified (Corbin and Strauss, 2014). The two waves of interviews – from 27th March 2020 to 12th May 2020 (i.e. phase I) and, then, from 19th May 2020 to 30th July 2020 (i.e. phase II) – were performed to comprehend the change in the informants' personal and professional lives during and after the first phase of lockdown. The interviews were conducted via Skype or Zoom. They were all recorded and manually transcribed. In addition, many informal conversations with several experts in the CCIs back the findings of this book chapter.

The interviewees were not affected physically by COVID-19, and none of their close relatives or friends were affected either. This constitutes a limitation of this chapter, as we could not observe and interview people who had experienced the emergency first-hand.

Table 6.1 reports the interview data maintaining the anonymity of informants.

The data analysis aimed at elaborating theory rather than at generating a completely new theoretical framework (Fisher and Aguinis, 2017), building on existing concepts in psychological resilience research to develop a more comprehensive understanding of how cultural workers adapt in the face of COVID-19. We performed a thematic analysis on interview data to identify emerging patterns (Yin, 2009). The most important categories, such as resilience and feelings of cultural workers, work reorganization practices, their perception of the upcoming future, and life lessons learned, contribute to the themes of this chapter.

Findings

This section reports the main findings of the chapter. In particular, we describe the feelings experienced by cultural workers during and immediately after the first lockdown. During the lockdown the following process took place: (1) cultural workers experienced a moment of reflection, and

Table 6.1 Data.

Informant	Gender	Age	Industry	Profession	Date and length of interview	Rounds of interviews	Location of the informant
1	Male	30–35	Film	Film director, film producer	27/03/2020 51' 23/05/2020 43'	2	Italy
2	Male	30–35	Film & Theatre	Actor	27/03/2020 31' 19/05/2020 26'	2	Italy
3	Male	45–50	Film	Executive producer	08/04/2020 44' 21/05/2020 43'	2	Italy
4	Female	40–45	Fashion	Creator, fashion designer	10/04/2020 36' 08/07/2020 77'	2	Italy
5	Male	35–40	Film	Film director, cameraman	23/04/2020 48'	1	Italy
6	Male	40–45	Fashion	Designer, owner of a brand	24/04/2020 37' 03/06/2020 24'	2	Italy
7	Male	40–45	Film	Special effects specialist	01/05/2020 75' 25/06/2020 33'	2	Italy
8	Male	35–40	Film & Theatre	Teacher, sound technician	12/05/2020 32' 10/06/2020 28'	2	Italy
9	Male	30–35	Film	Film director, film producer	01/04/2020 34' 26/05/2020 25'	2	Italy
10	Male	40–45	Film	Teacher, film producer	05/05/2020 54'	1	Italy
11	Female	25–30	Film	Film producer	08/05/2020 47'	1	Italy
12	Female	25–30	Film	Assistant	08/05/2020 58'	1	Italy
13	Male	35–40	Film	Film director, film producer	12/05/2020 44'	1	Italy
14	Female	30–35	Film	Project developer	08/05/2020 60'	1	Italy
15	Male	25–30	Film &Video	Program manager	07/04/2020 30' 27/05/2020 22'	2	Germany
16	Female	40–45	Journalism	Writer	09/04/2020 28' 30/07/2020 56'	2	Spain

(2) then, they started adapting to new circumstances. After the lockdown cultural workers felt stronger and eager to restart their work. Different types of supporting resources were uncovered. Regarding their professional life, during the lockdown, cultural workers worked on some backlog work, work that could be performed from home or they tried to transfer their work online. After the lockdown, they reported new solutions and opportunities created by digital technology and online interaction. In addition, cultural workers' prospects for the future and life lessons learned are reported.

Resilience and feelings of cultural workers

During the lockdown, most cultural workers started experiencing a profound state of reflection. Informant 1 reported:

> I was shaken by Nature and how much it could flourish without our intrusion. In the first week of lockdown, I noticed that birds were flying at a lower level, there were more bees, there was more nectar in flowers. All this made me emerge in a profound meditation mode ... I am having a moment of reflection, creative inspiration.
>
> *(Informant 1)*

Informant 9 explained that being able to stop and reflect could be considered as a gift:

> It is a moment of reflection. Having to stop without wanting or asking for it is a great gift.
>
> *(Informant 9)*

Several cultural workers (e.g. Informant 3, Informant 14) stressed their ability to adapt to new circumstances.

> I spent the first few weeks thinking that I would like to go back to life before and then I got used to it. It was impressive to think we all got used to it.
>
> *(Informant 14)*

Besides perpetuating in the reflective state, cultural workers described their feelings as stable, lucky, conscious, sad, acceptive, and adaptive to changes.

In line with the resilience literature (e.g. Bonanno et al., 2007; Brennan, 2008; Dunn et al., 2008; Martínez-Martí and Ruch, 2017), our empirical findings unveiled the strengths and supporting resources of our informants. The following categories were uncovered, namely personality, interpersonal relationships, work, and material resources. With regard to personality, many informants perceived the following traits as their strengths: curiosity (Informant 1); self-awareness, self-criticism, optimism (Informants 2 and 9); being a dreamer (Informant 9); adaptability (Informant 3); positivity, hope (Informants 16 and 5); resiliency (Informant 5); instinct, concreteness, knowing what you want (Informant 6). Informant 7 stated that faith was also helping him in overcoming the emergency. Informant 3 stressed how the decision to feel good or bad is a part of our DNA, implying that despite adverse events you can always decide how to feel. Informant 2 confirmed the same:

> The only thing you can control is whether to be strong or weak. It is something you have to decide.
>
> *(Informant 2)*

Interpersonal relationships with a family or colleagues were considered as important supporting resources. Cultural workers in a relationship reported:

> I am happy because I am in a happy relationship with my wife.
>
> *(Informant 15)*

> I feel quite lucky, my husband is my reference point, he gives me strength.
>
> *(Informant 4)*

Cultural workers without a partner were feeling more frustrated than those with a partner. For instance, Informant 16 reported:

> I feel frustrated ... Of course, I have learned how to be alone, but I miss a person next to me.
>
> *(Informant 16)*

Collaboration with colleagues acted as a relevant resource (Informant 5, Informant 8).

Employment was reported by some informants (e.g. Informant 8) as an important work resource during the COVID-19 lockdown.

Material resources such as good living conditions and material support acted as an additional supporting factor for cultural workers.

> I am fortunate to live in a large house.
>
> *(Informant 3)*

> I must admit that I am in a privileged position. I have a family that can help me in times of financial difficulty and not everyone has the same luck.
>
> *(Informant 2)*

In the follow-up interviews, cultural workers announced that they felt stronger than in the first phase of the lockdown (i.e. during the lockdown). They were anxious to restart their work.

> I feel risen from the ashes ...
>
> *(Informant 1)*

> My state of mind is of restart.
>
> *(Informant 2)*

> I feel stronger psychologically because I was tired and now I am more lucid and rested.
>
> *(Informant 3)*

Those cultural workers that continued working during the lockdown (e.g. those working for streaming service companies) declared they felt more relaxed after the lockdown as they learned to manage the increased workload, longer working hours, and separate better their life from their work.

> I am more relaxed for the fact that I can have more flexibility at work.
>
> *(Informant 15)*

Work reorganization of cultural workers

The following changes have been observed among informants: their work, whenever possible, went online, their working infrastructure switched to smart working. Any physical activity was suspended. One cultural worker decided to close his company and reopen a new one once the emergency was over. Cultural festivals and teaching also went online.

> Now there are no film festivals, no teaching. Actually, it is a big change to have festivals online. I am a bit afraid that people will get used to this change.
>
> *(Informant 9)*

Many cultural workers mentioned that they were in a waiting mode, working on some backlog work or some activities that could be performed from home, such as reading screenplays (Informants 4 and 11), writing (Informants 5 and 11), teaching (Informant 8) and training online (Informant 2).

Cultural workers that suffered the least were those working for big companies, such as streaming service companies. Informant 15 reported:

> More people are spending their time in streaming and now we see a huge increase in subscription ... I mean for streaming it is a huge potential, which needs to be managed properly.
>
> *(Informant 15)*

In the second wave of interviews, cultural workers reported more concrete solutions to their problems. For instance, Informant 1 decided where and how to open his new film production company. Informant 9 dedicated his time to writing screenplays, applying for public funds, and thinking of launching a new digital platform to screen short movies. This finding is in line with some recent studies defending the paradoxical nature of resilience: on the one hand cultural workers tried to understand and adapt to new circumstances; on the other hand, they looked at the jolt as an opportunity to learn and do something new (Giustiniano et al., 2020; Lombardi et al., 2021).

> I am thinking of opening a new film production with a new formula this time: digital, focused on documentaries, based in Ireland.
>
> *(Informant 1)*

> I have used my time wisely: I wrote 2 scripts, applied for a public fund...I want to organize a festival online and launch a new digital platform for short movies.
>
> *(Informant 9)*

Informant 7 reported that: "there is more concreteness in the work".

Informant 2, an actor, announced that he invested his time heavily in training and getting ready for the post-COVID-19 period.

> I continue to invest heavily in acting ... even if things are at a standstill. An actor must always keep training, keep a relationship with agencies, understand what is around, talk to colleagues.
>
> *(Informant 2)*

An executive producer of a big film production company in Italy mentioned that his company was using the time to invest in the training of the whole crew.

> These courses cost 400 euros per person, but they (i.e. crew) did them for free. They did 4 hours of general safety and then a course on COVID-19.
>
> *(Informant 3)*

Cultural workers that did not deal with online interaction and smart working in normal times started rediscovering opportunities created by digital technologies.

> Remote work opportunities are emerging. These are normal things, not artistic, in the field of communication and distance learning.
>
> *(Informant 2)*

Our findings revealed an interesting, although quite a predictable fact: cultural workers were already used to unstable, challenging, and precarious working conditions even before COVID-19. They reported their experience as freelancers, working on projects with unstable and low wages. These conditions contributed to building their resilience before facing the adversity of COVID-19.

> I've never had a long contract, I've always had a project contract. I have been precarious for 25 years and now I have signed the contract for the first time and a planetary disaster has happened.
>
> *(Informant 3)*

> Being a freelancer and coming from the cinema, I am used to working with a small crew, with little money, unlikely situations where anything can happen.
>
> *(Informant 12)*

In support of the recent creative industry literature (Gaim, 2018; Cinque et al., 2020), we found that cultural workers persisted with their job despite hardship.

> Work gives me satisfaction. If someone told me: from tomorrow you can no longer think about work, what would I do?
>
> *(Informant 3)*

Looking ahead

Cultural workers reported the harm caused by the pandemic to CCIs. For instance, the film industry and theatre require human interaction, without which it is hard to move on. Informant 2 reported: "Theatre is like a disco; it requires people". Informant 3 confirmed: "One metre of social distancing is impossible to respect in the cinema".

The fashion industry was also badly hit. Two informants stated that they could not see any benefits brought by COVID-19 but only harm, as their collections remained unsold.

> I was not ready for this. I have already produced the collection and now it is in stock.
>
> *(Informant 6)*

> The company is closed and there are many unsold goods. The collection 2021 was not sold and who knows if we are going to sell it in 2022.
>
> *(Informant 4)*

Many cultural workers were comparing the pandemic to the war, however, with some connotation of hope.

> After the plague there was a Renaissance. After the war there was a Neorealism. There will be a new phase, a new spring.
>
> *(Informant 9)*

> I think about the rebirth of cinema after the war. I wonder who knows if we will not have a post-pandemic cultural rebirth.
>
> *(Informant 12)*

Despite visible damages, cultural workers did not despair and communicated their expectations of a better future. Many were convinced that entering market conditions would improve after the emergency.

> After the crisis, starting conditions will be similar for everyone. The production system will change as it did in 2008 with the digital.
>
> *(Informant 1)*

> There is a great enthusiasm, everything is questioned. It is a starting point.
>
> *(Informant 9)*

COVID-19 made cultural workers aware of the opportunities created by digital technologies and online interaction. One informant mentioned that he was in the process of launching his streaming platform for short movies, an idea that came to him during the lockdown. He also announced the idea of creating an online festival and carrying out an online dubbing of a film. Another interviewee, a film director and producer, told of his idea of creating a new film production company with a focus on digital. A programme manager of a big streaming service company stated that subscriptions sky-rocketed enormously during the lockdown.

However, informants reported that the benefits of technology had to be balanced with its risks. Informant 9 stated:

> Technology is useful for work but not for close contacts. It works for work without emotions ...
>
> *(Informant 9)*

Cultural workers working in the film industry were envisioning the death of cinemas due to streaming service companies.

> On the one hand, I'm worried about distribution. I'm afraid that cinemas will die.
>
> *(Informant 12)*

Overall, cultural workers hoped that COVID-19 induced people to care more about the CCIs.

> What would your quarantine look like without music, cinema, books? In great moments of crisis, perhaps, what keeps you company the most is a book and not a new dress. I hope someone has realized that we exist.
>
> *(Informant 12)*

Learned life lessons

This brief section unveils the life lessons learned by cultural workers during and after the first COVID-19 lockdown. During home confinement the biggest life lessons related to the themes of time, luck, simplicity, relationships, and society. Cultural workers realized the importance of a better use of their time, which did not imply the need to rush but, on the contrary, to clear their lives of unnecessary meetings and occupations and to have more time to focus on what mattered. Cultural workers acknowledged the necessity of not procrastinating over important things. Yet, time does not need to always be productive. As conveyed by one informant, even an empty moment can make a lot of sense. Several cultural workers reported that they felt very lucky to live in contemporary society. One informant communicated an enhanced civic sense. Cultural workers started appreciating more their relationships and simplicity. Many realized that they liked staying at home without being bored. Their imagination and dreams were keeping boredom away. COVID-19 gave time to rediscover old passions.

After the first COVID-19 lockdown, life lessons were around topics of risk, time, relationships, opportunities. Cultural workers stressed once again the preciousness of time and relationships. However, a small change compared to phase I could be noted: life lessons in phase II were more concrete, positive, and action oriented. Cultural workers learned the importance of being positive, transparent, and direct, being able to risk, follow one's own instinct and search for new opportunities.

> You must be willing to risk everything, always.
>
> *(Informant 1)*

> It is important to consider new opportunities. I do not want to wait. But there is time, no need to rush and run after people.
>
> *(Informant 9)*

Discussion, implications, and opportunities for further research

Our chapter advances novel insights into CCIs by exploring cultural workers' feelings and well-being, work reorganization practices, and lessons learned during and after the first COVID-19 lockdown that took place in Europe. Our evidence confirms that cultural workers encounter various unexpected events during their artistic careers. Their days have an unpredictable pattern. However, the COVID-19 pandemic found everyone unprepared. Our findings reveal the role of several resource endowments in helping cultural workers face the adversity. In line with previous studies on psychological resilience (e.g. Bonanno et al., 2007; Brennan, 2008; Dunn et al., 2008; Martínez-Martí and Ruch, 2017), we uncover the importance of personality traits (e.g. self-awareness, self-criticism, optimism, positive thinking, faith), interpersonal resources (e.g. social support from family, colleagues), material resources (i.e. living conditions) and work resources (i.e. employment). Cultural workers engaged in improvisation, using the available resources rather than planned ones (Giustiniano et al., 2018; Giustiniano and Cantoni, 2018).

This book chapter confirms the presence of psychological resilience in cultural workers. Most of them were in a reflective, contemplative mode in the first weeks of lockdown, followed by the acceptance and adaptation to new circumstances. Resilience implies a positive adaptation and reaction to an adversity. Our book chapter is in line with the recent research suggesting that resilience has a paradoxical nature, e.g. "gardening" – understanding, preparing, and adapting to the unique environment – vs. "learning" – looking at the jolt as an opportunity to learn something new (Lombardi et al., 2021). Resilience requires paradoxical actions involving the capacity to maintain normal functioning in extraordinary times (Giustiniano et al., 2020). Our chapter shows that, in the first phase of lockdown, cultural workers suspended activities requiring social interaction, living in a waiting mode and dedicating their time to the backlog of work, creative work from home, and coming up with a plan. In the second phase of lockdown, most of the creative workers were satisfied with how they spent their home confinement, and they reported more concrete plans and creative solutions. They looked at the pandemic as an opportunity to grow. The importance of digital platforms, online interaction and remote work opportunities were highly acknowledged by cultural workers that decided to push their businesses in that direction. In terms of prospects, cultural workers reported the harm caused by the pandemic to the CCIs; however, they were proactively getting prepared for the future. The future that this time would be different but would still require creativity and adaptability of cultural workers, quite used to challenging conditions. In addition, we examined what lessons cultural workers learned during and after the COVID-19 lockdown. Most of them were based around the topics of time, relationships, and society. COVID-19 provided a chance to appreciate the importance of own time and relationships, caring more about societal issues. After the lockdown, the life lessons were more positive and action-oriented, reflecting the improvement in cultural workers' resilience.

This book chapter contributes to the research on CCIs (e.g. Gaim, 2018; Cinque et al., 2020;) and the individual resilience literature (e.g. Fletcher and Sarkar, 2013; Giustiniano et al., 2020) by (1) exploring the impact of COVID-19 on cultural workers' personal and professional lives; (2) by applying a holistic view of resilience intended as both a paradoxical capacity and a process; (3) by revealing the role of several resource endowments in helping cultural workers to overcome severe adversities; (4) by stressing how the past experience with challenging working conditions contributes to the spirit of adaptation of cultural workers.

The insights of this chapter can be of relevance for cultural workers to improve their self-awareness about the paradoxical nature of resilience (i.e. requiring adaption to new circumstances but also the search for new opportunities) and resources necessary to positively adapt and react to adversities. In line with previous studies (Giustiniano et al., 2020; Lombardi et al., 2021), we suggest looking at improvisation as an important capacity to empower individual resilience. The chapter can be interesting for other professionals who are facing personal and professional challenges due to COVID-19. We believe that such pandemic times induced many precarious, project-based workers to rethink their usual ways of working and made them appreciate the use of digital technology and online interaction, the changes that will persist after COVID-19.

Further work may continue our research in the upcoming phases of COVID-19, exploring the second lockdown that occurred in autumn 2020, or the recovery phase after vaccination. CCIs have always been characterized by creativity and innovation. They constitute a fertile ground to explore new ways of organizing, and COVID-19 provided plenty of occasions for rethinking what the future of CCIs would look like.

References

Bennett, T. (2018), "'Essential – passion for music': Affirming, critiquing, and practising passionate work in creative industries", In: Martin, L., & Wilson, N. (Eds.), *The Palgrave handbook of creativity at work*, Palgrave Macmillan, Cham, pp. 431–459.

Bonanno, G. A. (2004), "Loss, trauma, and human resilience: Have we underestimated the human capacity to thrive after extremely aversive events?", *American Psychologist*, Vol. 59, No. 1, pp. 20–28.

Bonanno, G. A., Galea, S., Bucciarelli, A., & Vlahov, D. (2007), "What predicts psychological resilience after disaster? The role of demographics, resources, and life stress", *Journal of Consulting and Clinical Psychology*, Vol. 75, No. 5, pp. 671–682.

Brennan, M. A. (2008), "Conceptualizing resiliency: An interactional perspective for community and youth development", *Child Care in Practice*, Vol. 14, No. 1, pp. 55–64.

Cinque, S., Nyberg, D., & Starkey, K. (2020), "'Living at the border of poverty': How theatre actors maintain their calling through narrative identity work", *Human Relations*, Vol. 70, No. 8, pp. 1–26.

Corbin, J., & Strauss, A. (2014), *Basics of qualitative research: Techniques and procedures for developing grounded theory*, Sage, Los Angeles.

DCMS (2001), *Creative industries mapping document,* Department of Culture, Media and Sport, London.

Dunn, L. B., Iglewicz, A., & Moutier, C. (2008), "A conceptual model of medical student well-being: Promoting resilience and preventing burnout", *Academic Psychiatry,* Vol. 32, No. 1, pp. 44–53.

Duymedjian, R., & Rüling, C. C. (2010), "Towards a foundation of bricolage in organization and management theory", *Organization Studies,* Vol. 31, No. 2, pp. 133–151.

Eikhof, D. R., & Haunschild, A. (2006), "Lifestyle meets market: Bohemian entrepreneurs in creative industries", *Creativity and Innovation Management,* Vol. 15, No. 3, pp. 234–241.

Eikhof, D. R., & Haunschild, A. (2007), "For art's sake! Artistic and economic logics in creative production", *Journal of Organizational Behavior,* Vol. 28, No. 5, pp. 523–538.

Ekman, S. (2015), "Win-win imageries in a soap bubble world: Personhood and norms in extreme work", *Organization,* Vol. 22, No. 4, pp. 588–605.

Endrissat, N., Islam, G., & Noppeney, C. (2016), "Visual organizing: Balancing coordination and creative freedom via mood boards", *Journal of Business Research,* Vol. 69, No. 7, pp. 2353–2362.

European Commission (2018), 2018–2020 call on inclusive and sustainable growth through cultural and creative industries and the arts, retrieved from: https://ec.europa.eu/eurostat/cros/content/2018-2020-call-inclusive-and-sustainable-growth-through-cultural-and-creative-industries-and-arts_en.

Fisher, G., & Aguinis, H. (2017), "Using theory elaboration to make theoretical advancements", *Organizational Research Methods,* Vol. 20, No. 3, pp. 438–464.

Fletcher, D., & Sarkar, M. (2013), "Psychological resilience: A review and critique of definitions, concepts, and theory", *European Psychologist,* Vol. 18, No. 1, pp. 12–23.

Florida, R. (2002), *The rise of the creative class and how it's transforming work, leisure, community and everyday life,* Basic Books, New York.

Gaim, M. (2018), "On the emergence and management of paradoxical tensions: The case of architectural firms", *European Management Journal,* Vol. 36, No. 4, pp. 497–518.

Gill, R. (2014), "Academics, cultural workers and critical labour studies", *Journal of Cultural Economy,* Vol. 7, No. 1, pp. 12–30.

Giustiniano, L., & Cantoni, F. (2018), "Between sponge and titanium: Designing micro and macro features for the resilient organization", In: Boccardelli, P., Annosi, M. C., Brunetta, F., & Magnusson, M. (Eds.), *Learning and innovation in hybrid organizations,* Palgrave Macmillan, Cham, pp. 167–190.

Giustiniano, L., Clegg, S. R., Cunha, M. P., & Rego, A. (2018), *Elgar introduction to theories of organizational resilience,* Edward Elgar Publishing, Cheltenham, Northampton.

Giustiniano, L., Cunha, M. P., Simpson, A. V., Rego, A., & Clegg, S. (2020), "Resilient leadership as paradox work: Notes from COVID-19", *Management and Organization Review,* Vol. 16, No. 5, pp. 971–975.

Huberman, A. M., & Miles, M. B. (1994), "Data management and analysis methods", In: Denzin, N. K., & Lincoln Y. S. (Eds.), *Handbook of qualitative research,* Sage, Thousand Oaks, pp. 428–444.

ILO (2020), ILO Monitor: COVID-19 and the world of work. Seventh edition. Updated estimates and analysis, retrieved from: https://www.ilo.org/wcmsp5/groups/public/@dgreports/@dcomm/documents/briefingnote/wcms_767028.pdf.

Kidd, S., & Shahar, G. (2008), "Resilience in homeless youth: The key role of self-esteem", *American Journal of Orthopsychiatry*, Vol. 78, No. 2, pp. 163–172.

Lampel, J., Lant, T., & Shamsie, J. (2000), "Balancing act: Learning from organizing practices in cultural industries", *Organization Science*, Vol. 11, No. 3, pp. 263–269.

Lombardi, S., Cunha, M. P., & Giustiniano, L. (2021), "Improvising resilience: The unfolding of resilient leadership in COVID-19 times", *International Journal of Hospitality Management*, Vol. 95, pp. 1–13.

Luthar, S. S., Cicchetti, D., & Becker, B. (2000), "The construct of resilience: A critical evaluation and guidelines for future work", *Child Development*, Vol. 71, No. 3, pp. 543–562.

Martínez-Martí, M. L., & Ruch, W. (2017), "Character strengths predict resilience over and above positive affect, self-efficacy, optimism, social support, self-esteem, and life satisfaction", *The Journal of Positive Psychology*, Vol. 12, No. 2, pp. 110–119.

McRobbie, A. (2015), *Be creative: Making a living in the new culture industries*, Polity, Cambridge.

OECD (2020), OECD Policy Responses to Coronavirus (COVID-19). Culture shock: COVID-19 and the cultural and creative sectors, retrieved from: http://www.oecd.org/coronavirus/policy-responses/culture-shock-covid-19-and-the-cultural-and-creative-sectors-08da9e0e/.

Townley, B., Beech, N., & McKinlay, A. (2009), "Managing in the creative industries: Managing the motley crew", *Human Relations*, Vol. 62, No. 7, 939–962.

Tugade, M. M., & Fredrickson, B. L. (2004), "Resilient individuals use positive emotions to bounce back from negative emotional experiences", *Journal of Personality and Social Psychology*, Vol. 86, No. 2, pp. 320–333.

UNESCO (2019), Culture and Sustainable Development: The Key Ideas, retrieved from: http://www.unesco.org/new/en/culture/themes/culture-and-development/the-future-we-want-the-role-of-culture/the-key-ideas/.

UNESCO (2020), COVID-19 hits culture sector even harder than expected, warns UNESCO, retrieved from: https://en.unesco.org/news/covid-19-hits-culture-sector-even-harder-expected-warns-unesco.

Vera, D., & Crossan, M. (2004), "Theatrical improvisation: Lessons for organizations" *Organization Studies*, Vol. 2, No. 5, pp. 727–749.

Wright, D. (2018), "Hopeful work" and the creative economy, In: Martin, L., & Wilson, N. (Eds.), *The Palgrave handbook of creativity at work*, Palgrave Macmillan, Cham, pp. 311–325.

Wu, Y., & Wu, S. (2016), "Managing ambidexterity in creative industries: A survey", *Journal of Business Research*, Vol. 69, No. 7, pp. 2388–2396.

Yin, R. K. (2009). *Case study research: Design and methods.* Sage, Thousand Oaks.

7 The COVID-19 pandemic, coworking spaces, and cultural events

The case of Italy

Federica Rossi and Ilaria Mariotti

Introduction

The spread of the COVID-19 pandemic in Europe during 2020 has pushed the national governments to implement special restrictive measures, drastically changing citizens' lifestyles. In Italy, the progressive closure of non-essential economic and institutional activities at the national level started with the Prime Minister Decree of 4 March 2020 (GU Serie Generale n.55/2020), which, among others, established the interruption of congresses, meetings, and social and cultural events. In addition to global networks, indeed, COVID-19 found favourable circulation conditions through super-spreading events which had an accelerating effect: a religious meeting in Eastern France, a football game in northern Italy, carnival festivities in Western Germany, a night event in a ski resort in the Austrian Alps (Bourdin and Rossignol, 2020).

Given this background, the present chapter explores the changes in the cultural events' organization by coworking spaces (from now on, CSs) in Italy due to the COVID-19 pandemic, analyzing data from the national survey by Italian Coworking, and presenting the case study of Milan, based on the local survey of the project *Milano Collabora* (Pais et al., 2021; Mariotti et al., 2021c).

The proliferation of CSs started in the late 2000s, with the first space named "Hat Factory" established in San Francisco (USA) in 2005. From that year on, we have witnessed a sprawl of this type of new working space worldwide: in 2015, there were 8,900 CSs worldwide, while in 2019 they were more than 22,400 with over 2 million members (Deskmag, 2019). The majority of coworkers (CS users) are professionals belonging to the creative and cultural industries (Akhavan et al., 2019; Mariotti and Pacchi, 2021); therefore, the CS could be seen as a catalyst, which boosts these sectors' growth by increasing interactions, creating new business opportunities.

As for many other economic activities, the restrictions imposed by the COVID-19 pandemic have heavily affected the CSs businesses. The first estimates by Deskmag (2021) show that the European CSs lost on average one-fifth of their leasable desks compared with the start of 2020, and they

DOI: 10.4324/9781003128274-10

lost members (about one-quarter). Therefore, the COVID-19 restrictions have forced the CSs to rethink their business strategies. As argued by Migliore et al. (2021: 21) "CSs have evolved rapidly to welcome additional user categories (potentially including students and common citizens), to add new services to members (e.g., food delivery), and to re-arrange meetings into virtual workshops and events" allowing for extraordinary resilience. Specifically, CSs were encouraged to develop new ways of communication and promotion of their activities, among which the organization of the cultural events.

Before the pandemic, the CSs' main communication tools were their websites and social media pages (e.g. Facebook, Twitter). The lockdown has strengthened this tendency: starting from March 2020 some CSs promoted online events mainly addressed to their coworkers. However, the organization of public online events could represent a sustainable strategy throughout coexistence with the virus, since 45% of the world's population has a social media account, and the social media penetration in Italy is at 42% (We Are Social, 2019).

The role of social media and digital technology in disseminating cultural material during the COVID-19 pandemic has been recently discussed in the paper by Agostino et al. (2020), who focused on the Italian state museums' online initiatives. They analyzed the 100 most significant Italian state museum activities during the lockdown (March–May 2020), and they observed an increase in online cultural materials and initiatives taking place through social media, which had attracted significant interest, as demonstrated by the rising number of followers. Besides, Amorim and Teixeira (2020) presented how four case studies (an artist-run space, an art gallery, a museum, and an art biennale) reacted to COVID-19 pandemic restrictions by moving their activities to online platforms.

Against this background, the current chapter aims to answer the following research questions: has the COVID-19 affected the activities of CSs, particularly the organization of cultural events? How have the CSs reacted to this shock?

The chapter is structured into four sections. The Introduction is followed by a literature review paragraph, divided into the definition of CSs, and the description of cultural events studies. Section 3 provides an overview of coworking spaces in Italy, focusing on the organization of cultural events and communication channels before and during the COVID-19 pandemic, analyzing data by Italian Coworking, and presenting the Milan case study. The last section concludes the chapter and discusses some policy implications.

Literature review

This section provides an overview of the academic literature on the two combined issues explored in the chapter: coworking spaces and cultural events. First, it presents a definition of CS and some recent papers on its activities. Then, it describes previous socio-economic studies focusing on cultural events.

The coworking space

According to the literature, a CS is a social practice that has in common some social (community), cultural (sharing), and economic (saving) characteristics of other sharing activities (Merkel, 2015). The CS is also defined as a physical space (office) provision, where the users 'work- alone- together' (Spinuzzi, 2012; Capdevila, 2014; Bilandzic, 2016), and where a community is established, based on the willingness to cooperate with others to create shared values (Fuzi et al., 2014).

CSs offer flexible spatial and virtual solutions, favouring different individual working times, diversity of functions co-located in the same place, and a unique mix of the domestic and business atmosphere (Migliore et al., 2021; Kingma, 2016). For this reason, many studies associate CSs to the so-called 'third places' (Oldenburg, 1997), which are neither workplaces/ offices (second place) nor private homes (first place), but represent the heart of a community's social vitality, conviviality, and inclusion. Indeed, by offering geographical proximity and non-hierarchical relationships among coworkers, CSs may encourage socialization, collaboration, individual/ team creativity and, therefore, they may foster business opportunities for self-employed professionals, freelancers, and digital nomads (the main users of CSs), who otherwise would not enjoy the relational component associated with a traditional corporate office (Mariotti et al., 2017). According to a recent study conducted in Italy by Akhavan et al. (2019), 74% of people hosted by CSs are professionals belonging to the creative industry sectors, such as architects, designers, software developers, ICT professionals, media professionals, but also cultural workers.

Besides the core business (renting a desk to the coworkers), many CSs host multiple activities other than work, such as events (i.e. workshops, cultural events, charity events, training courses, networking events), which could be public or specifically addressed to coworkers. Thanks to these activities, CSs can attract and retain people in their spaces when they would normally be elsewhere than in the office, and they can enrich their communities by triggering engagement (Migliore et al., 2021). The results of the survey addressed to Italian coworkers in the year 2018 underlined that the organization of cultural, charity, and community events, together with the agreements with local services and participation in a Social Street,[1] are perceived to have a very positive impact on the urban context (Mariotti et al., 2021a).

Moreover, by promoting public events, CSs may strengthen their economic sustainability by making profits. They may enlarge the network, gain visibility, finance specific private activities, enhance the relationship with the neighbourhood, and strengthen the area's attractiveness. As stated by Mariotti et al. (2017) and Akhavan et al. (2019), the organization of events may show a positive impact on the neighbourhood where the CS is located because it might: (i) modify the daily and weekly cycles of use within the neighbourhood (i.e. sponsoring evening and night activities or weekend events); (ii) affect the traditional services by revitalizing existing retail and commercial activities, bars, and cafés; (iii) offer business discount schemes for coworkers in the neighbourhood's shops and services. Therefore, to a more considerable extent, the organization of events within the CSs may contribute to the strengthening of community ties at the neighbourhood level.

Cultural events studies

Previous socio-economic studies focusing on cultural events could be classified into two groups, depending on their approach: (i) research adopting a macro-level perspective, which investigated the socio-economic impacts of cultural events on the hosting regions/cities; (ii) literature using a micro-level perspective, which analyzed both the effects of socio-demographic characteristics on people's attitudes towards cultural events, and the link between attending cultural events and individual well-being/happiness.

As concerns the first group of studies, it is well known since the work of Porter (1989) that the presence of flourishing cultural facilities contributes to the regions' quality of life and plays a significant role in the regional development by improving attractivity for firms, workers, and residents. Previous studies confirm that public cultural events enhance the neighbourhood's image, add life to city streets (Richards and Wilson, 2004), and increase residents' sense of place and pride, quality of life, accessibility, and inclusion (Liu, 2014).

Moreover, due to an event's ability to generate new flows of people, they often represent an opportunity for local development and location promotion, pushing economic growth, especially when the cultural event has an international value. For example, many studies evaluated the cultural and social effects of hosting the European Capital of Culture (among others, see Ebejer et al., 2021 for the case of Malta; Žilič Fišer and Kožuh, 2019 for the case of Slovenia; Herrero et al., 2006 for the Spanish case; Richards and Wilson, 2004 for the case of the Netherlands).

As mentioned above, the second strand of literature focuses on the individual characteristics of participants to cultural events. Specifically, previous studies underlined that women participate more actively in cultural activities than men (Bihagen and Katz-Gerro, 2000; Seaman, 2006). In addition, middle-aged and young people were found to be the typical audiences of cultural activities (Stafford and Tripp 2000); and more highly educated individuals have a more positive attitude towards cultural events (Žilič Fišer and Kožuh, 2019).

Instead, looking at the effect of cultural activities on happiness and subjective well-being, there is an empirical consensus – across different countries – on an existing positive relationship (Lee and Heo, 2021; Vegheş, 2020; Hand, 2018; Wheatley and Bickerton, 2017; Pagán, 2015; Grossi et al., 2012). Specifically, Lee and Heo (2021) examined the relationship between attending arts and cultural activities and individual happiness in Korea, distinguishing among four categories: visual arts, performing arts, movies, and sporting events. They found a positive relationship, which is particularly high for attending performing arts.

Vegheş (2020) explored the links between the cultural participation and the quality of life of the European Union consumers, highlighting that "higher cultural participation results in a better quality of life and, vice-versa, improved quality of life creates a favourable background for extended cultural participation" (p. 134).

By analyzing the German Socio-Economic Panel data, Pagán (2015) observed a strong positive correlation between life satisfaction and joining cultural events. Besides, attending cultural events has a higher impact than other leisure activities, such as social interaction, sport, etc.

Hand (2018) investigated the relationship between the frequency and types of leisure activities and happiness, using data from the Taking Part survey commissioned by the UK government in 2012–2013. They showed that both frequency and diversity of arts attendance positively influenced happiness, but this relationship is strongly significant only in the lower quartile.

Finally, the results by Grossi et al. (2012), who analyzed an Italian representative sample, highlighted that, among the various potential factors considered, cultural access was the second most important determinant of psychological well-being, immediately after the absence of diseases.

Evidence from the empirical analysis

This section presents the results of two surveys addressed to coworking managers in Italy (in 2018 and 2020, by Italian Coworking) and in Milan (in 2020 by Pais et al., 2021), focusing on CSs' cultural events management and communication strategies. These surveys provide helpful evidence to answer the research questions: (i) Has the COVID-19 affected CSs' activities, particularly the organization of cultural events? (ii) How have the CSs reacted to this shock?

Coworking spaces in Italy and cultural events, before and during the COVID-19 pandemic

As described in Mariotti et al. (2021b), in 2018, there were 549 CSs recorded in Italy, which include all (at that time) active privately owned and managed workplaces. Figure 7.1 shows the geographical distribution

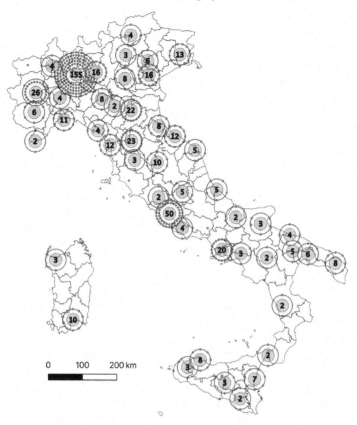

Figure 7.1 The geographical distribution of CSs in Italy.

Source: Authors' elaboration.

of CSs across Italian municipalities. Northwest (42%) and Center macro-areas (23%) hosted most CSs, while South and Islands accounted for 19%, and Northeast for 16%. Thus, about half of Italian CSs are in metropolitan cities: Milan city was the most attractive, hosting 99 CSs in 2018 (raised to 119 CSs in 2021), followed by Rome (46), Turin (18), and Florence (16).

To analyze possible changes in the cultural events management before and during the COVID-19 pandemic, we rely on secondary data about CSs in Italy, collected by Italian Coworking (from now on IC), which is an online platform.[2] Indeed, starting from 2017, IC has developed a yearly survey to coworking managers to gather information about CSs' business strategy, characteristics, services provided, profitability, problems encountered, expectations for the future, etc. Specifically, the first contact was done by telephone to engage the coworking managers, then a link to an online survey was sent by e-mail.

This chapter focuses on two waves of this survey, the 2018 and 2020 ones. The 2018 IC survey resulted in 107 complete questionnaires. The interviewed sample reflected the geographical distribution of the overall CSs in Italy, with an overrepresentation of Northeast (25%), while Northwest accounted for 29%, Centr 26%, and South and Islands 18%.

84% of the interviewed CSs had at least one event room, running meetings, courses, and cultural events. The cultural events hosted in the CSs can be organized by external professionals, cultural/creative coworkers, or CS managers.

Only 7% of respondents did not organize any event during the previous year, while 48% organized from one to ten events, 32% from eleven to fifty events, and 9% more than 51 events in a year (with one coworking space organizing 200 events). Moreover, 80% of CSs organized training courses and workshops. These events could also promote the CS activities and attract new users, as confirmed by the respondents: 39% claimed that they have moderately or often used events as a marketing strategy. However, only 10% of CSs frequently organized events in partnership with other CSs.

Looking at the financial revenues deriving from cultural events organization, 31% of respondents stated they had no revenues from events organization; instead, events represented more than 20% of previous year total revenues for 29% of CSs.

Finally, looking at the CSs' communication strategy, in 2018, social media represented an important channel: 48% used them very often, 30% used them moderately, 20% only a few times and 2% did not use them. Facebook is the most used (93%), followed by LinkedIn (46%), Instagram (40%), and Twitter (38%). Besides, the majority of the CSs interviewed used more than one social media at the same time.

The 2020 IC survey aimed to collect information on CSs' activities and management during the lockdown of March–April 2020. Seventy-one organizations,[3] which managed 188 CSs (almost 25% of Italian CSs), completed the questionnaire. The respondents were geographically distributed as follows: 24% (representing 18 CSs) were in the Northeast, 36.6% (representing 131 CSs) in the Northwest, 21% (representing 25 CSs) in the Center, and 18.4% (representing 14 CSs) in South and Islands.

About 60% of interviewed organizations were closed during the lockdown due to the imposed restrictions; 70% entirely cancelled their training courses, and 79% annulled all their events. However, thanks to social media and messaging channels, 93% of the interviewed could keep in touch with their community members. About 20% of respondents organized online training courses and webinars, and 27% organized virtual events. Only 8.5% of the organizations forecasted to close the spaces due to the economic damages linked to the restrictions.

The survey also collected the CSs initiatives to react to the imposed closures of office spaces. For example, besides the "classical" webinars and online cultural events, to hold together their communities, some CSs organized daily 20 minutes "online coffee breaks" with members, who can informally chat and share difficulties and needs. This type of initiative indirectly supports the creative industry activities since most coworkers belong to this sector (Akhavan et al., 2019). Finally, other cultural initiatives were promoted, such as live talks on social media pages, articles reviews, online interviews, and short videos, which had populated the CSs' websites.

The Milan case study

In Italy, the first CSs were opened in Milan in 2008, while 2012, 2013, and 2014 are considered "boom years". At the end of 2014, there were 68 CSs in the city. About half of them were specialized in the following sectors: architecture and design (18%), digital professions (10%), communication and information technology (8%, respectively), social innovation (5%), and other sectors (3%).

The CSs were mainly agglomerated in the northern part (Viale Monza, Isola-Sarpi, and Lambrate-Città Studi, which host about 67% of CSs), followed by central districts (Brera-Centrale-Porta Venezia, with 20%), and by south-western neighbourhoods (Tortona-Navigli, with the remaining 13%). The main creative urban districts, which participate in the well-known Milan Design Week,[4] are the most attractive areas for CSs (Mariotti et al., 2017), as presented in Figure 7.2a.

Specifically, the CSs located in the "creative neighbourhoods" are specialized in the media sector and architecture and design. As underlined by literature, the activities relying on symbolic knowledge (artistic and aesthetic) tend to prefer lively urban atmospheres (Asheim and Hansen, 2009) and, specifically, environments with a distinct and urban identity (Florida, 2008), like the Tortona-Navigli and Isola-Sarpi areas (Mariotti et al., 2017).

In 2021, Milan hosts 191 CSs (+75% compared to the year 2014), which are agglomerated in the more creative areas (see Figure 7.2b), while new locations in less central areas arise (Mariotti et al., 2021c). As it has happened in 2014, even in 2021, larger CSs – mainly settled in the north of the city in former productive or commercial buildings – offer several facilities to their coworkers (e.g. meeting rooms, kitchens, spaces to relax) and to external users (e.g. cafés and restaurants), and they often organize events (e.g. meetings, exhibitions, seminars, or training courses) open to the outside community. The organization of events contributes to create effects at the urban scale, as Mariotti et al. (2017) identified, since they are mainly addressed to urban communities of knowledge, creative, and digital workers (both self-employed and freelance). Specifically, events and services contribute to increasing the traditional Milan attractiveness for local and international new workers. Moreover, even at the local scale, the organization of events (e.g. readings, workshop, concerts, art performances, and

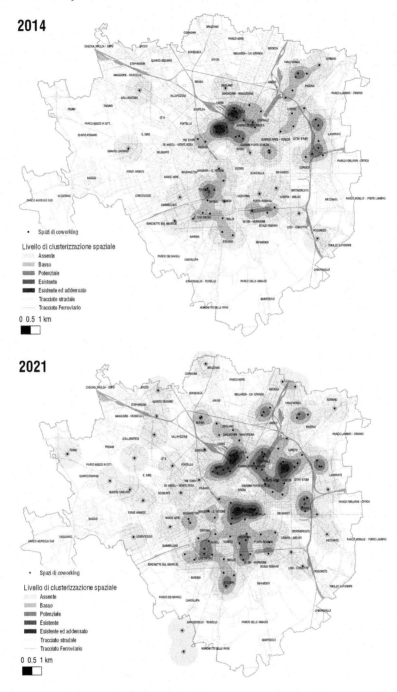

Figure 7.2 The agglomerations of CSs in Milan in 2014 (a) and 2021 (b).

Source: Mariotti et al. (2021c).

exhibitions) hosted in the larger CSs can affect the episodic transformation of the public space with new urban equipment, space to rest or for leisure, art, and cultural installations.

The recent survey carried out within the *Milano Collabora* project by Pais et al. (2021) concerns 87 out of 191 CSs in Milan. It results that 36% of the spaces experienced a reduction of the physical interactions inside the CS due to the adopted measure to guarantee physical distancing and to the contagion fear. Moreover, to maintain the community alive, the coworking managers have undertaken innovative solutions to keep the coworkers' social interaction. As concerns the organization of events, in 2020 compared to the year 2019 (before the pandemic) 36% of the CSs have cancelled them, 44% have reduced the number of events, 10% have maintained them steady and 10% have increased the events. As described in previous studies about Milan, the events organized by the CSs are usually related to their specialization (i.e. events about design are organized by CSs specialized in design and architecture) and/or to the demand of the neighbourhood (i.e. cultural, charity, and community events) (Akhavan et al., 2019).

Moreover, 17% of the CS managers have carried out online events addressed to the coworkers to maintain the community. These events have been formal (meeting with policymakers and experts about how to face the COVID-19 pandemic) and informal (breakfast, aperitive, coffee break).

The survey explored the turnover decrease in 2020 compared to 2019. Since the organization of events provides a significant share of the CSs' turnover, it results that in the period of March to May 2020 the CSs have declared, on average, a reduction of about 46% of the turnover (reaching 100% in case of closure of the space during the lockdown). On June–August 2020, the drop was about 41%, while the CS managers were expecting on October–December 2020 to organize events with a positive impact on the turnover. Nevertheless, this has not happened due to the new lockdown that started at the end of 2020.

Discussion, conclusions, and policy implications

The organization of events represents one of the main items of the CSs' turnover, and it is part of the leading practices' effects at the urban scale, contributing to increased traditional local attractiveness for new workers. Moreover, even at the local scale, the events hosted by the large CSs can affect the neighbourhood via the episodic transformation of the public space.

The surveys described above allowed us to answer the research questions: has the COVID-19 affected the activities of CSs, particularly the organization of cultural events? How have the CSs reacted to this shock?

Most Italian CSs had at least one event room, running meetings, courses, and cultural events; moreover, events represent a positive marketing strategy and contribute to the financial revenue increase. However, the

COVID-19 pandemic has had a strong negative impact on events and training courses, with 70% CSs that cancelled their training courses and 79% annulled all their events. Similarly, CSs in Milan experienced a reduction of the physical interactions inside the CS and a significant drop in the number of events. The events' cancellation has impacted the CSs' turnover in the period March–May 2020 (first pandemic wave in Italy) with, on average, a reduction of about 46% (reaching also 100% when in case of closure of the space).

Italian and Milanese CSs have massively used social media and messaging channels to keep the community alive and have organized online training courses, webinars, and virtual events to cope with this situation.

Therefore, tailored policy tools are advocated. A recent ESPON report by Bourdin and Rossignol (2020) describes the several compensating and circumventing measures about culture and leisure underlying that some cities and NUTS3 regions have enhanced online cultural services, such as online virtual tours of zoos (Warsaw-PL), museums (Leipzig-DE, Cuenca-ES), online streamed cultural programs (Bologna-IT, Cuenca-ES) and performances of plays and classical concerts (Warsaw-PL). Another interesting measure consists of physically bring small cultural events in the neighborhood to allow the vulnerable people to enjoy culture from home (Goteborg-SE) or help all the residents overcome isolation difficulties where lockdowns have been implemented (Bologna-IT). In addition, direct financial support (including grants) for cultural associations, institutions, and individual artists, along with financial compensation for the organizers of cultural events, have also been widely reported: "some public authorities delivered direct financial support to relief financial difficulties (Ghent-BE), whilst others launched calls with new regulations enhancing innovative forms (including digital) which enable everyone to enjoy culture (Goteborg-SE, Warsaw-PL)" (Bourdin and Rossignol, 2020: 32). At least to our knowledge, no evidence concerns measures subsidizing CSs to organize cultural events, and this might be promoted.

Another issue to be considered is the importance of the CS size of indoor and outdoor space to host events. During the COVID-19 pandemic, several cities worldwide have allowed private sectors to use the open-air public space for their activities (i.e. bars, restaurants, etc.). As stated by Florida et al. (2021), under an extended, multi-year lockdown, cities and towns might increasingly become cultural and civic gathering places, hosting outdoor events, in city streets and plazas, as part of the transformation of city centers into pedestrian and bike havens.

Finally, policymakers should solve the existing digital gaps specific to some countries. In this context, the more peripheral CSs or those without broadband access are undoubtedly penalized in online activities and events.

Further research might investigate, through appropriate surveys, if and how the digital work, fostered by the pandemic conditions, is complementary or substitute to traditional activities within the CSs spaces. Specifically, concerning the organization of cultural events, it will be necessary to verify whether the mixed online/in-person model will be sustainable from a CS's turnover point of view and whether tailored policy measures enhancing the organization of events within the CS will be successful (as for the CS itself, as for the local context). Moreover, special attention will be paid to the emerging collective work dynamics using digital technologies among the creative workers who populate the CSs.

Acknowledgements

The book chapter is supported by COST Action CA18214 'The geography of New Working Spaces and the impact on the periphery', which is funded by the Horizon 2020 Framework program of the European Union (project website: http://www.new-working-spaces.eu/; European Union Website: https://www.cost.eu/actions/CA18214). ⊃coſt

Notes

1. A Social Street is always a Facebook born from the desire of the residents of an anti-social street to seek and create participatory and collective meeting points in their neighborhood, i.e. places to meet and to know each other; to do things together and help one another (Akhavan et al., 2019). The idea of "Social Street" in Italy originates from the experience of the Facebook group "Residents in Via Fondazza-Bologna", born, in September 2013, from the observation of the general impoverishment of social relationships, which causes feelings of loneliness and loss of sense of belonging, urban degradation, and lack of social control of the territory (www.socialstreet.it).
2. See: https://www.italiancoworking.it/.
3. The percentages reported in the paragraph referred to the 71 organizations interviewed.
4. The Milan Design Week is a temporary fringe event taking place every year since the early 1990s and involving several Milan neighborhoods.

References

Agostino D, Arnaboldi M, and Lampis A (2020) Italian state museums during the COVID-19 crisis: from onsite closure to online openness. *Museum Management and Curatorship* 35(4): 362–372.

Akhavan M, Mariotti I, Astolfi L, and Canevari A (2019) Coworking spaces and new social relations: a focus on the social streets in Italy. *Urban Science* 3(2): 1–11.

Amorim JP, and Teixeira L (2020) Art in the digital during and after Covid: aura and apparatus of online exhibitions. *Rupkatha Journal on Interdisciplinary Studies in Humanities* 12(5): 1–8.

Asheim B, and Hansen H (2009) knowledge bases, talents, and contexts: on the usefulness of the creative class approach in Sweden. *Economic Geography* 85(4): 425–442.

Bihagen E, and Katz-Gerro T (2000) Culture consumption in Sweden: the stability of gender differences. *Poetics* 27(5–6): 327–349.

Bilandzic M (2016) Connected learning in the library as a product of hacking, making, social diversity and messiness. *Interactive Learning Environments* 24(1): 158–177.

Bourdin S, and Rossignol N (2020) ESPON STUDY-Geography of COVID-19 outbreak and first policy answers in European regions and cities. Report, Espon, Bruxelles.

Capdevila I (2014) Different entrepreneurial approaches in localized spaces of collaborative innovation. *SSRN Electronic Journal.* Epub ahead of print 3 December 2014. DOI: https://dx.doi.org/10.2139/ssrn.2533448

Deskmag (2019) The 2019 global coworking survey. Deskmag. Available at: https://coworkingstatistics.com/number-of-coworking-spaces-and-members-worldwide-througout-the-years (accessed 10 March 2021).

Deskmag (2021) How the pandemic is affecting coworking spaces. Deskmag. Available at: https://www.deskmag.com/en/coworking-spaces/covid19-pandemic-impact-on-coworking-spaces-market-report-corona-statistics (accessed 10 March 2021).

Ebejer J, Xuereb K, and Avellino M (2021) A critical debate of the cultural and social effects of Valletta 2018 European Capital of Culture. *Journal of Tourism and Cultural Change* 19(1): 97–112.

Florida R (2008) *Who's Your City?* New York: Basic Books.

Florida R, Rodríguez-Pose A, and Storper M (2021) Cities in a Post-COVID World. *Papers in Evolutionary Economic Geography* 2041.

Fuzi A, Clifton N, and Loudon G (2014) New in-house organizational spaces that support creativity and innovation: the co-working space. In: *R&D Management Conference*, Stuttgart, June 2014, pp. 3–6.

Grossi E, Blessi GT, Sacco PL, and Buscema M (2012) The interaction between culture, health and psychological well-being: data mining from the Italian culture and well-being project. *Journal of Happiness Studies* 13(1): 129–148.

Hand C (2018) Do the arts make you happy? A quantile regression approach. *Journal of Cultural Economics* 42(2): 271–286.

Herrero LC, Sanz JA, Devesa M, Bedate A, and José del Barrio M (2006) The economic impact of cultural events: a case-study of Salamanca 2002, European Capital of Culture. *European Urban and Regional Studies* 13(1): 41–57.

Kingma FS (2016) The constitution of "third workspaces" in between the home and the corporate office. *New Technology, Work and Employment* 31(2): 176–193.

Lee H, and Heo S (2021) Arts and cultural activities and happiness: evidence from Korea. *Applied Research Quality Life* 16: 1637–1651. DOI: https://doi.org/10.1007/s11482-020-09833-2

Liu YD (2014) Socio-cultural impacts of major event: evidence from the 2008 European Capital of Culture, Liverpool. *Social Indicators Research* 115: 983–998.

Mariotti I, Akhavan M, and Di Matteo D (2021a) The geography of coworking spaces and the effects on the urban context: are pole areas gaining? In Mariotti I, Di Vita S, and Akhavan M (eds.) *New workplaces: Location patterns, urban effects and development trajectories. A worldwide investigation.* Cham, Switzerland: Springer, pp.169–194.

Mariotti I, Akhavan M, and Rossi F (2021b) The preferred location of coworking spaces in Italy: an empirical investigation in urban and peripheral areas. *European Planning Studies*. Epub ahead of print 9 March 2021. DOI: https://doi.org/10.1080/09654313.2021.1895080

Mariotti I, Manfredini F, and Giavarini V (2021c) La geografia degli spazi di coworking a Milano. Una analisi territoriale. Report, Comune di Milano, Milano Collabora

Mariotti I, and Pacchi C (2021) Coworkers and coworking spaces as urban transformation actors. an Italian perspective. In Mariotti I, Di Vita S, and Akhavan M (eds.) *New Workplaces: Location Patterns, Urban Effects and Development Trajectories. A Worldwide Investigation*. Cham, Switzerland: Springer, pp. 53–63.

Mariotti I, Pacchi C, and Di Vita S (2017) Coworking spaces in Milan: location patterns and urban effects. *Journal of Urban Technology* 24(3): 47–66.

Merkel J (2015) Coworking in the city. *Ephemera | Theory & Politics in Organisation* 15(1): 121–139.

Migliore A, Manzini Ceinar I, and Tagliaro C (2021) Beyond coworking: from flexible to hybrid spaces. In Orel M, Dvoulety O, and Ratten V (eds.) *The Flexible Workplace. Coworking and Other Modern Workplace Transformations*. Cham, Switzerland: Springer Nature, pp. 3–24.

Oldenburg R (1997) *The Great Good Place: Cafes, Coffee Shops, Bookstores, Bars, Hair Salons and Other Hangouts at the Heart of the Community*. Cambridge: Da Capo Press.

Pagán R (2015) How do leisure activities impact on life satisfaction? Evidence for German people with disabilities. *Applied Research in Quality of Life* 10(4): 557–572.

Pais I, Manzo C, and Gerosa A (2021) La trasformazione dei coworking di Milano nell'emergenza pandemica. Le interviste ai coworking manager. Report, Comune di Milano, Milano Collabora.

Porter ME (1989) *The Competitive Advantage of Nations*. New York: Free Press.

Richards G, and Wilson J (2004) The impact of cultural events on city image: Rotterdam, Cultural Capital of Europe 2001. *Urban Studies* 41(10): 1931–1951.

Seaman B (2006) Empirical studies of demand for the performing arts. In Ginsburgh V, and Throsby D (eds.) *Handbook of the Economics of Art and Culture*. Amsterdam: North-Holland Publishing, pp. 415–472.

Spinuzzi C (2012) Working alone, together: coworking as emergent collaborative activity. *Journal of Business and Technical Communication* 26(4): 399–441.

Stafford MR, and Tripp C (2000) Age, income, and gender: demographic determinants of community theatre patronage. *Journal of Nonprofit and Public Sector Marketing* 8(2): 29–43.

Vegheş C (2020) cultural consumption as a trait of a sustainable lifestyle: evidence from the European Union. *European Journal of Sustainable Development* 9(4): 125.

We are Social (2019) Global Digital Report 2019. Available at: https://wearesocial.com/global-digital-report-2019 (accessed 28 October 2020).

Wheatley D, and Bickerton C (2017) Subjective well-being and engagement in arts, culture and sport. *Journal of Cultural Economics* 41(1): 23–45.

Žilič Fišer S, and Kožuh I (2019) The impact of cultural events on community reputation and pride in Maribor, The European Capital of Culture 2012. *Social Indicators Research* 142: 1055–1073.

8 Freelance classical musicians in Austria and the COVID-19 pandemic

Dagmar Abfalter and Sandra Stini

In spring 2020, the COVID-19 pandemic hit the Austrian freelance music scene with unprecedented and unpredictable vehemence. Social media effective balcony concerts and virtual performances organized at short notice could not hide the shock of an entire professional field within the Cultural and Creative Industries. The aim of this chapter is to shed light on the situation of freelance classical musicians during the COVID-19 pandemic in Austria. To this end, we start with an estimation of the economic importance of the cultural sector in general and classical music in Austria in particular. Second, structural inequalities in the field of classical music between orchestra musicians with fixed positions and freelance musicians are identified. The third section shortly describes the containment and relief measures that have been taken by the Austrian government so far. Drawing on an early explorative online survey among freelance musicians in Austria in March/April 2020, we then present perceptions of the impact of COVID-19 on job portfolios and income. After some notes on the data and methods used, the results of the thematic analysis show how the pandemic has further exacerbated these inequalities during the pandemic.

The economic importance of music and the cultural sector in Austria

Music and especially classical music (or Western art music) play an important role in the Austrian Culture and Creative Industries, both from an economic and cultural identity point of view. It shapes the brand image of Austria, fuelling the notion of a "cultural nation" (Meinecke 1908) where common culture forms the basis of coexistence. As such, classical music is an important part of the discursive construction of Austrian national identity (Wodak et al. 2009) after 1945 until today. Furthermore, it is an important contributor to Austria's economy and tourism income. Precise data on the overall economic impact of classical music are not available for Austria. Therefore, information on the cultural and tourism sectors that are both fuelled by the music industry are used as proxies.

DOI: 10.4324/9781003128274-11

In 2017, a total of 32,445 companies were assigned to the cultural sector (5.8% of non-agricultural companies). Of these, 19% belonged to the domain "performing arts". The share of the cultural sector in the gross value added of the production and services sector was 2.7% or 5.7 billion euros in 2017 (Statistik Austria 2020). According to Eurostat (2021), cultural employment in Austria amounts to 181,300 persons or 4.2% of total employment in 2019. The Austrian labour force survey finds that 4.6% (200,600) of the workforce were employed in a cultural occupation in 2018. As in other European countries, workers with a cultural occupation in the cultural sector had a higher level of education than the workforce as a whole and were far more likely to be self-employed: 80.5% had a baccalaureate or university-level degree, and nearly half (46.9%) were self-employed (Statistik Austria 2020).

In 2019, the direct value-added effects of tourism amounted to 21.69 billion euros representing 5.5% of Austria's GDP. Including the indirect effects calculated on the basis of a tourism satellite account, the value-added amounts to 29.74 billion euros and 7.5% of GDP (Statistik Austria 2021a). Within the tourism job market, 5% of jobs are attributed to the cultural tourism sector (BMLRT 2021). Cultural tourism is considered one of the fastest-growing segments in the tourism industry, with 36% of total tourism worldwide and approximately 4% more growth (over 5 years) than global tourism in 2017 (WTO 2018).

Austria offers production, education, and training facilities of high number and reputation, many of which are publicly subsidized. In 2018, the combined public cultural expenditures of the territorial entities (state, federal provinces, and municipalities) amounted to approximately 2.69 billion euros, or 0.70% of GDP. The focus on focus is clearly on education and training (30% of cultural expenditure) and the performing arts (17%) (Statistik Austria 2020).

The cultural industry in Austria is not limited to urban areas but extends across the nine federal provinces. However, some specialized cultural activities such as opera houses, orchestras, or music halls are usually located in large cities and the tourist centres of a country. In Austria, the capital Vienna as well as Graz, Linz, and Salzburg, are key centres in this regard (Trippl et al. 2013). Some of the most prestigious cultural brands in the form of established institutions include the Wiener Staatsoper, the Wiener Philharmoniker, or the Wiener Symphoniker, all of them associated with the so-called "Wiener Klang" (Viennese sound). Although free groups, orchestras, multi-purpose halls, etc. are an important part of the musical portfolio, they are not currently systematically recorded by Statistik Austria (2020).

Civil service versus precarious work conditions

In 2020, about 12 professional orchestras in Austria were regulated by collective agreements and offered about 1,000 permanent positions with regulated income and a certain degree of planning security. Frequently, these orchestras are generously subsidized or connected to subsidized major arts institutions, such as the Wiener Staatsoper.

Historically, in the Habsburg Monarchy musicians of the Hofmusikkapelle were civil servants and employed for life. A look into, for example, the collective labour agreement of the Wiener Symphoniker indicates that many orchestra musicians are still treated similar to civil servants in the case of salary valorisation, travel allowance regulations, or child benefit allowance. These fixed positions, even when full-time, frequently entail multiple employment. For example, a member of the Wiener Staatsopernorchester would always be a member of the Wiener Philharmoniker, organized as a private association (they were counted as a single orchestra in the number of 12 professional orchestras). An orchestra position can open further employment opportunities in the form of additional engagements, solo performances, university professorships, or teaching activities (Abfalter & Stini 2021). It should be noted that the fixed positions are dominantly occupied by middle-class men and that "Western classical music is in many ways connected with Whiteness" (Leppänen 2015: 19).

Alongside this group of privileged musicians, precarious work prevails in the freelance orchestra musician scene. A study on the social situation of artists and cultural mediators in Austria (n = 1,757) shows that complex employment situations with high rates of self-employment, multiple jobs both in the artistic field and in fields of activity related to or unrelated to art, irregularity due to short-term commissions or employment were and are characteristic of the working situation of many of the artists interviewed. Securing social security in old age, securing social security in the event of unemployment, and income insecurity and irregularity were perceived as particularly stressful factors for musicians. In sum, 70% of the respondents also undertake arts-related and/or non-arts-related activities creating a striking divergence between the idealistic and financial focus of their work (Wetzel 2018). So-called portfolio careers involving a breadth of activities are characteristic of the classical music sector. They are marked by low incomes, uncertainty, and lack of workplace benefits such as pensions (Scharff 2018). Much entrepreneurial risk such as advance payments for travel or sheet music is transferred from subsidized institutions to freelance musicians. The next section deals with the impact of the COVID-19 pandemic in Austria.

Freelance musicians and the COVID-19 pandemic in Austria

While Austria initially did not appear to be affected by the viral infection at the beginning of 2020, after a first diagnosis of coronavirus on 25 February, first actions and announcements of restrictions by the Austrian government started on 10 March, resulting in the first hard lockdown on 16 March 2020, that – for the live performing arts – should last until the end of April 2020. Two more hard lockdowns were imposed from 7 November to 6 December 2020 and from 26 December 2020 to 7 February 2021. Between these periods, containment measures were relaxed or tightened, frequently at short notice. While cable cars and restaurants could reopen relatively soon, cultural events with audience were banned almost continuously until May 2021 or had to move into the digital space. Many projects were cancelled or postponed. Even the prestigious New Year's Concert 2021 of the Wiener Philharmoniker took place without a hall audience. Re-openings were associated with difficulties of international travel, security constraints, and capacity limitations.

On 3 April 2020, the advocacy group representing the independent cultural work in Austria IG Kultur argued that according to a survey at least 4.5 million euros have been lost to the sector in just one month, more than 3,000 employees were at risk of losing their livelihoods, and the continued existence of many cultural associations and institutions was in acute danger. Continuing the measures until the end of July 2020 would lead to an estimated damage of 10.7 million euros (IG Kultur 2020).

Although the Austrian government had promised quick and unbureaucratic relief measures, the first months of the pandemic were characterized by uncertainty about eligibility and formal procedures for freelance artists to access relief schemes. This led, in part, to the resignation of the Secretary of State for Arts and Culture in May 2020. Finally, freelance musicians were able to submit applications for funding measures to various agencies starting in the summer of 2020. The government aid funds most frequently used by musicians were the *Hardship Fund of the Austrian Chamber of Commerce* for EPUs and micro-companies compensating 80–90% of the profit from the comparable month in the previous year up to a maximum of 2,000 euros; and the *Bridging Fund for self-employed Artists* with a maximum of 1,000 euros per month. Further aid funds for freelance musicians affected by the ban on events were set up by the collecting societies in the music sector and other regional authorities such as federal provinces and municipalities.

The duration of the payout varied greatly. Some aids were disbursed after only a few months, as the funds earmarked for them had been fully spent. Others, such as the Hardship Fund and Bridging Fund, were extended every three months. These are currently scheduled to continue as support measures until fall 2021. In the course of the pandemic, a comprehensive portfolio of relief measures was established. Direct support measures include the relief funds, which have already been extended from a sum of 38 billion euros announced by the Austrian chancellor on 18 March 2020 to 52.18 billion euros in September 2020, but also lockdown bonuses or a "protective umbrella" for event organizers, a 300 million euros endowment allowing for more security in planning in-person events. Indirect support measures contain the deferral of social security contributions, fiscal reliefs, or voucher redemptions for events. Finally, support and goodwill solutions for cancelled or deferred subsidized projects have been developed (BMKOES 2021).

What will happen after the end of the relief measures is completely uncertain at present. In the following, we focus on early perceptions and fears of freelance musicians during the pandemic.

Survey on early financial consequences of the pandemic

When the first ban on events was announced in 2020, we started a short explorative online survey with closed and open questions and asked freelance musicians in Austria about the expected loss of earnings for this first pandemic month from 13 March to 13 April 2020. Sampling and questionnaire distribution was effectuated through musicians' networks at Facebook, and the survey was administered via Unipark (QuestBack). The questionnaire (in German) focused on lost earnings for individual events/organizers known at that time until the communicated end of the first lockdown. The feedback clearly showed the desperate situation in which many freelancers found themselves at the beginning of the crisis. The actual losses incurred are significantly higher in the meantime, but so are financial measures taken by the government to support individuals economically affected by the pandemic.

Method

In total, 228 persons completed the online questionnaire. After the cleaning of double entries, incomplete questionnaires, and questionnaires filled out by event organizers rather than individual freelance musicians, the sample consists of 200 freelance musicians of all genres in Austria. The sample description including gender, age, main residence, university degree, and dependence on freelance musical income is depicted in Table 8.1. We specifically consider the subsample of classical musicians that represents the majority of respondents (70.5%).

A total of 135 participants of the survey completed an open question on the expected effects of COVID-19 (*How does COVID-19 affect your work as a freelance musician?*). These answers were analyzed with thematic coding. In the following, we focus on the 85 responses from the classical field. Interview statements and references to event organizers are anonymized, respondents' characteristics such as gender, age, main residence, university degree, and occupational dependency (in %) of the respondents are added in brackets.

Results

The survey respondents are a small, non-representative sample of those affected by COVID-19 containment measures; still, the information they provided is sobering. In total, 2,552 cancelled event dates and loss of

Table 8.1 Sample description.

		Total (n = 200)	Classical music (n = 141)
Gender	Male	53.5% (n = 107)	44.7% (n = 63)
	Female	46.5% (n = 93)	55.3% (n = 78)
	Diverse	0	0
Age (years)	≤25 years	8.0% (n = 16)	10.6% (n = 15)
	26–35 years	51.5% (n = 103)	50.4% (n = 71)
	36–45 years	17.5% (n = 35)	19.1% (n = 27)
	46–55 years	17.0% (n = 34)	14.9% (n = 21)
	56–65 years	4.0% (n = 8)	2.8% (n = 4)
	≥66 years	2.0% (n = 4)	2.1% (n = 3)
Main residence (Federal province)	Burgenland	1.0% (n = 2)	0.7% (n = 1)
	Carinthia	1.5% (n = 3)	1.4% (n = 2)
	Lower Austria	8.5% (n = 17)	9.9% (n = 14)
	Upper Austria	6.5% (n = 13)	7.1% (n = 10)
	Salzburg	4.5% (n = 9)	5.7% (n = 8)
	Styria	9.5% (n = 19)	4.3% (n = 6)
	Tyrol	2.5% (n = 5)	2.8% (n = 4)
	Vorarlberg	2.0% (n = 4)	2.1% (n = 3)
	Vienna	58.5% (n = 117)	61.0% (n = 86)
	Outside Austria	5.0% (n = 10)	4.3% (n = 6)
	missing	0.5% (n = 1)	0.7% (n = 1)
Highest music-related university degree	No university degree	8.5% (n = 17)	3.5% (n = 5)
	Still studying	9.5% (n = 19)	10.6% (n = 15)
	Bachelor/1st diploma	22.5% (n = 45)	22.7% (n = 32)
	Master/2nd diploma	52.5% (n = 105)	56.0% (n = 79)
	other	7.0% (n = 14)	7.1% (n = 10)
Dependency of freelance work (% of income)	≤25%	4.0% (n = 8)	4.3% (n = 6)
	26–50%	19.0% (n = 38)	19.9% (n = 28)
	51–75%	11.5% (n = 23)	14.2% (n = 20)
	≥75%	64.0% (n = 128)	59.6% (n = 84)
	missing	1.5% (n = 3)	2.1% (n = 3)

earnings per organizer or client of 40 to 40,000 euros (overseas performances in Japan) were listed, amounting to a total of almost 550,000 euros. At the time of the survey, according to the respondents only 15 organizers have compensated at least partially (e.g. rehearsals) or announced compensations.

As early as April, many respondents speak of an "existence-threatening situation" in which they cannot cover their running expenses and criticize the "high level of uncertainty". Main themes arising from the answers on how COVID-19 affects the respondents' work as freelance musicians centre on the precarious and seasonal nature of freelance work, a feeling of being unemployed and jobless, the impact on several parts of the portfolio, as well as uncertainty and existential fears due to the pandemic.

Precarity and seasonal work

The quotes contain diverse accounts of precarious work where even little income can make a difference.

> Normally I have several marginal jobs, work contracts and freelance jobs on the side. Unfortunately, I've been completely unemployed since the beginning of the year, except for a small job paying 150€per month, and have been dependent on this little income from concerts and masses. The Covid situation unfortunately hit me at a very inopportune time–luckily friends and family can support me a little. (female; 26–35 years; Vienna; other; 26–50%)

The first lockdown affected the lucrative Easter and summer business and its traditional church masses and festivals. Seasonality of musical work further accentuates individual risk.

> Loss of 41% percent of my annual earnings by having at least 8 performances (and 12 rehearsal days) within the ministry-ordered closure of the theatre. (female; 46–55 years; Overseas; Master/Diploma; >75%)

Unemployed entrepreneurs

A recurring expression is being "arbeitslos", German for being "unemployed". As in the context of at least partially self-employed the equivalent of "jobless" would have been more accurate, we interpret a specific sentiment of situation dependency. As one respondent states:

> All concerts and opera productions, church music performances were cancelled. Possible replacement dates are in prospect, however, I will not have time there, I am therefore for 1 month without income through no fault of my own, as a freelancer I am also not entitled to unemployment benefits. (male; 46–55 years; Lower Austria; Bachelor; >75%)

This is all the more remarkable as freelance musicians bear the risk of entrepreneurial activity and in many cases have already made investments in terms of advance expenses that will not be reimbursed.

> There are no more spontaneous requests, I have booked trains to travel to Switzerland, the insurance booked does not cover, no one pays the costs incurred (200€). Instead of 1500€+ I now have 200€- in the account and no other orders. (female; 26–35 years; Vienna; Master/Diploma; 51–75%)

Often, rehearsals and practice times are not compensated for freelance musicians, while they are part of regular working hours for employed musicians.

> Many hours of work, including preparation, go into nothing. After all, the fees aren't even a great hourly wage if you include preparation, buying sheet music, renting instruments and similar expenses. One is faced with a certain void, and not knowing how long the cancellations will last, and whether more concerts will be cancelled, is tough. I've never realized as clearly as I do now how thin the ice is on which we stand as freelance artists. With a wave of the hand, everything can collapse. (female; 36–45 years; Lower Austria; Master/Diploma; >75%)

Affecting several parts of income portfolio

A portfolio career relies on diverse sources of income which usually reduces risk. The pandemic simultaneously affected several or even all parts of freelance musicians' income portfolios.

> In addition to my income as a musician, I also lack income from private lessons, as 3 students understandably want to stay at home during the weeks and I can't work in my part-time job as a ticket collector at [event organizer]. So, I miss out on a month's salary. (female; 26–35 years; Vienna; Master/Diploma; >75%)

The containment measures affected not only performances of all kinds but also music lessons and non-music-related jobs in cultural organizations and many more.

> All dates also for April and May are wobbling from the side of the organizers (opera tour, concerts, church services,…). I also teach in elementary schools as part of a special music project – even here the income is currently in question for April/May/June […]. (female; 36–45 years, Carinthia; other; 51–75%)

Uncertainty

The inability to predict the future and to plan relate to the temporal dimension of precarity (Scharff 2018).

> All concerts and performances were cancelled without compensation. Other projects [example of a festival] are still planned with performances in July, but of course there are no guarantees. As a result, I am preparing for projects at home and learning texts and vocal parts of roles that may not even take place. (male; 26–35 years; Styria; Master/Diploma; >75%)

Even in the case of postponements, coordination is difficult due to overlaps, so that these incomes are also not considered secure.

> It is not only the last-minute cancellations that have caught me completely off guard, but also the uncertainty about how long this situation will last. At the moment it seems unlikely that after the end of the first period of measures (in Austria April 3) cultural activities can be fully resumed. Therefore, I am forced to ration my savings and keep my head above water until July. However, if normality has not returned by then, I will no longer have any financial resources at my disposal. Also, it is already complicated or impossible to coordinate events that are postponed [...] with already confirmed engagements. This inevitably leads to collisions, which in turn cause a further loss of income. (female; 36–45 years; Vorarlberg; Master/Diploma; >75%)

Performances are at the heart of a classical music career. In consequence, the containment measures exert a negative impact on study and career.

> You get depressed. Artistically it's a disaster for my career. I missed out on very important events ... (male; 46–55 years; Overseas; Master/Diploma; >75%)

Apart from a lack of performance opportunities, daily practice, which is so important for musicians, is often impeded. Confined or urban housing situations further aggravate incompatibility with family or care duties.

> Fortunately, since February I have a weekend domicile at which I now stay. If I had stayed in the city, I would certainly not have been able to practice, since [my] partner with a much higher salary does home office. [So] I take care of our child. I urgently need to write mails for future projects & engagements, put together programs, submit projects etc. and I almost don't get to practice. I hope we can find a better time management for me. [... M]uch of my income flows mainly to expenses for partial payments for long overdue equipment and student loan repayment, as well as social security. [...] Since I can't do any canvassing now, things won't get any better next season. I have all kinds of ideas about what I could do artistically (online) during the crisis, I just don't have the time. (female; 26–35 years; Vienna; Master/Diploma; >75%)

Lack of financial reserves and fear for one's existence

Finally, a recurrent theme is a lack or low level of financial reserves or cash flow needed to cover running expenses.

> My main source of income is on standby for an unknown amount of time. Since I work at home most of the time, apart from concerts, I

don't notice it as much in everyday life, until the time comes when I have no more money for food and rent ... (male; 26–35 years; Vienna; Bachelor; >75%)

Highly skilled musicians, frequently with renowned university degrees, find themselves in an unexpected emergency situation in which they would even accept unskilled work.

I have lost all my income. I do not know how I will pay my rent the next months. I will end up in debt and can now already register myself [as] unemployed. I would take any unskilled job now to avoid the debt even though I have 2 BA and MA and will get a second MA title next semester. It's horrible. I have nothing saved for a case like this, the next 3 months would have to be highly profitable. I have no idea how to make the most necessary payments. It is extremely threatening. (female; 26–35 years; Salzburg; Master/Diploma; >75%)

Uncertainty and threatening poverty create fears for freelance musician's existence. Surveys such as the UK COVID-19 Impact Polls by the Musicians' Union (2020) already warn that a significant number of freelance musicians are thinking about giving up their careers, presumably also outside the UK.

Intensification of structural inequalities in the orchestra music scene

The COVID-19 pandemic hit the Austrian economy in 2020 with –6.3% in real terms. Due to lockdowns, accommodation and food service activities (–35.8% in real terms), arts, entertainment, and personal services (–18.3% in real terms) as well as transportation (–13.8 in real terms) suffered the strongest losses (Statistik Austria 2021b). All of these sectors are closely related to the freelance orchestra scene.

According to a recent study by Ernst & Young (EY consulting 2021) building on impact surveys, interviews, and additional market research, the cultural and creative economy is one of the most affected in Europe. The shockwaves of the COVID-19 crisis are felt in all Cultural and Creative Industries in 2020 with a loss of 31% of its turnover. Most impacted were the performing arts (–90% between 2019 and 2020) and music (–76%). Within the Austrian music industry, the prohibition of live concerts and events led to massive revenue loss in 2020, sales of physical recordings, and royalties for public broadcasting collapsed due to closed shops and gastronomy. Austrian production showed a drop in revenue of 40% in 2020. Only music streaming subscriptions showed an increase (IFPI Austria 2021). In a recent online survey on music creators, 86% of 1,777 respondents and 93% of freelance musicians stated that they had suffered financial losses due to the COVID-19 pandemic between 15 March 2020 and 14 March 2021.

The majority claimed losses of more than 10,000 euros for this period (Tschmuck 2021).

This crisis has further exacerbated the structural inequalities in the freelance music scene. The holders of fixed positions were hindered in their professional practice for a long time and cut off from additional business. However, almost all Austrian service orchestras were able to put their musicians on job retention schemes at the beginning of April, leaving them with at least 80% of their salary for hours not worked and their financial security including pension payments. In order to secure international touring, the Wiener Philharmoniker (95 out of 148 orchestra members; Tošić 2021) was even given priority in the hard-to-obtain vaccination by the City of Vienna. Larger institutions such as the Wiener Staatsoper could more easily draw on existing infrastructure for digital events. While monetizing digital offerings is still difficult, these offerings allow certain performances and continuity of professional practice during lockdown.

In contrast, almost all income opportunities had disappeared in the freelance orchestra scene. No short-time work schemes were available to them, and the establishment of financial assistance by the public sector was slow to take off, despite intensive lobbying by advocacy groups. A lack or the nature of contractual agreements impeded easy access to relief schemes. Substitute replacements for professional orchestras were left empty-handed. Events had mostly been cancelled without compensation, or at best postponed. Digital music lessons were often not accepted by private students. Marginal employment opportunities in cultural institutions had disappeared.

As the data of our early study reveal, many musicians had to draw on their reserves, which were frequently small due to the precarious working conditions and low salaries in the freelance music scene. Furthermore, opportunities for artistic development and practice were drastically reduced.

Overcoming structural inequalities after the crisis

During the COVID-19 pandemic structural inequalities in the classical music scene in Austria have been intensified. The results of our early study on the effects of the pandemic on the situation of freelance musicians stress their precarious and vulnerable position. While relief measures have finally been made accessible, the long-term effects on the sector are uncertain. Political measures that go beyond short-term relief of the pandemic impacts would need to consider the structural framework conditions for freelance musicians such as labour contract provisions to avoid bogus self-employment and minimum wage standards, at least for the subsidized sector. Improved access to social security and pension funds could reduce uncertainty and existential fears especially for those dependent on precarious seasonal and portfolio work. Avenues for the sustainable monetarization of digital music offers are highly needed. Finally, collecting and publishing reliable data on the work of orchestras and freelance musicians would not only provide a valuable basis for the development of concrete and sustainable measures but also shed more light on the reproduction of privilege and disadvantage by gatekeepers in the sector (Tatli & Özbilgin 2012). Such efforts have been recently announced by politicians and interest groups.

At the time of writing, the end of the pandemic is not yet in sight.

References

Abfalter, D. & Stini, S. (2021) An independent career in classical music? A comparison of market valuation practices of classical music and higher music education in Vienna and Berlin. *Paper presented at the 11th International Conference on Cultural Policy Research (ICCPR 2020) "Resilience of Cultural Policy"*, March 23–26, 2021, online.

BMKOES (2021) *FAQ: Auswirkungen des Coronavirus auf Kunst und Kultur.* https://www.bmkoes.gv.at/Themen/Corona/Corona-Kunst-und-Kultur.html [accessed: June 25, 2021].

BMLRT (2021) *Kulturtourismus in Österreich.* https://info.bmlrt.gv.at/themen/tourismus/tourismuspolitische-themen/Tourismus-und-Kultur/Kulturtourismus-in–sterreich.html [accessed: June 14, 2021].

Eurostat (2021) *Cultural employment by sex.* https://ec.europa.eu/eurostat/databrowser/view/cult_emp_sex/default/table?lang=en [accessed: June 25, 2021].

EY consulting (2021) *Rebuilding Europe – The Cultural and Creative Economy before and after the COVID-19 Crisis.* Brussels: GESAC.

IFPI (2021) *Österreichischer Musikmarkt.* https://ifpi.at/website2018/wp-content/uploads/2021/03/ifpi-musikmarkt2020.pdf [accessed: June 21, 2021].

IG Kultur (2020) *Auswirkungen der COVID-19 Maßnahmen auf unabhängige Kulturvereine und -einrichtungen.* https://www.igkultur.at/sites/default/files/news/downloads/2020-04-03/Covid19-Auswirungen%20auf%20Kulturvereine_Die%20Ergebnisse%20im%20Detail.pdf [accessed: June 05, 2021].

Leppänen, T. (2015) The west and the rest of classical music: Asian musicians in the Finnish media coverage of the 1995 Jean Sibelius Violin Competition. *European Journal of Cultural Studies*, 18(1), 19–34. doi: 10.1177/1367549414557804.

Meinecke, F. (1908) *Weltbürgertum und Nationalstaat*, München: Oldenbourg.

Musicians' Union (2020) *Coronavirus Presses Mute Button on Music Industry.* https://musiciansunion.org.uk/news/coronavirus-presses-mute-button-on-music-industry [accessed: June 18, 2021].

Scharff, C. (2018) *Gender, Subjectivity, and Cultural Work: The Classical Music Profession.* Oxon: Routledge.

Statistik Austria (2020) *Kulturstatistik 2018.* Wien: Statistik Austria.

Statistik Austria (2021a) *Tourismus-Satellitenkonto – Wertschöpfung.* https://www.statistik.at/web_de/statistiken/wirtschaft/tourismus/tourismus-satellitenkonto/wertschoepfung/index.html [accessed June 21, 2021].

Statistik Austria (2021b) *GDP in 2020: Historic decline of 6.3%.* http://www.statistik.at/web_en/statistics/Economy/national_accounts/gross_domestic_product/annual_data/index.html [accessed 22 June, 2021].

Tatli, A., & Özbilgin, M. (2012) Surprising intersectionalities of inequality and privilege: the case of the arts and cultural sector. Equality, Diversity and Inclusion: An International Journal, 31(3), 249–265.

Tošić, L. (2021): Wiener Philharmoniker wurden bei Corona-Impfung vorgereiht. Der Standard, 17 April, 2021, https://www.derstandard.at/story/2000125915161/vorgereiht-wiener-philharmoniker-bekamen-die-corona-impfung?ref=rss [accessed June 18, 2021].

Trippl, M., Tödtling, F., & Schuldner, R. (2013) Creative and cultural industries in Austria. In: Lazzeretti, L. (ed.) *Creative industries and innovation in Europe.* London: Routledge, pp. 86–102.

Tschmuck P. (2021) *der österreichische musikarbeitsmarkt in der covid-19-pandemie.* https://musikwirtschaftsforschung.wordpress.com/2021/05/14/der-osterreichische-musikarbeitsmarkt-in-der-covid-19-pandemie/ [accessed June 18, 2021].

Wetzel, P. (2018): *Soziale Lage der Kunstschaffenden und Kunst- und Kulturvermittler/innen in Österreich. Ein Update der Studie "Zur sozialen Lage der Künstler und Künstlerinnen in Österreich"* 2008 (with collaboration of Lisa Danzer, Veronika Ratzenböck, Anja Lungstraß und Günther Landsteiner). Wien: L&L Sozialforschung; österreichische kulturdokumentation.

Wodak, R., de Cillia, R., Reisigl M. & Liebhart K. (2009) *Discursive Construction of National Identity.* 2nd ed., Edinburgh: Edinburgh University Press.

World Tourism Organization (2018) *Tourism and Culture Synergies*, Madrid: UNWTO, doi: https://doi.org/10.18111/9789284418978.

9 Artists in the COVID-19 pandemic

Use of lockdown time, skill development, and audience perceptions in Colombia and Spain

Javier A. Rodríguez-Camacho, Pedro Rey-Biel, Jeremy C. Young and Mónica Marcell Romero Sánchez

The effects of the COVID-19 pandemic have been felt in different ways across the creative industries. On the one hand, the performing arts almost completely ceased normal operations, since performance and rehearsal venues closed with no clear reopening date (Chuba 2020). In the music industry, the losses due to the impossibility of performing and presenting live music shows during 2020 were estimated at $8.9 billion worldwide (Pollstar 2020). On the other hand, some creative sectors adapted to the new context faster, finding ways to restore some type of operations or even thriving in the so-called "new normal". For example, the growth of the video streaming market during the pandemic has been estimated at around 55%, increasing from $104.11 billion in 2019 to $161.37 billion in 2020 (Ball 2020). Similarly, music streaming platforms such as Spotify increased their number of paying users by 21% between March 2020 and March 2021 (Nicolau 2021). Outside the arts, other creative industries have also boomed in this period; for instance, about 30% of adults reported having tried a new gaming activity during the lockdown (Arkenberg 2020).

These disparate outcomes aside, one arguably uniform effect has taken hold across the creative industries in the form of a surplus of available time. The reduction in commuting time, social commitments, and other activities curtailed by the pandemic, particularly during the lockdown periods, gave nearly everyone additional free hours. It was not unusual, especially in the initial stages of the pandemic, to find people sharing in their social media the creative objectives they were pursuing, the lectures they had attended (remotely), or even the TV shows and reading they were catching up with. On the supply side, creators may have faced a similar situation. Indeed, evidence from a survey of Spanish artists and workers in the cultural sector found that they continued to spend significant amounts of time during the lockdown on activities related to their creative practice – starting new projects, adapting existing ones, picking up others, and even splitting some of that time with more market-oriented activities, such as rethinking their

DOI: 10.4324/9781003128274-12

business models or increasing their marketing efforts (Abeledo Sanchís 2020). The situation was paradoxical in one sense, as artists may have had more time to spend on creative activities but limited access to circulation and distribution spaces, resulting in fewer chances to present their work, commercialize it, and gauge audience reactions.

This study examines the net effects of these shocks, linking artists' use of time to the reactions that the works they created during the pandemic generated from an audience. We exploit the unexpected shock of the time surplus described above to investigate the strategies that artists used to deal with the effects of the pandemic. Among the many ways in which artists could have used their lockdown time, we focus on two types of activities: developing artistic skills and improving business, marketing, and entrepreneurship skills. These two are not mutually exclusive, as improvements in one of these areas could have affected the other, and some artists may have worked on both types of skills. We propose three mechanisms for the development of these skills: formal training by following a structured program, autonomous training (e.g. reading on one's own, attending webinars, rehearsing), and teaching others one's practice. We used a survey to understand and measure these activities during the lockdown, including two kinds of questions. The first type asked respondents for their subjective perception of the changes experienced in these activities because of the lockdown; we then asked them to indicate the exact number of hours spent in a typical week on activities connected to the development of their artistic and business skills.

A non-probabilistic sample of 345 artists from Colombia and Spain participated in the survey. These two countries were chosen because of the size and characteristics of their creative industries, cultural and linguistic proximity, and the research team's access to artists and audiences. We found that a majority of artists in both countries reduced the time spent on production, distribution, and circulation activities during the pandemic. The capacity to adapt and the access to digital creation, production, and circulation spaces seems to have been essential for the continuation of creative activities. Nevertheless, many artists devoted more time to reflection, research, and preparation of creative works during the lockdown, irrespective of their field or material restrictions. Learning activities were also among the ones most frequently mentioned by the artists. Furthermore, the Colombian artists in our sample invested a statistically significant additional amount of time in autonomous learning related to business, marketing, and entrepreneurship. The differences in time allocations for the Spanish subset of the sample were not statistically significant.

A second stage of our study applied an experimental design to assess the audience reactions to the work of 18 Colombian visual artists who participated in the survey. Each artist chose two works, one created before and the other after the start of the pandemic, both of which they considered equivalent in format, material, technique, and effort. These works were randomly and anonymously presented to 290 experiment participants in Colombia, recruited from a pool of university students, who were asked for their subjective evaluation and emotional reactions. Additionally, a panel of experts evaluated these works to provide a more objective measure of their quality and characteristics. We found that the ratings of pre- and post-pandemic works created by a specific artist were statistically different, whereas there was no similar difference in the total sample of audience and expert scores. That is, the overall field of painting or digital illustration has not been changed by the pandemic, although some artists' work has been affected in ways that observers can notice. On average, audience and expert ratings of post-pandemic works were lower. Changes in the creators' skill level may explain these differences, as all the cases where an artist's post-pandemic work obtained a higher audience rating involved creators who used their lockdown time to develop their artistic and/or business skills.

Furthermore, when we estimated an econometric model with the post-pandemic audience rating as the dependent variable and skill levels and use of time during the lockdown as independent variables, we found that higher-quality work was created by artists who had spent time developing their skills in the past, though not necessarily during the pandemic. However, the time when newly developed skills materialize in one's work is not obvious, making it harder to parse the short-term effect of lockdown time allocations. There were, however, strong and evident links between training, work quality, and ratings. Moreover, selection effects were involved in the decision to use time developing a certain type of skills: 67% of the artists who worked on their artistic skills had a below-average self-assessed skill level, while 89% of those who focused on business skills reported already having an above-average business skills level. It is also possible, however, that choosing to use lockdown time to develop one's skills may negatively affect artists' work, if they reduce their creative time to perform market-related activities or even for further training.

The rest of this chapter is organized as follows. First, we present some contextual information on the state of the creative industries in Colombia and Spain in the wake of the pandemic. Next, we introduce our model and its theoretical foundations, the research instruments, and the empirical strategy. We then discuss the results, beginning with the survey findings and continuing on to the experimental study, including the estimation of the econometric model. We close with brief concluding remarks and recommendations.

An overview of the creative industries in Colombia and Spain

Despite the many macroeconomic and sociopolitical differences that may exist between Colombia and Spain, their creative industries share several similarities in their development and magnitude. Between 2014 and 2019, the contribution of the creative industries to Colombia's GDP was 3.2% on average (Departamento Administrativo Nacional de Estadísticas 2020); in Spain during the same time period, it averaged 3.27% (Ministerio de Educación, Cultura y Deporte 2020). On the demand side, a national survey in 2017 showed that 40.5% of Colombians age 12 or older had gone to the cinema at least once, 53.9% had listened to recorded music, and 67.9% had watched other types of audiovisual content in the past year (Sistema de Información de Economía Naranja 2021). In Spain, a similar survey conducted in 2018 and 2019 found that 57.8% of the population age 15 and over had gone to the cinema at least once in the past year, 85.8% listened to recorded music at least once a month, and 65.1% had watched videos or other types of audiovisual content in the past 12 months (MECD 2019). Although there are certainly important differences between the two markets (for instance, Spain's access to a common European market finds no parallel in Colombia), a macroeconomic look at both countries suggests a proximity that may not be as transparent for other countries in their regions, such as Argentina (where creative industries made a 2.5% contribution to GDP in 2017) or the UK (5.9% in 2019) (Department for Digital, Culture, Media and Sports 2021; Ministerio de Hacienda 2018).

Although detailed statistics on the effects of COVID-19 on the creative industries are still being developed, it is already possible to find evidence indicating the impact of the pandemic. Colombia's GDP decreased 6.8% in 2020 relative to the previous year (DANE 2021), whereas in Spain the estimated reduction in GDP was around 11% (Instituto Nacional de Estadística 2021). Between January and September 2020, the number of creative industry workers in Colombia decreased by 11.9%, compared to the same period in 2019 (DANE 2020). In Spain, the number of these workers decreased by 5.9% from 2019 to 2020 (MCUD 2021b).

Less systematic accounts paint a similarly complex picture. In April 2020, the Observatorio de la Cultura, a Spanish think tank specializing in the creative industries, surveyed a sample of 476 creative workers, finding that 23% of them had completely stopped their activities, with 66.7% continuing their work remotely, albeit with significant reductions in output. Moreover, the average expected loss of revenue for the year was 36%, with more than 35% of respondents claiming that they would lose between half and all their revenue for 2020 (Observatorio de la Cultura 2020). More than three-quarters of organizations and workers in the creative industries in Spain stated that their plans for the year were affected by the pandemic. The strategies these organizations used to deal with this shock included working remotely and reducing their workforce, with 42.5% reducing their activity to the bare minimum. Those in the interdisciplinary and performing arts were the most heavily affected, with larger organizations and those in the editorial business or cultural management facing the greatest reductions in the size of their workforce (Abeledo Sanchís 2020). In Colombia, up to 34% of the activities in the punk rock circuit had still not resumed in either live or virtual formats as of late 2020 (Campion & Rodríguez-Camacho 2020), a figure that was probably approximately applicable to live music in general. For their part, Colombian art galleries and museums lost more than 60% of their income, and some were facing the threat of permanent closure, despite increasing their audience in 2020 through digital channels (Noriega & Lizarazo 2021).

Some of these effects were unavoidable, given the restrictions on circulation and gatherings entailed by the obligatory lockdowns. In Colombia, a strict national lockdown started on 24 March 2020 (Symmes Cobb 2020) and, after many extensions, ended on 1 September 2020 (Mercado 2020; Taylor 2020), after which selective lockdowns continued. In Spain, a strict national lockdown started on 13 March (Hernández 2020) and continued until 21 June (Martinez 2020). The two-month difference between the lockdown periods is amplified by the fact that some cultural activities returned in Spain during the summer until the second wave of the pandemic forced new restrictions, whereas in Colombia activities such as concerts or live theatre performances did not return until very late in 2020. In this study, our artist-level approach helps us bypass the heterogeneities between countries and artistic fields that we would otherwise face when trying to make cross-country comparisons regarding the effects of the pandemic. That is, we compare each artist with himself or herself by comparing the same artist's works before and after the start of the pandemic, thereby isolating the variable pertaining to their use of time and enabling us to explore its correlation with audience ratings of the works created.

Theoretical foundations of the study

Our approach to this study is grounded in three streams of prior literature. The first concerns the role of creative and business skills in the career outcomes of artists. Since at least the 1990s, several US universities have been supporting different types of initiatives aimed at developing the business skills of their arts students (Beckman 2007). In more recent years, these efforts have become widespread and systematic. In 2018, more than 30 major US universities had arts-business incubators or arts ventures competitions, with a growing number offering dedicated arts entrepreneurship programs or certificates (Mullaney 2018). Similarly, in Colombia and Spain, arts entrepreneurship programs are being offered in increasing numbers, and several business-oriented courses can be found in arts schools' curricula. Our research extends this line by empirically investigating the role of both creative and business skills in the market performance of artists, in the context of how these artists used their time during the lockdowns.

The second stream pertains to audience evaluation of cultural goods through user reviews. Artistic works are defined as experience goods, meaning that their quality is unknown to buyers until after they have purchased or consumed them (Nelson 1970). This literature postulates that expert and/or user reviews offer information on an artistic work's quality, such that higher quality goods obtain better reviews and therefore attain superior market results. A very fertile research line has explored these ideas (Basuroy et al., 2003; Gemser et al., 2007; Liu, 2006; McKenzie, 2012; Souza et al., 2019). Our model measures the number of hours artists invested in various activities during the lockdown and uses that number as an independent variable when examining the audience ratings of the works these artists created before and after the pandemic. We hold that artists who improved their artistic skills during the pandemic should attain better ratings for their post-pandemic work. Similarly, artists who developed their business skills should have become better at marketing and promoting their own work. The role of promotion and customer engagement via marketing strategies is positively correlated with the market performance of artistic and entertainment goods (Elberse & Eliashberg 2003; Hackley & Tiwsakul 2006; Hennig-Thurau & Houston 2019; Ho-Dac et al., 2013). Therefore, we propose that by improving their artistic skills, artists can offer a higher quality of work and hence obtain better ratings. Similarly, or in conjunction, by improving their business skills, artists could understand and engage their audiences in a more meaningful way, resulting in higher ratings of their work.

We are interested in measuring the different responses to the pandemic observed among artists, specifically their use of time during the lockdown, to understand the market outcomes to which these actions could lead. We propose a model in which our dependent variable, representing market results, is based on user reviews (ratings) of a work, and we explore the correlation of this variable with our measure of the artistic and business skills of its creator. Participants in an experimental design provided the ratings of these works. In this way, we draw on the third relevant research stream, which approaches consumer behaviour using experimental methods (Gneezy et al., 2012; Hennig-Thurau et al., 2006; Kalwani & Yim 1992; McKenzie et al., 2019).

By combining these three approaches, we can analyze the pandemic's effect directly on artists, since we obtain audience ratings for the works they created before and after the beginning of the pandemic. Moreover, we can discuss the implications of the strategies used by the artists to deal with the pandemic lockdowns and how these strategies impact audiences' perceptions of their work. We can characterize the emotions these works generate in the audience and whether respondents can determine if a work has been created before or after the pandemic. Furthermore, we obtain primary evidence on the role of artistic and business skills in the market performance of artworks, shedding light on the role these types of skills play in an artist's career.

Methods and materials

In this section, we present our hypotheses and empirical strategy, the experimental design, the survey used to collect data, and the econometric model we estimated.

Hypotheses

Building on the works cited in the preceding section, we formulated the following hypotheses:

1 Audience ratings will increase with the (self-reported) level of artistic skills of the creator.
2 Audience ratings will increase with the (self-reported) level of business skills of the creator.
3 Audience ratings will increase with the quality of a work (as rated by a panel of experts).
4 The audience rating of works created by artists who used their time during the lockdown to develop their artistic skills will increase relative to the rating of their works before the pandemic.
5 The audience rating of works created by artists who used their time during the lockdown to develop their business skills will increase relative to the rating of their works before the pandemic.

We test these hypotheses by (1) comparing the audience's ratings of the works created by a given artist before and after the pandemic (H4, H5), and 2) estimating an econometric model in which the dependent variable is the audience's ratings of an artist's post-pandemic work (H1, H2, H3).

We chose audience ratings of the work created by the artists as our dependent variable because actual market outcomes could be affected by the economic impacts of the pandemic, perhaps on a lagged basis. Moreover, if we asked participants a question like "Would you buy this work?" the validity of the findings might be limited by the hypothetical nature of the purchase decision, since no real money would be involved in the experiment. However, audience ratings are a good proxy for the market performance of a cultural good. User reviews in the form of ratings or evaluations have often been used as indicators of the quality of such goods (Chintagunta et al., 2010; Dhar & Chang 2009; Zhou & Duan 2016). We also sought to address the often-idiosyncratic nature of popular ratings by including in our analysis an expert assessment of the works, which provided us with a more objective evaluation of the goods. Other researchers have applied a similar strategy, obtaining expert ratings from websites or databases and analyzing them in combination with user reviews. We asked a panel of art critics and educators to anonymously rate the works presented to the experimental participants, and we included this control in our model.

Our identification strategy rests on the fact that the pandemic has given us a natural quasi-experimental setting in which to study the effect of artistic and business skill development on the market performance of artists. Categorical responses can be established based on how artists used their time during the lockdown, and these may be identified as treatments into which they self-select. Those who did not alter their pre-pandemic time allocations or used their time to study or work on unrelated subjects would function as the control group. Additionally, we have self-reported measurements of the artists' skill levels, as well as expert ratings of their current and past work, variables we include in our model in order to isolate as much as possible the time-allocation effects.

Data collection and experimental design

This study comprised two stages: an analysis of the artists' responses to the pandemic in terms of their use of the surplus of time derived from the lockdown, and audience and expert evaluation of the works created by the artists before and during the pandemic. In this section, we present the instruments developed to obtain the data in each stage.

Artist survey

The information from the artists was collected by means of an online survey. It was distributed, using a targeted approach, in Bogotá from 2 to 18 December 2020 and in Barcelona from 25 January to 10 February 2021. In Colombia, the survey was posted on Pontificia Universidad Javeriana's social media accounts, sent to faculty in the relevant departments (Arts, Design, Media), and shared with associations of artists (musicians, illustrators). In Spain, the survey was shared with professors in the arts faculty at Universidad de Barcelona, Universidad de Sevilla, Universidad Complutense de Madrid, Universidad de Vigo, Universidad de Salamanca, Universidad del País Vasco, Universidad de Granada, Universidad Politécnica de Valencia, and Universidad de Zaragoza, as well as with associations of artists (magicians, musicians). Additionally, research team members used their informal social networks to distribute the survey. A non-probabilistic, convenience sampling method was followed. A total of 345 artists and workers in the creative sector received the survey, 202 from Colombia and 143 from Spain. After the exclusion of participants who did not complete the survey, our final non-representative sample included 123 artists, 68 from Colombia and 55 from Spain. Given the exploratory nature of this stage of the study, we consider the size of the sample adequate, particularly since the study also involved a larger number of participants who evaluated these artists' work. The descriptive information obtained from the survey helps us to establish a context for our analysis, but the estimations and statistical analysis take place at the level of the artist, drawing on a pool of over 2,500 audience ratings.

The research team developed the artist survey. It included questions on how the artists used their time during the lockdown, specifically in relation to activities that may lead to changes in artistic and business skills. These activities fell into the following categories: Creation/Reflection/Exploration (i.e. time to think about and work on their art), Formal Learning, Autonomous Learning, and Teaching. We based these mechanisms on the work of Fiorella and Mayer (2013, 2014), who explored the relative effects of learning by teaching others and found that teaching leads to greater persistence of learning in those performing the activity. In other words, artists could improve their artistic skills by teaching others their practice, aside from taking courses or training on their own. We measured the weekly number of hours devoted to each of the aforementioned activities, comparing these to the hours they reported having dedicated to the same activities before the pandemic. For instance, we asked, "How many hours did you spend in a typical week, before the pandemic, teaching others your artistic practice?" We then repeated the same question for the period during the lockdown. Subjective measures of artists' perception of how the pandemic changed their use of time were also included.

With regard to business skills, since the heterogeneity in the responses could be so great and specific to each field and context, we decided to use training in business as a proxy for the time allocated by each artist to developing the business side of their creative practice. That is, we asked the artists if they had taken formal training on business-related topics during the lockdown (e.g. registering for a course on marketing), or if they informally searched for and learned from information or training on business-related topics (e.g. attending webinars, watching videos, reading, searching for mentors).

We also asked the artists to assess their own skills before and after the pandemic, as well as their experience, professional training, past achievements, and some market performance indicators during the pandemic (e.g. "Did you generate any income from works created during the pandemic?"). We controlled for the artistic discipline as well, since not all artists could have used the time to continue creating, due to technical challenges or lack of access to equipment or appropriate spaces. Questions on the artists' ability to use the spaces where they most often created and circulated their work were also included. We asked the participants to focus on a representative period before the pandemic when responding to these questions; otherwise, some of the possible forms of cultural participation would have been affected by the lockdown and restrictions.

The survey was validated by means of a protocol analysis with 12 academicians and artists. We showed them the survey form and asked them to answer the questions with us, suggesting adjustments in how the questions were worded, options we may have forgotten in multiple-choice questions, or possible additional questions. Some minor adjustments were made following this process, to make the instrument easier to understand for participants in each country, using regional versions of Spanish.

Experimental design

The experimental stage of this study sought to link the ways artists used their time during the lockdown with potential market results. To achieve this, we asked the artists who participated in the survey to share their works with us and then presented these to some participants using an experimental design. These were Colombian adults recruited from a pool of university students, faculty, graduates, administrative staff, and others in the personal networks of research team members. No qualification was required other than residing in Colombia and having Internet access. A total of 290 individuals participated in this phase.

To obtain the works needed for the experimental stage, the artists who had expressed interest were invited to voluntarily share with the researchers two comparable works of art, one created before and another during the pandemic. We screened these works to confirm that they were indeed comparable. The works deemed suitable for the experimental study were coded and randomly presented to the participants, without indicating the artist, whether the work was created before or after the lockdown, or any other information. After observing each work, the participants completed a quantitative questionnaire. These scores were used as proxies for the market performance of such works. Our goal was to understand the role artistic skills and business skills play in the audience evaluation of cultural goods. Hence, obtaining an indicator from the audience such as their subjective valuation of the works allowed us to make suitable comparisons between artists who used their time during the lockdown differently and who have different levels of artistic and business skills.

The experimental design was developed based on Gross and Levenson (1995), Ray and Gross (2007), and Gilman et al. (2017), who have presented audiovisual works to participants and recorded their emotional reactions using original questionnaires. We used Ray and Gross's (2007) scale for emotion elicitation for film, translated it into Spanish, and included an item to measure each participant's valuation of the works presented. This new item was analogous to the scales presented on websites where individuals can rate a cultural good (IMDB, Filmaffinity, Rate Your Music, Discogs, Goodreads, etc.). Often these scales do not include any instructions next to them, implying that they are meant to capture a subjective valuation of the good in question. Instead of the usual five stars found in such cases, we used a scale from 0 to 8 to maintain consistency with the emotion elicitation scale.

The experimental sessions were conducted remotely by sending the participants an anonymous link to access an online form created using

Qualtrics. The participants were presented with the instructions, followed by a trial run to familiarize them with the experimental setting and procedure. The experiment comprised three rounds. In each round the participant was shown a work of art and was then asked to answer the experimental questionnaire (rating and emotional reactions). A round was completed when five different artworks, all randomly taken from the pool, had been presented to a participant. Therefore, each participant rated 15 works. Participants were not shown the same artwork a second time. A 30-second mandatory break followed the completion of each round, to allow the participants to rest and to reduce their emotional and cognitive demands. The next round started immediately after that. After the third round was completed, a post-experimental survey was presented, including questions on cultural participation and their demographic information.

The experiment contained two (implicit) treatments related to whether the work a participant was presented had been created by an artist who developed his or her (1) artistic and (2) business skills during the pandemic. We followed a within-subject design; that is, the works viewed by each participant were completely randomized and could include pre- and post-pandemic works by artists who did or did not use lockdown time to develop their business or artistic skills. This design minimized potential biases due to the order of presentation.

A representative screenshot of the experimental setting, including a work of art from our pool, the subjective valuation question, and the scale included in the experimental instrument, is shown in Figure 9.1.

When asked for their emotional reaction, participants were given a list of 18 emotions, such as *amusement, pride, fear, contempt, joy, interest, surprise, happiness,* and *confusion,* and were instructed to select, on a scale from 0 to 8, the number best indicating the intensity of the emotion they felt when observing the work. They could choose as many or as few emotions as they wished. Next, they were asked whether they felt any other emotion not included on the list and, if so, to report the name and intensity of that emotion on the same 0–8 scale. After this, participants were asked when they believed the work had been created – either before or after the beginning of the pandemic. Finally, they were asked if they had previously seen the work.

Results

In this section, we present the results from the different stages of the study, beginning with the artist survey and continuing with the audience reactions.

Demographic information and descriptive statistics

As noted above, we received 68 valid artist survey responses from Colombia and 55 from Spain.[1] Table 9.1 summarizes the artistic work and training of the respondents.

En la siguiente escala elige el número que mejor represente cuánto te gusta esta obra.

Nada 0	1	2	3	Más o menos 4	5	6	7	Mucho 8
○	○	○	○	○	○	○	○	○

→

Figure 9.1 Representative screenshot of the experimental setting presented to each participant when asked to rate a work (in Spanish). Gabriel Angel with permission for its anonymous use in the experiment and its inclusion in this chapter.

The Colombian sample was 39.7% female, with 3% of respondents not identifying as binary or preferring not to answer. The overrepresentation of male respondents aligns with the gender distribution of the creative industries in Colombia. The mode of the sample's age distribution was the 41–45 age group (22.9%), followed by the 18–24 age group (18.0%). The Spanish sample was only 16.3% female, with 4.6% of respondents not identifying as binary or preferring not to answer. Although female participation in the creative industries in Spain continues to be below the average across all productive sectors, in 2020 it was estimated at around 41.4% of the total workforce (MCUD 2021a). Our sampling bias with regard to gender could be an effect of the age distribution of the respondents: 33.3% of them were 51 or older, followed by 14.3% at age 36–40 and 14.3% at 41–45. In the last decade, the gender gap in the Spanish workforce was the largest in the 55–64 age bracket. This gap was 14.2% in 2019, with a national average of 10.8% (INE 2020). The remaining demographic variables in the Spanish sample were consistent with those found in the Colombian sample.

Table 9.1 shows the largest group of Colombian respondents who worked in the visual and cinematographic arts (44.1% including visual arts, film, video, and photography). In the Spanish sample, nearly half of all respondents were working in the performing arts, with the visual and

Table 9.1 Distribution of fields of artistic specialization in the sample.

	Proportion of respondents in the sample (%)	
	Colombia	Spain
Artistic field of work		
Visual arts	23.53%	14.55%
Music	17.65%	16.36%
Film and video	14.71%	1.82%
Performing arts	11.76%	47.27%
Dance and ballet	8.82%	0.00%
Photography	5.88%	5.45%
Electronic and transmedia arts	4.41%	0.00%
Literature	4.41%	5.45%
Traditional arts and artisanship	1.47%	1.82%
Others	7.36%	7.28%
Education		
Professional training in the artistic field of their practice	68.79%	65.45%
Other artistic training	7.01%	3.64%
Other type of training	24.20%	30.91%
Experience		
Less than five years	23.56%	27.27%
Five to ten years	34.39%	25.45%
More than ten years	42.05%	47.28%

cinematographic arts (visual arts, film, video, and photography) ranking second at 21.8%. The proportion of musicians was nearly identical in both samples. This distribution generally aligns with recent surveys of the creative industries in Spain, such as that of Abeledo Sanchís (2020), in which the performing arts (including music) represented the largest cultural sector in their sample (33.2%), followed by the visual arts (17.3%). Our somewhat different percentages may be an effect of the sampling frame, since the survey was shared with networks of stage performers (magicians, musicians, actors) in Spain and faculty in the Department of Visual Arts in Bogotá. We do not claim representativeness of the samples but simply that the two subsets of the sample are sufficiently similar to enable comparisons between them.

Despite these differences in the fields of specialization, the samples are consistent with regard to the artists' training and experience. A large majority of the Colombian respondents (70.6%) had professional training in their field of practice, and over 63% used more than half of their weekly productive time to work on their creative practice. About 41.2% of the respondents started devoting that amount of time to their work within the last five years (2015–2019), whereas 35.3% started doing so in 2009 or earlier. In the Spanish sample, 65.45% had professional training in their field, a figure comparable to the 71.9% determined by the Spanish Ministry of Culture across the industry (MCUD 2021a), and 38.2% used more than half of their weekly productive time to work on their creative practice.

Use of time during the lockdown and the effects of the pandemic

Our survey included two types of questions regarding the use of time. The first set was based on subjective measures (perception), and the second asked respondents to specify the number of hours spent on certain types of activities (objective). The activities covered in these questions roughly correspond to those entailed by the creative industries value chain (*Creation, Production, Distribution,* and *Participation*) and were intended to register the time used in learning activities concerning their artistic and business skills. Table 9.2 presents the results from the first type of questions.

As Table 9.2 shows, more than 51% of the Colombian artists felt they had allocated more or a lot more time to training or studying during the lockdown. Looking exclusively at creation activities, 41.2% claimed they used more time or a lot more time, with 19.1% indicating they had used the same time as before the lockdown. These results seem to suggest that overall, extra time was allocated to learning and training activities, whereas the preparation and actual creation of new works did not seem to be affected as clearly in either direction. In our sample of Spanish artists, 41.8% reported using more or a lot more time on learning and studying, while 47.3% allocated more or a lot more time to research, reflection, and preparation. This behaviour is consistent with the evidence that artists

Table 9.2 Artists' self-reported perception of the time allocated to different activities connected to their creative practice during the lockdown.

Activities	Colombia					Spain				
	A lot less	Less	Same	More	A lot more	A lot less	Less	Same	More	A lot more
Research, Reflection, and preparation	10.29%	25.00%	23.53%	26.47%	14.71%	20.00%	10.91%	21.82%	34.55%	12.73%
Training or study	14.71%	19.12%	14.71%	30.88%	20.59%	18.18%	12.73%	27.27%	25.45%	16.36%
Creation	16.18%	23.53%	19.12%	25.00%	16.18%	16.36%	21.82%	21.82%	29.09%	10.91%
Production	22.06%	27.94%	10.29%	25.00%	14.71%	23.64%	25.45%	27.27%	16.36%	7.27%
Distribution and circulation	38.24%	19.12%	10.29%	22.06%	10.29%	47.27%	14.55%	27.27%	7.27%	3.64%
Managerial or entrepreneurial tasks	20.59%	25.00%	20.59%	22.06%	11.76%	38.18%	20.00%	23.64%	14.55%	3.64%

continued working, albeit remotely, during the lockdown. Indeed, the creation of "new ideas, products, and projects I had no time to work on before" was the action most frequently reported in the survey conducted by Abeledo Sanchís (2020) on the use of time during the lockdown. The same study found that education, training, and the acquisition of new skills were among the activities that artists most frequently undertook during the lockdown.

Along the same lines, 35.3% of the Colombian sample reported having continued to create and produce works that were similar or comparable to those before the pandemic. Among the Colombian artists sampled, 79.4% said they regularly create their work in their home or their own workshop, with 66.2% stating that they had access to that space during the lockdown. Thus, it is not entirely unexpected that more than one-third of them were able to continue creating. The same cannot be said of production, distribution, and circulation, with 49.5% and 57.4% of the Colombian artists in the sample saying they used less or a lot less time in those activities during the lockdown, respectively. Looking at the use of time in production activities reported by the Spanish artists, we see that their answers skew toward a reduction; 49% claimed to have used less or a lot less time, with another 27.3% reporting that they used the same amount of time as before the lockdown. This was also the case for circulation, with 61.8% using less or a lot less time for such activities. Since the circulation spaces available for performing artists (nearly half of the Spanish sample) are strongly connected to public, physical locations such as theatres, concert halls, and venues with stages, which were largely inaccessible during the lockdown period and even afterward, this finding is predictable.

In Colombia, 51.5% of the sample reported not generating any income through their creations during the lockdown. Among those who did, for 20.6% of them the income came from works created before the pandemic, while 19.1% generated this income with works created during the lockdown. These figures merit consideration by social planners, given that 22.1% of the sample said they had no other sources of income. Regarding government initiatives supporting the creative sector in the pandemic, only 1.5% of Colombian respondents received state funds. The proportion of Spanish artists in our sample who did not generate income during the lockdown was 61.8%, higher than the Colombian case, perhaps due to the prevalence of performing artists in the sample, as this group had a harder time replacing their circulation spaces during the lockdown. Additionally, the 20% who generated economic resources in the period did it with works predating the pandemic, and only 1.8% had access to government funds. Moreover, at least 26% of the respondents in the Spanish sample did not have income sources other than those connected to their creative practice. These results resonate with other works on the effects of the pandemic on the creative industries, in both Spain and Colombia, and attest to the economic impacts of the pandemic on the sector.

Time allocations to improving artistic or business skills during the lockdown

We now turn to the results of the second type of questions, regarding how the artists used their time during the lockdown. We asked the participants to indicate the exact number of hours they spent on each of seven activities on a representative week both before the pandemic and during the lockdown, as shown in Table 9.3. The seven activities were presented in a list and the participant needed simply to write in the number of hours. Respondents could leave fields blank. The difference between self-study and formal study was made clear in each question; the latter entailed participation in a structured program at an institute, university, conservatory, or online, whereas the former referred to watching videos, reading on their own, or attending webinars or mentorship sessions.

There was a small increase in the time dedicated to improving artistic skills autonomously in both countries and a decrease in the number of hours used to teach others. In Colombia, the time used for the formal study of artists' practice decreased, whereas it increased in Spain. This difference may be due to the different distributions of fields and ages between the two samples. Spanish artists reported that they devoted less time to improving their business skills, both through formal and/or autonomous

Table 9.3 Use of time by Colombian and Spanish artists before the pandemic and during the lockdown.

| | Activities | Hours spent in a representative week | | | |
| | | Colombia | | Spain | |
		Pre	Post	Pre	Post
Artistic skills	Formal study of your creative practice	6.28	6.06	3.24	3.74
	Self-study, rehearsal, and autonomous improvement of your creative practice	7.94	8.62	8.62	8.88
	Teaching others your creative practice	7.53	7.20	4.47	3.54
Business skills	Formal study of topics related to business, marketing, and entrepreneurship	2.51	2.87	1.48	1.11
	Self-study of topics related to business, marketing, and entrepreneurship	3.02	4.42	2.41	2.31
Other skills	Formal study of topics other than arts or business	3.29	3.37	4.27	3.80
	Self-study of topics other than arts or business	3.78	4.31	3.02	6.76

study, in contrast to the Colombian results, which show an increase in the two allocations related to business skills. This difference may reflect the availability of broader welfare programs in Spain but not in Colombia, where artists had to search for alternative sources of income during the lockdown. Interestingly, there was a noticeable increase in the hours the Spanish artists devoted to autonomous study of topics other than arts or business. However, none of the differences was statistically significant. The only statistically significant difference concerned the self-study of topics related to business, marketing, and entrepreneurship among Colombian artists, with a greater number of hours being used during the lockdown. This reinforces our intuition on the changes in income-generating activities and the economic preoccupations artists in the two countries faced during the pandemic, with those in Colombia feeling more strongly compelled to explore new ways to make money.[2]

In both countries, several artists claimed to have experienced changes in their skills as a consequence of the pandemic. The participants were asked to rate themselves on certain aspects of their creative work (i.e. technique, experience, promotional skills, commercial skills, teamwork, creativity, awards and accolades, learning capacity, teaching capacity, innovation, and research), using a scale from 1 (lowest) to 5 (highest). Next, they were asked whether they believed some of those scores had changed due to the pandemic. More than 40% of the Colombian sample reported an increase in their skills. Another 11% said they improved their technique, 9% said they strengthened their creativity, and 7% improved their marketing and business skills. The reason provided was the extra time available to focus on a specific task. In the Spanish case, 47% reported a change in their skills after the lockdown. Technique improvement was reported by 14.5% of respondents, though none mentioned business skills at all. Asked about the reasons for this improvement, the Spanish artists primarily cited the extra time to think, practice, read, research, and create.

On the other hand, 25% of the Colombian and 20% of the Spanish respondents reported a decrease in their skill level. In Colombia, 9% claimed their experience and access to awards and grants had decreased. An additional 6% mentioned that their business skills declined. The Spanish participants reported a reduction in their teamwork skills (5.4%) and experience (3.6%). The reasons reported were the lack of access to their teams and equipment, social distancing due to healthcare restrictions, and the absence of circulation spaces. Emotional and psychological issues such as depression, lack of motivation, and concerns about the future were frequently mentioned, particularly in the Spanish sample.

The increase in the time used by Colombian participants in the informal study of business cannot be explained in a simplistic manner. The experimental stage of our study allows us to comment on such changes from the perspective of their potential market performance, as measured through audience ratings.

Experimental results

The experimental stage of the study took place between April and May 2021 in Colombia only, comprising three phases.[3]

Twenty-eight Colombian artists accepted the invitation to participate and shared their works with us, around 41% of those who participated in the survey. From this pool, we selected 36 works created by 18 different artists, based on their comparability and ease of presentation (e.g. we excluded videos over 5 minutes long or functional designs that could not be embedded in the experimental software). All artists were offered a participation incentive of 100,000 Colombian pesos (about 23 EUR).[4] Figure 9.2

Figure 9.2 The two works provided by one artist for our experiment: pre-pandemic (top), post-pandemic (bottom). Andrés Kal with permission for its anonymous use in the experiment and its inclusion in this chapter. (*Continued*)

Figure 9.2 (Continued)

shows two representative works shared by one of the artists who took part in the experiment.

In the second phase, to obtain expert evaluations of the 36 works used in the experiment, we contacted 12 evaluators with highly recognized careers in the arts, who have been involved in processes of evaluating artworks for awards or grants. None of these had taken part in the survey or the experiment. Each evaluator was presented with seven works, randomly selected from our pool, and asked to rate them using a quantitative instrument based on the criteria applied by the Colombian Ministry of Culture in its grant competitions. These criteria were *Technique* (dexterity in the use and transformation of artistic materials), *Investigation* (evidence of research in the creation process), *Experimentation* (critical and creative appropriation of the formal and conceptual practices of the discipline), and *Impact* (contributions to the artistic and cultural fields in the context in which the work was created). A link to a questionnaire programmed on Qualtrics was shared with the experts, using an environment and design similar to the one shown in Figure 9.1 above. The expert rating of a work, our proxy for an objective evaluation, was calculated as the average of the four evaluation criteria for all experts rating that work, on a scale from 0 to 8. We obtained 84 observations (full ratings of different works) from the 12 experts.

The final phase of the experiment comprised audience interactions with the selected works. A total of 290 Colombian adults participated in this phase. We obtained 2,516 observations, or an average of 8.68 per participant. The 18 works received an average of 69.88 observations (minimum 60, maximum 81). An observation consisted of a participant's rating of a work, on a scale from 0 to 8, as shown in Figure 9.1. Participants were additionally asked to indicate the emotions they felt when observing the work, rating the intensity of each emotion on the same scale. Finally, the participants were asked to state whether they believed the work had been created before or after the start of the pandemic. Each person spent an average of 26.7 minutes participating in the experiment, which was accessed remotely using a Qualtrics link at the participants' convenience and using the device of their preference. Demographic characteristics of the participants are presented in Table 9.4.

The average pre-pandemic expert rating for the works was 5.47, with a maximum of 7.50 and a minimum of 3.70. The audience pre-pandemic ratings were distributed between 6.30 and 3.43, with a mean of 4.80. There were no statistically significant differences between the two distributions. Moreover, the highest-rated work for the audiences was in the top five expert ratings and vice versa. This could mean that both the experts and

Table 9.4 Demographic characteristics of the experiment participants.

Gender	
Male	40.29%
Female	58.27%
Others	1.44%
Age	
18–24	73.05%
25–30	8.51%
31–35	2.84%
36–40	2.13%
41–45	2.84%
46–50	4.96%
51 or more	5.67%
Occupation	
Undergraduate student	70.71%
Graduate student	5.01%
Other type of student	11.43%
Full-time worker	2.14%
Other	10.71%

audiences can identify a high-quality pre-pandemic work and are aligned in their appreciation of it. We observed some divergence at the lower end of the rating distributions, since some of the works rated highest by the audience received below-average ratings from the experts. We will further discuss possible reasons for these potential discrepancies when presenting the results of the econometric model. For the post-pandemic works, the expert ratings averaged 5.40 with a maximum of 7.25 and a minimum of 3.08. For the audiences, the minimum was also 3.08, but with a maximum of 6.00 and an average of 4.74. The distributions were not statistically different. Interestingly, the top expert and audience-rated works from the pre- and post-pandemic groups were all created by different artists. The low scores were consistent across the two groups, with experts and audiences picking the same works. Hence, we could say that both could agree on what is a relatively low-quality post-pandemic work. In contrast, there was greater divergence as to who received the highest post-pandemic ratings.

A correlation analysis reveals that pre- and post-pandemic audience scores were strongly and positively correlated, signalling a consistency in the artistic preferences of the audience. On the other hand, there was almost no correlation between the pre- and post-pandemic expert ratings. We believe this is a consequence of the type of evaluation performed by experts, who (unlike the taste-driven audience members) may rate a work unfavourably if it fails to meet some objective criteria such as technique or innovation, even if it fits their individual preferences. In contrast, audiences may stick with their preferred artist even if the post-pandemic work has suffered relative to some objective and/or technical standard. Nevertheless, the post-pandemic expert and audience ratings were strongly and positively correlated. The literature proposes a positive link between high-quality experience goods and their audience reviews. We hold that the correlation just described confirms the link between our measure of quality (expert ratings) and audience ratings, one of our modelling assumptions.

Looking at how the artists responsible for the top- and bottom-rated works fared across time, we see that the creator of the highest audience-rated post-pandemic work was also the creator of the lowest expert-rated pre-pandemic work. Again, this result might point to disparities in quality evaluation criteria between the audience and experts. Strikingly, the creator of the highest expert-rated pre-pandemic work was also the creator of the lowest-rated post-pandemic work according to the experts, and the creators of the lowest expert-rated post-pandemic works were also responsible for two of the top four pre-pandemic works as rated by the experts. Thus, these changes in performance by the same creator over time may not indicate differences in evaluation capacities between experts and audiences as much as possible loss of skill during the lockdown, limitations in the creation or production processes, or even thematic disparities. Indeed, artists' own perception that their skills decreased during the pandemic was correlated with the post-pandemic expert ratings.

Regarding thematic differences in the works, the emotions most frequently reported in the observations of pre-pandemic works were *interest, surprise, confusion, joy, fun,* and *happiness.* For the post-pandemic counterparts, Interest and Confusion were the leaders, with Fun and Joy also appearing rather frequently. However, the post-pandemic works also induced more frequent reactions of Anger, Anxiety, and Misery, which were not mentioned in pre-pandemic works. The prevalence of Confusion may indicate that these works were hard for the audience to analyze and rate, whereas the experts may not have faced such problems. This explanation would be similar to that offered above for some of the rating differences, where the experts rated works poorly when the audience did not.

Table 9.5 presents the results of artist level *t*-tests performed to check if there were differences between their works' pre- and post-pandemic ratings. The table also shows the change in the weekly number of hours the artists used to develop their artistic and/or business skills, to help us identify potential cases of skill development and/or loss.

There are ten cases where the differences between the pre- and post-pandemic audience ratings are statistically significant; six of these have a higher pre-pandemic evaluation. This comparison is harder to make for

Table 9.5 Artist-level differences in the pre- and post-pandemic ratings of their work and time invested in developing their skills.

| Artist code | Differences in ratings (pre-pandemic score minus post-pandemic score) | | Differences in use of time (pre-pandemic hours minus post-pandemic hours) | |
	Audience	Experts	Artistic skills	Business skills
ach	0.4876	−2.2083*	8.00	−2.00
ac	−0.2148	−1.3333	−8.00	0.00
ad	−1.0935***	1.2500**	3.50	−1.50
ag	−1.4236***	−1.7500	9.00	−1.00
ap	1.1850***	0.3750	10.00	−18.00
ar	1.1296***	0.1667	−6.00	4.00
cd	0.4338	2.2917*	−3.00	4.00
fb	1.1638***	3.4167	1.00	0.00
js	−0.7244**	0.3750	−6.00	−7.00
ka	0.8205**	0.8750	−1.00	0.00
mb	−0.1084	1.7500**	9.00	2.00
pa	−0.3676	−0.8750	0.00	−7.00
pl	0.0044	−0.9167	8.00	0.00
rc	0.7755**	0.2917	−9.00	−1.00
rs	0.5607*	−0.6250	5.00	1.00
rj	−0.2347	−0.7500	−50.00	−10.00
ss	−1.3901***	−0.0417	−6.00	4.00
sg	−0.0306	−1.1250	−15.00	−4.00
Group	−0.0210	−0.1910	−2.81	−2.03

Notes: *p-value < 0.1, **p-value < 0.05, ***p-value < 0.01.

the expert ratings, since the number of observations is very small (between one and three, compared to the average of 69 audience ratings per work). When testing for differences in means for the whole group of pre- and post-pandemic scores, we found that the pre- and post-pandemic audience ratings were not statistically different, nor were the pre- and post-pandemic expert ratings. This supports our intuition to focus on the artist-level effects of the pandemic as a determining factor in the differences. Indeed, the hypothesis that the two sets of audience scores and expert scores are different is rejected, with p-values 0.823 and 0.283, respectively, at 95% certainty. Thus, we can conclude that the average quality of the pre-pandemic works in our sample is not different from the average quality of the post-pandemic works.

Looking at the specific artists, we see that in three of the six cases where the pre-pandemic work had a superior audience rating, the artists used less time to develop their artistic skills during the lockdown than before the pandemic. On the other hand, in all the cases where the post-pandemic work had a superior audience score, the artists used their lockdown time to develop at least one type of skill (artistic skills for one artist, business skills for two artists, and both skills in one instance). Therefore, we confirm hypotheses H4 and H5, concerning an anticipated increase in post-pandemic audience ratings for the artists who spent their lockdown time developing one or both types of skills.

It is also interesting that all the artists with a superior pre-pandemic audience rating had above-average artistic skills in the self-assessment requested from them in the survey, and none of them reported perceiving a loss in artistic skills. This could hint at selection effects in the decision to spend time developing a particular type of skill. Two-thirds of the artists who worked on their artistic skills started at self-reported below-average levels. On the other hand, 89% of the artists who worked on their business skills started at an above-average level in that area. Half of the artists who used time to develop both artistic and business skills already had a baseline level above average on both types. No artist of the 18 involved in the experimental stage reported perceiving a decrease in artistic skills, while one-third indicated that their business skills suffered through the lockdown. Moreover, 30% mentioned perceiving an increase in their technique, 25% in their experience, and 15% in their creativity, all of which are part of their artistic skills. Many said that having extra time to work and think was the reason for that increase. Nevertheless, an even larger proportion referred to the prevailing uncertainty, isolation, severe lack of funds, and economic hardship as factors affecting their work. A study by Spiro and coauthors (2021) conducted in the UK during the first 2020 lockdown similarly found a prevalence of uncertainty, vulnerability, and anxiety among performing artists, with implications for their emotional wellbeing. All these factors should be considered when contemplating the possible occurrence of skill loss during the lockdown and its potential effect on audience or expert ratings and perceptions.

Our data suggest that skill development and loss are complex processes, which may not necessarily be represented by continuously increasing or decreasing functions, nor do the slopes of their development and loss necessarily match each other, even taking into account that the timing of the manifestation of a skill gain or loss in one's work may vary. Maintenance of a basic skill level may require time too, not to mention the presence of emotional and health elements at play in the learning and/or training processes, as well as in the creative work itself. The mood of the creators, their environment or context of creation, and the thematic elements present in the work are intertwined, as one could surmise from the examples shown in Figure 9.2. The audience and expert ratings support the hypothesis that these differences can be perceived, although the underlying mechanisms are not obvious.

However limited, our insights align with theoretical and empirical predictions on the relevance of skill level in the rating of a creative work. We further explored this relationship by estimating the econometric model. From our pool of experimental results, we took the 1,246 observations corresponding to post-pandemic audience ratings as our dependent variable. We then combined these with the information on the creator obtained from the survey conducted in the first stage of the study. Next, we added the expert ratings for the specific works. Finally, since we had only 500 paired observations due to the within-subject randomization – that is, ratings from the same participant for both the pre- and post-pandemic works of a given artist – we used the following procedure to complete the missing pre-pandemic values: (1) For artists with statistically non-significant differences in their pre- and post-pandemic audience ratings (Table 9.5), we used the same rating as the post-pandemic rating that the participant assigned to the work. (2) For artists with statistically significant differences, we imputed a value that maintained the same difference from the participant's post-pandemic value. Thus, we had 500 observations with both ratings from the participants, and for the remainder we had an actual post-pandemic rating from the participants and a value we computed for the pre-pandemic score.[5]

The dataset we constructed by combining results from the survey, the expert evaluations, and the experiment had some limitations. The main limitation was that it represented an individual-level dataset built from work-level observations. This had implications for the variability and correlations of the variables, in the first case due to the repetition of certain values (e.g. all 65 observations for one artist had different user ratings but repeated the values for skills, experience, and use of time), and in the second due to the construction of some variables (the hours allocated to each type of skill added up to the total of hours used before or after the pandemic). A correlation analysis was used to determine the exclusion of the problematic variables, which we omitted. Table 9.6 presents the results of our econometric model.

We estimated four variants of the main model and found in all of them that the pre-pandemic audience rating was strongly and positively correlated

Table 9.6 Effect of skill levels and lockdown time allocations: regression results for the post-pandemic audience ratings.

	A	B	C	D
Audience rating pre	0.7525***	0.7456***	0.7562***	0.7555***
	(0.0184)	(0.0216)	(0.0210)	(0.0214)
Expert rating pre	−0.1968***	0.1540	−0.1005*	−0.5879***
	(0.0584)	(0.1148)	(0.0596)	(0.1651)
Expert rating post	0.1162**	0.1263	0.2994***	0.4750***
	(0.0590)	(0.0852)	(0.0661)	(0.1013)
Education	0.5264***			
	(0.1158)			
Art skills	−0.3710***	−0.2845**		−0.2601**
	(0.1023)	(0.1327)		(0.1305)
Business skills	−0.0601	0.3832***		−0.5231***
	(0.0540)	(0.1308)		(0.2008)
Learning skills	−0.0840	0.0151		−0.6757***
	(0.0759)	(0.1128)		(0.1575)
Male	0.3733***	0.2589	0.4239***	1.4624***
	(0.1151)	(0.2332)	(0.1530)	(0.3004)
Experience				
Between 5 and 10		0.7736***	0.9922***	1.0054***
More than 10 years		(0.1527)	(0.1486)	(0.1549)
		0.5759***	0.5341***	0.6378***
		(0.1685)	(0.1613)	(0.1667)
Total hours pre			0.0316***	0.0632***
			(0.0074)	(0.115)
Total hours post			−0.0165***	−0.0349***
			(0.0035)	(0.0057)
Constant	2.8835	−1.0553	−1.0549	4.9282
	(0.6821)	(1.1089)	(0.5633)	(1.4585)
N	1,245	969	969	969
R^2	0.5849	0.5869	0.5892	0.6028

Notes: *p-value < 0.1, **p-value < 0.05, ***p-value < 0.01; numbers in parentheses are standard errors.

with the post-pandemic score, which is to be expected since the works were created by the same artists in a short span of time and since they went through a selection process focusing on their comparability. Post-pandemic expert ratings were also positively correlated with the post-pandemic audience score, which supports our hypothesis that higher-quality work obtains superior audience ratings (H3). As discussed in the theoretical section, this is what the literature predicted. On the other hand, it is somewhat surprising that the pre-pandemic expert score was negatively correlated with the post-pandemic audience score. Some studies have found discrepancies between the audience and expert evaluations of experience goods, with the former centring on taste or enjoyability while the latter offer more technical assessments (Holbrook 2005; Thrane 2019; Wallentin 2016). The media and many film fans have noted that the opinions of critics and audiences can diverge, such as in the case of critically praised films that receive luke-warm audience reviews and vice versa, as can be seen in review aggregators such as Rotten Tomatoes or Metacritic (Moore 2018). Something along these lines may be happening in our experimental sample.

These factors may also be at play in the case of skill levels and audience ratings, since we found that artistic, business, and learning skills were negatively correlated with post-pandemic audience scores. A higher skill level may entail more complex work, the quality of which may be harder for audiences to appreciate. Simpler experience goods, which appeal to the senses to communicate their quality rather than to expertise or critical authority, are known to perform better among untrained consumers, as would be the case with the students who participated in our experiment (Schiefer & Fischer, 2008). Nevertheless, the education and experience of the artists were strongly and positively correlated with the post-pandemic audience rating. These findings suggest that simply possessing highly developed skills may not be all one needs to create highly-rated artworks. Instead, one must put those skills to specific uses and develop them within the structure of a discipline or line of work, as evidenced by the relevance of the experience variable in our model. Even the gender variable aligns with this intuition, since being male is correlated with having earned accolades and prizes (something that may have long-standing gender biases at its root as well). Therefore, although we reject our hypotheses on the influence of artistic and business skills on the audience ratings (H1, H2), these factors may still be involved through other mechanisms.

Finally, the total number of hours spent developing an artist's skills before and after the pandemic were both strongly correlated with the post-pandemic audience rating. However, whereas the pre-pandemic time allocation showed a positive correlation, the use of time during the pandemic appears to have exerted influence in the opposite direction. We find in these results a paradoxical effect that, nonetheless, may be connected to matters of skill development. To be precise, the time used to develop skills before the pandemic may be reflected only in the work created after the crisis began. Similarly, while undertaking other tasks during the lockdown and perhaps increasing their total time allocation to these activities, artists may actually have been reducing their creative time in order to devote it to education (reading about digital distribution channels, following training programs) or market-related activities. Even if these new activities may increase their experience or develop their skills, with potential eventual effects on audience ratings, this may happen over a longer time frame than the one afforded to them by the pandemic and this study.

Having considered all the results, we conclude that our findings align with theoretical predictions that higher-quality works should obtain better ratings from consumers and experts, potentially performing well in the market even within the unprecedented context of the pandemic. Moreover, such works are often created by artists who have spent time in the past developing their skills, whether through practice (experience), education, or self-development. Thus, our empirical evidence confirms to some extent the extant literature in the context of the pandemic. Regarding the specific impacts of the pandemic on artist creation, both experts and audiences rated pre-pandemic work higher. The emotional reactions of the audience to post-pandemic creations, due to changes in the themes of the works and the mood of the artists, seem to be more relevant to that perception than skill development or loss.

Concluding remarks

This study shows that skill development and loss are part of complex processes intertwined with creative activities. Indeed, skilled artists tend to produce works that obtain positive reviews from both audiences and experts, but the exact mechanism connecting artistic and business skills with the ratings remains to be more fully explored, both within and outside the context of the pandemic. Our study, which is among the first to take works of art, created under defined conditions, to an audience and then measure their reactions, may lead to further research along similar lines.

In our argument, audience scores serve as proxies for the market performance of the works considered. Hence, understanding the role that artistic and business skills play in the audience evaluation of cultural goods, in the context of the pandemic, allows us to explore artist-level effects of COVID-19. The combination of two methodological approaches, experimental with the audience and exploratory with the creators, lets us analyze the effects of the pandemic using novel and primary information obtained from potential consumers. We can observe how the works created during the lockdown, amidst the material and symbolic restrictions imposed by the global healthcare emergency, are perceived and rated by their consumers. Our contribution is hence twofold, moving beyond the immediate realm of COVID-19 to discuss the role of artistic and business skills in the audience evaluation of artistic works. This analysis could provide insights for the development of curricular plans for artists or could lead to the design of training programs with targeted characteristics that more efficiently benefit certain types of artists, thus facilitating the reactivation and recovery of the cultural industries after the pandemic.

Our main limitations derive from the experimental nature of the work, constrained to a laboratory-type setting instead of actual circulation and distribution processes, and the closeness in time of the lockdown, the creation of the works, and their evaluation. Future studies could look at longer time frames, which may allow for the skills developed during the lockdown to fully materialize in the artworks. Concerning the circulation dimension, over 70% of audience participants in the experiment were undergraduate students, with about one-quarter belonging to creative fields. We are aware that students may not be the core consumers of the works used in our design. However, although experimental studies drawing on student samples for marketing research are considered acceptable, if not widespread, for the examination of when examining causal models (Barsade 2002; Hennig-Thurau et al., 2006), it may be worthwhile to consider participants in the actual target audiences of the artists. Similarly, it is not possible to estimate our model using expert ratings as the dependent variable, keeping skills and/or use of time as independent variables – which could have provided a potential robustness check – since the number of expert observations is too small. Involving more experts would bypass this problem in upcoming research efforts.

Regarding the artists, the experimental stage of the study included only those working in the visual arts in Colombia, and specifically the subset of artists who could continue creating under lockdown conditions. Expanding this pool is necessary before our findings can be generalized. Objective measures of the skills would also be useful, since we are currently limited to collecting self-reported values on a Likert scale. Likewise, a greater variability in the artists' time allocations would allow us to include clearer and more robust treatments in the experiment. In the present study, we used the experimental design to capture audience valuations and emotional reactions, without manipulations such as having some participants observe only the works of artists who did not change their routines during the pandemic or only those who increased the time allocated to a given type of skill. As for the emotional reactions, non-quantitative elements must be considered with regard to both creators and audiences, since a systematic way to compare emotional reactions using these quantitative scales has not yet been developed.

The immediate practical implications of our results indicate that artists would be wise to work on the development of their artistic and business skills, whether in formal programs, through their practice, or in self-study, as long as these activities do not reduce their dedication to creation or production. They must also understand that the results of their time investment may be perceived only on a delayed basis or only by a sufficiently qualified segment of their audience. Further work on audience and expert ratings, and their relation to skills, themes, experience, and formats will help bring light to these issues in the future.

Acknowledgements

This study would not have been possible without the generous contributions from all the artists, experts, colleagues, students, and friends who participated in the different stages of the project – sharing their work and knowledge with us, helping to distribute the surveys, discussing ideas, and kindly supporting the study through all its challenges. Among them, we especially wish to recognize the outstanding work of our research assistants, Sebastián Balcucho and Mariana Álvarez, who were our symbolic and practical connections to the quantitative and artistic worlds. This chapter benefitted from the valuable comments of two anonymous reviewers and the editors.

Notes

1. The low response rate was a pervasive problem during data collection. Only one-third of the participants completed the survey, including the requested information on their use of time. Fewer than half of those who completed the survey expressed interest in providing examples of their works for the experimental stage. However, we were able to include 41% of the Colombian artists in the experimental stage.
2. The fact that most of the differences in the time allocations were not statistically significant in either the Colombian or Spanish samples could be related to the small number of observations and the heterogeneity within the samples in terms of experience and fields.
3. We decided to limit the experimental stage to the Colombian subset of the sample because of the number of artists with comparable works, and within fields suited for the experimental design, who expressed interest in participating. Another factor was our access to a large pool of Colombian students with consistent demographic characteristics. Despite these limitations, since our analysis looks at the individual artist level for its comparisons and interpretations, we believe the findings can be generalized to other contexts, including Spain.
4. The small monetary compensation was offered to the artists in exchange for their time and the opportunity to share their work with a limited number of experiment participants. The artists retained ownership of their work, and this "loan" entailed no risk for their copyright or the originality of the work, given that it did not amount to a circulation activity since it took place in a private setting.
5. We opted for a complete, within-subject randomization to avoid potential biases resulting from the order of presentation (pre- or post-pandemic works being presented before the other) or due to the proportion of either type in each of the three experimental rounds. Therefore, not all participants observed a given artist's pre- and post-pandemic work.

References

Abeledo Sanchís, R., 2020. *Análisis del impacto del COVID-19 sobre las organizaciones y agentes culturales en España*. Econcult. Universitat de Valencia, Spain.

Arkenberg, C. 2020. Will gaming keep growing when the lockdown ends?, *Deloitte Insights*, https://www2.deloitte.com/us/en/insights/industry/technology/video-game-industry-trends.html

Ball, M. 2020. The impact of COVID-19 on Pay-TV and OTT Video, https://www.matthewball.vc/all/covidvideo

Barsade, S.G., 2002. The ripple effect: Emotional contagion and its influence on group behavior. *Administrative Science Quarterly*, 47(4), pp. 644–675.

Basuroy, S., Chatterjee, S. and Ravid, S.A., 2003. How critical are critical reviews? The box office effects of film critics, star power, and budgets. *Journal of Marketing*, 67(4), pp. 103–117.

Beckman, G.D., 2007. "Adventuring" arts entrepreneurship curricula in higher education: An examination of present efforts, obstacles, and best practices. *The Journal of Arts Management, Law, and Society*, 37(2), pp. 87–112.

Campion Canelas, M. and Rodríguez-Camacho, J.A., 2020. Efectos del coronavirus en el circuito punk de chapinero a partir de la cartografía de la territorialidad nómada: producción, consumo y participación. *Análisis Político*, 33(100), pp. 27–54.

Chintagunta, P.K., Gopinath, S. and Venkataraman, S., 2010. The effects of online user reviews on movie box office performance: Accounting for sequential rollout and aggregation across local markets. *Marketing Science*, 29(5), pp. 944–957.

Chuba, K. 2020. Will live events ever return? There may be no "back to normal". *Billboard*, https://www.billboard.com/articles/business/9463344/will-live-events-return-no-back-to-normal/

Cultura. 2020. Lanzan fondo para apoyar a la industria audiovisual en Colombia. *El Tiempo*, https://www.eltiempo.com/cultura/cine-y-tv/netflix-crea-fondo-para-ayudar-a-equipos-de-rodaje-en-colombia-491878

Departamento Administrativo Nacional de Estadística (DANE). 2020. Cuarto reporte de Economía Naranja y del sistema de consulta de información. Noviembre 2020, https://www.dane.gov.co/files/investigaciones/pib/sateli_cultura/economia-naranja/presentacion-rp-4to-reporte-economia-naranja.pdf

Departamento Administrativo Nacional de Estadística (DANE). 2021. *Producto Interno Bruto. PIB*, https://www.dane.gov.co/files/investigaciones/boletines/pib/cp_PIB_IVtrim20.pdf

Department for Digital, Culture, Media & Sports. DCMS. 2021. DCMS Economic Estimates 2019 (provisional): Gross value added, https://www.gov.uk/government/statistics/dcms-economic-estimates-2019-gross-value-added/dcms-economic-estimates-2019-provisional-gross-value-added

Dhar, V. and Chang, E.A., 2009. Does chatter matter? The impact of user-generated content on music sales. *Journal of Interactive Marketing*, 23(4), pp. 300–307.

Elberse, A. and Eliashberg, J., 2003. Demand and supply dynamics for sequentially released products in international markets: The case of motion pictures. *Marketing Science*, 22(3), pp. 329–354.

Fiorella, L. and Mayer, R.E., 2013. The relative benefits of learning by teaching and teaching expectancy. *Contemporary Educational Psychology*, 38(4), pp. 281–288.

Fiorella, L. and Mayer, R.E., 2014. Role of expectations and explanations in learning by teaching. *Contemporary Educational Psychology*, 39(2), pp. 75–85.

Gemser, G., Van Oostrum, M. and Leenders, M.A., 2007. The impact of film reviews on the box office performance of art house versus mainstream motion pictures. *Journal of Cultural Economics*, 31(1), pp. 43–63.

Gilman, T.L., Shaheen, R., Nylocks, K.M., Halachoff, D., Chapman, J., Flynn, J.J., Matt, L.M. and Coifman, K.G., 2017. A film set for the elicitation of emotion in research: A comprehensive catalog derived from four decades of investigation. *Behavior Research Methods*, 49(6), pp. 2061–2082.

Gneezy, A., Gneezy, U., Riener, G. and Nelson, L.D., 2012. Pay-what-you-want, identity, and self-signaling in markets. *Proceedings of the National Academy of Sciences*, 109(19), pp. 7236–7240.

Gross, J.J. and Levenson, R.W., 1995. Emotion elicitation using films. *Cognition & Emotion*, 9(1), pp. 87–108.

Hackley, C. and Tiwsakul, R., 2006. Entertainment marketing and experiential consumption. *Journal of Marketing Communications*, 12(1), pp. 63–75.

Hennig-Thurau, T. and Houston, M.B., 2019. *Entertainment science. Data Analytics and Practical Theory for Movies, Games, Books, and Music.* Springer Nature, Cham.

Hennig-Thurau, T., Groth, M., Paul, M. and Gremler, D.D., 2006. Are all smiles created equal? How emotional contagion and emotional labor affect service relationships. *Journal of Marketing*, 70(3), pp. 58–73.

Hernández, M. 2020. Pedro Sánchez anuncia el estado de alarma para frenar el coronavirus 24 horas antes de aprobarlo. *El Mundo*, https://www.elmundo.es/espana/2020/03/13/5e6b844e21efa0dd258b45a5.html.

Holbrook, M.B., 2005. The role of ordinary evaluations in the market for popular culture: Do consumers have "good taste"?. *Marketing Letters*, 16(2), pp. 75–86.

Ho-Dac, N.N., Carson, S.J. and Moore, W.L., 2013. The effects of positive and negative online customer reviews: do brand strength and category maturity matter?. *Journal of Marketing*, 77(6), pp. 37–53.

Instituto Nacional de Estadística (INE). 2020. Mujeres y hombres en España: Empleo. https://www.ine.es/ss/Satellite?L=es_ES&c=INEPublicacion_C&cid=1259924822888&p=1254735110672&pagename=ProductosYServicios/PYSLayout&param1=PYSDetalleGratuitas&param4=Ocultar

Instituto Nacional de Estadística (INE). 2021. *Contabilidad Nacional de España. Crecimiento en Volumen, variación anual*, https://www.ine.es/prensa/pib_tabla_cne.htm

Kalwani, M.U. and Yim, C.K., 1992. Consumer price and promotion expectations: An experimental study. *Journal of Marketing Research*, 29(1), pp. 90–100.

Liu, Y., 2006. Word of mouth for movies: Its dynamics and impact on box office revenue. *Journal of Marketing*, 70(3), pp. 74–89.

Martinez, P. 2020. Spain lifts national state of emergency after 3-month coronavirus lockdown. *CBS News*, https://www.cbsnews.com/news/coronavirus-spain-lockdown-lifted-national-state-emergency/

McKenzie, J., 2012. The economics of movies: A literature survey. *Journal of Economic Surveys*, 26(1), pp. 42–70.

McKenzie, J., Crosby, P., Cox, J. and Collins, A., 2019. Experimental evidence on demand for "on-demand" entertainment. *Journal of Economic Behavior & Organization*, 161, pp. 98–113.

Mercado, L. (2020). El 1° de septiembre termina cuarentena y empieza aislamiento selectivo. *El Tiempo*, https://www.eltiempo.com/politica/gobierno/ivan-duque-anuncia-aislamiento-selectivo-desde-el-primero-de-septiembre-532872

Ministerio de Cultura y Deporte (MCUD). 2021a. *Empleo Cultural 2020: Principales resultados.* CULTURAbase.

Ministerio de Cultura y Deporte (MCUD). 2021b. *Impacto del Covid-19 en el empleo cultural. Avance Enero-Diciembre 2020.* CULTURAbase.

Ministerio de Educación, Cultura y Deporte. (MECD). 2019. Encuesta de hábitos y de prácticas culturales en España 2018–2019, http://www.culturaydeporte.gob.es/servicios-al-ciudadano/estadisticas/cultura/mc/ehc/2018-2019/presentacion.html

Ministerio de Educación, Cultura y Deporte. (MECD). 2020. Anuario de estadísticas culturales 2020, https://www.culturaydeporte.gob.es/dam/jcr:52801035-cc20-496c-8f36-72d09ec6d533/anuario-de-estadisticas-culturales-2020.pdf

Ministerio de Hacienda. 2018. Informes de cadenas de valor: Industrias culturales. February 2018, https://www.argentina.gob.ar/sites/default/files/sspe_cadena_de_valor_industrias_culturales.pdf

Moore, N. 2018. The biggest divide between audience and critic scores on Rotten Tomatoes. *Looper*, https://www.looper.com/136024/the-biggest-divides-between-audience-and-critic-scores-on-rotten-tomatoes/

Mullaney, T. 2018. The big changes colleges are making to help art students snag jobs in America's gig economy. *CNBC*, https://www.cnbc.com/2018/11/16/the-arts-degree-gets-an-overhaul-to-help-us-students-snag-jobs.html

Nelson, P., 1970. Information and consumer behavior. *Journal of Political Economy*, 78(2), pp. 311–329.

Nicolau, A. 2021. Spotify added 3m subscribers in first three months of 2021. *Financial Times*, https://www.ft.com/content/d2050b0e-5ee5-436b-8cf1-9f70894a60a7

Noriega Ramírez, M. J. & Lizarazo M. P. 2021. La humanidad y el arte en crisis: ¿qué sigue para nosotros? *El Espectador*, https://www.elespectador.com/noticias/cultura/la-humanidad-y-el-arte-en-crisis-que-sigue-para-nosotros-ii/

Observatorio de la Cultura. 2020. *Consulta Urgente: Abril 2020*. Fundación Contemporánea; La Fábrica, http://fundacioncontemporanea.com/wp-content/uploads/2012/10/Observatorio_de_la_Cultura_URGENTE_.pdf

Pollstar. 2020. Pollstar projects 2020 total box office would have hit $12.2 billion, https://www.pollstar.com/article/pollstar-projects-2020-total-box-office-would-have-hit-122-billion-144197

Ray, R.D. and Gross, J.J. 2007. Emotion elicitation using films. Handbook of Emotion Elicitation and Assessment, 9. Oxford University Press, New York.

Schiefer, J. and Fischer, C. 2008. The gap between wine expert ratings and consumer preferences: Measures, determinants and marketing implications. *International Journal of Wine Business Research*, 20(4), pp. 335–351.

Sistema de Información de la Economía Naranja SIENA. 2021. Consumo cultural de personas de 12 años y más de contenido audiovisual, por región. https://siena.dane.gov.co/#/consultar_sistema_siena

Spiro, N., Perkins, R., Kaye, S., Tymoszuk, U., Mason-Bertrand, A., Cossette, I., Glasser, S. and Williamon, A., 2021. The effects of COVID-19 lockdown 1.0 on working patterns, income, and wellbeing among performing arts professionals in the United Kingdom (April–June 2020). *Frontiers in Psychology*, 11, p. 4105.

Souza, T.L., Nishijima, M. and Fava, A.C., 2019. Do consumer and expert reviews affect the length of time a film is kept on screens in the USA?. *Journal of Cultural Economics*, 43(1), pp. 145–171.

Symmes Cobb, J. 2020. Colombia to hold 19-day quarantine to fight coronavirus. *Reuters*, https://www.reuters.com/article/us-health-coronavirus-colombia-quarantin/colombia-to-hold-19-day-quarantine-to-fight-coronavirus-idUSKBN218068

Taylor, L. 2020. Colombia implemented a six-month lockdown to control coronavirus but there was a steep price to pay. *ABC News*, https://www.abc.net.au/news/2020-11-09/colombia-six-month-coronavirus-lockdown-price-to-pay/12855242

Thrane, C., 2019. Expert reviews, peer recommendations and buying red wine: Experimental evidence. *Journal of Wine Research*, 30(2), pp. 166–177.

Wallentin, E., 2016. Demand for cinema and diverging tastes of critics and audiences. *Journal of Retailing and Consumer Services*, 33, pp. 72–81.

Zhou, W. and Duan, W., 2016. Do professional reviews affect online user choices through user reviews? An empirical study. *Journal of Management Information Systems*, 33(1), pp. 202–228.

Section 3

Institutional strategies

First responses in the arts and culture sectors to the strict lockdown of March 2020

10 The COVID-19 pandemic and structural change in the museum sector

Insights from Italy

Enrico Bertacchini, Andrea Morelli and Giovanna Segre

Introduction

Among the Cultural and Creative Industries, museums and heritage sites have been one of the most hit sectors by the COVID-19 pandemic. According to UNESCO (UNESCO, 2020), 90% of museums worldwide have been temporarily closed for weeks or months during the emergency due to sanitary restriction measures, and 10% have reported being at risk of permanent closure. Similarly, the closure of borders and the block of international and within-country mobility has led to a sharp decrease in cultural tourism, with significant income losses (up to 75–80%) for museums and heritage sites in touristic areas (NEMO, 2020). While some institutions benefit from public subsidies, the economic consequences of the pandemic have been severe as most of the cultural heritage sector relies greatly on financial contributions from visitors and donors.

The cultural heritage sector has been commonly recognized as one of the Cultural and Creative industries characterized by both a slow change in semiotic code and material base (Jones et al., 2015). Still, the COVID-19 has potentially unveiled the necessity for a radical change and restructuring of strategies by museums and heritage institutions. The emergency, in some respects, has accelerated a long-lasting trend towards innovative practices, especially related to the digital domain, but that suffered from cultural and organizational barriers in their adoption (Bakhshi and Throsby, 2012). In other cases, the pandemic is deeply questioning the development model of museums and heritage institutions, especially regarding audience target and revenue sources.

In this chapter, we address how the impact of the COVID-19 crisis is obliging museums to rethink their strategies towards new models of audience involvement and economic sustainability. Crucially, amid supply and demand shocks brought by the pandemic, we identify two main dimensions of structural change: the convergence between the digital and physical experience and the increased importance of local audience and proximity tourism as a source of stability for museum activities. To cope with such

DOI: 10.4324/9781003128274-14

a structural change, we argue that museums need to shift from a trans-actional to a relationship orientation towards their audience, where the emphasis is no longer on attracting visitors for single experiences under traditional pricing models but on proactively developing and maintaining loyal audiences through novel membership schemes. At the same time, to fully grasp the opportunities of providing digital and physical access to their collections, museums should rely on new network governance models.

We use the Italian context as a seminal case study for illustrating these arguments. Drawing from the current debate on the economic sustainability of the Italian museum system during and after the COVID-19 crisis, we discuss the application of a universal membership scheme for State museums as a novel tool of audience involvement and test its economic viability as an alternative financing mechanism.

Most of the debate on the effects of the pandemic in the cultural heritage sector has concentrated on short-term recovery interventions or digital activities as the main focus of the response to the crisis. Our contribution provides instead a prescriptive and policy-oriented discussion on the possible strategies and solutions supporting the sector and its economic viability in a longer-term and post-pandemic scenario.

Structural change in museum and heritage sector after COVID-19

As highlighted in the organization studies and innovation literature (Drazin et al., 2004), structural change results from complex dynamics involving the interaction of technological, social, and economic patterns at the macro level and reflects the organizational change at the micro level. We argue that the pandemic has brought to light two potential dimensions of structural change affecting the cultural heritage and museum sector.

A first dimension is a more profound convergence between the digital and physical experience provided by heritage-related services. As stewards of cultural heritage, museums and heritage institutions have increasingly seen in the last decades at the core of their mission the transmission and communication of knowledge related to their heritage (Anderson, 2004). Cultural heritage organizations have traditionally accomplished this mission by providing physical access to their collections and artefacts, coupled with onsite learning and educational activities. Still, the digital revolution has led to new opportunities to access and transmit such valuable knowledge (Bertacchini and Morando, 2013). Today, there is a clear understanding of such opportunities. In particular, online access to digital collections may be seen as an innovation in audience reach. In many cases, it has enhanced accessibility to authoritative and trusted content and related information by complementing the user's physical visit (Marty, 2008, Navarrete and Borowiecki, 2016). Moreover, Navarrete (2013) underlines how digitization has often represented a solution to exhibiting the museums' collection, as physically displayed objects are just a minor share of the entire collection.

In this perspective, it is not unexpected that during the COVID-19 outbreak, with the closure of physical access to their collections, museums and cultural institutions have signalled the need to invest in digital infrastructure striving for online visibility and maintaining ties with their audiences (NEMO, 2020; Samaroudi et al., 2020).

Yet, a relatively overlooked aspect is how the effect of this crisis can lead to better integration of the digital and physical experience within museums and heritage institutions. In many cases, the necessity of visitors' tracing made compulsory the online reservation of the onsite visit, with the possibility for the institution to know beforehand the characteristics of its audience and establish a digital interaction with prospective visitors. If properly managed, such a small change can radically alter physical and digital heritage consumption patterns enhancing the experience (Ballina et al., 2019). Having an advance-tracking system for their future visitors, museums can provide a broader and long-lasting experience of their collections, leveraging on versioning of their physical and digital output (i.e. free access vs. premium content). For example, the visitor begins the experience online through the contents and digital services related to the collection. She can deepen the visit to the museum, which continues online with further post visit insights or proposals for new experiences. Moreover, integrating the digital and physical experience could enable better profiling of visitors and their habits, leading to more personalized cultural heritage experiences (Nuccio and Bertacchini, 2021).

These conditions undoubtedly represent opportunities in the heritage sector as they can favour an acceleration of data-analytics innovation processes that would have taken several years. At the same time, it remains an open question whether the very fragmented digital strategies of heritage institutions, coupled with lack of resources or cultural barriers towards new technological innovation by some organizations, might enable all the museums to exploit the new data-driven potential of the convergence.

The second dimension of structural change refers to proximity tourism and local audiences' increased importance as a source of stability for museum activities. Amid unprecedented global travel restrictions and the very high uncertainty on the end of the pandemic worldwide, the tourism industry and particularly long-haul tourism have been deeply affected by the pandemic. The COVID-19 is not only posing a severe challenge to the sustainability of regions with high tourist specialization, but a growing number of observers (Farzanegan et al., 2020; Gössling et al., 2020; Prideaux et al., 2020) suggest that, in analogy with the ongoing climate crisis, it questions the volume-growth tourism model advocated till recently by several organizations and stakeholders in the tourism sector.

As cultural tourism has represented in the last two decades, a significant driver of the demand for museums and heritage institutions (Richards,

2018), the pandemic has equally unveiled the fragility of the sector in leveraging on tourism models driven by long-haul mobility and the attractiveness of single masterpieces or iconic museums facilities.

In a post-pandemic scenario, addressing proximity tourism and catering to local audience demand could offer an alternative sustainable strategy to stabilize museum activities in the future volatile context (Romagosa, 2020). Nevertheless, proximity tourism has been a neglected field in tourism research and has only recently gained attention in the scholarship debate (Jeuring and Diaz-Soria, 2017; Bertacchini et al., 2021). Similarly, while repeat visits have been one of the main targets of the museum and cultural attractions managers, investing in the attraction of repeat visitors as a promotion strategy has often been overshadowed by the opportunities of attracting ever-increasing flows of first-time visitors. While literature addressing loyalty in tourism behaviour has often considered satisfaction as the main element for inducing repeat visitation, research on repeat visits to cultural attractions indicate more complex motivational and behavioural factors at play, where the choice to revisit is more a process of enculturation that is not necessarily based on the novelty of the cultural supply (Brida et al. 2014). This implies that to cater to the demand of local audience and visitors from proximate areas, museums and heritage institutions must leverage on the cultural value of the available collections and objects, but through designing activities and experiences seen by the repeat visitors as novel chances to enhance their cultural capital (Black, 2016). This implies a deep change in museum programming, from expensive blockbuster exhibitions to modular and replicable activities linked to single aspects, perspectives, or items of the museum collection.

Moreover, while the local audience might constitute a more homogeneous set, at least from the point of view of the motivations, it might express specific needs or diversified preferences. Timing of the repeat visit, jointly with the propensity of loyal visitors to attend other cultural events in the local area, suggests the need for an adequate promotion of events at different times of the day, raising the attention towards the museum as a place of "cultural production", and consequently stimulate the repeat visit of a place where cultural capital can be enhanced (Black, 2013). Similarly, a shift towards the local audience and proximity visitors suggests that museum activities should be tailored to target the needs of entire households rather than the visitor profile characterizing long-haul tourism (Lang et al., 2006)

Italian cultural heritage organizations and COVID-19

The Italian cultural heritage is often considered one of the largest and most diversified globally, characterized by a vast and heterogeneous set of museums and heritage organizations, which differ from the type of collection, geographical location, institutional features, and number of visitors.

According to the Italian museum census, about 5,000 museums and similar institutions are active in Italy, made up of 3,882 museums, galleries or collections (80.5%), 630 monuments and monumental buildings (12.8%), and 327 archaeological and historical parks (6.7%). One peculiar feature of the Italian cultural heritage system is its high territorial dispersion. Museums and heritage institutions are present in all regions, with a relatively higher density (related to resident population or surface size) in the northern–central regions and in both large metropolitan areas and small cities (one in three municipalities has at least a museum or heritage site). The spatial distribution is rooted in the historical political fragmentation of the country. However, today it allows, unlike other European countries, to have a more geographically articulated offer of cultural heritage sites and museums, even if more challenging to manage due to the high fragmentation.

From an institutional viewpoint, the ownership structure of the heritage institutions is governmental primarily (63.4%), at the level of State, Regions, local public administrations (provinces and municipalities), public schools, and universities. However, there is a significant heterogeneity regarding the size and characteristics of heritage institutions depending on ownership and control by public sector authorities.

While most public museums and cultural institutions are owned by local government and municipal authorities, only 448 are owned and managed at the state level. This group which constitutes less than 10% of the total, alone attracts about 40% of visitors as it includes some of the most internationally known museums, monuments, and archaeological parks that attract a large flow of visitors, like the Galleria Degli Uffizi, Pantheon, the Flavian Amphitheatre (Colosseum), the Archaeological Area of Pompeii and the Museum and Park of Capodimonte. At the same time, besides the main attractors, is a large number of less-visited state-owned museums and heritage institutions, whose management and conservation are under central government control due to the national significance of their cultural heritage.

Overall, the cultural heritage sector has been experiencing a positive trend in visits in recent years. From 2006 to 2018, visits to Italian cultural heritage increased by almost a third (32.2%), growing on average at a rate of over 2.5 million visitors per year. In particular, the number of admissions to state-owned museums, monuments, and archaeological areas almost doubled, from 34.6 million to 54.1 million, and the number of visitors to non-state facilities also grew, even if more slowly, from 62.7 million in 2006 to 74.5 million. In 2018, a record number of 128.6 million admissions were therefore reached. Growth is mainly driven by the significant share of foreign tourists who visited the cultural institutions, 46% of the total public in 2018.

Compared to the buoyant growing demand for onsite visits, digitization and the provision of digital services by Italian museums and heritage institutions still show wide margins for improvement. According to data from the 2018 museum census, only 10% of state-owned museums and similar institutions have digitally catalogued their heritage, and only 37.4% of these have completed the digitization process. The use of interactive technologies and digital tools to enrich the visiting experience and the visitors' engagement is still limited, with only one institution out of ten (9.9%) offering the possibility to visit their collections or heritage sites virtually. Similar limitations emerge when considering standard digital communication: only about half of the museums report having a website and a social media account (51.1% and 53.4%, respectively, and only 14% provide online ticketing services.

As in other European countries, in recent decades, the cultural heritage sector, characterized by a relevant component of public ownership, has been subject to reforms aimed at greater autonomy and administrative decentralization (Bertacchini et al., 2018). In particular, a major reform by the Italian Ministry of Cultural Heritage in 2014 has provided some state museums with a more considerable degree of managerial and technical-scientific autonomy, but also introducing measures that may favour the implementation of network governance models for all cultural heritage institutions at the national and regional level (Marzano and Castellini, 2018). In particular, the reform granted to 32 state museums and heritage sites financial and managerial autonomy and introduced 17 regional hubs to coordinate clusters of the non-autonomous state museums and drive the development of networks among social and institutional bodies in the area (Baia Curioni, 2018).

Besides administrative decentralization and network governance, another key objective of recent reforms by the Italian Ministry of Cultural Heritage has been to enhance the digital infrastructure coordinate activities within the museum and heritage sector and give centrality to digital technologies in further stimulating the transformation of museums for audience involvement and relationship (Agostino et al., 2020b). This objective is currently pursued by implementing a national museum system (*Sistema Museale Nazionale*), an online platform aimed at connecting the cultural heritage of nearly 5000 museums and institutions in Italy, as well as at presenting and promoting them and their collections through a nation-wide network.

As clear from the arguments above, the COVID-19 outbreak had impacted the Italian museum and heritage sector when the effects of the reforms and transformations in recent years began to be evident. Like in many other countries, museums have undertaken several digital activities, focusing on online activity and social media engagement to maintain or develop the relationship with their audience. For example, by analyzing data of about one hundred state museums, Agostino et al. (2020a) illustrate how there has been a sharp rise in online cultural material and initiatives through social media during the first lockdown period in Italy.

The apparent success of such initiatives has stimulated a debate on the potential of the digital offer and how future directions of digitally enabled approaches can be used to find new strategies for the sustainability of Italian cultural heritage institutions in post-pandemic scenarios.

A first proposal that has received particular attention in the media, being supported by the Italian Ministry of Cultural Heritage, has been that of envisioning the creation of a "Netflix" of Italian culture, a platform for the distribution of digital content produced and offered by cultural institutions (Agostino et al. 2020b).[1]

With less ado, one of the most interesting contributions in the debate has come from James Bradburne, Director of the Italian state museum Pinacoteca di Brera,[2] proposing a manifesto to accelerate the change induced by COVID-19 in the sector by revolutionizing museums' strategies for audience relationship and engagement. The heart of the proposal is to create an economic model that replaces the purchase of a single visit with the purchase of a subscription for the contents and services that museums offer, both virtual and onsite. This vision has already been implemented in experimental form by launching BreraPlus+, a subscription-based online platform that enriches the experience with digital multimedia content.

Membership schemes of museum networks: A new subscription model for accessing the physical and digital heritage

The two proposals that emerged in the Italian debate and reviewed in this chapter indicate the need to find new strategies for audience involvement and the economic sustainability of heritage institutions. Although still in an embryonic state, the proposals illustrate different approaches, with advantages and limitations, in responding to the trajectories of structural change in the cultural heritage sector.

In the first case, the "Netflix" model, while representing a mere digital solution to the reduction of physical access, emphasizes the opportunity to exploit platform economies of scale from a network of cultural institutions to convey digital cultural content in a scenario where users of creative products and services increasingly use streaming and on-demand content platforms. However, as it has already emerged in the Italian debate, in a very competitive environment such as that of online digital content provision, the creation of a brand-new dedicated platform casts some doubts on the return on investment and the opportunity to monetize digital content related to Italian arts and cultural heritage. The BreraPlus+ model, in turn, emphasizes the integration between the physical and digital experience of the museum, with a potential attractiveness for repeat visits of local audiences. However, if replicated by many other institutions in an uncoordinated way, it leads to a risk of over-fragmentation, with perspective visitors being obliged to subscribe to several programs proposed by different museums. Moreover, platform economies of scale and network externalities would not be fully exploited.

Notwithstanding the limitations of the two approaches taken individually, we argue that it is possible to combine their positive aspects by identifying strategies that pursue:

- a shift from a transaction to a relationship orientation in the museum sector
- platform economies of scale through innovation in the role and functions of museum networks

As highlighted in the scholarship debate, the relationship orientation means "proactively creating, developing and maintaining committed, interactive and profitable exchanges with customers over time" (Garrido and Camarero, 2014). In contrast to the transaction orientation, which centres on increasing revenues at a single purchasing occasion, the relationship orientation adopts a longer-term perspective in the audience involvement that can innovate and extend traditional friends' and membership schemes (Slater, 2004). These schemes are mainly conceived as a club solution for supporting museums by creating a community of actively engaged members that usually represent a relatively small group compared to the whole audience of a heritage institution (Frey and Steiner, 2012). A novel relationship orientation addressing a broader audience base could be better suited to provide stability in museums' activities in a context where heritage institutions have to cope with the volatility of long-haul tourism demand while relying on less mobile local cultural consumers. At the same time, as the Pinacoteca di Brera initiative suggests, a relationship orientation would not leverage so much on the pro-social behaviour of a minority, but rather on the interest of the large audience to have continuous access to the museum's activities both online and onsite.

Besides a shift towards a more substantial relationship orientation, innovation in the role and functions of museum networks could enhance the exploitation of platform and network externalities deriving from the integration of digital and physical access by visitors to collections and sites. In their primary forms, museum networks may be described as an "ordered group of heritage institutions that, by inter-relating with one another, help accomplish a series of established objectives" (Bagdadli, 2003). Networks have often been established to improve museums' competitive and profitability capacity by exploiting economies of scale in organization input and visitor services or enhancing their cultural potential by building a stronger collective image through collaboration.

One particular form of museum networks addressing audience demand arises from destination cards and museum passes, where visitors, both tourists or residents, through the purchase of a single pass, have access to the cultural offer of all the institutions included in the network. Notable cases of schemes applying a bundling pricing strategy coupled with unlimited access are the Dutch Museum pass or the Carta Musei Piemonte (Werff et al., 2014; Bertacchini et al., 2019). These initiatives already have the purpose of establishing a stable relationship with local audiences and favouring cultural proximity tourism. However, they have mainly focused on physical access to the museum network without fully grasping the opportunity of a shared digital platform for subscribers where museums can become digital content producers and providers. To cope with the current challenges and opportunities posed by the COVID-19 crisis, we suggest that membership schemes for museum networks can represent a promising option that helps to realize museums' relationship orientation and enhances the integration between digital and physical access to cultural heritage.

Exploring the economic viability of a universal membership scheme for Italian state museums

The Italian context allows us to explore this policy proposal by considering the implementation of a universal membership scheme for state museums and cultural heritage institutions.

State museums, monuments, and archaeological parks represent the most organized network of heritage institutions in Italy. Despite the recent reforms towards greater autonomy of some of the most important museums and archaeological areas, this network has an established coordination system and enough organizational capacities to maintain a shared strategic vision. Moreover, the network is also at the core of the new strategy for creating a national museum system, of which one of the most important cornerstones is a shared digital platform.

Similar to museum passes, a universal membership scheme could be designed to provide one-year access to online content and onsite visits for both Italian and foreign visitors. While individual entrance fees could still be charged, we envision a scheme that gives free and unlimited access to all museums of the network for 12 months, bundled with services provided through the shared digital platform where subscribers can enjoy extra digital content and virtual experiences produced by the museums about Italian cultural heritage. It can be purchased freely at any time in anticipation of future visits to museums or for access to digital content. The information about the pass-holders, collected both at the registration and through the tracking of the use of the pass, can be helpful to profile their experience and enhance opportunities of relationship with the museums of the network. In a post-COVID-19 scenario, reservation of onsite visits could become the standard even with the membership scheme. However, as previously discussed, this new policy would enhance the integration between the digital and physical experiences of a diversified cultural offer available through the pass. As with the Pinacoteca of Brera pioneering initiative, but extended to more than 400 museums and heritage sites, this move would represent a radical shift in audience relationship and engagement by favouring repeated access to the collections and the content provided by the institutions as producers of digital cultural experiences.

Arguably, the universal membership scheme enables the state museums to take advantage of network and platform externalities online and onsite. Firstly, the size of the network ensures a critical mass of digital content on Italian cultural heritage conveyed in a single platform that can be attractive for both national and international audiences. Secondly, the reduced competition between museums to attract visitors can potentially trigger cooperative solutions. For example, the circulation of artworks and objects within the system (especially from major museums to minor ones) can enable visitors to enjoy them at different locations or enhance curatorial possibilities in exhibiting collections. In addition, another potential economic advantage of introducing a universal membership scheme would be reducing transaction costs in the management of admissions for museums. In contrast, reduction of transaction costs for pass-holders is less certain as it is very likely that onsite visits should still be reserved in advance when the pandemic will be over or under control.

One of the main challenges for implementing such a novel scheme is to assess its economic viability in terms of potential revenues and consumer demand. For instance, financial resources collected from the membership scheme should compensate for the foregone revenues of standard entrance fees and possibly grant new funds to invest in the digital infrastructure of the museum network and the production of new digital services and content.

In illustrative terms, it is possible to test the feasibility of this proposal using the data and statistics available on Italian museums and their visitors. Table 10.1 shows key economic facts of Italian State museums and heritage institutions relevant for the analysis.

For 2018, the last year with available data before the COVID-19 outbreak, the state museum system had around 30 million free admissions and 24 million paid admissions. Free admissions are mainly made up by visitors under 18, visits to structures that do not charge an entrance fee (34%) or from those to all state museums occurring on the first Sundays of each month following the free admission policy in force since 2014 (Cellini and Cuccia, 2018). The paid admissions generated gross revenues of 229 million euros and, excluding ticketing services concessions, 188 million euros. The net average ticket price is 7.55 euros, a relatively low value that is potentially due to discounted rates applied to visitors up to 25 years of age.

The Census of Italian museums, archaeological sites, and monuments reports each institution's estimated share of foreign visitors. With this information, it is possible to derive the share of paid admissions and revenues generated by Italian and foreign visitors. As shown in Table 10.1, the share of paid admission by foreign visitors is about 50%, consistent with the fact that there are some of the most iconic and attractive institutions for foreign visitors among the state museums and archaeological areas.

Table 10.1 Characteristics and economic facts of Italian state-owned museums and heritage institutions – 2018.

	Values	%
Museums, monuments, and archaeological sites	448	
With free admission	153	34.2%
With admission fees	295	65.8%
Total number of visits	55,313,772	
Free visits	30,329,887	54.8%
Fee-paying visits	24,983,885	45.2%
Total number of fee-paying visits	24,983,885	
Italians[a]	11,843,436	47.4%
Foreigners[a]	13,140,448	52.6%
Total gross revenues	€229,631,099	
Total net revenues	€188,524,664	
Total net revenues from Italian visitors[a]	€89,360,691	47.4%
Total net revenues from foreign visitors[a]	€99,163,973	52.6%
Average gross ticket price	€9.20	
Average net ticket price	€7.50	

Source: The Statistical Office of the Ministry of Cultural Heritage.

[a] Estimates on Italian and foreign visitors based on information reported on the Census of Italian Museums and Heritage Institutions, 2018 (ISTAT).

Since a universal membership scheme would apply to single individuals, one methodological challenge posed by the available data is to infer how many paid admissions are repeated visits to any museum or heritage institution belonging to the network. For foreign visitors, it is only possible to make some speculative hypotheses on how many state museums they visit during their trip to Italy. Conversely, for Italian visitors, cultural participation data on the yearly frequency of attendance to museums, archaeological areas, and monuments could provide a more grounded indication.

Figure 10.1 presents the number of visitors per frequency of attendance and the number of paid admissions of each group to the state museum system, assuming that the same distribution of visits per individual inferred through cultural participation survey for the Italian population aged 18 and over also holds for the subpopulation of Italian visitors to State museums. As expected, the distribution of visitors and visits per frequency of attendance is skewed. However, while visitors who have made up to three visits correspond to about 50% of the total of Italian visitors, the share of visits by this group is only 20% of the total admissions, accounting for the relative contribution of more frequent visitors.

From this elaboration, it can be easily estimated that a total of 2,272,608 individuals have made at least once a paid admission to Italian state museums. Dividing the revenues from admission fees attributed to Italian visitors by this figure leads to an amount of 39 euros.[3] This amount represents the breakeven price of the membership scheme that should be charged to obtain the same revenues collected through paid admissions of Italian visitors.

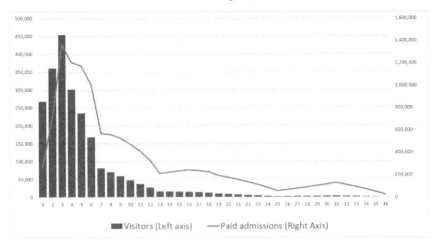

Figure 10.1 Distribution of visitors aged 18 and over and paid admissions to Italian State museums, per frequency of visit, year 2018.

Note: Visitors (right axis), Visits (left axis); Data estimated from cultural participation statistics reporting the frequency of attendance to museums, archaeological sites, and monuments for the Italian population aged 18 and over in the last 12 months. Reference year: 2018.

This calculus is based on some rigid assumptions and can be criticized for oversimplifying a complex reality that requires more data collection to be understood. Further, it can be objected that it does not consider relevant aspects of museum visitors' behaviour. Nevertheless, it represents a starting point for a more reasoned discussion on the economic opportunities of implementing a universal membership scheme. The price obtained is first in line with, if not lower than, existing annual museum passes targeting residents.[4] If the same price of the annual membership scheme were applied to foreign visitors, this would barely correspond to the sum of the entrance tickets to some of the museums, which often represent a must on foreigners' trips to Italy.[5] Moreover, according to the estimated revenues generated through entrance fees by foreign visitors, a price of 39 euros for a universal membership scheme implies that at least 2.5 million foreigners should purchase the pass, which corresponds to the 12% of foreign cultural tourists visiting Italy.[6]

The economic feasibility of the pricing proposal is strongly dependent on the number of people potentially interested in subscribing to the universal membership scheme. Starting from this breakeven scenario, there are several factors related to individual preferences that can negatively or positively influence the demand for the scheme, both for the Italian and foreign audience:

• *Preferences of occasional visitors:* people who expect to visit state museums only a few times a year and do not derive enough utility from the bundled digital goods provided through the online platform may find the pass not worth and would still prefer to purchase single admissions. Alternatively, those that currently make few onsite visits may consider it worth paying a premium price for exclusive access to the online cultural content. Considering the proposed price of the membership schemes, this argument applies to subjects with up to four visits, making their preferences and choice relevant for determining the size of the potential base of pass-holders.

- *Preferences for flat-rate pricing:* visitors might prefer a flat rate even if it is higher than the pay-per-visit price. Behavioural research has identified several explanations for this bias, such as mental accounting or risk aversion (Lambrecht and Skiera, 2006). As a result, risk-averse individuals may choose to purchase the museum membership scheme for the option value it provides to visit any number of times museums and heritage sites. Further, individuals who used to visit state museums only during free-admittance special days may be willing to pay the pass for more flexibility in planning their visits. Overall, these effects would increase the base of potential pass-holders.
- *Preferences for variety and bundled products:* Without a membership scheme, the observed demand is that of visits to museums for which individuals had a reservation price higher than the admission fee. However, the same individuals could express lower but positive reservation prices for visiting other museums in the network. As a mixed bundling strategy combining access to several museums and information goods content at a lower price than if the visitor were to purchase each ticket individually (Bakos and Brynjolfsson, 1999), the membership scheme could partly address such unsatiated demand and be attractive for individuals who have preferences for greater variety in cultural heritage experiences.
- *Preferences for voluntary contributions:* The universal membership scheme could trigger individual support to cultural heritage regardless of the utility arising from visits and online content. Subscription to the annual pass could be then considered not merely for the advantage of accessing collections and sites, but for some people as a form of crowd-patronage (Swords, 2017). Paying for the membership scheme would then be a form of voluntary price discrimination for those willing to support the network of state museums (Hansmann, 1981).

The economic sustainability of the universal membership scheme depends on the above-listed factors concerning individual preferences, which may influence its adoption. Although a museum pass is already theoretically applicable today, we believe that the real success of this initiative depends on whether it will be able to represent an alternative funding tool for museums in a post-COVID-19 scenario.

Finally, there are other relevant issues to consider regarding the effective implementation of this proposal. These aspects do not concern the potential demand of pass purchasers, but economic factors affecting the provision of the service within the new membership scheme.

- *Management costs:* ticketing services currently amount to 40 million euros, about 20% of revenues from paid admissions. Implementing the new universal membership scheme while maintaining the option of single entrance fee available should reduce the management costs of ticketing services. If this were not the case, adopting a universal membership scheme would risk being a lower option than the current ticketing service system.
- *Equity concerns:* Italian state museums are not evenly distributed over the territory but are more concentrated in some regions (i.e. Tuscany, Lazio or Campagna). While geographic distribution should not pose a problem for foreign visitors, it could create inequalities in access opportunities for locals. Residents in areas far from state museums face higher costs to use the pass, which can only be partly lessened by the circulation of artworks and objects exhibited at different museums in the network.
- *Allocation rules:* the choice of the allocation rule of the joint proceeds from the pass sales can lead to distributional concerns, and it might become particularly relevant if the pass program is extended to other museums and heritage institutions, because it can generate divergent incentives to participate in the universal membership scheme. According to Ginsburgh and Zang (2001), a sharing rule based on the relative contribution of each museum to the overall income generated by the joint pass program is superior to other sharing rules (i.e. those proportional to losses from forgone admission fees or proportional only to the number of visits) as this rule rewards attractiveness but also allocate income to free entry museums.

Conclusion

In this chapter, we have analyzed how the pandemic has impacted the heritage sector, leading to a structural change that obliges museums and heritage institutions to pursue new strategies for audience involvement and economic sustainability.

Among the major transformations, we claim COVID-19 has accelerated the convergence between the digital and physical experience of heritage-related services and will give the local audience and proximity tourism more prominence as a source of stability for museum activities.

Two seminal proposals that emerged in the Italian debate during the COVID-19 crisis provide insights as to how museums and heritage institutions, to cope with such structural change, need to shift from a transactional to a relationship orientation towards their audience and explore new network governance models to fully exploit the opportunities provided by the integration between digital and onsite services. Crucially, we argue that membership schemes to museum networks have the potential to reach these complementary objectives.

The illustrative application of a universal membership scheme for Italian State museums as a novel tool of audience involvement suggests that this policy proposal might be, in principle, viable, representing a starting point for a more reasoned discussion on the economic opportunities of implementing innovative subscription models in the heritage sector.

While the impacts of COVID-19 on the heritage sector can be reasonably generalized, our contribution offers a policy perspective and normative arguments that fit the Italian context, but do not exhaust a discussion on the alternative strategies that museums and heritage institutions can pursue for audience involvement and economic sustainability in these new times. For example, we focused on the pricing of a membership scheme applied to museum networks. However, dynamic pricing adopted by single institutions to respond to temporal demand fluctuations can represent another potential option of financial sustainability under the newly volatile conditions (Seaman, 2018). At the same time, it is difficult to assess to what extent the advantages of implementing novel subscription models for museum networks could are sensitive to scenarios where pre-pandemic conditions and behaviours are restored.

Notes

1. After the initial proposal, the project has developed with the start-up of a new company called ITsART. In June 2021, the platform has been officially launched at www.itsart.tv
2. https://ilgiornaledellarte.com/articoli/l-orgoglio-di-esserci-di-nuovo-brad-burne-brera/133577.html
3. We use revenues net of ticketing service concessions. Using gross revenues, the price of the membership scheme is 42 euros.
4. The Netherlands Museum Pass charges a full rate at 64 euros. The newly introduced annual pass by the Galleria degli Uffizi is priced at 50 euros, including also temporary exhibitions.
5. For example, the entrance fee to Colosseum and Palatino is 16 euros, that to Pompei Archeological Park is 14.5, while for Galleria degli Uffizi is 20 euros.
6. Estimate based on Bank of Italy statistics on international tourism flows. In 2018, 40.2 million foreigners visited Italy for holiday and 19.4 million motivated their holiday for visiting cities of art or other cultural reasons.

References

Agostino, D., Arnaboldi, M., & Lampis, A. (2020a). Italian state museums during the COVID-19 crisis: from onsite closure to online openness. *Museum Management and Curatorship, 35*(4), 362–372.

Agostino, D., Arnaboldi, M., & Lorenzini, E. (2020b). Verso un "new normal" dei musei post-COVID 19: quale ruolo per il digitale?. *Economia della Cultura, 30*(1), 79–83.

Anderson, G. (Ed.). (2004). *Reinventing the museum: Historical and contemporary perspectives on the paradigm shift*. Rowman Altamira, Lahnam, MD.

Bagdadli, S. (2003). Museum and theatre networks in Italy: Determinants and typology. *International Journal of Arts Management*, 6(1),19–29.

Baia Curioni, S. (2018). "I've seen fire and I've seen rain". Notes on the state museum reform in Italy. *Museum Management and Curatorship*, 33(6), 555–569.

Bakhshi, H., & Throsby, D. (2012). New technologies in cultural institutions: Theory, evidence and policy implications. *International Journal of Cultural Policy*, 18(2), 205–222.

Bakos, Y., & Brynjolfsson, E. (1999). Bundling information goods: Pricing, profits, and efficiency. *Management Science*, 45(12), 1613–1630.

Ballina, F. J., Valdes, L., & Del Valle, E. (2019). The Phygital experience in the smart tourism destination. *International Journal of Tourism Cities*, 5(4), 656–671.

Bertacchini, E., & Morando, F. (2013). The future of museums in the digital age: New models for access to and use of digital collections. *International Journal of Arts Management*, 15(2), 60–72.

Bertacchini, E. E., Dalle Nogare, C., & Scuderi, R. (2018). Ownership, organization structure and public service provision: the case of museums. *Journal of Cultural Economics*, 42(4), 619–643.

Bertacchini, E., Nuccio, M., & Durio, A. (2021). Proximity tourism and cultural amenities: Evidence from a regional museum card. *Tourism Economics*, 27(1), 187–204.

Black, G. (2013). Developing audiences for the twenty-first-century museum. In *The International Handbooks of museum studies*, 123–151, Oxford: Wiley Blackway.

Black, G. (2016). Remember the 70%: Sustaining "core" museum audiences. *Museum Management and Curatorship*, 31(4), 386–401.

Brida, J. G., Disegna, M., & Scuderi, R. (2014). The behaviour of repeat visitors to museums: Review and empirical findings. *Quality & Quantity*, 48(5), 2817–2840.

Cellini, R., & Cuccia, T. (2018). How free admittance affects charged visits to museums: An analysis of the Italian case. *Oxford Economic Papers*, 70(3), 680–698.

Drazin, R., Glynn, M. A., & Kazanjian, R. K. (2004). Dynamics of structural change. In *Handbook of organizational change and innovation*, 173, Oxford University Press, New York.

Farzanegan, M. R., Gholipour, H. F., Feizi, M., Nunkoo, R., & Andargoli, A. E. (2020). International tourism and outbreak of coronavirus (COVID-19): A cross-country analysis. *Journal of Travel Research*, https://doi.org/10.1177/0047287520931593

Frey, B. S., & Steiner, L. (2012). Pay as you go: A new proposal for museum pricing. *Museum Management and Curatorship*, 27(3), 223–235.

Garrido, M. J., & Camarero, C. (2014). Learning and relationship orientation: An empirical examination in European museums. *International Journal of Nonprofit and Voluntary Sector Marketing*, 19(2), 92–109.

Ginsburgh, V., & Zang, I. (2001). Sharing the income of a museum pass program. *Museum Management and Curatorship*, 19(4), 371–383.

Gössling, S., Scott, D., & Hall, C. M. (2020). Pandemics, tourism and global change: A rapid assessment of COVID-19. *Journal of Sustainable Tourism*, 29(1),1–20.

Hansmann, H. (1981). Nonprofit enterprise in the performing arts. *The Bell Journal of Economics*, 12(2), 341–361.

Jeuring, J., & Diaz-Soria, I. (2017). Introduction: proximity and intraregional aspects of tourism. *Tourism Geographies, 19*(1), 4–8.

Jones, C., Lorenzen, M., & Sapsed, J. (Eds.). (2015). *The Oxford handbook of creative industries.* Oxford University Press, Oxford, UK.

Lambrecht, A., & Skiera, B. (2006). Paying too much and being happy about it: Existence, causes, and consequences of tariff-choice biases. *Journal of marketing Research, 43*(2), 212–223.

Lang, C., Reeve, J., & Woollard, V. (Eds.). (2006). *The responsive museum: working with audiences in the twenty-first century.* Ashgate Publishing, Ltd, Hampshire, UK.

Marty, P. F. (2008). Museum websites and museum visitors: Digital museum resources and their use. *Museum Management and Curatorship, 23*(1), 81–99.

Marzano, M., & Castellini, M. (2018). The reform of the Italian ministry of cultural heritage: Implications for governance of the museum system. *The Journal of Arts Management, Law, and Society, 48*(3), 206–220.

Navarrete, T. (2013). Museums. In *Handbook on the digital creative economy.* Edward Elgar Publishing, Cheltenham, UK.

Navarrete, T., & Borowiecki, K. J. (2016). Changes in cultural consumption: Ethnographic collections in Wikipedia. *Cultural Trends, 25*(4), 233–248.

Network for European Museums Organization. (2020). Survey on the impact of the COVID-19 situation on museums in Europe. Retrieved from https://www.ne-mo.org/fileadmin/Dateien/public/NEMO_documents/NEMO_COVID19_Report_12.05.2020.pdf

Nuccio, M., & Bertacchini, E. (2021). Data-driven arts and cultural organizations: Opportunity or chimera?. *European Planning Studies,* 1–18. https://doi.org/10.1080/09654313.2021.1916443

Prideaux, B., Thompson, M., & Pabel, A. (2020). Lessons from COVID-19 can prepare global tourism for the economic transformation needed to combat climate change. *Tourism Geographies, 22*(3), 1–12.

Richards G (2018) Cultural tourism: A review of recent research and trends. *Journal of Hospitality and Tourism Management 36,* 12–21.

Romagosa, F. (2020). The COVID-19 crisis: Opportunities for sustainable and proximity tourism. *Tourism Geographies, 22*(3), 1–5.

Samaroudi, M., Echavarria, K. R., & Perry, L. (2020). Heritage in lockdown: Digital provision of memory institutions in the UK and US of America during the COVID-19 pandemic. *Museum Management and Curatorship, 35*(4), 1–25.

Seaman, B. A. (2018). Static and dynamic pricing strategies: How unique for nonprofits?. In *Handbook of Research on Nonprofit Economics and Management.* Edward Elgar Publishing, Cheltenham, UK.

Slater, A. (2004). Revisiting membership scheme typologies in museums and galleries. *International Journal of Nonprofit and Voluntary Sector Marketing, 9*(3), 238–260.

Swords, J. (2017). Crowd-patronage – Intermediaries, geographies and relationships in patronage networks. *Poetics, 64,* 63–73.

UNESCO (2020). Museums around the world in the face of COVID-19, UNESCO report.

Werff, S., Koopmans, C., & Boyer, C. 2014. The effects of the Dutch museum pass on museum visits and museum revenues. *SEO Discussion Paper, 79. SEO Economisch Onderzoek.*

11 The COVID-19 pandemic and cultural industries in Spain

Early impacts of lockdown

Raúl Abeledo-Sanchis and
Guillem Bacete Armengot

Introduction

The resilience of the Cultural and Creative Sectors (CCSs) has been put to the test once again, not only because of the sequence of disruptive changes and drawbacks that cultural SMEs and entrepreneurs have faced in recent years (Pratt, 2009; De-Peuter, 2011; Donald *et al.*, 2013), but also because of the limited resources they have had at their disposal to do so. While the role of culture and creativity as a driver of economic growth (Potts and Cunningham, 2008; de-Miguel-Molina *et al.*, 2012; Boix *et al.*, 2013; Boix-Domenech *et al.*, 2021) and their contribution to social fairness, active citizenship and identity in the European nations (List *et al.*, 2017; European Commission, 2018a), has been widely recognized, policymakers have only paid attention to the CCS in times of crisis, when their conditions have been exposed (Comunian and Conor, 2017; Comunian and England, 2020).

In this context, the Cultural Economics Research Unit of the University of Valencia (Econcult) surveyed 780 cultural agents from Spain from 16 April to 17 May 2020 to measure the impact of the COVID-19 outbreak on the CCSs (Abeledo *et al.*, 2020). The main objective of this survey was to collect data on the effects that the strict lockdown measures implemented by Royal Decree on 14 March 2020 had on Spanish CCS organizations. The aim was to establish whether these organizations had access to support schemes and determine what measures they thought could help them recover. The survey provided relevant information on the actions they had taken to deal with the crisis, the availability and access to public subsidies, and their future prospects. The results revealed that the extremely uncertain environment generated by COVID-19 had forced cultural agents to adjust rapidly to ensure their short-term survival with limited access to public support.

This chapter examines how Spanish cultural and creative organizations reacted to the lockdown measures, looking at the impact on their operational structure, the actions they took to adapt, and the resources at their disposal, as well as their prospects in the medium and long term.

DOI: 10.4324/9781003128274-15

The first section of this chapter examines the effects of lockdown on CCS organizations from a short-term operational perspective, comparing expected revenue losses in the first and second quarters of 2020 and highlighting the needs identified by the survey respondents. The second section looks at the time allocated by respondents to activities related to short-term sustainability, paying special attention to the digitalization of activities and business models. The third section analyses the respondents' views on their future prospects and the most effective measures to deal with the effects of the COVID-19 crisis. The chapter concludes by reflecting on the fragile condition of the CCS and the effectiveness of the subsidy scheme deployed by the Spanish government to support them. The survey results point to the need for a coordinated and systematic response to overcome the effects of the pandemic.

Survey and sample details

This chapter analyses the results of a survey carried out between 16 April and 17 May 2020, nearly one month after the beginning of the Spanish lockdown. The survey was addressed to organizations belonging to the CCSs, defined in the Creative Europe programme as those sectors whose activities are based on cultural values or artistic and other individual or collective creative expressions (European Commission, 2018b). Although the survey was mainly distributed to SMEs and freelance professionals, NGOs and informal workers were also included to achieve representation of a wider range of agents.

The snowball sampling technique, a non-probabilistic sampling procedure, was used to obtain a significant number of responses in a short period of time (Abeledo *et al.*, 2020). The resulting analysis should be considered exploratory, as it was only intended to provide a quick snapshot of the situation at a time when there was no information on how the cultural sectors were coping with the lockdown. Further research will be required in the future to fully understand the extent of the impact of COVID-19 on the Spanish CCS.

As shown in Table 11.1, the total number of valid responses for the survey was 784. The survey adopted the definition of CCSs used in the Creative Europe programme, as it was based on a survey developed for the InterregMed "Chebec" project.[1] However, as the definition of Cultural Sectors provided by Creative Europe was not broad enough, an "other" option was included to capture any sectors that fell outside of that definition, such as advertising or journalism.

Performing arts were the most represented sector, accounting for one-third of the sample (33.2%), followed by visual arts, cultural heritage, and design. These four sectors alone accounted for 79.08% of the sample. The size of these groups was large enough to warrant an individual analysis, since their behaviour could present variations from the average.

Table 11.1 Distribution of the survey sample according to sectors.

Sector	Count (N)	Percent (%)
Performing arts	260	33%
Visual arts	136	17%
Cultural heritage	128	16%
Design and applied arts	96	12%
Multidisciplinary (at least two sectors)	53	7%
Literature, books, and reading	41	5%
Consultancy, research, and education	17	2%
Cultural communication	16	2%
Architecture	14	2%
Ancillary services	6	1%
Other (advertising, journalism, branding, cultural tourism, NGOs, etc.)	17	2%
Total	784	100%

Source: Own elaboration.

Impact of the COVID-19 outbreak: Revenue losses and short-term impact

The impact of lockdown on the Spanish population manifested itself in different ways, including an increase in psychological disorders stemming from fear of contagion, social isolation or loss of employment (Sandín et al., 2020), and widening social inequalities that especially affected women (Rodríguez-Rivero et al., 2020).

The Spanish economy, heavily reliant on tourism-related activities, was turned upside down due to the mobility restrictions. The CCSs were also among the hardest hit by the pandemic, which affected venue-based activities and supply chains the most (Travkina and Sacco, 2020). The economic impact of the crisis bore some similarities to that of the 2008 financial crisis in terms of its asymmetric effects on the cultural ecosystems, which varied depending on geographic context and sectoral specialization (Escalona-Orcao et al., 2021). CCS organizations had to deal with delays or cancellations of events, loss of sales or business opportunities, and workforce reductions, among others. Table 11.2 shows how lockdown affected the activities of the survey respondents on a scale of 1 to 5, where 1 means "strongly disagree" and 5 means "strongly agree".

The standard deviation (SD) values tend to be far from the mean, which reveals a dispersed pattern that can be explained by the heterogeneous nature of the CCS. However, if the mean values are considered, delays and postponement of events are the most common issues highlighted by respondents (Mean = 4.38, SD = 1.17), followed closely by lost sales and cancelled orders (Mean = 4.30, SD = 1.23) and loss of business opportunities and collaborations (Mean = 4.08, SD = 1.27), all of which are linked to the immediate effects of the mobility restrictions implemented by the

Table 11.2 Lockdown impact assessment.

Variables (1 = strongly disagree; 5 = strongly agree)	Most frequent value	Mean	Standard deviation (SD)
Delays in the organization of events managed by my organization	5	4.38	1.17
Lost sales/cancelled orders	5	4.30	1.23
Loss of business opportunities with other partners	5	4.08	1.27
Impossibility of participating in or attending a major trade fair or exhibition	5	3.91	1.55
Physical limitations (e.g. to produce works of art, perform, attend workshops, etc.).	5	3.83	1.53
Workforce reduction and staff downsizing	5	3.02	1.65
Many suppliers are not able to secure short-term supply	5	2.98	1.55

Source: Own elaboration.

Spanish government. These three variables display a similar standard deviation, which means that these issues affected the CCS irrespective of sector. This does not apply to the rest of variables, as the higher standard deviation, which reveals a polarized behaviour among respondents, could be attributed to differences between sectors. For instance, the impossibility of participating in trade fairs and exhibitions may have had a more significant impact on the literature sector. The same applies to physical limitations, since some activities require specific conditions and spaces and are therefore less likely to "go digital".

The severity of the short-term effects of COVID-19 becomes apparent when we look at the income perceived by cultural workers in the first half of 2020. The results for the first quarter were already available at the time of the survey (April 2020), while the figures for the second quarter represent the losses expected by respondents. Figure 11.1 compares the revenue losses experienced by cultural organizations.

The comparison reveals that the impact on income intensified during the second quarter, which is consistent with the fact that Spanish organizations were able to operate almost normally until March. In the first quarter, 13.27% of respondents experienced no income loss, while a third of those surveyed (34.82%) reported an income loss of more than 75%. In contrast, almost half (49.49%) of the organizations surveyed estimated losses of more than 75% in the second quarter. Moreover, the percentage of respondents who expected no income loss during this period decreased to 4.34%.

These income losses had a significant impact on the fixed costs of cultural organizations and aggravated the fragility of their productive and management structure, threatening their survival and the sustainability of

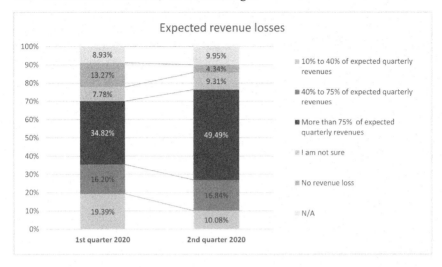

Figure 11.1 Expected revenue losses in the first half of 2020.

Source: Own elaboration.

the cultural ecosystem. The restrictions put in place to stop the spread of the virus limited production in unprecedented ways and created a "new normal" that forced organizations to make substantial changes in order to continue operating. Respondents were asked to assign levels of priority to the need for information on the support available, liquidity, and the need to adapt to remote working on a scale of 1 to 5 where 1 meant "minimum need" and 5 meant "maximum need". The results are shown in Table 11.3.

The aggregated analysis reveals that information stands out as the highest priority need, followed by liquidity. The need to adapt to remote working and the digital environment was seen as secondary. These results are in line with what could be expected in a changing context, although it is worth noting that response patterns are quite dispersed for all variables (with SD values ranging from 1.32 to 1.42) due to sectoral differences. Although the majority of respondents assigned maximum priority to the

Table 11.3 Assessment of priority needs.

Variables (1 = minimum need; 5= maximum need)	Most frequent value	Mean	Standard deviation (SD)
Clear information on available subsidies	5	3.85	1.32
Information to reschedule activities	5	3.79	1.40
Liquidity	5	3.77	1.38
Remote working and home-life balance	5	3.24	1.42
Adapting to the digital environment	3	3.19	1.40

Source: Own elaboration.

need for information on available subsidies, a divergence can be observed in the responses from venue-based sectors (performing arts and heritage) and design and applied arts. In the first case, having access to information that allowed them to reschedule their activities was essential due to their fixed costs and their reliance on visitors and spectators as their main source of income. It makes sense for those in design and applied arts to prioritize access to funding and liquidity schemes, although further research would be required to explore their assessment in more detail.

Coping with lockdown: Adaptive strategies and available support instruments

This section provides aggregated information on how the CCS coped with lockdown and does not delve into sectoral differences, as such analysis would require further research and therefore falls outside the scope of this piece of work.

The COVID-19 pandemic has created an environment of extreme uncertainty and has had significant implications for the economic and financial sustainability of cultural organizations. The short-term responses shown in Figure 11.2 reveal the different conditions that cultural and creative organizations found themselves in, particularly when it came to implementing digital processes.

Practically half of the survey respondents (48.47%) indicated that they had implemented remote working in response to lockdown measures, while almost 24% invested in the digitalization of their activities, which could mean either setting up a workspace at home or looking at alternative ways

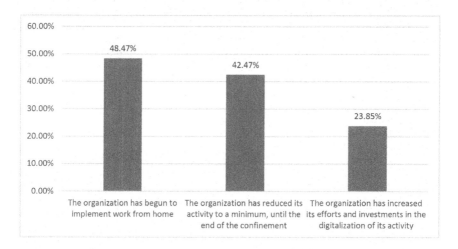

Figure 11.2 Actions deployed in response to lockdown.

Source: Own elaboration.

to meet the potential demand (e.g. online portfolios, websites, streaming contents, etc.). The COVID-19 outbreak accelerated digitalization trends, introducing structural transformations in cultural production that will run parallel to changes in consumption patterns in the medium and long term. However, venue-based sectors were not able to deploy digital solutions as easily as other sectors such as those depending on bulk creative capacity. For instance, half of the performing arts respondents (50.38%) were forced to reduce their activities to a minimum. The restrictions on live events and practice and rehearsal spaces, combined with the uncertainties around cultural programming, have led performing artists to an unsustainable situation that has aggravated their already precarious conditions (Bonnin Arias and Rubio Arostegui, 2019).

The reduction in activities altered the productive dimension of CCS organizations, suddenly interrupting their productive routines and forcing them to remain idle. Table 11.4 shows how these organizations re-allocated time to different productive tasks during the lockdown on a scale of 1 to 5, where 1 means "minimum time" and 5 "maximum time".

The activity to which respondents allocated most of their time was working on new ideas or projects they had no time to work on before (Mean = 3.39, SD = 1.28), followed by rethinking their business model or work processes to adapt to the new situation (Mean = 3.19, SD = 1.39). Although 4 and 5 are the most repeated values on the scale, the responses are quite dispersed, which results in a lower mean value for both variables (3.39 and 3.19, respectively).

Table 11.4 Activities/actions carried out during lockdown (time allocation).

Variables (1 = minimum time; 5 = maximum time)	Most frequent value	Mean	Standard deviation (SD)
Work on new ideas and products or projects I had no time to focus on before	4	3.39	1.28
Rethinking the business model and working processes	5	3.19	1.39
Administration and management work, including searching for subsidies	3	3.10	1.43
Increased communication efforts: dissemination, online marketing	3	2.96	1.40
Adapting services/products to the new medium-term scenario	1	2.95	1.44
Archive management, catching up on postponed work	3	2.90	1.39
Training and acquiring new skills	3	2.77	1.35
Market analysis (diagnosis of the situation, prospects for demand, etc.)	1	2.59	1.34

Source: Own elaboration.

Administration and management work related to available subsidies (Mean = 3.10, SD = 1.43) was also a priority for some of the respondents, especially those belonging to the heritage and visual arts sectors. It is important to note that although the most frequent value for this variable is 3, which is in the middle of the scale, the response pattern is also quite dispersed.

Something similar happens with communication efforts (Mean = 2.96, SD = 1.40). In this case, the low ratings for performing arts and design, which are highly represented in the sample, lower the mean. However, 38% of respondents from the literature and publishing sectors allocated a significant amount of time (4) to communication efforts. At a time when libraries were declared non-essential businesses, these values could point to a shift towards digitalization and online sales.

Surprisingly, the most frequent value for the variable "adapting services and products to the medium-term scenario" (Mean = 2.95, SD = 1.44) was 1, although the mean is almost in the middle of the scale (2.95). The concentration of responses from the performing arts sector around the lowest value contributed significantly to this phenomenon. On the other hand, 32% of respondents from the heritage and literature sectors spent most of their time (5) adapting their business models to the new scenario brought about by COVID restrictions.

In terms of market analysis (Mean = 2.59, SD = 1.34), the response pattern shows a general concentration on low values, following the trend of the most repeated value. This clearly indicates that it was too soon for cultural organizations to carry out such an analysis. Only the books and publishing sector show more moderate response patterns, concentrated around 3.

The productive constraints of lockdown triggered an immediate need for financial assistance for the cultural and creative workers and organizations. Although the Spanish government implemented measures to offset the economic impact of the pandemic, these were aimed at workers and SMEs irrespective of sector. Although cultural and creative organizations could file a Record of Temporary Employment Regulation (ERTE, in Spanish) to reduce their workforce, these subsidies were available to organizations from any sector. Support schemes specific to cultural organizations were deployed in May 2020. These included measures such as extraordinary access to unemployment benefits for intermittent cultural workers as well as soft loans and guarantees, advances and compensation for artists who had not perceived any income due to event cancellations, and the creation of support funds for the audio-visual and performing arts sectors. Figure 11.3 shows the extent to which respondents had access to these types of subsidies.

At the time of the survey, only 11% of respondents had actually received some kind of public financial assistance, while 22% stated that they were waiting for it and 44% had not had any.

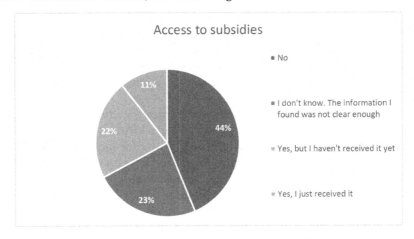

Figure 11.3 Access to COVID-19 subsidies.

Source: Own elaboration.

Future prospects and vision

The magnitude of the social and economic changes triggered by the lockdown measures suggests that their effects may be felt for a long time. Therefore, it is quite surprising that only 9.06% of respondents stated they would likely have to close down. However, practically all respondents (92.09%) acknowledged that they would be affected by the COVID-19 crisis to some extent in the long term. The current situation threatens the integrity of the Spanish cultural ecosystems due to job shedding and the related decrease in diversity and the financial stress that cultural and creative organizations are under.

Respondents were asked about the expected effects of the COVID-19 outbreak on the cultural ecosystem. They were asked to assess the likelihood of a series of changes on a scale of 1 to 5, where 1 was "least likely" and 5 "most likely". The results are shown in Table 11.5.

Overall, the results paint a pessimistic picture defined by a generalized mistrust in society and policymakers. Respondents thought that the recovery of the cultural ecosystem was more likely to stem from the sector itself than from public bodies.

According to the cultural organizations surveyed, the likeliest change in the CCS will be an intensification of the precarious working conditions (Mean = 4.17, SD = 1.18) that had already been a regular descriptor before COVID-19 (De-Peuter, 2011; Donald, Gertler and Tyler, 2013; Serafini and Banks, 2020). The severe consequences of the pandemic have exposed the fragile conditions of art and creative workers, which have only been acknowledged by policymakers in times of crisis (Comunian and Conor, 2017; Comunian and England, 2020). The emergence of new business

Table 11.5 Expected long-term changes in the cultural ecosystem.

Variables (1 = least likely; 5 = most likely)	Most frequent value	Mean	Standard deviation (SD)
Increased precariousness of work in the cultural and creative sectors	5	4.17	1.18
Emergence of new business models in the cultural and creative sectors	5	3.81	1.13
Changes in consumption patterns towards digital models	4	3.58	1.14
Increased CCS internationalization strategies after recovery (long term)	5	3.40	1.34
Improved perception of the economic and social value of cultural and creative activities	3	3.07	1.20
Improved sectoral structuring of CCS, creation of sectoral networks and territorial creativity hubs	3	2.98	1.27
Increased public-private partnerships and collaboration	3	2.84	1.31
Increased support for CCS through public policies	3	2.78	1.34

Source: Own elaboration.

models (Mean = 3.81, SD = 1.13) and changes in consumption patterns (Mean = 3.58, SD = 1.14) were also considered moderately likely, although the most frequent value for the latter was 4, a slight deviation from the average. These variables show the effects of the economic freeze on the supply and demand for cultural goods and services. A comparison between the two reveals a more proactive approach on the supply side.

An increase of internationalization strategies in the CCS post-COVID (Mean = 3.40, SD = 1.34) was also seen as moderately likely given the proactive image of cultural organizations. However, it is important to note that not all sectors agree with this assessment, as inferred from the increase in the deviation.

The last four variables show some degree of mistrust in the response expected from society and particularly policymakers. According to respondents, it is only moderately likely that the CSS will see an improvement in the perception of the economic and social value of culture (Mean = 3.07, SD = 1.20), followed by an improvement in the structuring and collaboration between CCS (Mean = 2.98, SD = 1.27). The same happens with variables related to public support for the CCS, with low levels of confidence in public-private collaboration (Mean = 2.84, SD = 1.31) and support through public policies (Mean = 2.78, SD = 1.34).

Respondents were also asked about the most effective measures to counter the long-term effects of COVID-19. A series of measures were presented

Table 11.6 Preferred measures to counter the effects of COVID-19 on cultural ecosystems.

Measures	1st option	2nd option	3rd option
A strategic plan to promote the recovery of the cultural and creative sectors (e.g. establish priorities, resources, etc.)	35%	17%	16%
Increase of public procurement of cultural organizations (e.g. funding of cultural projects, open calls, etc.).	17%	21%	15%
Financial support for businesses (loans, grants, etc.)	17%	17%	14%
Measures to support employment in the cultural sectors (e.g. short-term work allowance)	14%	11%	19%
Consumer vouchers or VAT reduction on cultural products and services to stimulate demand	6%	14%	15%
Tax deferment	8%	12%	9%
Communication campaign to stimulate local demand	3%	8%	12%
Total (option)	100%	100%	100%

Source: Own elaboration.

in a matrix in descending order, from most to least effective. Table 11.6 summarizes the perceived effectiveness of each of these measures.

A supply-side approach stands out as the preferred option. The need for comprehensive action through a strategic plan to promote the recovery of the CCSs was chosen by 35% of respondents as the first option. In this sense, the CCS organizations surveyed demand more attention from policymakers, particularly in terms of the planning of cultural activities. Other issues identified as relevant are subsidies and soft loans for businesses and an increase in public procurement, both of them with 17%.

As for the second option, an increase in public procurement was selected by 21% of respondents, followed closely by financial subsidies for businesses and a strategic plan, with 17% each. Finally, 19% of respondents chose measures to support cultural employment as the third option, followed by a strategic plan (16%).

On the demand side, measures such as consumer vouchers or VAT reduction on cultural products and services to stimulate demand were not considered effective in overcoming the crisis.

Conclusion

This chapter presented a descriptive analysis of the early-stage impact of the lockdown measures deployed in March 2020 on the Spanish CCSs, as well as their short-term response. Beyond the economic and organizational impact analyzed in this chapter, the COVID-19 outbreak has evidenced the need for a structural and systemic transformation of the cultural sector.

In recent years, the CCS have faced significant difficulties, and cultural and artistic work has received little attention from policymakers (Comunian and Conor, 2017), despite becoming strongly associated with precariousness (De-Peuter, 2011; Donald, Gertler and Tyler, 2013). The spread of COVID-19 and the effects of the lockdown measures have further exposed the fragility of workers in the CCS (Comunian and England, 2020).

However, lockdown measures have had an uneven impact on the CCS, especially affecting venue-based sectors and those whose production processes are characterized by a low degree of digitalization. Given the asymmetric impact caused by the heterogeneous nature of the CCS, it is expected that each sub-sector will recover at a different pace (Escalona-Orcao *et al.*, 2021). This raises questions about the future of the Spanish cultural ecosystems, which may be threatened by job losses and worsening working conditions in the short term.

The restrictions put in place to prevent the spread of the virus have halted production and caused significant losses, generating an extremely uncertain environment in which organizational choices carry high risks. This explains the importance given to the flow of information related to the availability of subsidies and the rescheduling of activities. Almost half (49.49%) of the respondents estimated income losses of more than 75% in the second quarter of 2020, when strict lockdown measures were still in place. While the pandemic has triggered the acceleration of digitalization, stimulated by changes in consumption patterns in the medium and long term, the reduction of activities has altered the productive dimension of CCS organizations, which found their productive routines being suddenly interrupted and their resources and time remaining idle.

Against this backdrop, the Spanish government deployed cross-sector measures for workers and SMEs. Although the Records of Temporary Employment Regulation (ERTE, in Spanish) had the potential to help cultural and creative organizations deal with workforce reductions, these subsidies were made available to organizations from any sector. While the decision to provide subsidies and support measures to a large group of beneficiaries seems rational from the government's perspective, cultural workers were already facing significant difficulties to consolidate their careers and make a living (Pérez Ibáñez and López-Aparicio, 2018; Bonnin Arias and Rubio Arostegui, 2019). The lack of a support scheme specific to CCS organizations may explain why respondents showed a generalized mistrust in policymakers and thought that support from the public sector was very unlikely in the long term. The organizations surveyed believed that the most effective solution would be a comprehensive and structured set of actions involving the whole cultural ecosystem delivered through a strategic plan. These organizations made it clear that policymakers should pay more attention to the CCS, particularly in terms of cultural planning.

Note

1. A survey was conducted as part of the InterregMed Chebec Project to explore how lockdown was affecting the participant CCS organizations. The University of Valencia later took the initiative to extend the survey to Spain on a voluntary basis.

References

Abeledo, R. *et al.* (2020) *Análisis del impacto del Covid-19 sobre las organizaciones y agentes culturales en España.* Valencia: Econcult. Available at: http://www.econcult.eu/es/publicaciones/analisis-del-impacto-del-covid-19-las-organizaciones-agentes-culturales-espana/ (Accessed: 10 November 2020).

Boix-Domenech, R., Peiró-Palomino, J. and Rausell-Köster, P. (2021) "Creative industries and productivity in the European regions. Is there a Mediterranean effect?", *Regional Science Policy & Practice*, pp. 1–19. doi: 10.1111/rsp3.12395.

Boix, R., de-Miguel-Molina, B. and Hervas-Oliver, J. L. (2013) "Creative service business and regional performance: Evidence for the European regions", *Service Business*, 7(3), pp. 381–398. doi: 10.1007/s11628-012-0165-7.

Bonnin Arias, P. and Rubio Arostegui, J. A. (2019) "Vocación y precariedad laboral en la profesión de la danza en España: Efectos de una política cultural ineficaz", *AusArt*, 7(2), pp. 105–114. doi: 10.1387/ausart.21132.

Comunian, R. and Conor, B. (2017) "Making cultural work visible in cultural policy", in Durrer, V., Miller, T., and O'Brien, D. (eds) *The Routledge Handbook of Global Cultural Policy.* Abingdon: Routledge, pp. 265–280.

Comunian, R. and England, L. (2020) "Creative and cultural work without filters: Covid-19 and exposed precarity in the creative economy", *Cultural Trends*, 29(2), pp. 112–128. doi: 10.1080/09548963.2020.1770577.

de-Miguel-Molina, B. *et al.* (2012) "The importance of creative industry agglomerations in explaining the wealth of European regions", *European Planning Studies*, 20(8), pp. 1263–1280. doi: 10.1080/09654313.2012.680579.

De-Peuter, G. (2011) "Creative economy and labor precarity: A contested convergence", *Journal of Communication Inquiry*, 35(4), pp. 417–425. doi: 10.1177/0196859911416362.

Donald, B., Gertler, M. S. and Tyler, P. (2013) "Creatives after the crash", *Cambridge Journal of Regions, Economy and Society*, 6(1), pp. 3–21. doi: 10.1093/cjres/rss023.

Escalona-Orcao, A. *et al.* (2021) "Cultural and creative ecosystems in medium-sized cities: Evolution in times of economic crisis and pandemic", *Sustainability (Switzerland)*, 13(1), pp. 1–24. doi: 10.3390/su13010049.

European Commission (2018a) "A New European agenda for culture". Available at: https://eur-lex.europa.eu/legal-content/EN/TXT/PDF/?uri=CELEX:52018DC0267&from=EN.

European Commission (2018b) "Regulation of the European Parliament and of the council establishing the Creative Europe programme (2021 to 2027) and repealing Regulation (EU) No 1295/2013", *COM/2018/366 final – 2018/0190 (COD).* Brussels, pp. 1–43.

List, R. A. *et al.* (2017) "Cultural participation and inclusive societies. A thematic report based on the Indicator Framework on Culture and Democracy". Available at: https://edoc.coe.int/en/culture-and-democracy/7285-pdf-cultural-participa-tion-and-inclusive-societies-a-thematic-report-based-on-the-indicator-frame-work-on-culture-and-democracy.html.

Pérez Ibáñez, M. and López-Aparicio, I. (2018) "Actividad artística y precariedad laboral en España: análisis a partir de un estudio global", *Arte y Políticas de Identidad*, 19, pp. 49–66. doi: 10.6018/reapi.359771.

Potts, J. and Cunningham, S. (2008) "Four models of the creative indus-tries", *International Journal of Cultural Policy*, 14(3), pp. 233–247. doi: 10. 1080/10286630802281780.

Pratt, A. C. (2009) "The creative and cultural economy and the recession", *Geoforum*, pp. 495–496. doi: 10.1016/j.geoforum.2009.05.002.

Rodríguez-Rivero, R. *et al.* (2020) "Is It Time for a Revolution in Work–Life Balance? Reflections from Spain", *Sustainability*, 12(22), p. 9563. doi: 10.3390/su12229563.

Sandín, B. *et al.* (2020) "Impacto psicológico de la pandemia de COVID-19: Efectos negativos y positivos en población española asociados al periodo de confinamiento nacional", *Revista de Psicopatología y Psicología Clínica*, 25(1), p. 1. doi: 10.5944/rppc.27569.

Serafini, P. and Banks, M. (2020) "Living precarious lives? Time and temporality in visual arts careers", *Culture Unbound: Journal of Current Cultural Research*, 12(X), pp. 1–21. doi: 10.3384/cu.2000.1525.20200504a.

Travkina, E. and Sacco, P. L. (September 2020) "Culture shock: COVID-19 and the cultural and creative sectors – OECD", p. 55. doi: https://doi.org/10. 1787/08da9e0e-en.

12 The COVID-19 pandemic and cultural industries in the Nordic region

Emerging strategies in film and drama productions

Terje Gaustad and Peter Booth

Introduction

When COVID-19 struck Nordic film and drama productions in March 2020, it carried all the hallmarks of a crisis (Lee et al., 2020; Pearson and Clair, 1998). Like elsewhere, producers across all five countries of the Nordic region experienced that the survival of their projects was threatened by the pandemic and shutdown responses. The production environment assumptions underpinning their projects were shattered, leaving filmmakers and their stakeholders in a highly ambiguous situation with little time to respond with emergency strategies for how to save and complete their projects. From a project management perspective, the crisis provides an opportunity to gain insight into how emergency project strategies develop, helping productions sustain shocks and rebound from disasters. More specifically, this once-in-a-lifetime event offers the opportunity to consider how all film and drama producers, across national borders, respond by adjusting their project strategies, first to a disruptive surge in uncertainty when the crisis hit, and then to a state of more foreseeable and continuous heightened uncertainty when producers learned to live with this environment. This chapter therefore seeks to identify and contextualize these emergency and emergent project strategies that are a direct response to challenges brought about by the COVID-19 pandemic.

The COVID-19 crisis is different from the type of crises that typically strike film and drama productions, as well as other projects within the creative and cultural industries from time to time. Typically, a crisis originates *within* the project organization or its immediate environment (illness, injury or death among lead cast members, loss or damage of recorded materials, etc.), and a crisis is normally limited to a single production (Brook, 2005). In contrast, the COVID-19 outbreak is a disaster caused by factors *outside* the production that are collectively experienced by the whole society, causing millions of organizations, large and small and in most countries, to suspend normal operation (Lee et al., 2020). It offers a rare opportunity to observe crisis management and identify patterns of responses across a

DOI: 10.4324/9781003128274-16

full population of project organizations reacting to disturbances caused by the same event. Despite certain warnings (see e.g. GPMB, 2019), the COVID-19 pandemic is best described as a Black Swan event, which is a low-probability, high-impact event that is almost impossible for decision makers to forecast (Phan and Wood, 2020; Taleb, 2007). In these events, normal project strategies are unlikely to contain the relevant risk assessments and crisis management plans that would have prepared project organizations for its consequences (Dempster, 2009; Taleb et al., 2009).

The pandemic severely affected most film and drama series projects. First, similar to other creative and cultural sectors such as live music and theatre, film and drama projects depend on a physical production requiring near crew contact. Animated films and series are the sole exception, more similar to gaming in this sense. Government and industry restrictions, and COVID-19 itself, rendered physical production work difficult and in some instances impossible. Challenges included:

- lockdowns forcing projects to delay or pause production,
- rescheduling challenges when ambiguous conditions prevented fixing new start dates,
- losing access to production insurance,
- travel restrictions holding up access to foreign cast, crew, and filming locations,
- essential team-members dropping out without notice due to illness or quarantine rules, and
- social distancing regulations impeding intimate and mass scenes.

Furthermore, projects suffered from market disturbances. Here the audiovisual sector is different from live music and theatre in that consumption occurs outside public arenas, apart from cinemas. When cinemas close, or operate with limited capacity, theatrical films lose full or partial access to their most important market channel (Gaustad, 2019). In contrast, drama series experience increased demand from audiences spending more time at home. However, drama series, animation projects, and film all suffered from disturbances to intermediate channels such as film and drama festivals and markets which are important for profiling, sales, and dissemination of finished projects. These are also important networking arenas for setting up new projects. All these market disturbances indirectly affect production, primarily in terms of demand, financing, and scheduling.

Faced with challenges that originate from a highly unpredictable environment, producers have responded to the initial disruption with emergency strategies that are gradually developing into new emergent strategies, which is to say they are developing new patterns of work that are "realized despite, or in the absence of, intentions" (Mintzberg and Waters, 1985, p. 257). Emergency strategies, as a catchall term to reflect organizations' immediate response to the initial complete disruption, primarily address how to secure the assets already created at the time of the disruption. In relation to the initial COVID-19 outbreak and restrictions, these assets include the creative works but also the project organization. When productions have had to delay or pause, assets relating to the organization typically include future access to lead cast, key crew, unique locations, and other essential resources. While disasters are typically time delimited, the COVID-19 crisis has lingered with partial and gradual reopening and closing of society, creating a production environment of more foreseeable heightened and enduring uncertainty. Hence, emergency strategies have been gradually adjusted and turned into emergent strategies. These are more complete strategies than the emergency strategies since they develop from learning that occurs from actions already taken, one by one, after the initial lockdown triggered the film and drama series production crisis.

The nature of the crisis, as experienced by filmmakers in 2020, varied across several parameters, but two were particularly important. First, the project phase mattered and especially so for the distinction between emergency and emergent strategies. Projects that were in the intense execution phase of pre-production or principal photography when the first round of lockdowns hit on 12 March 2020 faced a different and more immediate set of challenges than those that were still in their planning phase. Henceforth, we refer to the first category as in-production projects and to the second as ante-production projects. Second, around the world there have been national differences in the intensity of the pandemic's impact. Differences are reflected in the number of contaminations and deaths relative to population size and, most importantly for film and series production, in the official restrictive and mitigating measures. Among the Nordic countries, Sweden had by far the highest number of cases and deaths per capita, but still its measures were at times less restrictive for film and drama productions.

Based on a survey of theatrical film and documentary as well as TV drama producers across the Nordic countries (Denmark, Iceland, Finland, Norway, and Sweden), and supplemented by in-depth interviews, we identify emergency and emergent strategies that were developed and how they were implemented.[1] This provides a unique insight into how producers and their initiated projects coped with the various degrees of shutdowns implemented in the Nordic countries amid the COVID-19 outbreak, and the unpredictable environments that followed.

The rest of this chapter is structured as follows. First, we review the relevance of project strategy for film and drama series production, as well as the distinction between emergency and emergent strategies. Then we briefly discuss the moderating effects of COVID-19 related government measures on the effectiveness of project strategies. Turning to our mapping of project strategies among Nordic productions, we describe our research design and present four generic strategies revealed by our data. Then we show how they were employed as emergency and emergent strategies and across the relative spectrum of low to high containment and closure stringency experienced in the Nordic region. Finally follows a discussion of the strategies and our concluding remarks.

Emergency and emergent project strategies for responding to COVID-19

Like much activity within the creative industries (DeFillippi, 2015), the production sector of the film and television industry is predominantly organized around projects. Networked and role-based project organizations are set up for each feature film, documentary, or series season produced (Bechky, 2006). Projects are thus the fundamental organizing unit for audiovisual production and our key unit of analysis when studying responses to COVID-19. The project organizations are set up and managed by film and TV production companies but bring together, on a temporary basis, artistic, creative, and 'humdrum' freelance personnel and suppliers, as well as financing typically drawn from several private and public sources. The licensing of project outputs, in the form of finished films or drama-series, is an integral part of the project as it often entails commitments related to content elements (such as director, cast members, approved script) and delivery time. All these elements are affected by COVID-19 and are common to audiovisual projects. The strategies employed by these project organizations therefore best reflect the production sector's response to COVID-19.

Project strategy may be defined as "a direction in a project that contributes to the success of the project in its environment" (Artto et al., 2008, p. 8). For a film or drama series project in the context of the COVID-19 pandemic, the 'direction' refers to the plans and methods employed to work around pandemic-related obstacles to reach the objectives behind making the film or series. "Success" refers to how well the film or series achieves its goals, while "contributes" assumes that the direction has an effect; that is to say, that it matters and makes a difference. In this chapter we concentrate on goals associated with completing a production, which include the project and project organization's survival. Another set of goals are normally associated with market performance, but many of these also relate to production matters (e.g. maintaining certain quality standards, including stars, delivery, and release dates). A film project's "environment" is the world outside the project's boundaries and in this context dominated by COVID-19. A project's immediate environment includes production and distribution companies, investors, and other direct stakeholders, which are affected by the pandemic in a variety of ways. For example, theatrical distributors contend with cinema closures or restrictions, which may in turn affect their relationship with producers (Øfsti, 2020), while public financiers may provide access to emergency funding (Noonan, 2020). A project's wider environment includes domestic and international markets, as well as competing films and audiences. However, most importantly in this context are government and industry restrictive and mitigating measures. Since the environment is exogenous to project strategy, restrictive and mitigating measures represent a given framework within which strategies are developed and implemented. Assessing the measures belongs to a policy level analysis and, beyond the high-level summary captured by the stringency index presented below, this falls outside the scope of our strategic project management approach.

Project emergency strategies are defined here as the immediate plans and methods employed to ensure completion of the production when the first lockdown marked the start of the crisis. They are employed as a reaction to the disruptive surge in uncertainty. We know from crisis management literature that these strategies are dependent on preparations made before a trigger event occurs and on reactions to that event (Bundy et al., 2016; Pearson and Clair, 1998; Weick, 1993). While no level of preparations could have prevented a crisis triggered by the pandemic, the degree of preparedness for any type of crisis affects the actions taken when it occurs. Actions based on the project organization's preparedness are carried out focusing on control, where producers seek to ensure that managerial intentions are realized in action. They thus add a deliberate element to the emergency strategy. Other actions originate from numerous sources: Some will be imposed through the environmental context, such as requirements to pause production and cancel international filming locations, while others will be ad hoc responses at a team and individual level. Strategic patterns emerge from these actions as they are taken one by one without pursuing a plan.

Project emergent strategies are defined here as the implemented plans and methods based on learning from the actions that were taken immediately and while continuing into a new state of more foreseeable but continuous and heightened uncertainty. Learning occurs within each project organization but also between projects. Production companies may adjust their strategies for new projects going into production based on experience from those already in production, and freelance workers moving from one project to another may contribute to similar learning processes. Projects also learn from their wider environment. Industry associations, such as unions and producer associations, play important parts in interorganizational learning by sharing experiences and preparing guidelines based on experiences. Some learning is also imposed, as for instance through requirements relating to quarantining and the employment of an infection control officer. While these strategies develop gradually and typically emerge from practice rather than planning, they may or may not be deliberate. But in those cases where producers have intentionally developed conditions for these strategies to emerge, they are best understood as 'deliberately emergent' (Mintzberg and Waters, 1985).

Both emergency and emergent strategies may involve changes to the organization of a production, the content created, or both. If we split the organization of production into issues affecting economy or schedule, we end up with three areas – economy, schedule, and content. An emergency project strategy may for instance be to increase the production budget and/or period to avoid undesirable script changes. Another may employ major script changes to avoid having a project go over budget and schedule. Adjusting strategies between these three areas are akin to making priorities across the common project management areas of time, cost, and performance (Larson and Gray, 2021). Some methods employed in a strategy will relate to more than one of these areas. For instance, exchanging team members may affect economy (if they differ in rate), schedule (if it is a way to avoid delays), and content (if they have another artistic style). Organizational changes affecting creative elements, such as cast and crew members, are likely to affect content beyond the elements in question, since it is the quality of the film or series depends not just on the individual elements but also on whether they fit together (De Vany and Walls, 1996).

The moderating effects of government measures

The COVID-19 pandemic is by definition global so, as a trigger event for crises in film and drama series productions, it is likely to cause similar challenges everywhere. Yet, the project environment is more directly affected by drastic government measures taken in response to the pandemic (Lee et al., 2020). It is thus the institutional environment, defining the formal rules of the game, that determines strategic options for project organizations (Williamson, 2000).

Following basic principles of the categorizations made in other studies (see e.g. Cabrera Blázquez et al., 2020), we distinguish between restrictive measures taken to contain the pandemic, on the one hand, and financial and other measures taken to mitigate negative effects of these restrictions on the other. Together these measures moderate the effects of the pandemic, and since measures differ at least somewhat from country to country, the moderating effect will also vary.

According to publicly available data[2] of the Oxford COVID-19 Government Response Tracker's stringency index (SI), the Nordic countries on average experienced lower restrictions in comparison to other European countries between 12 March 2020 and 20 November 2020 (Hale et al., 2021), the time frame that our producer survey concerns. While SI captures national containment and closure policies across nine broad factors and hence is not acutely attuned to the restrictions most relevant to film and series productions, the average of the SI index for the period of interest (12 March 2020–20 November 2020) indicates Sweden enjoyed far fewer freedoms than suggested by mainstream media, having a higher SI index than its Nordic neighbours. This is presented in Table 12.1. Much of the media attention towards Sweden's COVID-19 strategy occurred in the early phase of the pandemic when, as illustrated by Figure 12.1, Sweden's stringency was significantly lower than its neighbouring countries. However, the

Table 12.1 Comparison of national containment and closure policies, 12 March
2020 to 20 November 20.

	Denmark	Finland	Iceland	Norway	Sweden	EU average[3]
COVID-19 restriction stringency index (SI)[4]	56.7	43.7	45.2	49.2	57.8	60.9
Variance of SI	97.6	147.9	46.6	224.8	59.1	–

finding of relatively higher stringency in Sweden should be contextualized
against three additional factors. Firstly, the level of restrictions faced by
Swedish and Icelandic productions was significantly more stable throughout the period in comparison to restrictions experienced by the other Nordic
countries, Norway and Finland in particular. Higher volatility in national
containment and closure policies is assumed to have created greater production uncertainty for the latter two countries. Secondly, Sweden experienced
some important restriction exceptions of particular relevance to the audiovisual sector. Among the Nordic countries, Sweden stood out in terms of
liberal travel rules (no quarantine or isolation for those arriving from EEA
and EU countries), onset restrictive measures were to a much larger extent
introduced in the form of recommendations rather than prohibitions, and
cinemas were not forced to close (Gaustad et al., 2021). Thirdly, the methodology used by Oxford's SI requires information to be categorized into
3 to 5 step scales and has been criticized for overlooking subtle but important differences (for example, Sweden public recommendations versus
outright bans in other Nordic countries) that may have a meaningful impact
on film production (Book 2020).

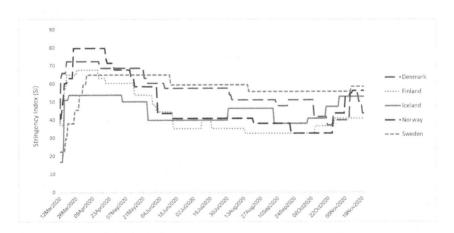

Figure 12.1 Variation in the stringency index across the Nordic countries,
12 March 2020–20 November 2020.

Mapping project strategies among Nordic productions

To map the project strategies employed by Nordic film and series productions facing the pandemic we have applied mixed methods including surveys, case studies, and document studies.

Project-oriented data, collected between 20 November 2020 and 10 December 2020 via a survey distributed by producer associations to their members in each of the Nordic countries, covers 155 feature film, drama series, and theatrical documentary projects. Compared to serial soaps, sitcoms, reality, entertainment, short films, commercials, and other audiovisual genres not included, the genres we examine are relatively resource intensive and complex productions demanding effective project strategies. Among other information, the survey captured data on the project itself, the impact of and response to COVID-19 restrictions, and the use and effect of government and industry mitigating measures. Based on data from each of the Nordic film institutes, we estimate 305 film, drama, and documentary projects were produced across the Nordic counties in 2020, and thus our survey response rate is estimated to be 51% (Gaustad et al., 2021).

Additionally, ten case studies of film and drama series projects were carried out in the fall of 2020 to gain a better understanding of how exactly the pandemic and government measures affected the industry. The projects were chosen to obtain a variety in terms of nationality, genre, format, size (budget and production period), commercial and artistic orientation, national or international scope, and project stage at the time when the pandemic struck. Each case study was limited in scope, with in-depth interviews of the producers as the main source of data collection. The insight gained from the case studies predominately guided our survey design but also helped in interpreting survey findings.

Document studies were also used to map government and industry restrictive and mitigating measures, and we collected data on measures introduced and adjusted between mid-March and mid-November 2020 in all Nordic countries.

Our analytical method begins from the assumption that, as a strategic decision, emergency and/or emergent responses tend follow patterns such that it is more meaningful to examine clusters of responses rather to analyze content, budget, schedule, or other organizational decisions on a stand-alone basis. Clustering methods involve exploratory analysis of a sample to maximize within cluster homogeneity when non-homogeneity of the overall sample is assumed (Hair et al., 2010). Of particular relevance to the chapter's aim, clustering can identify groups of people or projects with common characteristics and where the relations between variables may differ across groups (Chow and Kennedy, 2014).

A two-step cluster analysis technique was chosen because of its suitability for clustering categorical data (Norušis, 2011). Of the 155 projects with useable data, we began by excluding 37 projects that were in post-production or pre-release when the COVID-19 crisis struct on 12 March 2020 due to the non-necessity of emergency or emergent strategies for these projects. Project cancellation meant complete data was missing for a further 3 projects, and so clustering was based on data for 115 projects. Survey data contained 24 variables of potential relevance for identifying clusters of emergency and emergent responses, of which six continuous variables were converted in categorical ranges to reduce any higher weight given to categorical variables when combined with continuous variables (Bacher et al., 2004). Our strategy for clustering variable selection was then based on: previous knowledge of important audiovisual project strategies; decision variables that have significant association with our three moderating variables; exclusion of variables with low frequencies; and variables that diminished the quality of the clustering. This resulted in clustering projects around six key variables, each relating to a strategic area as indicated in Table 12.2:

i Number of countries where shooting occurs: A background variable providing an indication of production complexity in a COVID-19 environment.

ii Actual or estimated production period compared to the planned production period: Indicates to what degree project schedule is prioritized as an organizational strategic area.

iii Actual or estimate of production costs as percentage of original "locked budget": Indicates to what degree project economy is prioritized as an organizational strategic area.

iv Dropped international filming locations: Indicates to what degree project organization is prioritized as a strategic area, possibly with underlying objectives of protecting content (not dropping locations) or of reducing complexity to protect schedule and/or economy (dropping locations).

v Recasting and/or re-crewing: Also indicates to what degree project organization is prioritized as a strategic area, possibly with underlying objectives related to schedule, economy and/or content.

vi Made necessary changes to film script and/or content: The absence of changes indicates that content is a prioritized strategic area.

The optimal cluster solution was chosen based on Schwarz's Bayesian information criterion (Norušis, 2011), and then validated via three steps: ensuring the silhouette measure of cohesion and separation exceeds 0.0 (Norušis, 2011); ensuring Chi-square tests indicate significant association between each of the variables using in clustering and the cluster types; ensuring a similar proportion of cases spread across a not too large number of clusters (Norušis, 2011). Following validation, clusters were then identified via descriptive analysis against other moderating variables. In particular, we examined association between the clusters and (1) production stage at the onset of the COVID-19 pandemic; (2) country of sole or major producer; and (3) type of audiovisual production. Given the latter

Table 12.2 Clustering variables by clusters 1 to 4 (N = 115).

			Cluster 1: At all costs	Cluster 2: Content and time	Cluster 3: Team and place	Cluster 4: On time and budget
	Strategic area	Proportion	21.7%	38.3%	22.6%	17.4%
Actual or current estimated production period compare to the planned production period	Schedule	100%	32.0%	95.5%	80.8%	100.0%
		101–110%	24.0%	4.5%	15.4%	0.0%
		>110%	44.0%	0.0%	3.8%	0.0%
Actual or estimate of production costs as % of original "locked budget"	Economy	≤100%	0.0%	63.6%	7.7%	100.0%
		101–110%	44.0%	11.4%	88.5%	0.0%
		>110%	56.0%	25.0%	3.8%	0.0%
Dropped international filming locations	Organization	Yes	60.0%	0.0%	0.0%	55.0%
		No	40.0%	100.0%	100.0%	45.0%
Number of countries where shooting occurs	Complexity	1	52.0%	79.5%	80.8%	100.0%
		2	32.0%	18.2%	0.0%	0.0%
		3+	16.0%	2.3%	19.2%	0.0%
Recasting and/ or re-crewing	Organization	Yes	84.0%	40.9%	7.7%	90.0%
		No	16.0%	59.1%	92.3%	10.0%
Made necessary changes to film script and/or content (e.g. to drop crowded, indoor, intimate scenes)	Content	Yes	84.0%	0.0%	50.0%	95.0%
		No	16.0%	100.0%	50.0%	5.0%

variable was not found to be significantly associated with the clusters, it is not presented in the analysis that follows.

Four project strategies for producing with COVID-19

We identify four distinct strategic clusters by analyzing how projects prioritize the strategic areas of content and organization, with schedule and economy as subcategories of organization-related strategic areas (see Table 12.2):

At all costs strategy (1)

This strategy reflects a pattern of projects that make any changes necessary to complete the project, without any clear priorities between the different strategic areas. All parameters are kept flexible, and the costs are financial as indicated by higher budget overages, and artistic, as a result of making content changes.

Projects are less likely to complete production within the planned period and on budget, and extensions and overages are relatively likely to be more than 10%. Production team members are likely to be exchanged if needed due to COVID-19 complications.

A relatively high proportion of projects following this pattern are complex, with an international orientation, even after frequently dropping international locations. Changing co-producers is relatively common.

A flexible approach is also adopted with regards to content. Most projects make necessary changes to script and/or content.

Content and time strategy (2)

This strategy reflects a pattern of projects that give priority to content. None reported having made changes to script and/or content. In addition to keeping content fixed, the projects prioritize the schedule aspect of project organization and mostly complete production within the planned production period and without adding extra shooting days.

Projects following this strategy tend to be less complex in terms of having a limited international production orientation, and they do not drop any planned international locations to reduce complexity. Typically, principal photography is carried out only domestically.

Production team and costs are kept somewhat flexible but with relatively modest recasting and crewing. Mostly projects also stay on budget, but significant overages do occur.

Team and place strategy (3)

This strategy reflects a pattern of projects where organization is prioritized. Hardly any make changes to their plans for cast and crew, and they do not reduce complexity by dropping international locations despite having a relatively strong international production orientation compared to the *Content and Time* projects.

Production costs, time, and content are kept somewhat flexible. Projects typically add up to 10% to their original locked production budgets, but seldom more. There is also a little flexibility in time. Mostly projects stay on schedule. Some add time, but seldom more than 10%. Half of the projects falling into this strategic pattern make necessary changes to script and/or content, which is a bit more frequent than the average for all projects.

On time and budget strategy (4)

This strategy reflects a pattern of projects that also prioritize organization but with a clear focus on time and budget. All projects that complete production within the planned period and within the locked budget. With time and money fixed, projects are kept flexible across other parameters.

Reducing complexity by dropping international locations is common, and projects end up with a relatively modest international production orientation. Recasting and/or re-crewing is relatively common.

Projects also take a flexible approach to content. Making necessary changes to script and/or content is even more common for projects following this strategy than it is for those in the *At All Costs* cluster.

From emergency to emergent project strategies

The *At All Costs* response stands out as a clear emergency strategy. It was the second most common strategy employed by in-production projects, but it was rarely employed by ante-production projects (see Table 12.3). Given time to observe, learn and adapt to a COVID-19 environment, most producers of ante-production projects applied an emergent strategy with clear priorities regarding content and/or organization (*Content and Time, Team and Place*, or *On Time and Budget*).

Efforts to save project assets *At All Costs* may seem desperate, and some may question this response even as a rational emergency strategy. Yet, if the option is an exit strategy, abandoning the production, project salvage will still often be the economically most efficient strategy due to the nature of film and drama series production costs (Caves, 2000). The assets, created in the form of scripts, production designs, filmed scenes, sound designs, or similar pieces and contractual commitments, have no value unless the film or series is completed. As these assets represent sunk costs, completing a project will be economically desirable provided the cost to complete does not exceed estimated revenues from the project. The latter has, however,

Table 12.3 Project strategy clusters by production phase as of 12 March 2020 (N = 115).

	Cluster 1: All costs strategy	Cluster 2: Content and time strategy	Cluster 3: Team and place strategy	Cluster 4: On time and budget strategy	Chi-square p-value
Ante production: Not yet greenlighted or greenlighted only	6.4%[b]	42.6%[a]	27.7%[a]	23.4%[a]	0.009
In-production: Pre-production or principal photography	32.4%[b]	35.3%[a]	19.1%[a]	13.2%[a]	
Total	21.7%	38.3%	22.6%	17.4%	

[a,b] Where superscripts differ across row proportions, Z-test indicates significant difference between row proportions at the 0.05 level.

also become more uncertain as the pandemic has accelerated structural industry transformations linked to digitization, including less reliance on theatrical distribution (Hennig-Thurau et al., 2021). This is reflected in producers' estimates, especially for theatrical films. On average, producers reduced their estimated revenues by 20% for feature films, 23 for theatrical documentaries, and 7% for drama series.

The other three strategies were more frequently employed by ante-production than in-production projects, and thus represent the emergent strategies. Still, as they were employed as emergency strategies as well, they are emergency strategies adopted as emergent strategies. We note that *Content and Time* is most frequently employed as emergency strategy, but is applied even more frequently as an emergent strategy. Unlike the *At All Costs* strategy, each of the other three strategies shows clear priorities as to which elements of the organization or content to change, and this may reflect a more deliberate approach. While the *At All Costs* strategy is used to avoid an exit strategy and secure the survival of the project, the other strategies allow this goal to be combined with other goals such as preserving the content, the production budget, or a delivery date. Which of these goals is prioritized, and thus the choice of emergent strategy, is likely to reflect the originally formed pre-crisis strategy and the various stakeholders' influence over strategy implementation (Gaustad, 2018). Producers may for instance have limited strategic independence if the project financing is tied to specific objectives (meeting a delivery date, filming in a given location, and so forth).

Transnational strategies

Normally, a global crisis like the COVID-19 pandemic will have global and cross-border effects, requiring the same types of organizational responses from one country to another (Wenzel et al., 2021). Yet, one could expect to find a "Swedish strategy" – one that reflects the relatively unique Swedish project environment with more predictable and arguably more audiovisual production-friendly restrictive measures. But none stands clearly out (see Table 12.4). *On Time and Budget* is more frequently employed in Sweden than in any other Nordic country, but it is almost as frequently used in Norway and thus not unique for Sweden. Moreover, there is no evidence that Swedish productions have used any single strategy at a proportionally higher or lower rate than other strategies.

At All Costs was not employed as an emergency strategy by any Danish projects, but this can partly be explained by the low number of Danish in-production projects in our sample. *On Time and Budget* was not employed by any Icelandic productions. Among these, *Team and Place* was the most frequently used.

Another notable finding is that Norwegian projects had a significantly lower proportion employing *Team and Place Strategy*. With very few

Table 12.4 Project strategy clusters 1 to 4 by country (*N* = 115).

	Cluster 1: All costs strategy	Cluster 2: Content and time strategy	Cluster 3: Team and place strategy	Cluster 4: On time and budget strategy	Chi-square p-value
Denmark	0.0%[b]	61.5%[a]	23.1%[a,b]	15.4%[a,b]	0.017
Finland	28.0%[b]	32.0%[a,b]	36.0%[b]	4.0%[a]	
Iceland	15.4%[a,b]	38.5%[a,b]	46.2%[b]	0.0%[a]	
Norway	32.0%[a]	40.0%[a]	4.0%[b]	24.0%[a]	
Sweden	20.5%[a]	33.3%[a]	17.9%[a]	28.2%[a]	
Total	21.7%	38.3%	22.6%	17.4%	

[a,b] Where superscripts differ across row proportions, Z-test indicate significant difference between row proportions at the 0.05 level

changes to recasting and/or re-crewing, a *Team and Place* would have been a challenging strategy in the context of Norway's higher variability of stringency levels, particularly in regards to use of foreign crew. Further, Finish and Icelandic productions were notable for their reluctance to use the *One Time and Budget Strategy*. We assume this to be reflective of the makeup of the projects' financing arrangements, as well as the lower average restriction stringency in these two countries, which collectively averted the need to make content-related changes to meeting time and budget obligations.

Overall, we find that the strategies are relatively transnational in nature within the Nordic region, which has been less homogenic with regards to both COVID-19 intensity and measures than it typically is in most other matters. This may indicate that the moderating effects of government measures on the choice of project strategy are somewhat limited. Our case studies and survey data suggest this is partly because of transnational spillover effects from these measures. Projects are relatively seldom purely national; they often have international stakeholders. Almost a quarter of the film and drama series in our sample were filmed in two or more countries, and this was after almost a quarter had dropped international filming locations. Furthermore, only 30% were produced without foreign cast and crew, despite the pandemic. The multinational profile of many projects seems to reduce the moderating effects of government measures on project strategy choices.

Discussion

We have identified four strategic clusters, representing four types of strategic responses to the COVID-19 crisis. There is of course some heterogeneity within each cluster with regards to other variables, but the four strategies still suggest a set of similar approaches taken by projects within the Nordic region. The diffusion of emergency and emergent strategy types between projects may be a result of national and international guidelines developed by producer associations and other industry bodies. Evidence from our case studies also points to productions working directly together to shape and mitigate the consequences of the disaster in all Nordic countries. Hence, learning from the actions taken occurs among individual team members, within each project organization, but also between projects and within the whole sector, all contributing to more efficient emergent project strategies.

A distinctive feature of emergency strategies applied as a response to the immediate disruption of the pandemic, which we rarely observe in emergent strategies applied later to cope with the foreseeable but sustained high levels of uncertainty, is the overriding priority of project salvage. This is clearly seen in the *At All Costs* strategy, where producers compromise in all strategic areas of production, relating to both content and organization. With respect to the goal of project survival, it seems effective. Only 2% of the projects replying to our survey were cancelled. Given the scope of the crisis, this share may seem surprisingly low but reflects the cost structure of films and drama series. High first-copy costs combined with very low dissemination costs create strong incentives to complete a project once it enters the resource-intensive stages of pre-production and production. In other Cultural and Creative Sectors with higher dissemination or performance costs, like live music and theatres, one would thus expect to see higher cancellation rates. The *At All Cost* strategy's effectiveness with regards to other goals, including production quality and market performance, is unknown, but it is likely that projects have suffered in the areas that were not prioritized.

Other strategies are also applied as emergency strategies for in-production projects, but these clusters contain less complex projects. This may explain why producers in these cases were able to combine project salvage with other goals in their emergency strategies.

Being able to make such combinations is the distinctive feature of emergent strategies. With the exception of a small share relying on *At All Costs* as an emergent strategy, producers pursuing one of the other three strategies seem able to prioritize two strategic areas in addition to securing the survival of the project.

Effective strategic responses to the pandemic mitigate consequences for a project by minimizing both its financial and artistic costs. The four strategies identified take different approaches to balancing economic and creative priorities. The *Content and Time* strategy clearly prioritizes avoiding artistic costs, while the *Time and Budget* strategy clearly prioritizes financial cost control. The other two take more mixed approaches.

However, even when content is prioritized artistic costs are likely to occur. For instance, our case studies reveal that extra resources spent on required contingency planning have not been limited to production crew but have demanded close involvement of talent and creative personnel. The extra time key creatives divert to production questions has in many cases meant less time and attention spent on typical artistic considerations.

Some measures, like moving meetings and other work online, have also added directly to the artistic costs. While these costs are difficult to quantify, track, and control, creative goods like films and drama series have multiplicative production functions, and so artistic costs may have severe consequences for the value of the finished product (Caves, 2000). Plans and methods for making space for creative processes in the context of heightened demands for contingency planning have therefore become important and suggest an association between production period and content that goes beyond the time it takes to produce specific materials.

Concluding remarks

Producers of film and drama series are no strangers to production risk, and many have crisis management experience. Yet, they were not able to identify the potential risks of the pandemic due to the Black Swan characteristic of the COVID-19 crisis. When such a crisis hits, producers not only have to cope with the nature of the disaster, but, as we identify in this chapter, they must cope with an unpredictable institutional environment. Attempts by producers at traditional risk assessments are thus likely insufficient to provide protection against adverse events like COVID-19. However, resilience and crisis management are interrelated (Williams et al., 2017), and the ability to devise emergency and emergent strategies contributes to resilience. This is particularly important for the unstable project-based organizations that characterize much of the Cultural and Creative Industries.

Our chapter reveals how Nordic producers relaxed their priorities in many or all strategic areas as an emergency strategy to salvage their projects. The ability to relinquish strategic focus on all areas but project survival enhanced their resilience. However, while project survival is a necessary condition for artistic and commercial success it is not sufficient, and relaxing other priorities is likely to impair the ability of a film or series to achieve its goals. Therefore, in the emergent strategies that later transpired for dealing with a high but foreseeable level of uncertainty after the initial crisis disruption, strategic focus returns to normal areas of content, organization, economy, and schedule. They are thus not purely emergent but also coloured by the intentions behind the projects' original, pre-crisis strategies.

These patterns were observed across country borders, with divergent levels of intensity of the pandemic, different average levels of national containment and closure stringency, and a significant degree of variability in the levels of stringency between countries. Given these environmental and institutional variances, the strategic responses of the audiovisual projects were less country specific than we assumed would be the case. Contextualized against the higher average levels of containment and closure stringency across the EU, we are inclined to speculate that our finding of project strategy being more sensitive to project-specific variables than national ones also applies beyond the Nordics.

Notes

1. This research was carried out with financial support from the Nordisk Film & TV Fond.
2. The Oxford COVID-19 Government Response Tracker's stringency index is covered by a Creative Commons Attribution CC BY standard. https://www.bsg.ox.ac.uk/research/research-projects/covid-19-government-response-tracker.
3. Population-weighted average of the 27 EU countries.
4. The Oxford COVID-19 Government Response Tracker "Stringency index", daily average from 12 March 2020 to 20 November 20. The daily updated index reflects national containment and closure policies across nine variables including school closures, workplace closures, public event closures, restrictions on gatherings, public transport closures, curfews, restrictions on internal movement, international travel, and public information campaigns (Hale et al., 2021).

References

Artto, K., Kujala, J., Dietrich, P. & Martinsuo, M. 2008. What is project strategy? *International Journal of Project Management*, 26, 4–12.

Bacher, J., Wenzig, K. & Vogler, M. 2004. *SPSS TwoStep Cluster – a first evaluation.* https://www.ssoar.info/ssoar/handle/document/32715 (Accessed: 10 February 2021).

Bechky, B. A. 2006. Gaffers, gofers, and grips: Role-based coordination in temporary organizations. *Organization Science*, 17, 3–21.

Book, J. 2020. Oxford's Stringency Index is Falling Apart, American Institute for Economic Research. Available at: https://www.aier.org/article/oxfords-stringency-index-is-falling-apart/ (Accessed: 22 June 2021).

Brook, G. 2005. Surviving the roller coaster: worst practices in project management within the television production industry. *Project Management Journal*, 36, 5–14.

Bundy, J., Pfarrer, M. D., Short, C. E. & Coombs, W. T. 2016. crises and crisis management: integration, interpretation, and research development. *Journal of Management*, 43, 1661–1692.

Cabrera Blázquez, F. J., Cappello, M., Chochon, L., Fontaine, G., Milla, J. T. & Valais, S. 2020. *The European Audiovisual Industry in the Time of COVID-19.* Strasbourg: European Audiovisual Observatory.

Caves, R. E. 2000. *Creative Industries: Contracts between Art and Commerce.* Cambridge, MA: Harvard University Press.

Chow, K. F. & Kennedy, K. J. 2014. Secondary analysis of large-scale assessment data: an alternative to variable-centred analysis. *Educational Research and Evaluation*, 20(6), 469–493.

De Vany, A. & Walls, D. 1996. Bose-Einstein dynamics and adaptive contracting in the motion picture industry. *The Economic Journal*, 106, 1493–1514.

Defillippi, R. J. 2015. Managing Project-Based Organization in Creative Industries. In: Jones, C., Lorenzen, M. & Sapsed, J. (eds.) *The Oxford Handbook of Creative Industries.* Oxford: Oxford University Press.

Dempster, A. M. 2009. An operational risk framework for the performing arts and creative industries. *Creative Industries Journal*, 1(2): 151–170.

Gaustad, T. 2018. How Financing Shapes a Film Project: Applying Organizational Economics to a Case Study in Norway. In: Murschetz, P. C., Teichmann, R. &

Karmasin, M. (eds.) *Handbook of State Aid for Film: Finance, Industries and Regulation.* Cham, Switzerland: Springer.

Gaustad, T. 2019. How streaming services make cinema more important. *Nordic Journal of Media Studies*, 1(1): 67–84.

Gaustad, T., Booth, P., Offerdal, E., Svensson, L. E. & Gran, A.-B. 2021. *Nordic Mission Possible: An Assessment of Covid-19's Impact on the Nordic Audiovisual Industry and the Effectiveness of Government and Industry Measures.* Oslo, Norway: Centre for Creative Industries, BI Norwegian Business School.

GPMB. 2019. *A World at Risk: Annual Report on Global Preparedness for Health Emergencies.* Geneva: Global Preparedness Monitoring Board.

Hair, J. F., Black, W. C., Babin, B. J. & Anderson, R. E. 2010. *Anderson. Multivariate Data Analysis: A Global Perspective.* Englewood Cliffs, NJ: Prentice Hall.

Hale, T., Angrist, N., Goldszmidt, R., Kira, B., Petherick, A., Phillips, T., Webster, Samuel Cameron-Blake, E., Hallas, L., Majumdar, S. & Tatlow, H. 2021. *Oxford COVID-19 Government Response Tracker.* Oxford, UK: Blavatnik School of Government. https://www.bsg.ox.ac.uk/research/research-projects/covid-19-government-response-tracker (Accessed: 18 May 2021).

Hennig-Thurau, T., Abraham, R. S. & Sorenson, O. 2021. The economics of filmed entertainment in the digital era. *Journal of Cultural Economics*, 45(2), 157–170.

Larson, E. W. & Gray, C. F. 2021. *Project Management: The Managerial Process.* New York, NY: McGraw-Hill.

Lee, G. K., Lampel, J. & Shapira, Z. 2020. After the storm has passed: translating crisis experience into useful knowledge. *Organization Science*, 31, 1037–1051.

Mintzberg, H. & Waters, J. A. 1985. Of Strategies, deliberate and emergent. *Strategic Management Journal*, 6(3), 257–272.

Noonan, C. 2020. Public funding in a time of crisis: film funds and the pandemic. *Baltic Screen Media Review*, 8, 10–17.

Norušis, M. J. 2011. *IBM SPSS Statistics 19 Advanced Statistical Procedures.* New York: Pearson.

Øfsti, M. 2020. Distributor strategies in the face of closed cinemas: Norwegian responses to Covid-19. *Baltic Screen Media Review*, 8, 54–66.

Pearson, C. M. & Clair, J. A. 1998. Reframing crisis management. *Academy of Management Review*, 23, 59–76.

Phan, P. H. & Wood, G. 2020. Doomsday scenarios (or the Black Swan excuse for unpreparedness), *Academy of Management*. 34, 425–433.

Taleb, N. N. 2007. *The Black Swan: The Impact of the Highly Improbable.* London: Allen Lane.

Taleb, N. N., Goldstein, D. G. & Spitznagel, M. W. 2009. The six mistakes executives make in risk management. *Harvard Business Review*, 87, 78–81.

Weick, K. E. 1993. The collapse of sensemaking in organizations: The Mann Gulch disaster. *Administrative Science Quarterly*, 38, 628–652.

Wenzel, M., Stanske, S. & Lieberman, M. B. 2021. Strategic responses to crisis. *Strategic Management Journal*, 42, O16–O27.

Williams, T. A., Gruber, D. A., Sutcliffe, K. M., Shepherd, D. A. & Zhao, E. Y. 2017. Organizational response to adversity: fusing crisis management and resilience research streams. *Academy of Management Annals*, 11, 733–769.

Williamson, O. E. 2000. The new institutional economics: taking stock, looking ahead. *Journal of Economic Literature*, 38, 595–613.

13 The COVID-19 pandemic and cultural industries in the Czech Republic

Marek Prokůpek and Jakub Grosman

Introduction

Since March 2020, the COVID-19 pandemic has affected daily life worldwide, driving the global economy into turmoil not seen since the Second World War. Most governments have taken extraordinary and radical measures to mitigate the spread of the coronavirus, which has led, among other things, to the closure of most cultural organizations and venues, thus creating the loss of livelihoods for many cultural workers. Therefore, the majority of stakeholders faced significant challenges to maintain contact with their communities and diminish the negative economic results. The arts and cultural sector (ACS) remains one of the most influenced. This discussion analyses the situation of the Czech ACS and provides a comprehensive perspective of the aftermath of the early measures and the state assistance provided. To do so, the authors conducted research that includes a survey distributed among different stakeholders, from both institutions and individuals, from March to June 2020. During this period, the authors collected responses from 317 organizations and 860 individual cultural workers.

On 10 March 2020, all cultural events and performances were limited to audiences of only 100. On the 12th of the same month, the Czech Health Minister declared a national state of emergency. The following day, theatrical, musical, film and other art performances, sports, cultural, religious, traditional, and similar events and gatherings with the participation of more than 30 people were forbidden. Furthermore, it was ordered to close public spaces, including libraries, museums, and galleries. By the end of April, the government relaxed some of the more radical measures.

In May and June, a majority of Czech citizens believed that the pandemic was over and returned to new normal. With only a few hundred COVID-19 cases, the government decided, despite the warning from experts, to withdraw most measures. In May cultural organizations and venues gradually opened. From the 25th a maximum of 300 and from 8 June 500 visitors were permitted. However, the return to normalcy proved short lived with the second wave of the pandemic in early autumn. The results were

DOI: 10.4324/9781003128274-17

disastrous. Once considered an international poster child for its pandemic crisis management, the Czech Republic became a European epicentre. As the number of infected people skyrocketed, the government took again radical measures to deter the spread of the virus. From 5 October, theatres, concerts and other activities including singing ceased. A week later, all cultural events involving more than 10 people indoors and 20 people outdoors were banned. Concerts, theatres, and other performances were banned, as well as museums, galleries, exhibition spaces, castles, and other cultural venues.

ACS-related activities were not able to recover from the first and were now confronted with the second wave. Due to the ongoing pandemic and lockdowns, it is impossible to precisely measure and identify the long-term impact of the crisis.

Vulnerability of the ACS in times of crisis

Thanks to its structure and established practices, the culture sector is considered one of the areas most susceptible to crises (Carbonare and Prokůpek 2020). Banks and O'Connor (2020) suggest that although it is important to identify the immediate economic needs of cultural workers, organizations, and companies, the root cause of this vulnerability must be emphasized.

Based on observation of the behaviour of cultural actors, one may derive certain conclusions. The increased tendencies of instrumentalization of the arts and neoliberal policies and the privatization of culture render the sector less resilient towards crises. Paradoxically, many of these tendencies are consequences of the 2008 global financial crisis, when governments reduced their cultural funding. The growing trend to view culture as a source of economic contribution coupled with the upgrade global tendencies to upgrade cultural organizations to a more entrepreneurial level, thus creating less dependency on the state enfeebled cultural actors. Actors that heavily depend on earned income and private contributions experienced a more negative outcome than their counterparts benefiting from public subsidies.

Banks and O'Connor (2020) claim that the cultural sector steadily identifies itself as an industry: emphasizing growth and innovation, providing goods and services, is part of the problem. Sectors that intervene in both private for-profit and public non-profit spheres create value confusion (Banks and O'Connor 2020) and infuse tension (Meyrick and Barnett 2020). Governments continue to pressure cultural sectors to prove their value, in particular, the economic. Economic value remains a focal point in political discussions and has gained more relevance and importance than other values. Consequently, public support now focuses on prestigious cultural projects and events with the potential to create significant economic gain; hence cultural diversity suffers.

Comparing with other crises, such as the 2008 global financial crisis, is an option to estimate the impact of the pandemic; however, significant differences between these two exist. The pandemic is more visible and is the reason for the closure of major cultural organizations and venues. A stronger parallel is found in the area of economic impacts. In recent years, publicly subsidized cultural organizations faced a decline in contributions from their founders and the associated pressure to develop innovative funding and business strategies. Some of the particular economic characteristics of the cultural and art production explain, to some extent, specific opportunities, threats, and difficulties faced in economic crises. This is a risky sector of prototype products, with a high but subjective symbolic value (Throsby 1994). Simultaneously, the industry now experiences a massive transformation of its business models due to digital communication technologies (Rifkin 2000; Benghozi and Lyubareva 2014). Many cultural initiatives and activities survive due to public funding, generous support, and, in some cases, other philanthropic contributions. The crucial importance of government policies explains why the transformation of the welfare state and new socio-economic trends influence the ACSs. National entities, especially in the European context, therefore play a crucial role in this field, mainly as a result of direct but also indirect subsidies. States are expected to intervene in order to save cultural organizations but also to stimulate the economy. Thus, many countries increase government spending in various areas such as industry, healthcare, and the social welfare system. Normally, these interventions have a short-term effect, which is also crucial for the survival of many actors in the culture sector during the pandemic.

Context of the Czech ACS

Institutions in former Czechoslovakia were until 1989 were part of centrally planned economy and society. After the 1989 Velvet Revolution, which led to the fall of the Communist party leading role, Czechoslovakian society transformed into a free market economy. This unprecedented transformation created a variety of future sociological, political, and economic issues. In this respect, the oppressed cultural workers 'true' Bohemians, during 1948–1989, were mostly opposed to being associated with collective organizations. Therefore, post-1989 they formed a significant mass of independent cultural workers. Czechoslovakia, as with other former communist countries, incurred transformations of their cultural systems and policies when faced with the need for a radical change (Bonet and Donato 2011). These actions were similar to those imposed by a crisis such as that engendered by the COVID-19 pandemic. Nevertheless, the transformation of cultural organizations was not as significant as the private sector transformation. Thus, many relics from previous decades still influence the arts and culture ecosystem.

In 1993, following a mutual agreement by both entities, the Czech and Slovak Federative Republic divided into two independent states: the Czech Republic and the Slovak Republic. This internationally recognized transaction is often referred to as 'The Velvet Divorce'. During the early days of the Czech Republic, there was a minimum number of private donors, with the Czech state, one of the largest supporters of arts and culture.

Historically, culture has played an essential role in Czech society and has been always among the central change drivers. Yet its value has never been fully recognized and appreciated. Despite political proclamations addressed in the official cultural policy of the Czech Republic issued by the Ministry of Culture, the ACS was never a priority of the government agenda in the last 30 years. In spite of the first initial mapping of Cultural and Creative Industries (CCIs) in the Czech Republic (2011–2015), the Czech cultural sector is still partially unknown and subject to further exploration. In particular, the performing arts, except for the theatre sector, has never been adequately mapped and lacks the necessary data to advocate its social value. This uncharted situation is a significant threat for the individual self-employed cultural workers, who are partially 'out of the system'.

Moreover, a significant weakness of the Czech ACS is the lack of strong advocacy of the social and cultural value of arts and culture. Equally absent are strong professional associations and unions that would advocate sectors' needs and interests and lobby for more efficient legislative and economic development. Such lack of professional groups is obvious on both levels, organizational, and even more visible on the level of independent cultural workers.

The Czech ACS is very fragmented and was never properly delineated. There are no clear and data-based estimates of the entire cultural sector. The most advanced segment comprises theatres and dance, which regularly reports their key indicators, such as income, cost, employees, visitors, and number of shows, to the state agency the National Information and Consulting Centre for Culture (NIPOS). In doing so, there is a clear estimate of key indicators for this segment of the performing arts. Unfortunately, the music industry was never outlined and there are no relevant estimates for key indicators as for theatre and dance. In the case of fine arts, the situation is between the previous two. The Ministry of Culture has certain data on state-subsidized organizations such as museums that are obliged to report yearly key indicators. In the case of commercial art galleries and independent self-employed visual artists, the state does not have sufficient data.

The COVID-19 pandemic revealed systematic errors and the fragility of the Czech cultural sector and creative economy. The Czech Ministry of Culture is responsible for most cultural affairs and cultural policies. During the crisis, it became clear that the Ministry lacks cultural data, in particular, in regard to independent self-employed cultural workers, stakeholders that are impacted the most. Without data-based management, it is almost impossible to create efficient measures that mitigate the negative economic repercussions of any crisis. Freelance workers in the arts and culture are the backbone of cultural value chain and were the first to be confronted with a quick loss of jobs due to the venue closures. Even the short-term consequences might be disastrous (Banks 2020). The way by which the government behaves towards ACS actors in general reflects and influences how they are treated during the pandemic (Banks and O'Connor 2020). It is not surprising that countries with a higher GDP provided more generous support for the sectors than ones with a lower GDP. In the case of the Czech Republic, when compared to other EU countries of similar size, the country provided a larger amount of financial assistance wing to relatively low national debt (Betzler et al. 2020). The question remains as to how efficiently this aid was developed and allocated.

Immediate impact on the Czech arts and culture sector

The authors collected quantitative data from 317 arts and cultural organizations and 860 cultural workers from March to June 2020. Table 13.1 captures the number of organizations in various fields and the number of such organizations that participated in the survey. The respondents were approached through Czech ACS networks and associations. The survey was promoted by the Arts and Theatre Institute, a state contributory organization providing ACS services.

The research focused on the following topics:

1 Economic impact on organizations and cultural workers.
2 Resource Management.
3 Reaction to lockdown documented on cancelled shows and events and activities shifted to online.
4 Policy measures and strategies used during the lockdown.

For the research, subjects in theatre and dance, music, and fine art were chosen as a sample as these categories form one segment defined and grouped by the Czech Ministry of Culture titled professional art. This sample was chosen because of similarities in their funding and as organizations in these

Table 13.1 Size of the ACS in the Czech Republic vs. sample of the survey.

Organization type	Number of theatres in the sector	Number of theatres participating in the survey	Number of music organizations in the sector	Number of music organizations participating in the survey	Number of art museums and galleries in the sector	Number of art museums and galleries participating in the survey
State-subsidized	72	37	39	9	134	33
For profit organizations	113	11	253	34	69	0
Non-profit organizations	120	98	97	56	79	39
Total	305	146	500	99	282	72

Source: Compiled by the authors based on NIPOS and Czech Statistical Office (2020).

areas include all three types of organizations, state-subsidized, for-profit, and non-profit organizations.

About 48% of organizations were based in the Prague metropolitan area, 61% of organizations were registered as NGOs, 24% were state-subsidized organizations, and 15% were for-profit organizations. All responding organizations received some form of public support from central or local governments for individual projects or annual operational support.

Organizations participating in the survey reported cooperation with 30,352 cultural workers. A regular employment contract represented 57% of all forms of contracts. The remaining 43% were contracted with self-employed freelancers by April 2020. The music industry reported the lowest level of regular employment contracts; only 21% of all co-operators were regular employees. On the other hand, it is necessary to mention that for some cultural workers and organizations, the preferred method of cooperation is due to lower tax exposure and the flexibility for individual cultural workers. In the first wave of COVID-19 lockdown in spring 2020, no major employee layoffs or contract cancellation were reported. Organizations announced that if the lockdown prolonged, they would be forced to cancel subcontractors and dismiss some employees.

The group of individual cultural workers without a regular employment contract was the most exposed group. Out of the sample of 860 cultural workers, 44% possessed both an employee contract and worked as freelancers. In the arts and culture industry the average worker has 2.5 contracts as self-employed with varying organizations. That signifies that 1 self-employed cultural worker has contracts with an average of 2.5 organizations. The highest number of contracts as self-employed is reported in the music industry with 2.9 contracts per cultural worker. Moreover, many of the individuals involved in the research had at least one contract as self-employed with non-ACS organizations. The sample of cultural workers was quite senior in terms of the length of their professional career, with an average of 17–20 years active. Despite the seniority of these workers, the median of their financial reserve to survive without income was between 2 and 3 months. The highest financial reserve worth 3 months' median was declared by individuals in the music industry.

In August 2020, the Ministry of Culture, together with the Ministry of Industry and Trade, introduced a support program for self-employed cultural workers. Many did not succeed due to the complexity of the general scheme as it failed to accommodate the seasonality of ACS incomes. This call for support was repeated twice afterwards with the administrative and legal blockers removed.

All organizations reported 2019 annual income worth 329.8 mil EUR. Within the first two months of lockdown, March to April 2020, the organizations estimated lost income worth about 26% of their monthly average income when compared with their 2019 monthly average income. The highest loss in income was reported by organizations in the music industry with 49% of monthly average income, followed by theatres 24% of monthly average income, and the lowest lost income reported the sector of fine arts 17% of monthly average income. The reported loss in income for April 2020 increased about 37% in comparison with March 2020 and resulted in approximately 36% of total monthly average income. The authors estimate that the dynamics of lost income grew dramatically in the following months, given that March is historically a low-income month for the respondents, with the high season for the music industry being summer. The music industry suffered the worst decrease in income observed in March–April 2020 (Figure 13.1).

The lowest income decrease in the fine arts is not surprising. Many of these organizations are state-subsidized, and the earned income forms only a small part of their annual budgets.

On the other hand, a suspended cultural life and consequent activities triggered savings worth 10.3% in March 2020 and even increased savings worth 11.8% of the average monthly cost in April 2020.

In late summer a joint program of the Ministry of Culture and Ministry of Industry and Trade introduced guidelines to support art and cultural organizations to fund part of their lost expenses due to cancelled performances and other events. Usually, the smaller independent organizers, which form the majority in ACS, were able to cancel events or performances with limited or nil cost. Therefore, they were not eligible to apply for this assistance. The second call of this scheme was improved and focused on reimbursement of operational cost of cultural organizations

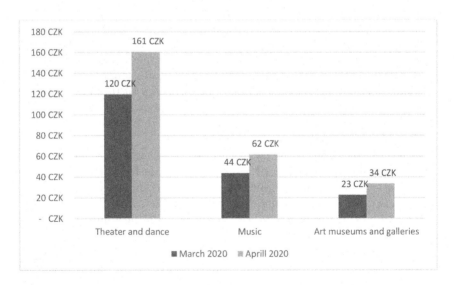

Figure 13.1 Missing income in March and April 2020.

Source: Authors.

and independent cultural workers. The latter included technical professionals, such as sound designers, light designers, and arts managers. In total, 99 million EUR were allocated to three calls of this support scheme for art and cultural organizations from August 2020 until March 2021. On 22 June, the government approved a new subsidy program, which was created to support businesses in the cultural sector. The program compensated for the costs associated with events and activities cancelled or relocated. Only those entities that had the affected action from 10 March to 31 August could apply for the subsidy. Recognized subsidies were paid only after the fact and in the amount of 50% of eligible expenses. The maximum amount of the subsidy was fixed at CZK 5 million per organizer, equal to 197,000 EUR (Figure 13.2).

In total, the responding organizations reported 3,884 cancelled events, performances, live shows, and exhibitions, in March 2020, which is reflected in the loss of 924,000 visitors. This included tickets not sold for live performances, art museums, and gallery visits. The dynamics of cancelled performances and lost audiences increased from March to April 2020 by 28% for cancelled events, totalling 1,551,000 visitors unable to attend arts and cultural events. The organizations reported 2,475,000 that could not attend these events in March–April 2020. About 44% of these visitors would have participated in theatre organizations, 34% art museums and galleries, and 21% to music events. For a country of a limited geographical footprint, with a total population 10,650,000 inhabitants, it signifies almost one-quarter of the population without considering the unique visitors more frequently visiting live performances and art museums and galleries (Figure 13.3).

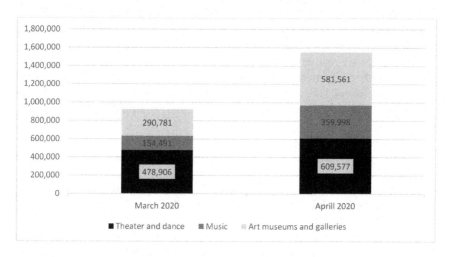

Figure 13.2 Lost audience in March and April 2020.

Source: Authors.

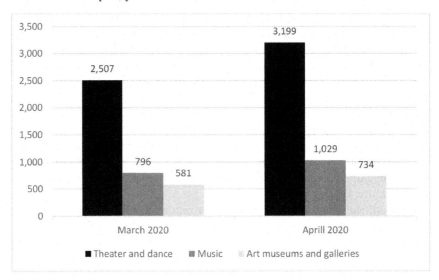

Figure 13.3 Cancelled performances in March and April 2020.

Source: Authors.

Theatres reported 5,706 cancelled performances in March–April 2020, which in comparison to all reported performances is about one-fifth of all annual theatre performances. Oppositely, theatres, clubs, music venues, and galleries promptly reacted to the measures and transferred part of their programs to digital space. Responding organizations reported 852 new performances in streaming and other forms of online presentation and presence. The leading sector of shifting to digital was theatres with 637 online performances.

The research results highlight the need for structural change and innovation for crisis resilience at both the institutional and individual levels. The research confirmed that institutions and individuals could not create financial reserves. In addition, multi-stream funding is not sufficiently developed. Individuals are exposed to excessive pressure due to:

1 A high share of contractual relations in lieu the usual labour scheme employer–employee due to missing regulations and a support framework.
2 A 37% share of self-employed in the cultural field compared to 17% of the entire Czech economy (Eurostat 2019).

For these reasons, the crisis revealed a possible future burden on the social system. There exist a large number of self-employed cultural professionals who are only partially covered by the social and welfare insurance system. This independent group of Bohemian cultural workers is the most vulnerable group of the pandemic. These professionals represent the most creative and innovated "behind the scene" contributors. Without them most organizations would not be able to create and operate. There is an urgent need to develop a supportive and legislative framework for these members. These independent experts understand the need for a collective body to advocate their interests.

In the case of organizations, the immediate impact varied across segments:

1 Theatres' cash flow did not suffer immediately due to the higher level of subsidies. The sector of theatres and dance indicates long-term stagnation.
2 The music industry experienced the heaviest immediate economic downturn as it receives the lowest state interventions and is more exposed to the market.
3 The impact on the art museums and galleries sector was not immediate as the income from admission is not a significant part of their budgets. A decrease in public as well as private funding is expected in the future.

These results are useful indications for policymakers to develop measures for CCIs.

Governmental support of the ACS

In the case of the Czech Republic, measures taken to mitigate the negative economic impact of the pandemic on ACS may be divided into:

a stimulus measures,
b employee-related measures, and
c tax measures.

Stimulus measures consist of compensation, guarantee schemes, loans, and others. These inject money into the economy and provide stability to enterprises and individuals with the aim of spillover effect. The Czech government provided stimulus measures for all self-employed citizens during the first wave of the pandemic in the form of one-time support. The Ministry of Culture in cooperation with the Ministry of Industry and Trade issued support in two waves. These programs focused on both non-profit organizations as well as for-profit organizations and individual freelancers. During the second wave, another stimulus support, specifically for self-employed arts professionals, was issued as a lump sum of 60,000 CZK, equivalent to 2,400 EUR. This support was designated for professionals in music, theatre, dance, visual arts, and literature. During the first call of the COVID-Culture program for organizations, 197 applications were paid the amount of CZK 95,234,457, equivalent to 3,745,335 EUR.

In the second call of the program, 4,061 applications for self-employed persons and 438 applications from entrepreneurs in the cultural sector were approved. A total of CZK 526,369,790, equivalent to 20,700,823 EUR, was paid as part of the second call.

Strategies initiated by the ACS

As part of this research the authors aim to capture also all aspects of the pandemic on the ACS and strategies adopted during this period by the organizations and individuals in ACS.

Players in the ACSs during the first and second waves were not motivated to create long-term changes in their business models for several reasons. First of all, the unclear communication from the government indicated that the closure of cultural organizations and venues would not endure. Second, the players dedicated most of their time to survival strategies to overcome the immediate impact. Naturally, all players extended their online activities and shifted to a virtual environment. The impact of digitalization on the sector is significant. Many subjects claim that the pandemic motivated to improve online activities and digital channels become the only media to contact with their communities. In many cases, this strategy did not resolve their financial losses, as many such activities were provided gratis. The measures to mitigate the spread of the COVID-19 virus did not permit them to step out of the digital environment. Only a few players came with innovative approaches to maintain communication with their communities.

In the case of state-subsidized organizations, most are not motivated to develop new income-generating activities. They claim that in the case of public funding reductions, they would rather revise and decrease costs and limit programs. This tendency results from the lower flexibility of state-subsidized organizations and a low level of options to develop income-generating activities due to the legal environment.

As the performing art sector was more impacted than the visual art, they were more active in developing new strategies to maintain contacts with their audiences and to increase their future funding streams.

The situation of the self-employed cultural workers is alarming. To survive and provide income for their families, many had to change their jobs with the uncertainty to never return. It is not unusual today to have opera singers, actors, and musicians working in supermarkets, delivery services, or taxis. It demonstrates that state support is not sufficient due to the missing legal framework and legislation.

Conclusion

The COVID-19 pandemic has affected ACS strongly. The sector had to immediately react and attempted to remain relevant to their communities while doing their best to mitigate the negative economic impact of the pandemic. Naturally, subjects relying on earned income have suffered more severely than the ones that benefit from public subsidies as major portion of their budgets. The research confirms that players in the fine arts have had the lowest income losses among the sample, as most are state-subsidized organizations.

The research also highlights that there is an urgent need for structural changes to develop a legal and economic framework for sustainable business models at both the institutional and individual levels. The research reveals that the ACS is highly exposed to crisis due to the lack of financial reserves, risk management, and the high share of self-employed cultural workers in the sector.

The central and local governments have already warned that public funding will decrease. Probably, some arts and cultural organizations and venues will not survive.

Individuals are no longer able to consume art and culture in the fashion to which they are accustomed. Alas, taken for granted for decades, it has disappeared. The question is whether such an interruption of personal contact with art and culture will in the long-term influence behaviour and whether demand and the way arts and culture are provided will change. The 'new normal' has yet to be defined.

The pandemic reintroduced the question about the relevance and value of culture. Furthermore, what will be the contribution and role of the ACS in support of education, economic development, environmental and cultural development? These, and many others, are questions the sector will need to be addressed to develop sufficient conditions for value creation. The current crisis is considered as an opportunity to reassess the ACS innovation potential.

Acknowledgement

The research and this chapter were realized with financial support from The Technology Agency of the Czech Republic, ETA programme, TL04000374.

References

Banks, M. (2020). The work of culture and C-19. *European Journal of Cultural Studies*, 23(4), pp. 648–654.

Banks, M. and O'Connor, J. (2020). A plague upon your howling: art and culture in the viral emergency. *Cultural Trends*, 30(1), pp. 40–51.

Benghozi, P. J. and Lyubareva, I. (2014). When organizations in the cultural industries seek new business models: a case study of the French online press. *International Journal of Arts Management*, 16(3), pp. 6–19.

Betzler, D., Loots, E., Prokůpek, M., Marques, L. and Grafenauer, P. (2020). COVID-19 and the arts and cultural sectors: investigating countries' contextual factors and early policy measures. *International Journal of Cultural Policy*, pp. 1–19.

Bonet, L. and Donato, F. (2011). The financial crisis and its impact on the current models of governance and management of the cultural sector in Europe. *ENCATC Journal of Cultural Management and Policy*, 1(1), pp. 4–11.

Carbonare, P. and Prokůpek, M. (2020). Cultural Business Models. In: A. Rurale, M. Addis, eds., *Managing the Cultural Business: Avoiding Mistakes, Finding Success - The 10 Most Common Mistakes in Arts Management*. Abingdon and New York: Routledge, pp. 32–77.

Eurostat (2019). Country Report the Czech Republic 2019. [online] Available at: https://ec.europa.eu/info/sites/info/files/file_import/2019-european-semester-country-report-czech-republic_en.pdf [Accessed 28 October 2020].

Meyrick, J., and Barnett, T. (2020). From public good to public value: arts and culture in a time of crisis. *Cultural Trends*, 30 (1), pp. 75–90.

NIPOS and Czech Statistical Office (2020). Results of the culture satellite account. [online] Available at: https://www.czso.cz/documents/10180/90577095/Z09000519.pdf/922c0d0b-cb4b-477d-ac1b-3df03df0f615?version=1.4 [Accessed 28 October 2020].

Rifkin, J. (2000). *The Age of Access: How the Shift from Ownership to Access Is Transforming Modern Life*. London: Penguin.

Throsby, D. (1994). The production and consumption of the arts: A view of cultural economics. *Journal of Economic Literature*, 32(1), pp. 1–29.

14 The COVID-19 pandemic and the European screen industry

The role of national screen agencies

Caitriona Noonan

This chapter will take as its starting point two intersecting realities. Firstly, whilst unprecedented in many ways, the experience of 2020 should be seen as one critical moment in a longer timeline of change for the film and television sectors. Many of the transformations taking place in the sector originated before the pandemic: the consolidation of power by transnational media and technology giants, the existence of an agile but resultantly precarious and unequal labour market, and squeezed funding and distribution opportunities for independent cinema. The pandemic further exposed persistent structural weaknesses within the European screen sector.

The second reality is that very few films or high-end television dramas would reach our screens without some form of direct or indirect public support (Doyle *et al.* 2015; McElroy, Noonan 2019; Sørensen, Redvall 2020) – a trend which continued in 2020/21 (European Audiovisual Observatory 2021b). One of the principal sources of funding has been national screen agencies.[1] There exists a dense global network of publicly funded bodies supporting national film and television, including: the British Film Institute, Det Danske Filminstitut (Danish Film Institute), Screen Ireland (Fís Éireann), Eesti Filmi Instituut (Estonian Film Institute), Ffilm Cymru Wales, and Centre National du Cinéma et de l'Image Animée (the National Centre for Cinema and the Moving Image, France), to name a select few. Whilst they differ in scale, the remit of these organizations is to support the filmmaking capacity of their nation, aid the global circulation of national cultural resources and provide domestic audiences with the opportunity to enjoy an array of audiovisual content. This role means they traverse the screen sector at local, national, and international planes, and at the same time engage at every stage of value chain for screen content. Therefore, screen agencies are key cultural intermediaries within the audiovisual sector.

The research draws on the conceptualization of "cultural intermediaries" from Bourdieu's (1984) theorization of workers who bridge production and consumption, whose articulation of value is central to their work. They do this work by drawing on both formal expertise and broader intellectual and cultural formations. Bourdieu's concept is helpful in understanding the

DOI: 10.4324/9781003128274-18

role of screen agencies during the pandemic as it conceives of power in different forms (i.e. economic, cultural, symbolic) and in different spaces (i.e. within nations, within industries, and within different spheres of policy). Screen agencies routinely exercise forms of mediation within the screen industry, but this has been particularly pronounced in their responses to the pandemic. This power will also need to be further mobilized as structural evolutions continue to take place in the sector.

Therefore, this chapter examines national screen agencies as key public bodies mediating the impact of the pandemic. It begins with a discussion of screen agencies and their occupational values before moving to the immediate responses of film funds across Europe and the political and financial threats that they themselves will likely face in the coming years. It concludes with a reflection on the role they might play as the challenges facing the screen sector and its workers continue, even once the lockdowns are lifted.[2]

Screen agencies as cultural intermediaries

In policy terms, screen agencies are labelled cultural actors as evidenced by their funding and governance, which is *generally* administered through the culture department of their national government. Table 14.1 includes an overview of the governance arrangements for the agencies in the first stage of this study.

However, to limit understanding of their contribution to a cultural agenda alone would misjudge their remit. In practice, their activities cross multiple fields of policy including the arts, economy, taxation, education, public planning and tourism. In line with wider developments in European film and cultural policy (Mingant, Tirtane 2018), their role has expanded to include a plethora of economic concerns related to securing inward investment, developing sectoral infrastructure and building labour capacity.

Yet, to position them as simply occupying the intersection between culture and economy, as Bourdieu's original interpretation framed cultural intermediaries, would again oversimply their position. *Some* screen agencies are actively attempting to secure a more inclusive, diverse and sustainable sector through, for instance, their purposeful redirection of funding (e.g. to female-led projects) or within their talent development initiatives (McElroy, Noonan, forthcoming). Here our research speaks to a "third" wave of studies on cultural intermediaries, building on calls by Perry et al (2015) and Cronin and Edwards (2021). These authors argue for greater emphasis on the socially engaged practices performed by cultural intermediaries which "operate between diverse cultural, creative and social worlds" (Perry *et al.* 2015: 14–15) and which mediate between multiple manifestations of the political (Cronin and Edwards 2021). Screen agencies negotiate a cultural, economic *and* social agenda within their national policy structures. The responses made by screen agencies to the pandemic illustrate some of this

Table 14.1 Overview of screen agencies in the project's research sample.

Agency	Country	Remit	Oversight and funding
Centre du Cinéma et de l'Audiovisuel/Cinema and Audio-visual Centre (CCA)	Belgium	Responsible for providing support in the creation and promotion of audiovisual works in the French-speaking community	Departmental organization within the Department of Culture of the Wallonia-Brussels Federation
Wallimage (WI)	Belgium	Economically driven, their objective is to create employment whilst fostering and sustaining the development of the local audiovisual industry within Belgium's French-speaking community	Public limited company that is funded by the government of Wallonia
Vlaams Audiovisueel Fonds/ Flanders Audio-visual Fund (VAF)	Belgium	Aims to stimulate and support independent audiovisual creation in Flanders, working on behalf of the Flemish government	Non-departmental, delegate organization of the Flemish Ministry of Culture, Youth, Sports and Media.
Hrvatski Audiovizualni Centar/ Croatian Audio-visual Centre (HAVC)	Croatia	Aims to stimulate a successful, vibrant audiovisual industry and to promote the widest possible enjoyment and understanding of audiovisual works throughout Croatia	Non-departmental, delegate organization of the Ministry of Culture, Croatia.
Danske Filminstitut/Danish Film Institute (DFI)	Denmark	Main task is to support and encourage Danish film and cinema culture	Non-departmental, delegate organization of the Ministry of Culture, Denmark
Screen Ireland/Fís Éireann (SI)	Ireland	The development agency for the Irish film industry investing in talent, creativity, and enterprise	Non-departmental, delegate organization of the Department of Culture, Heritage and the Gaeltacht
Northern Ireland Screen (NIS)	Northern Ireland	Committed to maximizing the economic, cultural, and educational value of the screen industries for the benefit of Northern Ireland	Non-departmental, delegate organization of the Department for Economy of the Northern Ireland Government
Screen Scotland (SS)	Scotland	Provides funding and support for the production, exhibition, and distribution of film, working within Scotland and internationally	Sits within Creative Scotland, but is a stand-alone agency, made up of a partnership with Scottish Enterprise, Highlands and Islands Enterprise, Skills Development Scotland and Scottish Funding Council
Ffilm Cymru Wales (FCW)	Wales	The development agency for Welsh film, supporting film development, production, education, exhibition, business development, and filmmaker career progression	Non-departmental, delegate organization of the Arts Council of Wales

expanded account of mediation and its value in understanding policymaking in the creative industries.

One must take care not to over-generalize the remits and structures of screen agencies. In each country they perform slightly different roles, have developed different relationships with their publics, and perform their mandate with various aesthetic, cultural, economic and social values in place. They vary in size and resources (European Audiovisual Observatory 2019), and in some European nations they are the sole provider of public funds to the film sector. They are informed by distinct histories and are shaped by key internal personalities. However, it is also clear that certain collective tendencies are discernible, and this has resulted in the homogenization of specific operating logics amongst screen agencies. This chapter focuses on and explains some of the commonalities in their interventions.

Our pre-pandemic interviews reveal three prevailing logics which characterize screen agencies. Firstly, staff, assessors and board members are generally drawn from the sector. This occupational profile establishes a credible knowledge base, which then underpins claims to authority and legitimacy amongst the sector, policymakers and other publics. The research interviews underscored the critical value of expertise and relational capital to the legitimacy of film funds and their ability to leverage and mobilize resources. Building a positive relationship with the sector is a normative concern for screen agencies and offers undoubtedly value, but it can also be a substantial obstacle when, for example, issues of equality and diversity are raised (see Liddy 2020, Nwonka 2020).

A second logic which infuses screen agencies is that the distribution of funding has been firmly established with recourse to ideas of "quality" in relation to cultural and artistic value and/or, more recently, "market growth". Scarcity of resources, coupled with the riskiness associated with screen outputs, means that agencies actively navigated and employ subjective ideals like auteurship and popularization and, whilst we don't have space to rehearse the arguments here, there is a long history of debate about the systemic application of ideas about what is "good art", what is culturally valuable and its relationships to questions of power (see for example Belfiore 2020).

A final value which infuses screen agencies is their focus on delivering a screen sector for the future – a common term seen in the parlance of screen agencies is "future-proofing the sector". This is in part due to the volatility and complexity of the screen sector, and inherent in the project-to-project mode of working that characterizes film- and TV-making. In response, screen agencies have purposefully orientated themselves both to respond to immediate needs, but to also expanding the temporal horizons of the sector. They routinely articulate visions for the sector's future as part of their mandate to serve the public interest. This vision is realized through establishing pipelines of creative work through, for example, delivering ongoing support to key talent and/or creative companies with substantial growth potential, as opposed to only funding individual film projects alone. In the pandemic this logic served their strategic response by framing their desire to also see beyond the immediate crisis and to what the audiovisual sector would become post-pandemic.

The chapter offers this account of screen agencies as an albeit brief contribution to extending Bourdieu's ideas of cultural intermediation, but also to contextualize the responses of screen agencies to the pandemic. What we can observe in their responses is the active realization of these values and the leveraging of different forms of power to navigate the potentially devastating impact of the shuttering of the screen industries during 2020 and 2021. However, as discussed later, such power is not without its limits.

The response of screen agencies to the pandemic

Screen agencies have been a critical part of the response to the pandemic in many European nations. This is not altogether surprising given that the efficacy of many is forged on the relationships they have cultivated with the sector over long periods of time. Many agency staff enjoyed careers in the sector meaning they empathize with the financial, logistical, and creative burdens those in the sector face. Whilst each country has had its own experience within the pandemic, there have been some general trends in the interventions formulated by screen agencies as summarized in Table 14.2. Indeed, one observation from the review of measures adopted by the agencies is that similarities outweigh differences. During the first months of the pandemic, agencies adopted very similar policies, often in the same sequence (e.g. support for the immediate cessation of production and then support for the long-term closure of exhibition spaces). The main areas of support were around financially supporting production and distribution, allowing greater flexibility in their contractual terms, providing training and skills development, and engaging in "crisis coalitions" to formulate collective responses and to advocate more effectively for public support.

In response to the pandemic, screen agencies adopted a multipronged approach delivering many of these categories of intervention simultaneously with the purpose of keeping the sector afloat until "business as usual" could resume – without knowing when that might happen and what a return might look like. Support evolved over the course of 2020 and 2021 as several waves of lockdown swept over each country, demanding different responses, firstly as filming and production was abruptly halted, and then as the long-term closure of venues and cinemas threatened their financial viability. Of course, all of this support also needed to be provided at a time when the agencies themselves were facing their own staffing and executive burdens due to the pandemic.

Through the funding strategies, development initiatives, and audience schemes outlined above, screen agencies have operated as key cultural intermediaries. They have distributed resources, shaped the response of

Table 14.2 Trends in the interventions from screen agencies to the pandemic.

Category of support	Remit	Examples
Production support	• Funding to complete productions and to cover additional costs associated with the pandemic (including emergency cash flow loans, the recruitment of COVID advisers, the purchase of safety and testing equipment, etc.) • Development funding for scripts, projects, and slates • Insurance guarantee funding • Advice on new safety guidelines • Logistical support for foreign crews because of border restrictions	NL Film Fonds (Netherlands) allocated €40m in new subsidies in the first half of 2020 including a pandemic guarantee scheme with €2.5m (NFF 2021) In Germany a €15m fund is established between Filmförderungsanstalt, regional funds, and the Federal Government Commissioner for Culture and Media (Filmförderungsanstalt 2020)
Distribution support	• Direct funding for cinemas, venues, and distributors impacted by lockdown • Extensions to existing distribution funding to support moves to online distribution • Creation of new online platforms, film festivals, and cultural projects • Creation of educational resources • Promotional campaigns • Additional funding linked to health and safety within venues • Reimbursement of costs for events, even if event cancelled due to lockdown	"Return to cinema" campaigns led by the Instituto de la Cinematografía y de las Artes Audiovisuales (Spain) and Polski Instytut Sztuki Filmowej (Poland) A campaign led by the Centre du Cinéma et de l'Audiovisuel de la Fédération Wallonie-Bruxelles, *Le Cinéma belge à la maison*, promotes new Belgian releases Svenska Filminstitutet (Sweden) allocates €35m to the film industry including cinemas, distributors, and film festivals Screen Ireland launches Cinema Stimulus Support Fund in which cinemas based in the Republic of Ireland could apply for up to €40K per cinema site with a maximum of up to €100K allowable to applicants with larger cinema chains

(Continued)

Table 14.2 Trends in the interventions from screen agencies to the pandemic. (*Continued*)

Category of support	Remit	Examples
Flexibility in contractual terms	• Greater flexibility in funding criteria in relation to release windows and platform distribution. • Greater flexibility with administrative and reporting procedures • Creation of digital application systems • Changes to the terms of funding, deferments of loans, and levy repayments	Instead of paying in three instalments, the Eesti Filmi Instituut (Estonia) makes payments to recipients in two Screen agencies in many nations including Italy, France, Portugal, Norway, and Spain amend criteria for funding, allowing films to bypass theatrical release
Training and skills development	• Online training and professional development courses are made available online • Training around new health and safety guidelines • Launch of talent development schemes launched aimed at under-represented groups (e.g. women) and around key creative roles (e.g. writers)	Screen Skills Ireland, the skills development unit within Screen Ireland, allocates funding worth over €130K to organizations to deliver skills development activities and initiatives for a diverse range of groups and roles across the screen sector
"Crisis coalition"	Formation of industry coalition to find solutions to issues raised in the pandemic and advocate to government on behalf of the sector and its workers	The British Film Institute coordinates a COVID-19 Response Screen Sector Taskforce, in which to discuss priority issues and concerns from across the sector. The BFI, in partnership with other screen agencies Ffilm Cymru Wales, Northern Ireland Screen and Screen Scotland, was also involved in the dialogue with government to present critical concerns from the film sector and propose solutions

the sector in pragmatic ways, and attempted to find innovative ways to connect producers with audiences. They have been an active part of the response measures to the pandemic and subsequently have shaped patterns of cultural consumption, production, and work, perhaps in the long term. We can also see their mediating role clearly through their active participation, and in some countries leadership, of the networks which have emerged to respond to the crisis, including in the UK, Ireland, and Denmark. By forming a "crisis coalition" which includes other local stakeholders (such as film companies, trade unions and guilds, government officials, and other cultural bodies), they have been part of efforts to respond quickly to the catastrophic impact of the pandemic and to find common purpose amongst different vested interests, whether it be around the safe resumption of filming or the reopening of venues. Screen agencies are particularly suited to this role as they are embedded within the habitus of policy. They routinely mediate complex policy structures and administrative geographies that do not always align with the natural structures of the screen sector. Therefore, screen agencies find themselves critical actors in coordinating activities and engaging in joint strategies to support the sector at a time of crisis.

At times this has meant adopting both a mediating and advocacy role. Despite decades of policymaking in relation to the creative industries, the specific structures of the screen sector are often neglected by policymakers. This is especially where flexible and freelance work has become normalized as the professionalizing mode of the sector and as a tax-efficient way of operating. As the financial burden of the pandemic intensified for workers, screen agencies often played a prominent role in discussions with government officials, in supplying relevant sectoral data and bridging cross-departmental dialogue in order to secure measures which would support small creative businesses and take account of the financial arrangements for those who were either self-employed or operating on a freelance basis. A glimpse into this mediating work is given in the submission by the British Film Institute to the Department of Digital, Culture, Media and Sports' inquiry into the pandemic in mid-2020:

> DCMS has provided regular engagement with both the BFI and the wider sector with policy officials and Ministers. As well as this, the department has supported the BFI as it repurposed the Brexit Screen Sector Taskforce for Covid-19, fielding senior officials to update screen representatives. The frequent ministerial meetings for the Creative Industries have been primarily used as a way of feeding back the immediate issues faced by the sector, and the BFI has responded to numerous commissions on specific areas from policy teams. [...] We are submitting a huge amount of information to DCMS on these policy concerns, and we believe early cross departmental dialogue might eliminate design flaws and ensure they work for the creative

sector. It is vital for our stakeholders and the screen and creative sectors that they know their concerns are being heard and understood across Whitehall.

(BFI 2020)

This outward-facing communication combined with less formal information-sharing activities shows us how mediation works in a policymaking crisis. Screen agencies didn't simply act as go-betweens but actively shaped the perception of screen and its value. As observed in their public statements related to the crisis, screen agencies actively constructed a narrative of value which included both screen outputs and the companies and workers who make it happen. They also underscored the importance of public finance to the screen sector. Whilst this intermediation wasn't entirely new – screen agencies have long been part of negotiating between policymakers and industry – it was the interdependent network of stakeholders, many under real financial threat, being able to collaborate quickly and directly, which is the critical feature of this coalition's activities.

However, the pandemic also highlights a non-causal relationship between the power of screen agencies and their ability to effect change in policy. As noted later in the evidence to the above inquiry, the British Film Institute lament:

> Given how well evidenced the scale of the problem is, it is disappointing that the two key support schemes [for workers] have not been amended to include these [self-employed and freelance] groups despite numerous representations to government on how this could be done.

(BFI 2020)

Whilst some governments have been more responsive to the issues faced by freelancers, the UK system of income support still had notable gaps well into 2021. Therefore, despite their prominence in discussions, political decision-makers and their broad ideological priorities can be impervious to some of the influence of cultural intermediaries.

This also suggests that it will be the political climate ahead that may be a significant threat to screen agencies and their efficacy in policy formation in the future. The susceptibility of these bodies to political change has been noted by several scholars, including Doyle et al (2015) in relation to the dissolution of the UK Film Council in 2011. Some international funds have already felt both the economic and political tide turning in their national context. Under its far-right government, Ancine, Brazil's main public-sector source of film funding, has had a long-term freeze on its funding (Hopewell 2020). The organization representing screen agencies in Europe, the European Film Agencies Directors (EFAD), also publicly expressed its concerns regarding the Slovenian Film Centre, which has been facing "administrative difficulties" over the past months resulting in a suspension of funding distribution, and "endangering film production in Slovenia" (EFAD 2020). The conditions of a crisis can be used by many political actors to remodel policymaking, and so the shape, remit, and even existence of screen agencies may be susceptible to political change. Therefore, the political landscape that emerges post-pandemic will be a significant element in the future of screen agencies.

Political change is only one factor impacting the future of screen agencies and of course another (overlapping) concern will be funding. Some screen agencies will face their own financial uncertainty. In many countries public financing for film and television will have to sit alongside more immediate needs such as funding for health and social care, and likely in the context of a deep global recession. As the European Audiovisual Observatory (2021b: 7) concludes, "reductions loom" for public funding within the screen sector. Many screen agencies have lost important sources of ancillary revenue from things such as cultural venues such as in the case of the Danish Film Institute and British Film Institute. Despite extra funding to ensure the liquidity of projects and film companies, there will likely be a long-term squeeze on the budgets of screen agencies. This will undoubtedly have an impact on the volume and range of new projects which agencies will be able to support and force some difficult decisions about the priorities for national cinema in the coming years.

Building a "new" European screen industry

This chapter opened with an observation that the screen industry was facing not one but several structural changes and that the pandemic simply exacerbated some pre-existing weaknesses. It concludes by reflecting on the future and the specific roles which screen agencies might productively play. The value of film, television, and creative arts more generally in a time of crisis is certainly not in question. Throughout the pandemic people cocooning in their homes sought relief from their daily ennui through new films and television programmes and took comfort in returning to their old favourites. As Banks (2020) observes, during the periods of enforced lockdown "[w]hile culture and arts may not be vital to the preservation of life, they are proving increasingly vital to preserving the sense of life being lived". Demand for screen content was high, as evidenced by the increasing subscriber numbers to many Subscription Video on Demand (SVOD) services (European Audiovisual Observatory 2021a), again, capitalizing on a longer-term trajectory of growth and consolidating their economic power across Europe. Yet whilst audience demand for some content might be high, the European Audiovisual Observatory (2021b: 6) also predicts that the audiovisual sector is unlikely to return in 2021 (at least) to its pre-pandemic levels. In 2020 the sector lost over 10% of its revenues compared to 2019, translating into a loss in the financing of original European production of over EUR 3billion (for the EU27 only) (ibid.). Amongst the many roles that screen agencies might perform within this context, there are three which will be very critical going forward.

The most obvious is the strategic distribution of limited public funds at a time when the costs of production will likely increase due to the logistical issues arising from the pandemic. Public funding at both national and pan-European levels (for example, via the Creative Europe MEDIA programme) will be as important as ever. Innovation in the deployment of public funding will be required if future opportunities are to be realized. Here, for instance, it is worth noting recent calls for funding from Vlaams Audiovisueel Fonds, the Flemish agency, and the Netherlands Film Fund, which both sought to use the cessation of production to rethink modes of storytelling offering funding and specialized support for R&D schemes and for the integration of new technologies such as Augmented Reality and Virtual Reality with traditional filmmaking practices (Vlaams Audiovisueel Fonds 2020; NFF 2021). In this way public funding can become an important catalyst for experiment and creativity at a time when the boundaries between screens and technology are growing ever more porous. The funding and support decisions of screen agencies will be critical in delivering an increasingly converged screen landscape. This will also likely impact the organizational logics within screen agencies, and, as it will require new knowledge and skills, the expertise within these bodies will likely change. Future research will need to consider how screen agencies and their staff are transformed after the pandemic.

More resources will also need to be directed to remedying the ongoing constraints within European exhibition and distribution following further consolidations and new business models emerging in this part of the value chain (European Audiovisual Observatory 2021b; Smits 2019). In the past screen agencies have prioritized their nation's production capacity despite the ongoing structural issues related to distribution (European Audiovisual Observatory 2019: 19). As theatrical distribution became even more problematic over the course of the pandemic, many agencies formulated interventions on the distribution and demand side. This included dedicated funds for local cinemas and exhibition hubs to ensure they could weather the economic storm. Some agencies have supported and cooperated on the launch of new online distribution initiatives attempting to rival global SVoDs (including www.filmas.lv created by the Latvian Nacionālais Kino Centrs, www.netikino.ee in cooperation with the Eesti Filmi Instituut, Estonia, and lecinemabelgealamaison.be from the Center du Cinéma et de l'Audiovisuel of the Wallonia-Brussels Federation). These digital platforms are designed to support national film distribution and seed local demand for content.

However, we are at the beginning of a major period of transformation for the screen sector, especially in the relationship between cinema venues and distributors (Chandler 2020; European Audiovisual Observatory 2021b). There is a long history of tension between film distributors (like Disney,

Universal, and Warner Brothers) and exhibitors over the "windows" in which films will be available in cinemas. The delayed release of high-profile titles (e.g. the Bond film *No Time to Die*) exacerbated tensions and further threatened the financial stability of many cinemas. There was also further anxiety as some distributors (notably Disney) used lockdown to experiment with direct-to-streaming releases. It is too early to say whether such release strategies will become the norm, but certainly it offers both opportunities and challenges for filmmakers, and by extension screen agencies. Many in the industry regard theatrical release as a much-needed opportunity for financial return and an indicator of quality and therefore, visibility. However, there also exist in this direct to steaming strategy opportunities for some players – Cineuropa (Salwa 2020) described the strategy of direct-to-streaming as "a blessing in disguise" for Polish horror film *W lesie dziś nie zaśnie nikt* (Kowlaski 2020, *Nobody Sleeps in the Woods Tonight*) which became one of the most-watched films in the country via Netflix. However, when the only pan-European SVOD platforms are US companies like Netflix, Amazon, and Apple, it also represents a conundrum to screen agencies, especially those in smaller nations or those from countries with minority languages, as they attempt to keep routes to international markets open.

A further role for screen agencies will be in declaring the screen sector as "open for business", a role which is especially important as we write in 2021 and when there are large epidemic waves continuing to break across Europe. In part this will be communicating to international productions, potential co-producers, and investors that the sector is ready to resume trade and indeed, in many parts of Europe there has been a return to filming. In this context screen agencies need to help productions navigate a way through local conditions and to harmonize transnational production. However, on a much more critical level it is also encouraging audiences back into cinemas and film spaces, hopefully with a greater appreciation for their own domestically produced content. Whilst the rise in subscribers' numbers to services like Netflix suggests a boon for filmmakers, the reality is that much of this content bears little cultural specificity, and these organizations become further gatekeepers for European filmmakers. Screen agencies need to make sure that the pandemic doesn't contribute to the further consolidation of big cinema chains and transnational SVODs and that independent cinema remains a visible and viable part of creative life in Europe.

Finally, a "new" European screen industry must be one that includes labour markets that are both sustainable *and* equitable. The pandemic revealed further the precariousness of the freelance economy in which the long-term consequences for equality, diversity, and inclusion are potentially even more devastating (Banks 2020; Eikhof 2020). Research points to the unequal economic and social impact that the pandemic will have on European citizens, with women and ethnic minorities predicted to be disproportionately harder hit by the economic fallout from the pandemic (Cookson, Milne 2020). Prior to the pandemic some screen agencies such as the Svenska Filminstitutet (Sweden) have attempted to lead change in relation to gender equality in the sector. However, the full realization of equity in the screen sector remains stubbornly slow across Europe (European Audiovisual Observatory 2020; Liddy 2020; Nwonka 2020; O'Brien 2019; Rollet *et al.* 2016).

Therefore, screen agencies will have a dual role in relation to equality: firstly, to ensure that any gains made in the last decade are not lost and that the economic recovery measures enacted protect *all* creative workers. Secondly, to create meaningful routes into and within the screen sector so that the sector which emerges post-pandemic is one which is egalitarian, inclusive, and diverse. The purposeful distribution of funding by screen agencies to disadvantaged groups will be a critical intervention in this goal, along with accessible talent development schemes and the strategic collection of data which unmasks ongoing problems. However, we must also note the informal and quotidian role that screen agencies staff play in disrupting the prevailing norms of the sector by leveraging their expertise, legitimacy, and power in their relationships with the sector and policymakers.

In each of these roles, screen agencies will need to bring together diversely positioned organizations and also establish "more vertical and horizontal solidarities" (Banks 2020) – something we began to see in the interventions outlined above. They will need to mobilize knowledge and broker compromises. Crucially, they will also need to continue to narrativize and advocate for the value of screen to those outside the industry. Many of the roles above will cross-cultural, economic, and social concerns, and it is in the realization of these ambitions that we will be able to see the full value of cultural intermediaries to the creative industries after the pandemic.

Notes

1. These bodies are alternatively titled film commissions, film institutes, or film funds. The choice of screen agencies here is purposeful, recognizing that these organizations rarely concern themselves with only film and increasingly supporting other screen forms such as high-end television and gaming. Funding, whilst important, is only one of their activities. It is also in recognition of the influence of New Public Management (NPM) on policy-making in Europe and the creation of a range of semi-autonomous "agencies" based on geography and/or remit through which many areas of policy, including cultural policies, are implemented (Pollitt and Talbot 2004; Verhoest 2018).
2. This chapter emerges from an Arts and Humanities Research Council (AHRC) funded project "Screen Agencies as Cultural Intermediaries: Negotiating and Shaping Cultural Policy for the Film and TV Industries within Selected Small Nations" (June 2018–August 2021). The focus of this project was on the experiences of screen agencies in small nations; the sample for this study included the following small nations: Belgium, Croatia, Denmark, Ireland, Northern Ireland, Scotland, and Wales. An overview of these

agencies is provided in Table 14.1. We conducted 46 semi-structured interviews within the national screen agencies before the pandemic (September 2018–February 2020) and undertook reviews of the institutional policies of the selected screen agencies and the national policy frameworks they inhabit. For this chapter we have continued to monitor and collate their updated support programs and follow closely their public responses to the pandemic. We have also gathered data on the responses of a wider sample of European agencies in order to see wider trends in the response measures of screen agencies. Whilst hugely important, the research focuses on national agencies, excluding regional and supranational bodies from the discussion at this time. More information about the research project can be found at www.smallnationsscreen.org.

References

Banks, M. (2020) The work of culture and C-19. *European Journal of Cultural Studies*, 23:4, 648–654. doi: 10.1177/1367549420924687.

Belfiore, E. (2020) Whose cultural value? Representation, power and creative industries. *International Journal of Cultural Policy*, 26:3, 383–397.

Bourdieu, P. (1984) *Distinction: A Social Critique of the Judgement of Taste*, English Translation. ed. Harvard University Press, Cambridge.

British Film Institute (BFI) (2020) *Written evidence submitted by the British Film Institution*. Response to DCMS Select Committee Inquiry. Impact of Covid-19 on DCMS Sectors. https://committees.parliament.uk/writtenevidence/4379/pdf/ (accessed 4 March 2021).

Chandler, C. J. (2020) No blockbusters: How COVID-19 has worsened the fraught relationship between cinemas and distributors. *The Conversation*. 7 October. https://theconversation.com/no-blockbusters-how-covid-19-has-worsened-the-fraught-relationship-between-cinemas-and-distributors-147622 (accessed 2 March 2021).

Cookson, Clive and Milne, Richard (2020). "Nations look into why coronavirus hits ethnic minorities so hard". – *Financial Times* April 29. https://www.ft.com/content/5fd6ab18-be4a-48de-b887-8478a391dd72 (accessed 13 August 2020).

Cronin, A. M. and Edwards, L. (2021) Resituating the political in cultural intermediary work: Charity sector public relations and communication. *European Journal of Cultural Studies*. doi: 10.1177/1367549421994239.

Doyle, G., Schlesinger, P., Boyle, R., Kelly, L.W. (2015) *The Rise and Fall of the UK Film Council*. Edinburgh University Press, Edinburgh.

Eikhof, D (2020) COVID-19, inclusion and workforce diversity in the cultural economy: What now, what next? *Cultural Trends*, 29(3), 234–250.

European Audiovisual Observatory (2019) *Mapping of Film and Audiovisual Public Funding Criteria in the EU*. European Audiovisual Observatory, Strasburg.

European Audiovisual Observatory (2020) Diversity and inclusion in the European audiovisual industries: Both on and off-screen. Workshop 10 December 2020. https://rm.coe.int/summary-workshop-2020-diversity/1680a14957 (accessed 1 March 2021).

European Audiovisual Observatory (2021a) European VOD revenues increased 30-fold over the last ten years. Report https://rm.coe.int/trends-in-the-vod-market-in-eu28-final-version/1680a1511a (accessed 2 March 2021).

European Audiovisual Observatory (2021b) Yearbook 2021/21: Key Trends. Report https://rm.coe.int/yearbook-key-trends-2020-2021-en/1680a26056 (accessed 26 May 2021).

European Film Agency Directors association (EFAD) (2020) EFAD in support of the Slovenian Film Centre. Press Release. https://europeanfilmagencies.eu/news-publications/our-press-releases/253-efad-in-support-of-the-slovenian-film-centre (accessed 3 March 2021).

Filmförderungsanstalt (2020) Corona-Krise: Bundes- und Länderförderer starten Hilfsprogramm für die Film- und Medienbranche. Press Release. https://www.ffa.de/aid=1394.html?newsdetail=20200327-1351_corona-krise-bundes-und-laenderfoerderer-starten-hilfsprogramm-fuer-die-film-und-medienbranche

Hopewell, John (2020). "Brazil's Government Funding Freeze Shakes up Film Business". – *Variety* May 11. https://variety.com/2020/film/news/brazil-government-film-crisis-pandemic-1234601330/ (accessed 10 August 2020).

Liddy, S. (Ed.) (2020) *Women in the International Film Industry: Policy, Practice and Power*. Palgrave Macmillan, Cham.

McElroy, R., Noonan, C. (2019) *Producing British Television Drama: Local Production in a Global Era*. Palgrave Macmillan UK, London.

McElroy, R. Noonan, C (forthcoming) "Film policy, social value and the mediating role of screen agencies". In: *Motion Pictures and Public Value*. Mette Hjort and Ted Nannicelli (Eds.).

Mingant, Nolwenn, Tirtane, Cecilia (Eds.) (2018) *Reconceptualising Film Policies*. Routledge, New York.

Nederlands Filmfonds (NFF) (2021) All COVID-19 updates from the Film Fund. Press Release 12 January. https://www.filmfonds.nl/page/8492/alle-covid-19-updates-van-het-filmfonds (accessed 4 March 2021).

Nwonka, C. J. (2020) *Race and Ethnicity in the UK Film Industry: An Analysis of the BFI Diversity Standards*. LSE, London.

O'Brien, A. (2019) *Women, Inequality and Media Work*. Routledge, Oxon.

Perry, B., Smith, K., Warren, S. (2015). Revealing and re-valuing cultural intermediaries in the "real" creative city: Insights from a diary-keeping exercise. *European Journal of Cultural Studies*, 18, 724–740.

Pollitt, C., Talbot, C. (Eds.) (2004) *Unbundled Government: A Critical Analysis of the Global Trend to Agencies, Quangos and Contractualisation*. Routledge, London.

Rollet, B., Paris-Saclay, U., Beuré, F. (2016) *Gender Equality for Directors in the European Film Industry*. European Women's Audiovisual Network. https://www.ewawomen.com/research/ (accessed 27 September 2021)

Salwa, Ola (2020) Review: *Nobody Sleeps in the Woods Tonight*. Cineuropa. 27 March. https://cineuropa.org/en/newsdetail/387357/ (Accessed 21 October 2021).

Smits, R. (2019) *Gatekeeping in the Evolving Business of Independent Film Distribution*. Palgrave, Cham.

Sørensen, I. E., Redvall, E. N. (2020) Does automatic funding suck? The cost and value of automatic funding in small nation screen industries in Northern Europe. – *International Journal of Cultural Policy* Online first. doi: 10.1080/10286632.2020.1724107

Verhoest, K. (2018) "Agencification in Europe", in: Ongaro, E., Van Thiel, S. (Eds.), *The Palgrave Handbook of Public Administration and Management in Europe*. pp. 327–346.

Vlaams Audiovisueel Fonds (2020) Call innovation workshop. 8 May. https://www.vaf.be/nieuws/call-innovatieatelier (accessed 2 March 2021).

15 Orchestrating change

The future of orchestras post COVID-19

John O'Hagan and Karol J. Borowiecki

Introduction

Ongoing challenges

The crisis created by COVID-19 for live orchestral music could be viewed as simply another challenge in the long line of difficulties that orchestras have had to face since their formation. The word 'orchestra' in fact is Greek in origin, but orchestras as we know them today have their roots from the 16th-century consorts employed in noble households and to groups of instrumentalists especially assembled for important occasions. In the following three centuries they evolved into much larger ensembles and playing in concert halls greatly expanded in size.[1]

Major technological changes in the 20th and 21st centuries posed further challenges for orchestras and raised the issue of how the value of a live classical music experience exceeds, if at all, listening to and watching recorded music in isolation. Live-streamed orchestral music became a further option in recent decades. And during COVID-19 lockdowns, live-streamed orchestral concerts with no live audience became a reality.

Thus, there has been a huge change in the options available on the demand side for orchestral music and also on the supply side. The emphasis in this chapter will be on these aspects of the issues facing orchestral music in the years ahead. The ongoing and long-documented financial problems facing orchestras will not be addressed here, except peripherally. The focus instead will be on the changing options for receiving and transmitting orchestral music.[2] Live streaming could increase greatly the potential audience, and hence revenue streams, as discussed in the conclusions. But, maybe not also.

COVID-19 though created severe short-term problems on the cost front, problems which – it is assumed – will not persist into the future. In total lockdowns there were no income streams at all, although the staff required for orchestral music had still to be paid. Emergency state borrowing and measures were put in place in different countries to address this problem, not just for orchestras but also across the whole economy (see European

DOI: 10.4324/9781003128274-19

Parliament, 2020). As this issue is not specific to orchestras and maybe just short-term in nature, they will be discussed only briefly here. What will be discussed more thoroughly are the likely implications for production and consumption of live orchestral music during COVID-19 and the long-term changes, if any, that these may bring about.

One last point, the focus here is on symphony orchestras, with little reference to orchestras needed for opera/ballet. These orchestras usually are smaller in size and are linked directly to the future of these art forms. This does not mean of course that a study of them is not warranted, but simply outside our terms of reference given space limitations.

Outline of chapter

The approach of this chapter is polemical in nature, reflecting the very fluid situation that lies ahead for orchestras post COVID-19. The chapter has four main research objectives. First, to put the current debate in context, we will look at the key challenges that orchestras have faced since the turn of the last century and in what way COVID-19 posed problems that impacted orchestral music. The following section addresses the second objective, which is to outline briefly some special short-term measures introduced to mitigate the impact of COVID-19, namely: (i) the income support measures needed to sustain orchestras during total lockdowns; and (ii) the extent to which orchestras could come together and practice, and in fact perform, even if only in front of no or very limited live audiences. Following this the chapter will address the third objective, namely, to speculate as to what possibly lies ahead for live orchestral music, post-COVID-19, and in a rapidly changing world regarding technological advances in the production and consumption of orchestral music.

The next section addresses the fourth research objective and briefly surveys some broad trends in the 'consumption' of orchestral music over time, particularly in terms of numbers attending live concerts and streamed concerts. The data at this stage are simply indicative, as even for one country it is difficult to get reliable time-series data of this nature. This should provide some indication of the possible future direction of orchestral music, which perhaps was well mapped out long before COVID-19, but which unquestionably COVID-19 may have accelerated. The final section concludes the chapter with some interesting possible scenarios to consider.

Orchestral music in an age of technology

Receiving

About a century ago, technological advancement brought about dramatic changes for orchestral music in terms of how and where it is consumed. Home radio enabled many people to hear live broadcasts and recordings of all kinds, including classical music performances. As Manzi (2017) points out, in the 1950s, the TV arrived, on which people could watch orchestras play live. Since then, he argues, we have eight-track cassettes, CDs, DVDs, MP3s, YouTube, and most recently, streaming. Alongside those advances in recording technology there was a rapid advancement in the capabilities of listening equipment, including personal headphones, portable Bluetooth speakers, and professional-grade speakers that put out sound with lifelike quality. Video has got to the point where the human eye can no longer pick out a single pixel on a computer or TV screen, not to mention the immersive experience of virtual reality.

In a similar vein, the Swiss American conductor and scholar Botstein (2020) argued more recently that viewing/listening to orchestral music was once just an adjunct to concert life and that recording in the past supported the culture of concert attendance. By the mid-1960s, however, the balance shifted, he argued. More money was to be made by artists through recording than live performances. Recordings became more important. And one could readily imagine staying at home, in a 'surround-sound' context, with or without headphones, and listening to one's favourite multi-phonic studio recording rather than going out and sitting uncomfortably in a concert hall.

These represent dramatic changes indeed in the ways in which orchestral music can be received. Whether or not they spell the 'end' for live orchestral music is an issue we return to later.

Producing

There are technological issues facing orchestras also on the supply side. It was argued in fact some decades ago, for example by Frederickson (1989), that technology had advanced to the point that performers' sounds can be not only recorded but analyzed, reconstituted, and simulated and that as the rationalization of technique continues to its logical conclusion, a specific musician might be no longer necessary. Keiichiro Shibuya, the Japanese composer, who wrote an orchestral piece, which was performed in the United Arab Emirates in 2020, was conducted by a robot, waving its arms and moving up and down with the rhythm of the seven-minute-long piece of music (Campbell, 2020). Not only the continuation of live orchestral concerts then is in question, but the very existence of an orchestra as we know it could be at stake. This is probably an exaggeration, but certainly apart from music performed by a full orchestra physically together, there will be options in terms of reconstituted and simulated music available – through digital tracking, mixing, and mastering – a practice very common in popular music for some time.

Over 30 years ago, Kramer (1996) also heralded that technology was already ubiquitous in music. It had, he argued, altered how music is transmitted, preserved, heard, performed, and composed. Less and less often, he states, do we hear musical sound that has not at some level been shaped by technology, broadly defined. For example, technology is involved in the reinforcement of concert halls, the recording and broadcast of music, and the design and construction of musical instruments. Instruments are now available that look like piano keyboards, feel like piano keys, and sound like piano timbres, but which are actually dedicated digital synthesizers; virtuoso performers whose instrument is the turntable are now part of not only the world of disco but also, albeit a small part so far, of the world of classical concert music.

COVID-19: New challenges and short-term responses

COVID-19 brought new challenges. Zero or limited audiences became the norm. But, for many months, orchestras could not gather to practice and perform, even in empty halls, due to the need for social distancing between the players. As Bibu et al. (2018) note there is no other activity in which 40, 80, or 120 people are doing the same thing together, side by side, with a precision of a tenth of a second, starting and finishing together. One outcome was smaller groups playing from home, synchronized across venues, but with limited success. Many more open-air free concerts were also provided. Theatre, concert and opera performances had to be cancelled, with different consequences for small private companies, as well as public ones and prestigious state-funded public venues.

Lost revenue streams

Many European states reacted quickly to counterbalance the consequences of COVID-19 with income support for cultural institutions and creative workers, as part of the wider supports for all sectors affected worst by COVID-19 restrictions (see European Parliament, 2020).

Individual countries introduced different measures at different times. One of the first measures though was to cancel major events and public gatherings. This meant museums, art galleries, theatres, opera houses, concert halls, cinemas, and festivals were the first to be shut down, together with restaurants and cafés. Some artists and creators remained active during the confinement period or streaming via digital messaging platforms. Those who were lucky enough to be employed by public theatres, opera houses, and concert halls could count on some state-designed solutions that cover all the staff. As a result, to address cultural needs, institutions such as concert halls, opera houses, theatres, and museums made their productions and exhibitions available online, free of charge (see European Parliament, 2020).

In some European countries, for example, Austria and Germany, the cultural sector had been better prepared to weather the crisis due to decades of heavy state investment and better social protection for performers. Besides, both countries took extensive new actions, for example, the launching of two new funds: one to pay a bonus to organizers of smaller cultural events, so they can be profitable even with social distancing, and another to provide insurance for larger events to mitigate the risk of cancellation. Many in the cultural sector were covered by various furlough schemes applied nationwide in most countries to compensate for lost income, up to 80% in some cases. But, as mentioned most of these schemes were part of the wider measures introduced by governments.

Safe social distancing and other requirements

The fact that orchestras could not meet, practice, and perform was the other pressing problem to be addressed, as seen above. This applied of course to many sectors of the economy as well, but for orchestras special measures specific to their operation were needed to make possible performance, even if initially only to empty concert halls.

It became a big event therefore when an orchestra was able to return to the concert hall, often after many weeks of isolation. However, for example, for the Berliner Philharmoniker, on their first return to the concert hall, only 15 players could be onstage at a time, the strings sat 2 metres apart, and the woodwinds and brass 5 metres apart (Barber, 2020). The latter had a longer gap because they could blow great quantities of air droplets much further. At the end of their performance they bowed, smiled to an empty, silent hall, and departed the stage.

Barber (2020) also refers to Konzerthaus, home of another Berlin orchestra. The orchestra had done its share of virtual experiments, such as a streaming concert, a series of one-to-one recitals between orchestra musicians and listeners who called them on the phone, and virtual tours of the 200-year-old concert hall. But the driving objective was to return to concerts, and the only issue then was how to do so safely. The problem is as Bibu et al. (2018) also point out that orchestras are a very large crowd of people, coming together in intimate proximity indoors, many of them blowing into instruments vigorously for hours at a time.

Thus, questions arose, for example, as to how the emissions from the enormous bell of a tuba compare with those of a flute? The coiled tubes of a French horn with an oboe? There are differences in the way the air flows through the instrument, and in how the players draw their breaths – do the droplets come from the mouth, or deep in the lungs? Some instruments require blowing through reeds, or wider metal mouthpieces. Those factors likely affect what kinds of particles are produced, how long those particles hang in the air, and the amount of infectious virus they ultimately bear.

Seven major German orchestras as a result, turned to epidemiologists at the Charité, Germany's top academic medical centre, to draft guidance (see Berghöfer et al., 2020). The players could get by with less distance, they suggested: 1.5 metres between each string player, and 2.0 metres for the brass and woodwinds. They also suggested putting up plexiglass between the wind and brass players to block the spread of droplets.

There was a host of other recommendations. For example, that in the music ensemble with wind instruments with aerosol production and formation of droplets, specific hygienic measures should be developed. The floor in the work area of the wind instrument group should be cleaned thoroughly after play. Protection with a transparent material should be set up for the string players or for others sitting in front of the wind players to avoid the distribution of aerosol in their direction. This should be tall enough to shield the horns of the respective instruments so that it provides protection even during movement of the instruments during play. After a rehearsal or a concert, music stands and other work surfaces all had to be cleaned thoroughly.

In a later study, researchers at Munich's Ludwig Maximilian University and the University of Erlangen, working with musicians from the Bavarian Radio Symphony Orchestra, found the risk from playing musical instruments to be manageable. For their experiment they placed musicians – individually – in a darkened room, where they were asked to take a puff from an e-cigarette containing nicotine-free fluid and begin playing.[3] Closely calibrated cameras and laser transmitters recorded what happened next or, more accurately, what didn't happen next. The aerosol transmission made visible by the smoke was less dynamic than researchers expected and fell well short of 2 metres in front of most musicians and less than 1.5 metres at the side.

When will though normality return was then the key question? In fact, there was a return to some sort of normality in Madrid from as far back as late summer 2020 (Dombey, 2021).[4] To accomplish social distancing, for example in the Teatro Real, nine brass players were moved to boxes to the right of the stage; six harps and a percussionist were on the opposite side; several violinists played flush against the wall. Everyone was regularly tested for the virus, and wardrobe and make-up were attended to in corridors or rehearsal rooms, to keep the cast apart. The audience was masked, and their temperatures were taken on arrival, and the ventilation system pumped out a minimum of 28 litres of filtered air for each member of the audience every second. Up to two-thirds of audience capacity was allowed and over 90% of venues opened this way in Madrid.

Long-term challenges and possible solutions

Few in the classical music world doubt that the orchestral music of Beethoven, Brahms, Mozart, Shostakovich, Tchaikovsky, and others will continue to be important in decades to come. But how will this music be produced and engaged with? Particularly, will trends which began long before COVID-19 in these respects continue or even be accelerated? Will orchestras as we know them exist if few of their performances were to live audiences? As a European Parliament report (2020) asks, will creative workers who have streamed their productions for free manage to monetize their work once life returns to normal? Will new creative workers emerge from this period of intense prosumer activity and be able to continue their creative work? Will cultural institutions increase their outreach to new audiences and be operational with potentially reduced public funding? Will small cultural venues be able to operate? Some recent papers addressed a few of these issues.

A new business model

Szedmák and Szabó (2020) point out that many companies during the lockdowns had to temporarily pause operations, universities and schools had to change to distance education, organizers had to postpone all kinds of events. Organizations which reacted quickly to these new circumstances will be able to survive this period, they argue. In the case of symphony orchestras, it is not enough to rely on the existing repertoire and follow traditional models. Without innovatively rethinking their operation and services, orchestras will find it difficult to survive. In other words, their 'business model' needs to be revised.[5]

Digitization they argue opens new ways for the orchestras to reach out and address audiences in an unusual way. The Berlin Philharmonic's *Digital Concert Hall* project was the first major initiative which used social media to broaden the audience globally by making the orchestra's concert recordings available to consumers around the world via the Internet (see also Uhl et al., 2013). Thus, the audience can access the orchestra's recordings or even live concerts anytime, anywhere. This also provides an opportunity to reach a new audience: the concept can be attractive to those who, while open to classical music, cannot appear in person for any reason (e.g. remote location, schedule, other tasks/programmes). Furthermore, it is a great way to reach out to young people who prefer listening to music at home and often consider the traditional concert form uncomfortable. Since the concert experience is not the same through the screen as live, no orchestra must worry about losing current audiences, they argue. The application of the concept is more likely to result in the involvement of new audience members, while the existing core audience may 'consume' more, they argue.

Another interesting example they provide of the exploitation of opportunities offered by digitalization is the San Francisco Symphony's 'SoundBox' programme, which aims to redefine the concert experience. Perhaps in ways that would not suit all tastes in Europe. The venue is one of the orchestra's rehearsal rooms, and the concert hall resembles a cosy bar where guests can enjoy the concert with a cocktail or beer in their hands. Thanks to the modern technological, audio-visual solutions and effects, viewers can feel as if they were in cathedral or – just a moment later – in an underground club, while the volume and complexity of the music is constantly changing.

The musical experience can be enriched by video installations projected on the walls. The musicians also put emphasis on interactions with and involvement of the audience.[6]

Focus on the 'Local'

The worry of Botstein (2020) is that the pandemic may have deepened the attachment to video and audio access to music at home. People have learned how to take advantage of the ease of computer-based technology and can even make listening more personal, tailored to personal tastes, and interactive.

After the pandemic has passed, why not be content, he argues, to watch performances at home, much like a soccer match or basketball game. So perhaps in post-pandemic circumstances, a concert or opera will be performed on the stage, with the singers facing an empty, multi-seat hall, while the performance is watched by a global audience comfortably settled in the privacy of their homes. In that case, one needs only one or two performances, from which an HD video can be made. Individual viewers, most likely, eventually will be able to programme their own visual angles so that they see what they wish. This will lessen further the incentive to attend a live event.

To sustain live orchestral music in this context, it must, he strongly argues, become intensely local and much less reliant on the international concert circuit. In the 19th century, touring raised standards and broadened horizons, but that is not needed anymore. Recording, internet access, and streaming give anyone in the world a sense of what is going on and what the reigning technical standards are. What is needed instead is nurturing excellence and a specific sense of meaning locally. Related to this is his suggestion to expand the repertoire and curate all concerts so that music for listeners is more deeply connected to the conduct of local life. And there is no reason not to recruit allies from local institutions such as colleges, universities, and museum institutions to help with the task of repertoire expansion, curating, and contextualizing.

Musical performance needs also, he elaborates, to become untethered from the concert hall. It should be performed in local public spaces, from churches to schools, to commercial and industrial sites, in museums and hospitals, prisons and on train platforms, and in the streets. Local people of all ages, at all levels, should be encouraged to take part in making music, from playing to composing, improvising, and writing about music.

Some relevant pre-COVID-19 trends

This penultimate section will examine some general recent trends to throw light on the proposals outlined earlier. Much more data work would be required though before any definitive conclusions can be reached, but nonetheless the trends identified here could be indicative of future change. A major issue is that it is almost impossible to get the required data, even for one country over time, let alone compare across countries. Nonetheless, the available data do reveal some interesting trends.

For example, Figure 15.1 highlights the contrasting experiences regarding live attendance at orchestral music concerts in the United States and some European countries. There was a steady decline in the United States up to around 2010, with attendance levelling off after that. In marked contrast, attendance in Germany increased significantly over the period. Attendance in Finland and Sweden also increased significantly from 2009. Thus, there was not a crisis in attendance at live orchestral music in Europe prior to COVID-19, contrary to the situation in the United States.

Figure 15.2 throws some light on the possible reasons for the more positive picture in relation to Germany. While the number of concerts, of various sorts, over the period remained steady, there was a dramatic rise in the number of music educational events. The latter include concerts for young people and children (25% of total in 2017–18), school concerts (20%), and workshops in schools (55%).

As Zieba and O'Hagan (2013) state, German orchestras have deep local and regional roots, arising from its decentralized system of government. Arising from this, German orchestras produce much more than symphony concerts but also run introductory matinées, explanatory concerts, literary

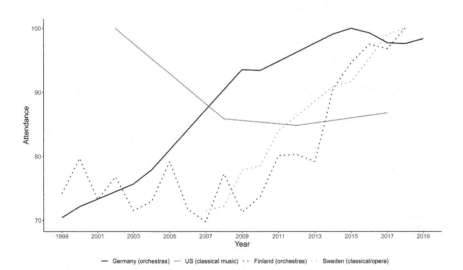

Figure 15.1 Trends in attendance at the live orchestra in Germany, the United States, Finland, and Sweden (normalized scale).

Source: Theater Statistics provided by Deutscher Buhnenverein (Germany), National Arts Administration and Policy Publications database (United States), Association of Finnish Symphony Orchestras (Finland), and Swedish Agency for Cultural Policy Analysis (Sweden).

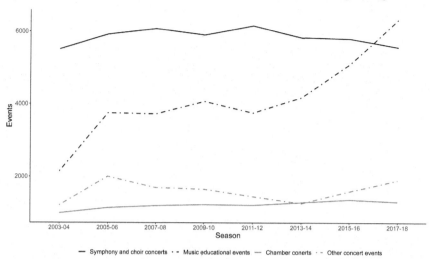

Figure 15.2 Events organized by publicly funded orchestras and radio ensembles in Germany, 2003–2004 and 2017–2018.

Source: Compiled by the German Music Information Center based on information from the German Orchestra Association (DOV).

musical-themed evenings, and thematically linked chamber music concerts. There has been particularly an upward trend in the area of orchestra activities for children, young adults, and families. Orchestra members are also extensively involved on a voluntary basis in the local musical community. It may be that Botstein's (2020) recommendations seen above for US orchestras were shaped by this German experience, which suggests that such innovations can 'work' in sustaining and increasing attendance at live orchestral music.

Turning now to the proposal by Szedmák and Szabó (2020), namely, to find new revenue sources, especially from streaming, the evidence so far is very limited and mixed. Figure 15.3 shows that income from orchestral concerts by the New York Philharmonic was robust over the period shown, but also that income from recording and broadcasting is very small, with no evidence of any increase from that source over the years. This does not bode well, perhaps for streaming as a solution to the crisis facing US orchestras.

Figures 15.4 and 15.5, though, highlight the possibilities regarding revenues from streaming. Figure 15.4 shows that streaming revenue in 2016 accounted for around 16% of global classical recorded music revenues, rising within two years to 37%. The highest percentage in 2018, as can be seen in Figure 15.5 was in the United States, at 60% of total revenue, with the figure for Europe at 22%. The US figure maybe then shows the potential perhaps for earning revenue from paid-for streamed orchestral

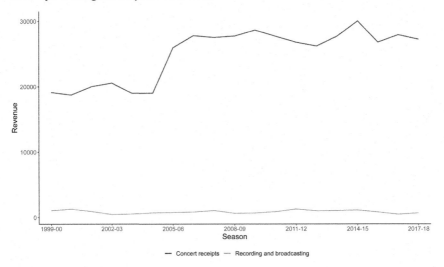

Figure 15.3 Income from orchestra activities, New York Philharmonics, 1990–2000 to 2017–2018.

Source: New York Philharmonic Annual Reports from 2000 to 2018.

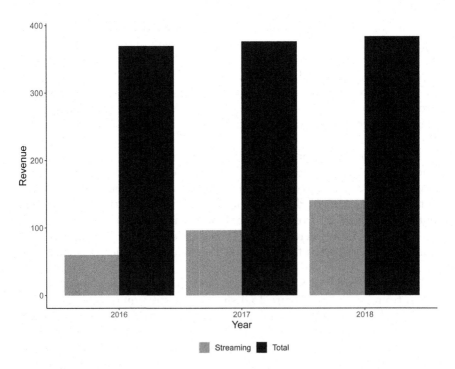

Figure 15.4 Global classical recorded music revenues 2016–2018 (millions $).

Source: Mulligan et al. (2019).

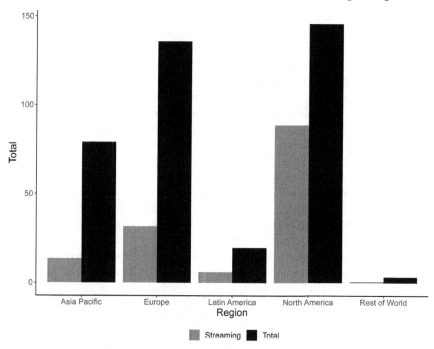

Figure 15.5 Global classical recorded music revenues by region 2018 (millions $).

Source: Mulligan et al. (2019).

concerts. Mulligan et al. (2019) are very positive in fact about the future of classical music in an age of streaming. They, like Szedmák and Szabó (2020), see streaming as a key factor in reaching the millennial classical music fan, the people who in older age will frequent concert halls.

Concluding comments

Being part of the educational sector, it is interesting for us to note that the COVID-19 pandemic has brought about major changes in the way how not only core services, like education and health, are provided and consumed, but also leisure supply, including orchestral music. In some ways, orchestral music was before COVID-19 way ahead of education and health in terms of engaging with technology. Streamed lectures and tutorials were possible decades ago, but few universities, including our own, embraced such technology before COVID-19. Likewise, for example, remote consultations with doctors were possible for decades but became only a reality during COVID-19. Orchestras as seen though had exploited such possibilities well before this, first through recordings and more recently through live-streamed performances.

How orchestras are financed in terms of earned revenue, sponsorships/ philanthropy, and state funding is an issue for another paper. However, the notion that there is a very limited paying audience for live orchestral music no longer applies. Take for example the case of another live entertainment industry, namely football. The same number of players as a century ago are still required for a football match, as they are for an orchestral concert. There is also a strict limit to how many people can watch a live football match in the stadium, as is true for a concert hall. However, live football matches are now streamed to millions of viewers each week, generating huge revenues for the sport. The same could apply, albeit to a much more limited extent, to orchestral music.

Moreover, the availability of high-quality transmission on large home TVs or wherever did not deter attendance in the stadium. In fact, the experience of watching a match or a concert would be greatly lessened without a full stadium/concert hall. As such, for live transmission to be effective for a concert or football match requires a full attendance in the stadium/concert hall: in other words, the two are complementary.

What orchestras might ask, but not only orchestra but perhaps other cultural sectors, is: why do people pay large sums, say, to watch a Champions League football match or a French Open tennis match, in the stadium, at great cost in terms of time and money, when they can do so at home at much lower cost and in more comfort? And how come, even though a huge part of revenues flow to superstar players, do they continue to attract large numbers of players and attendees in both sports at all levels? The answer may be that the cases of live orchestral concerts and football matches have no parallels, but COVID-19 has perhaps shown that whether they do or not is an issue to be explored with some urgency.

Notes

1. See Peyser (2006) on the origins of and other interesting issues relating to orchestras.
2. This is related to the so-called Baumol's disease, namely the issue of a fixed number of players required, over time, to perform orchestral music, which in turn with a fixed audience, means increasing relative costs and hence increased relative imputed, if not actual, prices. (see Flanagan, 2012).
3. https://www.irishtimes.com/news/world/europe/german-researchers-claim-risk-of-covid-transmission-at-live-classical-music-is-manageable-1.4420732
4. The Bolshoi opened for live audiences in September 2020, with 50% capacity (Foy, 2021).
5. See Flanagan (2012) for a detailed analysis of revenues and expenses profiles of fifty US orchestras, with little reference of course then to revenue possibilities from streaming, live and recorded.
6. Garcia-Maunez (2020) argues on similar lines. Like others she argues that orchestras should focus on telling stories and expand beyond traditional mediums (i.e. quiet, stuffy concert halls). Ultimately, orchestras can and should utilize virtual 'concert halls' to provide a novel experience, reach a wider audience, and tell stories in a new way. See also Bibu et al. (2018) for an interesting pre-COVID-19 discussion on how orchestras have adapted/should adapt to a changing world.

References

Barber, G. (2020). 'The science behind orchestras' careful Covid-19 come-back', *Wired* August 6, at: https://www.wired.com/story/the-science-behind-orchestras-careful-Covid-19-comeback/

Berghöfer, et al. (2020). *Policy Brief about Performances of Orchestras during the COVID-19 Pandemic*, Charité –University Medicine Berlin: Berlin, Germany.

Bibu, N., L. Brancu, G. Teohari (2018). 'Managing a symphony orchestra in times of change: behind the curtains', *Procedia - Social and Behavioral Sciences*, 238, pp. 507–516.

Botstein, L. (2020). 'The future of music in America: The challenge of the COVID-19 pandemic', *The Music Quarterly*, August, online. https://www.ncbi.nlm.nih.gov/pmc/articles/PMC7454821/

Campbell, M. (2020). 'A robot just conducted a human symphony orchestra by waving its arms around', Euronews, February 2.

Dombey, D. (2021). 'The show goes on in Madrid as cultural life continues despite pandemic' *Financial Times*, February 13. https://on.ft.com/3rR6Jha

European Parliament (2020). *EU support for artists and the cultural and creative sector during the coronavirus crisis*. European Parliament: Strasbourg.

Flanagan, R. (2012). *The Perilous Life of Symphony Orchestras: Artistic Triumphs and Economic Challenges*, Yale University Press: New Haven.

Foy. H. (2021). 'The jewel in Russia's artistic crown is no stranger to turmoil – but Covid-19 has inflicted a new kind of challenge', *Financial Times*, March 6. https://on.ft.com/3bofDxf

Frederickson, J. (1989). 'Technology and music performance in the age of mechanical reproduction', *International Review of the Aesthetics and Sociology of Music*, 20 (2), pp. 193–220.

Garcia-Maunez, A (2020). 'Orchestras' post-pandemic future', *Arts Management & Technology Laboratory*, December 3, at: https://amt-lab.org/blog/2020/12/orchestras-post-Covid-19-digital-future.

Kramer, J. (1996) 'The Impact of technology on the musical experience', *The College Music Society*, at: https://www.music.org/index.php?option=com_content&view=article&id=2675:the-impact-of-technology-on-the-musical-experience&catid=220&Itemid=3665

Manzi, Z. (2017). 'Why live streaming is not a solution for orchestras in a digital world', *The Startup*, December 7. https://medium.com/swlh/why-live-streaming-is-not-a-solution-for-orchestras-in-a-digital-world-de7a41e49b29

Mulligan, M., K. Joplin, Z. Fuller (2019). *The Classical Music Market: Streaming's next Genre?* MIDiA Research White Paper: London.

Peyser, J (editor), (2006). *The Orchestra: A Collection of 23 Essays on Its Origins and Transformations*, Hal-Leonard Corporation.

Szedmák, B., R. Szabó (2020). 'The value innovation of symphony orchestras and the triggering effect of Coronavirus', *Club of Economics in Miskolc'* MILWAUKEE: *TMP*, 16 (2), pp. 89–95.

Uhl, A., A. Schmid, R. Zimmermann (2013). 'From the concert hall to the web: how the Berliner Philharmoniker transformed their business model', August, at: https://www.researchgate.net/publication/265794566_From_the_Concert_Hall_to_the_Web_How_the_Berliner_Philharmoniker_Transformed_their_Business_Model

Zieba, M., J. O'Hagan (2013) 'Demand for live orchestral music: the case of German *Kulturorchester*', *Jahrbücher für Nationalökonomie und Statistik (Journal of Economics and Statistics)*, 235 (2), pp. 225–245.

Conclusions

The legacy of COVID-19 for the cultural industries

Trilce Navarrete

Undoubtedly, 2020 will be considered a pivot year where major shifts took place at policy, institutional and individual levels. The cultural and creative sector is large and presents many idiosyncrasies per sub-sector, which responded differently to the pandemic. Similarly, governments' emergency policy instruments reflected great variance in the structures and resources available, as well as differences in the understanding of the cultural ecosystem as a whole, curiously conceived within strict geographical borders. Overall, the cultural and creative sector came to a still stand, reinvented itself, and got up to date with plans that had not been given the time to develop. Some fundamental changes have taken place, in a line of transformations that have been shaping the cultural and creative industries sector long before the pandemic. It will be up to the sector to decide what awareness is kept and developed or left as temporary responses to a global crisis with no further implication.

The chapters in this book have documented numerous responses at individual, institutional, and policy levels across Europe. Three key common messages can be highlighted. First, culture was deemed as non-essential in our society. This is nothing new, as evidenced by the sustainable precarious labour conditions cultural and creative workers have had to endure, including a high rate of self-employment, unstable work, low wages, greater risk, and concentrated power centres accelerated by the dynamics inherent in the Internet and the continuous reduction of government support. Specialized staff, as well as those associated with the technical side of improving service provision, have little incentive to remain in the sector given the perilous conditions of work. Increasing evidence of the social role of culture as part of the economy, but most importantly to increase the overall wellbeing of participants, can be expected to change the social perception of culture. Further research and greater harmonization of methods will be key for such a shift at national levels. In this volume, evidence is provided that cultural workers who kept their work and understood their role as social healers or social servants were more innovative during the crises and contributed to the provision of essential functions associated with the creative and cultural industries (see Chapter 5).

DOI: 10.4324/9781003128274-20

A second common point documented has to do with the lack of sufficient data available from the cultural sector, in this case to inform policy response. Not all countries have a proper account of the creative and cultural sector, particularly regarding the self-employed and informal workforce. In many countries, cultural participation remains significant within the informal economy. Similarly, there is no national system to capture digital remote cultural participation, particularly to document the explosion of service provision experienced during the lockdown. The lack of definitions that consider a digital or hybrid variant for data collection remains a challenge, as has been argued for the digital heritage tourist (Navarrete, 2019). An example is museum online service provision, currently lacking a definition (what is a digital museum?), not monitored in production or consumption side, which may change as the heritage sector develops paid services and online payment infrastructures, comparable to the music or film industries. Clearly, data availability to understand the sector is beneficial for all economic actors, including institutions, producers, and the public at large. On the positive side, some temporary policy changes may become structural to better reflect the changing needs of the sector (see Chapter 3).

The third notable message is the extraordinary nature of the pandemic, disrupting all processes at the global level, which gave valuable insights to study and understand the culture and the creative sector. An important result can already be highlighted, regarding the fundamental gaps and divides within the sector associated with the level of physicality or remoteness at service point, the stage of digital transformation, the role of the participating consumer, as well as the degree of complexity in the production and distribution of the service. This raises the critical question of whether the cultural and creative sector can continue to be considered as *one sector*. The pandemic has highlighted the diverging needs and benefits of the sector, contrasting the successful video online services to the cancelled festivals and live events. Innovation and digital transformation are underway. It can be expected that much research will emerge from studying this period. The current volume has documented specific instances of a first and even second response to national measures reacting to the pandemic. A follow-up volume is invited to take advantage of the available data, insights, and time needed by the cultural and creative sector to redefine its course.

What have we learnt? While It is too early to say what the overall long-term implications of the pandemic will be, a few elements are already visible at individual, sectoral, and policy levels. Changes were not all caused by the pandemic, yet the lockdown provided a catalyst for accelerating processes previously initiated, including digital and hybrid service provision (Navarrete and Borowiecki, 2016; Massi, Vecco and Lin, 2020; Waldfogel, 2020). Drawing from the presented evidence in this book, we can confidently say that one major change revolves around the increased digital literacy across the sector. The forced remote nature of activities meant to sustain a certain level of normal functioning sharpened the preferences of consumers and mobilized creators to deliver (paid) services online. The cultural and creative sector gained market space, to deliver intermediate services (B2B) as well as new consumer services. Cultural and creative industries are re-considering the commercialization of their services, particularly those that have traditionally been free of charge such as provision of heritage content online.

The pandemic served to scout new products, markets, and levels of consumer participation. Museums are adopting online payment models for ticket sales as well as for other services while performing arts in turn are exploring the use of immersive technologies generally associated with heritage, such as virtual and augmented reality in dance and theatre. At the policy level there has been a need to expand coverage, including support to creative makers even if services provided are not part of the core arts or are not formally institutionalized. Revision of data collection methods to inform decision making at the policy level has become urgent, including the metric to establish the role and value of the cultural and creative industries in society: How can the singing in balconies or dancing in the street be accounted for? How to capture the value of re-enacting an art piece in social media?

If the current pandemic is compared to the previous crisis, a renaissance in the creative and cultural sector can be expected. The role of governments and the private contributor may shift, as individuals see the limits of government reach and as governments stimulate new frameworks for private support coordinated by non-governmental agencies. However, with the endemic poor infrastructure of the creative and cultural education, business and technology know-how will continue to limit the extent to which the sector can develop sustainably and equitably.

References

Joel Waldfogel (2020) Digitization in the cultural industries, in Towse and Navarrete (eds.) Handbook of Cultural Economics, 3rd Edition, Edward Elgar, Cheltenham, pp. 235–240.

Marta Massi, Marilena Vecco, and Yi Lin (Eds.) (2020) Digital Transformation in the Cultural and Creative Industries. Routledge, London.

Trilce Navarrete (2019) Digital heritage tourism: innovations in museums, World Leisure Journal, 61:3, 200–214, DOI: 10.1080/16078055.2019.1639920

Trilce Navarrete & Karol J. Borowiecki (2016) Changes in cultural consumption: ethnographic collections in Wikipedia, Cultural Trends, 25:4, 233–248, DOI: 10.1080/09548963.2016.1241342

Index

adaptability 23, 98, 104, 110
advertising 26, 54, 69, 71, 195, 196
architecture 28, 68, 121, 123, 196
arts, contemporary art 53
audience ratings 143, 158, 161
audiovisual 28, 31, 35, 37, 67, 69, 70, 76, 144, 150, 211, 216, 220, 239
Austria 17, 18, 20, 114, 128, 257

Belgium, Flanders 14, 16, 17, 241, 249, 251, 253
book industry and newspapers 13, 28, 30, 40, 54, 67, 69, 74, 86, 196, 201
Bulgaria 14, 17, 20, 67
business skills 142, 157

catalyst 40, 114, 249, 169
Colombia 141
concert halls 256
coworking spaces 114
crisis management 47, 48, 51, 208, 212, 223, 227
Croatia 19, 241, 251
cultural ecosystem, creative ecosystem 11, 21, 63, 196, 198, 202–204, 228, 268
cultural intermediaries 239, 240, 243, 251
cultural policy 27, 47, 57, 65, 229, 251
Czech Republic 14, 16, 17, 241, 251

dance 31, 51, 53, 75, 79, 85, 87, 89, 90, 153, 229, 235, 270
data collection 47, 51, 52, 58, 77, 148, 170, 188, 215, 269, 270
Denmark 14, 20, 210, 214, 221, 241, 246
design 54, 68, 102, 116, 121, 196, 199, 201, 219, 233

digital literacy 269
digitization 18, 40, 67, 94, 96, 178, 182, 220, 260, 270
disruption 12, 57, 99, 194, 208, 210, 212, 222, 223, 251, 269
drama 36, 74, 85, 90, 208

education 28, 30, 32, 38, 48, 53, 55, 60, 75, 77, 89, 92, 129, 156, 167, 168, 178, 196, 237, 244, 260, 261, 265, 270
entrepreneurship, entrepreneurial 49, 57, 58, 70, 76, 96, 130, 134, 142, 145, 155, 157, 158, 194, 227, 236
equity 190, 251
Estonia 14, 18, 20, 70, 239, 245, 249

fashion 101, 102, 107
festival 13, 30, 31, 33, 34, 50, 53, 55, 76, 89, 105, 209, 244, 257, 269
film, cinema 13, 19, 20, 26, 29, 30, 34, 56, 67, 69, 74–76, 96, 102, 144, 153, 209, 211, 239, 241, 257, 169
Finland 14, 17, 46, 210, 214, 221, 262
flexibility 78, 94, 98, 105, 189, 218, 231, 243, 245
fragility 36, 39, 98, 180, 197, 205, 229
France 14, 17, 19, 27, 114, 239, 245
freelance, self-employed 16, 30, 53, 54, 69, 70, 76, 84, 86, 128, 195, 221, 212, 215, 229, 231, 235, 247, 250
freeze 21, 83, 203, 247

Germany 14, 17, 20, 70, 101, 114, 244, 257, 258, 262, 263, 267

Heritage 28, 31, 32, 49, 52, 53, 55, 67, 177, 178, 187, 195, 196, 199, 201, 241, 269, 270

Iceland 7, 210, 214, 220, 221
infrastructure 12, 14, 17, 19–21, 66, 105, 138, 182, 186, 240, 269, 170
innovation 19, 22, 39, 49, 51, 90, 91, 96, 121, 158, 162, 178, 184, 227, 263, 269
Ireland 15, 17–19, 77, 108, 239, 241, 244–246, 251
Italy 15, 16, 18, 20, 99, 101, 102, 114, 177, 245

job satisfaction 84–86, 91, 93, 118, 180

labour, risk 21, 25, 32, 75, 96, 98, 109, 130, 134, 177, 183, 189, 205, 223, 242, 256, 259, 268
labour, wages 67, 69, 107, 268

museums 20, 30, 31, 38, 40, 48, 50, 52, 53, 55, 67, 73, 75, 85, 115, 124, 145, 176, 226, 229, 230, 233, 257, 261, 270

non-economic measures 13, 18, 20
Northern Ireland 241, 245, 251
Norway 84, 86, 96, 210, 214, 220, 245

online payment 269, 270
opera 35, 38, 56, 90, 129, 134, 236, 255, 257, 261
orchestras 35, 48, 55, 76, 128, 130, 138, 254

performing arts 13, 21, 23, 30, 31, 34, 38, 54, 74, 83, 89, 96, 118, 129, 137, 153, 195, 199, 229

photography 30, 89, 153, 210, 218
Portugal 15, 19, 20, 67, 245

Scotland 241, 245, 251
Slovakia 15, 20, 55
Spain 15, 17, 101, 102, 141, 194, 244, 245
streaming 29, 40, 67, 90, 95, 105, 117, 141, 183, 200, 250, 258, 261, 265
stringency index (SI) 212, 213, 221, 224
subscription models 105, 137, 183, 189, 191, 248
sustainability 19, 22, 116, 177, 179, 183, 189, 190, 191, 195, 197, 199
Sweden 15, 20, 210, 213, 220, 221, 224, 262

taxes, tax measures 18, 30, 33, 39, 65, 68, 70, 71, 73, 204, 231, 236, 240, 246
technology adoption 90, 91, 93, 95
television 29, 72–74, 221, 239, 248
tourism 67, 73, 76, 128, 177, 180, 184, 190, 191, 196, 240
transnational strategies 220

United Kingdom 11

visual arts 20, 24, 28, 34, 36, 51, 53, 145, 118, 153, 169, 195, 196, 201, 235

Wales 239, 241, 245, 251
wellbeing 85, 164, 268

Printed in the United States
by Baker & Taylor Publisher Services